NATUREGUIDE
BIRDS

SMITHSONIAN
NATUREGUIDE
BIRDS

David Burnie

LONDON, NEW YORK, MELBOURNE,
MUNICH, AND DELHI

DORLING KINDERSLEY

Editor Miezan van Zyl	**Senior Art Editor** Spencer Holbrook
Senior Editor Janet Mohun	**US Editors** Jill Hamilton, Rebecca Warren
Production Controller Erika Pepe	**Production Editor** Rebekah Parsons-King
Database David Roberts	**Jacket Designers** Laura Brim, Mark Cavanagh
DK Picture Library Claire Bowers, Harry Fabian, Emma Shepherd	**Picture Researchers** Jo Walton, Julia Harris-Voss
Managing Editor Camilla Hallinan	**Managing Art Editor** Michelle Baxter
Publisher Sarah Larter	**Art Director** Philip Ormerod
Associate Publishing Director Liz Wheeler	**Publishing Director** Jonathan Metcalf

DK INDIA

Editorial Manager Rohan Sinha	**Deputy Design Manager** Mitun Banerjee
Deputy Managing Editor Alka Thakur Hazarika	**Senior Art Editor** Anuj Sharma
Senior Editor Vineetha Mokkil	**Consultant Art Director** Shefali Upadhyay
Editors Roma Malik, Megha Gupta, Ritu Mishra	**Assistant Art Editor** Khundongbam Rakesh
Assistant Editors Neha Chaudhary, Jubbi Francis	**Designer** Vaibhav Rastogi
DTP Manager Balwant Singh	**Assistant Designers** Pooja Pawar, Sanjay Chauhan, Vritti Bhansal
DTP Designers Bimlesh Tiwary, Anita Yadav, Arjinder Singh, Jagtar Singh, Vishal Bhatia	**Production Manager** Pankaj Sharma
	Senior DTP Designer Harish Aggarwal

CONSULTANT

Craig Ludwig, Scientific Data Manager, Division of Birds,
National Museum of Natural History, Smithsonian Institution

First American Edition, 2012
Published in the United States by DK Publishing
375 Hudson Street, New York, New York, 10014

12 13 14   10 9 8 7 6 5 4 3 2
002 – 181830 – Apr/2012

Published in Great Britain by Dorling Kindersley Limited.

A catalog record for this book is available from the Library of Congress.

ISBN 978-0-7566-9041-0

DK books are available at special discounts when purchased in bulk for sales promotions, premiums, fund-raising, or educational use. For details, contact: DK Publishing Special Markets, 375 Hudson Street, New York, New York, 10014 or SpecialistSales@dk.com

Reproduced by Bright Arts, China, and MDP, UK
Printed and bound in China by Leo Paper Products

Discover more at **www.dk.com**

CONTENTS

HOW THE SPECIES PROFILES WORK

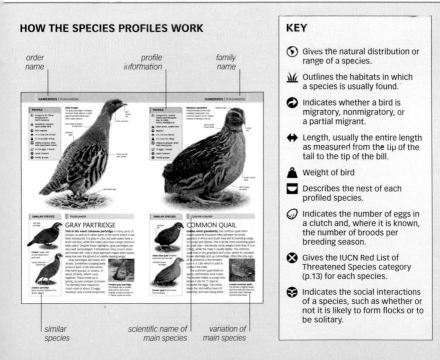

order name

profile information

family name

similar species

scientific name of main species

variation of main species

KEY

- **⊙** Gives the natural distribution or range of a species.
- **⩜** Outlines the habitats in which a species is usually found.
- **⮂** Indicates whether a bird is migratory, nonmigratory, or a partial migrant.
- **⟷** Length, usually the entire length as measured from the tip of the tail to the tip of the bill.
- **▲** Weight of bird
- **▭** Describes the nest of each profiled species.
- **⌬** Indicates the number of eggs in a clutch and, where it is known, the number of broods per breeding season.
- **✖** Gives the IUCN Red List of Threatened Species category (p.13) for each species.
- **✲** Indicates the social interactions of a species, such as whether or not it is likely to form flocks or to be solitary.

ANATOMY

Despite their great range in size and shape, birds all have the same underlying anatomy, with streamlined bodies and a pair of wings. Feathers keep them warm, and provide lift during flight.

UNDERSIDE
Seen from below, a bird's body is divided into three distinct regions—the head and body, the wings, and the tail. These are subdivided into smaller areas, such as the breast, and specific anatomical features, including the wrists and the bill. Most birds fly with the legs tucked in, but in some they trail behind the tail, creating a distinctive silhouette when seen from below.

underwing coverts

wrist

flank

breast

crown

belly

vent

foot

Feather types
Soft down feathers provide insulation, while contour feathers create a streamlined body or wing surface. Flight feathers generate lift, or—in the tail—help a bird brake and steer.

**DOWN
FEATHER**

**CONTOUR
FEATHER**

**FLIGHT
FEATHER**

**TAIL
FEATHER**

UPPERSIDE
In the air, the flight feathers are fully spread. Arranged in rows, their bases are overlapped by contour feathers called coverts, which smooth the flow of air. The primary flight feathers grow on the outer part of the wing, while the secondaries grow between them and the point where the wing meets the body. Body regions on the upperside include the shoulders, mantle, and rump.

primaries

secondaries

uppertail coverts

rump

mantle

tail

wingtip

COLORS AND MARKINGS

Birds include some of the world's most colorful animals, as well as others that are superbly camouflaged. Most of their colors are produced by pigments, giving their plumage a rich variety of patterns and hues. Some species also have iridescent colors, produced by the microscopic structure of feathers, and they change with the angle of view.

iridescent colors

ANNA'S HUMMINGBIRD

pigment colors

CIRL BUNTING

breeding plumage

nonbreeding plumage

ARCTIC LOON

male

female

PIN-TAILED WHYDAH

PLUMAGE VARIATION

In some birds, the sexes look identical, and the plumage is unchanged throughout the year. But in many others, plumage undergoes seasonal changes, and males and females can look very different, particularly when the time comes to breed. Once the breeding season is over, males often shed their colorful plumage, and resemble the females until the next breeding season begins. Young birds may also look different from adults.

BILL SHAPE

A bird's bill shape is intimately linked with the way that it feeds. Altogether, dozens of different bill shapes give birds access to an enormous range of food. Many songbirds, such as the blackbird, have short, slender bills for probing and picking up small animals, seeds, or fruit. Geese have broad, serrated bills for tearing up grass, while herons have daggerlike bills for spearing fish and frogs.

tears meat

GOLDEN EAGLE

pecks worms and fruit

BLACKBIRD

tears up grass

GRAYLAG GOOSE

stabs aquatic animals

GRAY HERON

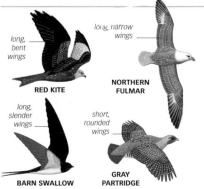

long, bent wings

long, narrow wings

RED KITE

NORTHERN FULMAR

long, slender wings

short, rounded wings

BARN SWALLOW

GRAY PARTRIDGE

WING AND TAIL SHAPE

Birds wings and tails have evolved to allow very different styles of flight. Birds with short, rounded wings, such as partridges, are shaped for short-distance flight, while ones with slender wings, such as swallows, usually fly faster, steering with tails that are sometimes forked. Birds of prey fly by flapping, gliding, or soaring—a form of flight also used by albatrosses at sea. Most small songbirds have compact wings for rapid takeoff and landing.

FLIGHT, MIGRATION, and BREEDING

Flight gives birds great advantages in the search for food, for partners, and for somewhere to breed. Not all birds can fly, but the ones that do include the greatest animal migrants.

FLIGHT

Bird flight involves a very complex set of movements, which vary from the moment of takeoff to the point where a bird comes in to land. In flapping flight, the wings generate upward and forward thrust. At the same time, the wing shape generates lift, in the same way as the wings of an airplane. Soaring birds fly without flapping their wings. Like gliders, they use lift to keep themselves airborne—a highly efficient way of flying that lets them scan the ground or sea below.

wings point forward

FLIGHT PATTERNS

Even from a distance, many birds can be recognized by the way they fly. Some have a level flight path, flapping their wings at a steady speed. Others flap their wings in bursts, tracing an undulating or random path as they move across the sky.

Fast flapping
Characteristic of small birds, with up to 200 beats a minute.

Slow flapping
Seen in many larger birds, including barn owls and herons.

Intermittent flapping
Typical of woodpeckers and their relatives, producing an undulating flight.

Random flapping
Common in aerial insect-eaters, such as swallows and swifts.

MIGRATION

Every year, millions of birds undertake long journeys between the areas where they overwinter and where they breed. Migrations are triggered mainly by the seasonal changes in day length, and they usually follow well-defined routes, some of which are shown here. Partial migrants include some populations that migrate, and others that stay in place; this is typical of species that have an extensive range, with wide variations in local climate.

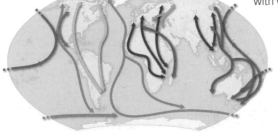

- American golden-plover
- Rufous hummingbird
- Short-tailed shearwater
- Arctic tern
- Common cuckoo
- Red-breasted goose
- Eastern curlew
- Eleonora's falcon

widely spread flight
feathers increase
wing's surface area

wings almost
meet at top of
upstroke

feet stowed
away, close
to body

Wing movement
During takeoff, a pigeon's wings
generate downward thrust to
counteract the pull of gravity.

BREEDING

All birds breed by laying eggs, but they develop in different ways. Some species, such as gamebirds and waterfowl, are well developed when they hatch. Their young can feed for themselves, although they still need parental care. In marked contrast, most songbirds hatch in a poorly developed state, without feathers and with their eyes closed. They are fed by their parents, and depend on them for warmth until their feathers begin to grow. However, their development can be rapid—some leave the nest when just 10 days old

Eggs
Birds eggs vary widely in their markings, shape, and color. Cliff-nesting murres have eggs that are pear-shaped, which prevents the eggs from rolling off ledges.

**PEAR
SHAPED**

SPHERICAL

ELLIPTICAL

CONICAL

cup shape

Nests
Most birds make nests to protect their eggs and young, but some lay their eggs directly on bare rock or open ground.

Courtship
Many birds have evolved complex courtship displays that enable a pair bond to be formed and maintained. Often, males display to attract females, but in these blue-footed boobies, both sexes join in "sky pointing" ceremonies. As well as visual displays, courtship can also involve songs and other sounds such as wing-clapping.

HABITATS

A bird's habitat provides it with everything that it needs to survive and breed. Most birds depend on a single habitat, while some species can use a wider range. Many migrants have two different habitats—each is used at a different time of the year.

- Mountains
- Temperate forest
- Coniferous forest
- Tropical forest
- Seas and oceans
- Wetland
- Polar regions
- Grassland
- Scrubland and heath
- Deserts
- Agricultural land
- Urban agglomerations

Coniferous forest
This type of forest covers large areas of the far north. Many birds, such as the crested tit, feed on insects and seeds.

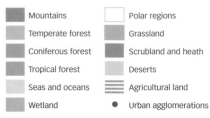

Tropical forest
A huge number of bird species live in this rich but rapidly shrinking habitat. Most, including the great blue turaco, are nonmigrants.

Ocean
Oceanic seabirds include albatrosses, petrels, and other pelagic species. They wander far from land, rarely returning except to breed.

Grassland
These are home to large flightless birds, as well as species such as guineafowl, which can fly but spend most of their time on the ground.

Temperate forest
This habitat attracts a huge wave of warblers, and other insect-eating migrants, when its trees burst into leaf during spring.

Polar regions
Many birds visit polar regions in the summer, but few, except penguins, remain there all year round.

Urban areas
For some species, such as rock pigeons and house sparrows, life in cities has led to worldwide success.

Scrubland and heath
A patchwork of trees and open areas creates ideal conditions for hoopoes, songbirds, and other migrants.

Coasts
Waders, gulls, and terns are common on coasts worldwide, while auks—including Atlantic puffins—are restricted to the Northern Hemisphere.

Mountains
High ground is patrolled by many birds of prey, including the Harris's hawk and large vultures.

Wetlands
Lush conditions make wetlands a rich habitat for waterfowl, which include ducks, geese, and swans. After breeding, many species migrate.

Deserts
Despite their harsh conditions, deserts and semi-deserts attract a wide range of seed-eating birds, such as this turtle dove.

BIRDWATCHING AND IDENTIFICATION

As well as being fascinating in its own right, birdwatching can contribute important information on the state of individual species. Identifying birds is easiest with the right equipment, and a knowledge of useful clues such as flight patterns and song.

WATCHING BIRDS

Some birds are instantly recognizable by their shape, color, or the way that they move. But when birds are small or far off, viewing aids (see panel, right) are crucial for making a correct identification and help reveal details that cannot be seen with the naked eye. Birds are wary animals, so they are best watched by avoiding sudden movements, or from the cover of a blind.

KEEPING RECORDS

Keeping a log is an ideal way of recording species observed, and seeing how they change with the seasons. The arrival of migrants is a particularly noticeable event, helping a birder keep track of the seasons. With experience, a log can build up into a personal species list—some of the world's best-traveled birdwatchers have "life lists" that are thousands of species long.

EQUIPMENT

Binoculars are essential aids to birdwatching, while telescopes and long-range lenses are for committed enthusiasts. Test binoculars before you buy. Select a pair that are light and shock-proof, but do not be tempted to go higher than 10x magnification, because they have a relatively narrow field of view.

Binoculars from 7x35 to 10x50 are ideal. The first figure is the magnification; the second figure gives the diameter of the lens.

A compact scope, mounted on a tripod, allows long-distance viewing.

Capture details with a single lens reflex (SLR) camera fitted with a long lens.

IUCN RED LIST

Since the 1960s, the International Union for Conservation of Nature and Natural Resources (IUCN) has published the Red List of Threatened Species. Species are assigned categories that show how much danger they face. The principal bird categories are shown here, and are featured in the species profiles that appear in this book. About 500 species of birds are endangered, of which 180 fall into the critical category. A further 1,500 species are listed as vulnerable or near threatened. Together, these species make up one in five of the world's birds.

Extinct Species for which there is no doubt that the last individual has died.

Extinct in the Wild Species that have died out in the wild, but exist in captivity.

Critically Endangered Species that face an extremely high risk of extinction in the wild.

Endangered Species that face a very high risk of extinction in the wild.

Vulnerable Species that face a high risk of extinction in the wild, unless prospects for their survival improve

Near Threatened Species that are close to qualifying for the above categories, or likely to qualify in the near future.

Least Concern Species that have been evaluated and are currently not at risk.

CLASSIFYING BIRDS

Like all living things, birds are classified to show how closely they are related, while giving each species a unique scientific name. Birds (Aves) are grouped into 29 orders, each with one or more families. The next subdivision is the genus, which contains one or more species, each with a two-part name. Some species are split into subspecies, indicated by a third name.

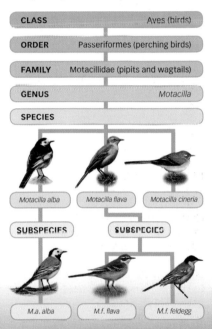

CLASS	Aves (birds)
ORDER	Passeriformes (perching birds)
FAMILY	Motacillidae (pipits and wagtails)
GENUS	Motacilla
SPECIES	

Motacilla alba   Motacilla flava   Motacilla cineria

SUBSPECIES   SUBSPECIES

M.a. alba   M.f. flava   M.f. feldegg

The long view
Open habitats are ideal places for using binoculars and telescopes, making distant birds easier to observe and identify.

SPECIES GUIDE

TINAMOUS

Common in Central and South America, tinamous are plump ground-dwelling birds with strong legs but small wings. Superficially similar to gamebirds (p.23), their skeletons show that they are more closely related to ratites (below).

Found in woodland, grassland, and scrub, tinamous feed on the ground, eating seeds and berries as well as insects and other small animals. Most members of this order can fly well over short distances on fast-beating wings, but if they are threatened they normally react by running away.

Tinamous typically live in small flocks, breeding in nests on the ground. Their eggs are some of the most remarkable of all birds, with a bright color and porcelain-like sheen. The male builds the nest and incubates the eggs alone, and the chicks are well developed when they hatch, able to run within a few hours.

ORDER	TINAMIFORMES
FAMILIES	1
SPECIES	47

Low profile
Like all its relatives, this red-winged tinamou is cryptically colored—a defensive adaptation for birds that feed and nest on the ground.

RATITES

Ratites include the world's largest living birds. Most common in the Southern Hemisphere, they all lack the bony keel that anchors flight muscles in other birds. Without this, and with poorly developed or tiny wings, none of them can fly.

The ratites include four related orders of birds—ostriches (struthioniformes), rheas (rheiformes), cassowaries and emus (casuariiformes), and kiwis (apterygiformes). From Africa, the ostrich is the world's biggest bird, while the rheas, cassowaries, and emus are the largest flightless species in South America and Australasia. All these birds react to danger by running. The ostrich is unique in having two toes on each foot, while other large ratites have three. Kiwis, which are much smaller and restricted to New Zealand, are the only ratites that are nocturnal.

Depending on species, ratites feed on plant food, small animals, or both,

ORDERS	4
FAMILIES	4
SPECIES	15

typically finding it by sight and pecking at it from plants or from the ground.

Kiwis are different from the other ratites, as shown by their long, downcurved bills. The kiwis feed on earthworms and other small animals, smelling their food with the help of nostrils, which are located at the tip of the bill. In addition to their normal diet, most ratites swallow stones. These lodge in the birds' digestive systems, and help grind up their food.

PROFILE

- Much of Argentina; scattered, small populations in E. Chile
- Arid and semi-arid grassland, dry savanna, open woodland, steppes, sandy areas
- Nonmigrant
- 15½ in (39 cm)
- 24–26 oz (675–750 g)
- Hollow in ground, often next to low bush
- 1–12 eggs; 1 brood
- Least Concern
- Flocks

Cryptic colors
Adapted to living in dry, open country, the elegant crested tinamou has camouflaged plumage for hiding in grassland and scrub.

long, thin, up-curled crest

white stripe from eye to base of neck

dark brown plumage

spotted wings

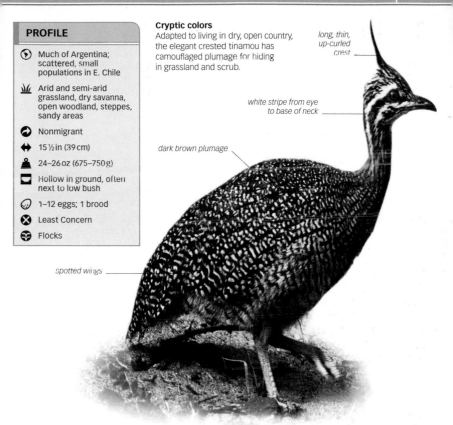

SIMILAR SPECIES

barred back

Ornate tinamou Small tinamou, living in high-altitude grasslands in the Andes

gray flanks

Solitary tinamou
Forest-dwelling tinamou from Argentina, Paraguay, and eastern Brazil

Eudromia elegans

ELEGANT CRESTED TINAMOU

One of more than 40 species of tinamous found in Central and South America, this ground-dwelling bird is distinguished by its slender, upturned crest. Like other tinamous, it resembles a gamebird (p.23), with short, strong legs, a broad body, and a relatively small head. Tinamous can fly, although some only weakly. This species is more likely to hide in case of approaching danger, taking to the air on whirring wings only as a last resort.

The elegant crested tinamou feeds on plants and insects. It is largely a solitary bird, except after the breeding season, when it is sometimes seen in family groups, which may coalesce to form small flocks. The breeding system is unusual, because either sex may have several mates. The nest is a simple scrape in the ground, near a low bush, and the male incubates the eggs. These have a glossy sheen—a characteristic that all tinamou eggs share.

PROFILE

- Across Africa from Senegal to Ethiopia, and as far south as Southern Africa
- Variety of open, semi-arid plains (from desert to savanna) and open woodland
- Nonmigrant
- 6–9 ¼ ft (1.8–2.8 m)
- 220 lb (100 kg)
- Large hollow in ground, formed by body pressure
- 2–12 eggs; 1 brood
- Least Concern
- Flocks

African giant
Found only in Africa, the ostrich is the world's largest living bird and is instantly recognizable by its size. The male is mostly black, with white wing feathers and a white tail.

white neck band

black plumage

two-toed feet

SIMILAR SPECIES

gray neck

Somali ostrich Found in East Africa, and often treated as a separate species

Struthio camelus

OSTRICH

Restricted to Africa's deserts and grasslands, the ostrich is the world's tallest and heaviest bird. It escapes enemies by running on its unique, two-toed feet and can sprint at up to 45 mph (70 kph). It also has great stamina, cruising at 30 mph (50 kph) for over half an hour. Although flightless, the ostrich has large, fan-shaped wings, which it spreads during courtship displays and also to keep cool.

Ostriches have a varied diet, and can go without water for several days. In the breeding season, males pair with a dominant female, but they also mate with subordinate females. Both sexes incubate the eggs, but the male usually takes the lead in protecting the young and teaching them to feed.

Female ostrich
The female is grayish brown, without any white on its plumage.

PROFILE

- South America, from Brazil south of the Amazon to C. Argentina
- Grassland and ranchland, often at edges of lightly wooded areas
- Nonmigrant
- 4–4½ft (1.2–1.4m)
- 44–88lb (20–40kg)
- Hollow in ground
- 2–6 eggs; 1 brood
- Least Concern
- Flocks

Camouflaged plumage
Known as the *ñandú* in Argentina, the greater rhea has gray-brown plumage, which makes excellent camouflage.

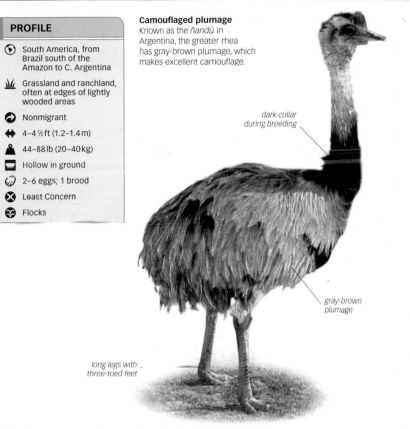

dark collar during breeding

gray-brown plumage

long legs with three-toed feet

SIMILAR SPECIES

gray plumage

Lesser rhea Smaller species found in the southern Andes and Patagonia

Rhea americana

GREATER RHEA

South America's largest flightless bird, the greater rhea lives in open plains and has a lifestyle similar to Africa's ostrich. It has a fully feathered head and neck, and shaggy, gray-brown plumage—often slightly darker in the male than in the female. A swift runner, it has strong legs with three-toed feet, and weak but comparatively large wings, which it uses for balance when running or making sharp turns. Each wing is equipped with a single claw, which can be used as a weapon against predators.

Greater rheas live in flocks, feeding on plant matter and small animals, and visiting rivers and lakes for water. For most of the year these groups are peaceable, but in the breeding season, males spar for the right to mate, pecking each other and trading heavy kicks. Successful males mate with several females, which lay their eggs in the same nest. Males incubate the clutch and care for the newly hatched eggs. The chicks leave the nest within a few hours of hatching.

Forest fruit-eater
The southern cassowary has black, hairlike plumage, red wattles, and a blue neck. It eats mainly fallen fruit, seeds, and plants.

coarse, black plumage

bright blue skin on neck and head

head casque

red neck wattles

strong, short legs

SIMILAR SPECIES

orange throat

Dwarf cassowary Smallest cassowary, found in the forests of New Guinea

Casuarius casuarius

SOUTHERN CASSOWARY

This sturdily built bird is the only cassowary to live in Australia as well as New Guinea. The tiny, feathered wings of the flightless southern cassowary are reduced to slender quills. They have short, strong legs and, as well as running, they also swim well. The adult develops a hornlike casque, which helps part the vegetation when running, head down, to escape from rivals or other threats.

Mainly solitary, southern cassowaries communicate in a variety of calls, from deep booming to coughing sounds. Females are larger than males, and lay a clutch of eggs on the forest floor. The male looks after the chicks until they are nine months old.

Juvenile cassowary
The juvenile has bold black-and-cream stripes on its body. It does not have the adult's head casque.

Long-range nomad
The emu is a semi-nomadic bird. It wanders hundreds of miles in search of food, sometimes going for several days without water.

grayish brown, shaggy plumage

bare skin on neck and head

long, scaly legs

PROFILE

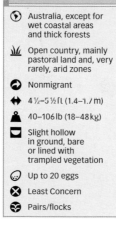

- 🧭 Australia, except for wet coastal areas and thick forests
- 🌾 Open country, mainly pastoral land and, very rarely, arid zones
- ↻ Nonmigrant
- ↔ 4½–5½ ft (1.4–1.7 m)
- ⚖ 40–106 lb (18–48 kg)
- ▭ Slight hollow in ground, bare or lined with trampled vegetation
- 🥚 Up to 20 eggs
- ✖ Least Concern
- 🐦 Pairs/flocks

Dromaius novaehollandiae

EMU

The world's second-tallest bird after the ostrich, the emu is native to Australia. Covered with loose, gray-brown to almost black, shaggy feathers, it has bluish bare skin on its head and upper neck—more colorful in the female—and tiny vestigial wings. It has long and powerful legs, with three-toed feet. A tireless runner if alarmed, it normally walks at other times.

A natural opportunist, the emu feeds on plants and insects, and sometimes congregates in great numbers on cropland and other places with good sources of food. It covers large distances when food gets scarce, often going without water. During the breeding season, the male calls using an inflatable throat sac, and flocks divide into breeding pairs, which fiercely defend a territory against competing pairs. After the eggs are laid, the female often leaves to find another mate, leaving the male to incubate the clutch and take care of the young. The male guards the striped chicks for over six months, until they become independent.

PROFILE

- 🕑 South Island, New Zealand
- 🌿 Forest, woodland, grassland, cultivated land
- ↻ Nonmigrant
- ↔ 26–28 in (65–70 cm)
- ⚖ 5 lb (2.3 kg)
- ▭ Bare hollow in ground or among tree roots
- ◒ 1 egg; 1 brood
- ✖ Vulnerable
- ✿ Pairs

Rare species
Once widespread, the tokoeka has been badly affected by introduced predators. It is now restricted to small populations in New Zealand's South Island, and on island refuges offshore.

brown plumage

humpbacked body

SIMILAR SPECIES

grayish plumage

Great spotted kiwi Largest kiwi, from New Zealand's South Island

mottled gray plumage

Little spotted kiwi Smallest kiwi, found in New Zealand's North Island

Apteryx australis

TOKOEKA

Also known as the southern brown kiwi, the tokoeka is one of five species of kiwis, all restricted to New Zealand. Like other kiwis, it is flightless, with a rotund, humpbacked body and hairlike feathers that completely conceal its tiny, nonfunctional wings. The tokoeka has a long, curved bill with sensory bristles around the base and nostrils at the tip. Both these adaptations help it find worms and other small animals that make up its food. It lives in forests, and emerges at night to forage and to breed. Once the sun sets, both sexes produce a shrill whistling sound that can be heard 1 mile (1.5 km) away.

The tokoeka is monogamous; once bonded it pairs for life. The female lays a single egg in a small, well-concealed burrow. For the female's size, the egg is enormous, equaling almost a quarter of its body weight. Both partners share the lengthy task of incubation, which lasts up to 80 days. The chick leaves the nest when a few days old, but remains in the parents' territory for several years.

GAMEBIRDS

With their muscular bodies and strong feet, gamebirds are adapted to life spent largely on the ground. Most can fly strongly, but if danger strikes, their first reaction is usually to run, bursting into the air only as a last resort.

Gamebirds include a range of different species traditionally hunted as food animals or "game." Among them are pheasants, quails, and grouse, as well as the domestic fowl. This group also includes some less familiar species, such as guans and currasows. Found on every continent except Antarctica, gamebirds live in a wide variety of habitats, from northern tundra to tropical rain forests. Most are terrestrial, although in some habitats they often roost in trees.

ORDER	GALLIFORMES
FAMILIES	5
SPECIES	290

ANATOMY AND DIET
Typical gamebirds have medium- to large-sized bodies, with thick legs and four well-developed toes. In some species, all four toes are level, but in many the hind toe is raised, and developed into a sharp spur. Gamebird wings are usually short and rounded, while their breastbone has a large, forward-pointing keel. The keel anchors the large flight muscles, which give many species an explosive takeoff in emergency situations. Although they fly well, they rarely travel far. Most are sedentary, spending their lives in one area, and only a handful migrate.

Gamebirds have short, blunt bills, and normally feed on plants and small animals, often scratching up their food with their feet. Many swallow grit and small stones to help grind up food.

PLUMAGE
Most gamebirds are cryptically colored in shades of brown, making it difficult to see them even in open ground. However, in pheasants and their relatives, males are often very different compared to females, with flamboyant colors that attract the female's attention. This reaches its peak in species such as the peafowl, where males compete with each other for partners, but play little or no part in raising the young.

NESTS AND YOUNG
With the exception of guans and currasows, gamebirds are ground-nesters, laying large numbers of eggs and producing well-developed young. Uniquely, mound-builders (p.24) use natural warmth to incubate their eggs. Their young are independent right away, but other gamebirds have young that need to follow their parents to learn how and where to find food.

Ready to run
Alert for any sign of danger, these northern bobwhites will run for cover first, rather than taking to the air.

PROFILE

- Semi-arid areas of W. and S. Australia
- Dry mallee bushland; woodland and scrub
- Nonmigrant
- 23½ in (60 cm)
- 3¼–4½ lb (1.5–2 kg)
- Compost mound
- 24 eggs; 1 brood
- Vulnerable
- Solitary/pairs

Mound maker
The malleefowl, a ground-dwelling bird, belongs to the mound-builder family. It builds "compost heaps" to incubate its eggs.

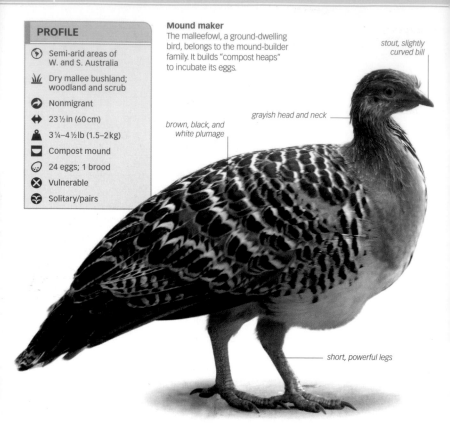

stout, slightly curved bill

grayish head and neck

brown, black, and white plumage

short, powerful legs

SIMILAR SPECIES

yellow throat wattle

Australian brush-turkey
Large, with a broad, flat tail, black feathers, and a red head

Maleo Indonesian species with pinkish breast and belly

Leipoa ocellata

MALLEEFOWL

A stocky bird, the malleefowl has black, brown, and white plumage on its back, upper tail, and wings. This omnivorous bird feeds on seeds, shoots, and insects. Pairs live in territories, and are thought to mate for life.

At the beginning of the breeding season, the male digs a wide depression in the ground, and then backfills it with twigs and fresh leaves to make a nest mound, until the heap is nearly 3 ft (1 m) high. When it rains, the moistened vegetation starts to rot, producing warmth that the male controls by adding or removing a covering of sand. The female lays eggs in the heap—as many as 24 in each season. The male monitors the temperature of the heap with its bill, keeping it within the correct range for incubation. When the chicks hatch, they scramble out of the mound, and immediately fend for themselves. They leave the vicinity of the nest within hours to take up life on their own, and are able to fly when just one day old.

forward-curling crest

yellow bill with bulbous base

black body

strong legs

long, heavy tail

Mobile crest
The great curassow has a distinctive crest of forward-curling feathers that adorns the length of its crown.

PROFILE

- 🌐 Mexico to Ecuador
- 🌾 Evergreen forests, mangroves
- 🔄 Nonmigrant
- ↔ 31–36 in (78–92 cm)
- ⚖ 6¾–11 lb (3.1–4.8 kg)
- ▭ Leaves and twigs in tree
- 🥚 2–3 eggs; 1 brood
- ❌ Vulnerable
- 🔗 Pairs/family groups

SIMILAR SPECIES

Bare-faced curassow
Found in tropical and subtropical forests; black facial skin

olive-brown body

Plain chacalaca
Gray head and neck; blackish tail with white tip

Crax rubra

GREAT CURASSOW

Standing almost 3 ft (1 m) tall, the great curassow is one of the most striking gamebirds in Central and northern South America. It uses its strong legs for walking, scratching up food, and perching. The curassow feeds on the ground, eating seeds, fruit, and small animals. It lives in pairs or family groups, led by an adult male, and roosts in trees to avoid nocturnal predators on the forest floor.

Unusual for gamebirds, the great curassow nests off the ground as well. The female lays 2–3 eggs. The eggs have coarsely granulated shells, and are large in relation to the female's size. The chicks develop rapidly, and leave the nest after three weeks. Curassows tame easily, and are sometimes kept among farmyard hens.

Female great curassow
One form of the female has bars on its neck, upperparts and tail, while two others are largely black or brown.

PROFILE

- Sub-Saharan Africa; introduced in the West Indies, Brazil, France
- Bush, savanna, and grassland, often near cultivation
- Nonmigrant
- 21–25 in (53–63 cm)

- 2¾ lb (1.3 kg)
- Unlined scrape
- 6–12 eggs; 1 brood
- Least Concern
- Flocks

Casqued head
The helmeted guineafowl gets its name from the helmetlike, bony casque on top of its colorful head. The shape of the casque varies between different individuals.

casque on head

red wattle

blue neck and facial skin

SIMILAR SPECIES

bald head

Vulturine guineafowl
The largest and most spectacular guineafowl

Numidia meleagris

HELMETED GUINEAFOWL

Widely kept as a domesticated species, the helmeted guineafowl is a handsome bird with boldly spotted plumage. It has broad wings, a short, sharply tapering tail, and streamlined feathers. This helps it push through dense vegetation.

Vocal and gregarious, helmeted guineafowl live in flocks of up to 24 birds, although hundreds sometimes gather at waterholes in times of drought. They feed on a variety of plants and small animals. If alarmed, they produce loud, metallic calls before running for safety. In emergencies they burst into the air, gliding for a short distance before dropping back to the ground.

Juvenile guineafowl
The eggs hatch after about a month and the young bird is soon able to run and flutter off the ground to roost in trees.

curled, brown crest

dark throat

white necklace

pure gray chest

scaly lower belly

Forward-facing crest
The California quail's plume is made of six slender, curved feathers. The crest is larger and darker in males.

streaked flanks

PROFILE

⊙	W. North America
〜	Grassland and scrub, farmland, open woodland, and chaparral
⊘	Nonmigrant
↔	9–10½ in (23–27 cm)
⬤	5–6 oz (150–175 g)
▭	Hollow in ground, lined with plant stems, often sheltered by vegetation
◔	10–12 eggs; 1 brood
✕	Least Concern
⬥	Flocks

SIMILAR SPECIES

grayish back

Gambel's quail Rust-colored crown, black spot on belly

thin, straight plume

Mountain quail Longest crest; brown throat patch

Callipepla californica

CALIFORNIA QUAIL

With its teardrop-shaped crest or plume, the California quail from western North America is only a distant relative of the quails of the Old World. Both sexes are brownish gray, with streaked flanks, and crests. Common in woodlands, scrub-covered hills, and open suburbs, this compact gamebird lives in parties or coveys, which can be 200-strong in fall and winter.

The California quail feeds on leaves, seeds, acorns, insects, spiders, and snails. While the flock feeds, males act as sentries—at the first sign of danger, a sentry gives a series of warning *pips*, sending the flocks either flying or running for cover. The young hatch after three weeks of incubation. Able to feed themselves, they swap their down for the juvenile plumage in 10 days.

Female California quail
The two female forms—gray or brown—lack the male's dark face and have slender, mid-brown plumes.

Field forager
The gray partridge's humped, compact body blends in well against plowed fields and other open places.

alert posture typical of male bird

streaked back

dull brown bill

brick-red face

finely barred gray breast

dull brown legs

SIMILAR SPECIES

ash-gray plumage

Chukar Larger, with an eye-stripe and a gray back

broad white line behind eye

Arabian partridge
Black-crowned species from desert regions

Perdix perdix

GRAY PARTRIDGE

This is the most common partridge in many parts of Europe, as well as in other parts of the world where it has been introduced. It is gray in color, but both sexes have a brick-red face, while the males also have a large chestnut belly patch. Despite these highlights, gray partridges are very well camouflaged. If threatened, they crouch down and remain still. Only a close approach makes them speed away low over the ground on rapidly beating wings.

Gray partridges eat seeds and shoots, sometimes scraping away snow to feed. In fall and winter, they form groups, or coveys, of about 20 birds, which roost together. These break up in spring, as pairs prepare to breed. The females have maximum clutch sizes of about 20 eggs. However, only a small proportion of the chicks survive.

Female gray partridge
The female has a smaller belly patch, and is less brightly colored, except for a darker eyebrow stripe.

PROFILE

- Europe to E. central Siberia and Mongolia; Iran, N. India, Africa, Madagascar
- Open areas, arable land
- Migrant
- 6 ½–7 in (16–18 cm)
- 2 ½–5 oz (70–150 g)
- Hollow in ground, lined with dried grass
- 12 eggs; 1 brood
- Least Concern
- Family groups

Miniature gamebird Predominantly brown with streaked upperparts, the common quail runs for safety instead of taking to the air.

striped crown

small bill

dark central throat stripe

small, rotund body

dark stripes on flanks

SIMILAR SPECIES

squared tail

Asian blue quail Smallest quail from the Far East

streaked brown plumage

Brown quail Good runner from Australia

Coturnix coturnix

COMMON QUAIL

Unlike most gamebirds, the common quail often travels several thousand miles between its winter quarters in Africa and South Asia and its breeding range In Europe and Siberia. This is all the more surprising given its small size—the female rarely weighs more than 4 ½ oz (130 g), while the male is usually lighter. The common quail lives in dry grassland and crops, where its streaked brown plumage acts as camouflage. Often the only sign of its presence is the female's *quic-ic-ic* call, which is used to contact the male.

The common quail feeds on seeds, and breeds once a year. The female makes a scrape nest where it sits for 21 days to incubate the eggs. The chicks leave the nest within hours of hatching, and start flying when they are about 11 days old.

Female common quail
The female is slightly larger than the male and does not have the male's blackish central throat stripe.

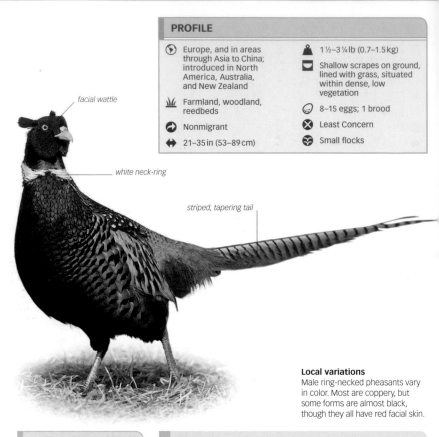

facial wattle

white neck-ring

striped, tapering tail

PROFILE

🜨	Europe, and in areas through Asia to China; introduced in North America, Australia, and New Zealand	⚖	1½–3¼ lb (0.7–1.5 kg)
🜁	Farmland, woodland, reedbeds	▭	Shallow scrapes on ground, lined with grass, situated within dense, low vegetation
➡	Nonmigrant	🥚	8–15 eggs; 1 brood
↔	21–35 in (53–89 cm)	✖	Least Concern
		⬡	Small flocks

Local variations
Male ring-necked pheasants vary in color. Most are coppery, but some forms are almost black, though they all have red facial skin.

SIMILAR SPECIES

very long gray tail

Lady Amherst's pheasant
Striking, multicolored plumage, with a long, barred tail

Phasianus colchicus

RING-NECKED PHEASANT

Originally from Central Asia and the Far East, the ring-necked pheasant has been introduced elsewhere for shooting and food. Compared to some gamebirds, this species flies readily. It bursts explosively into the air at the first sign of danger, beating its wings rapidly before gliding away. It feeds on fruit, seeds, and small animals. The male's loud *korr-kok* call is heard in the breeding season, along with the drumming of its wings.

The female lays a clutch of pale olive eggs. The chicks leave the nest when only a few hours old. In some regions, introduced pheasants become feral, breeding in the wild. In others, including Britain, large numbers are also raised and released each year.

Female pheasant
The female bird has a shorter tail than the male. Its brown plumage helps to conceal it when nesting.

PROFILE

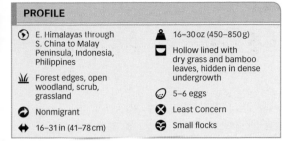

- ⊙ E. Himalayas through S. China to Malay Peninsula, Indonesia, Philippines
- ⩙ Forest edges, open woodland, scrub, grassland
- ◑ Nonmigrant
- ↔ 16–31 in (41–78 cm)

- ⚖ 16–30 oz (450–850 g)
- ▭ Hollow lined with dry grass and bamboo leaves, hidden in dense undergrowth
- ◔ 5–6 eggs
- ✖ Least Concern
- ✿ Small flocks

dark green
wing feathers

Wild cockerel
The male red junglefowl has red facial skin and hanging wattles, as well as a bright red comb. Each leg is armed with a sharp spur, used in combat with rivals.

SIMILAR SPECIES

pale bars on
gray-black neck
feathers

Gray junglefowl Species found in central and southern India

Gallus gallus

RED JUNGLEFOWL

The wild ancestor of the domestic chicken, this species lives in South and Southeast Asia, where it feeds on insects and plants. While the female is cryptically colored—a feature that allows it to hide when nesting—the ostentatious plumage of the male helps it attract females in the breeding season.

These birds live in small, mixed flocks until the breeding season begins. The strongest males then establish territories, and mate with several females. The females make nests, incubate the eggs, and also care for the young. Like many birds, they keep laying eggs if some are removed—a response that is used in chickens to produce a laying period that is many months long.

Female red junglefowl
The female is similar to a domestic hen, although it is more lightly built, with an upswept tail.

PROFILE

- Indian subcontinent
- Tropical forest, clearings, and cultivated fields
- Nonmigrant
- 3–7 ¼ ft (0.9–2.2 m)
- 7 ¾–11 lb (3.5–5 kg)
- Shallow hollow, bare or lined with sticks, leaves, and grass, hidden in thorny undergrowth
- 4–8 eggs
- Least Concern
- Small flocks

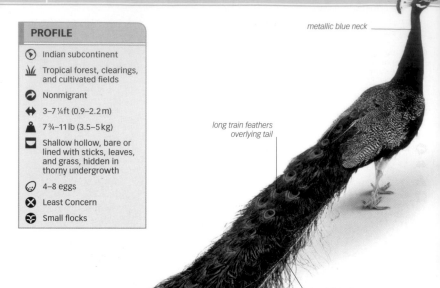

metallic blue neck

long train feathers overlying tail

true tail feathers concealed underneath train

Dazzling ornament
Peacocks molt their trains, or "tails," in late summer, when the breeding season finishes. A new train is fully grown by the end of the following winter.

SIMILAR SPECIES

tall, pointed crest

Green peafowl Strong flier from the forests of S.E. Asia

Pavo cristatus

COMMON PEAFOWL

Often known as the peacock—a name that applies to the male—the common peafowl is one of the best-known ornamental birds. The female has subdued plumage, but the male has a metallic blue neck and crest, and about 150 display feathers on its "tail." During displays, these feathers are spread out in a semicircular fan, revealing a collection of iridescent eyespots, or ocelli, in tones of copper and green.

Common peafowl feed on seeds, insects, lizards, and young snakes. They spend most of their lives on the ground, but roost in trees. During the breeding season, the male fans its train at a series of females, which briefly gather to form a flock. After mating, the female leaves the male to nest and incubate the eggs on its own.

Common peahen
The female peafowl has brown upperparts and a pale underside. It does not have a train.

PROFILE

- Throughout the Northern Hemisphere in Arctic tundra, from Iceland to Kamchatka in the Russian Far East

- Rocky tundra with sparse vegetation, also on high peaks above 6,500 ft (2,000 m)

- Nonmigrant

- 13–15 in (33–38 cm)

- 15–26 oz (425–750 g)

- Depression, lined with plant matter and feathers, often away from cover

- 8–10 eggs; 1 brood

- Least Concern

- Winter flocks

Cold-proof
The rock ptarmigan has highly insulating plumage, and also fully feathered feet, which help it walk across ice and freshly fallen snow.

small, delicate bill

red comb above eye

"salt-and-pepper" pattern on gray upperparts

white belly

feathered feet

SIMILAR SPECIES

rich red-brown body

Willow ptarmigan Larger, lacks red comb in winter

Lagopus muta

ROCK PTARMIGAN

Ptarmigans are medium-sized gamebirds adapted to cold conditions. The rock ptarmigan is one of the hardiest species—its range includes some of the most inhospitable parts of the Arctic, only a few hundred miles from the North Pole.

Its appearance changes with the seasons. In summer, it is largely mottled brown, but in winter it is almost pure white, except for some black tail feathers and pronounced red combs in males. Its diet also changes throughout the year: in summer, it eats the leaves of dwarf willows and other low-growing shrubs, switching to berries in fall. In winter, it mainly eats twigs and bugs, sometimes digging into the snow to reach its food. The female incubates the eggs and looks after the young.

Changing plumage
The rock ptarmigan changes its plumage with the changing seasons, but has white wing tips year-round.

PROFILE

🕑 Scotland, N. Spain, Scandinavia, from Alps eastward to Russia

🌿 Mostly coniferous forest; sometimes mixed forest with conifers or other evergreens

🔄 Nonmigrant

↔ 23½–34 in (60–87 cm)

⚖ 4½–9¾ lb (1.8–4.1 kg)

▭ Hollow on ground, at base of tree, lined with grass, pine needles, twigs

🥚 4–15 eggs; 1 brood

❌ Least Concern

🐦 Family groups/flocks

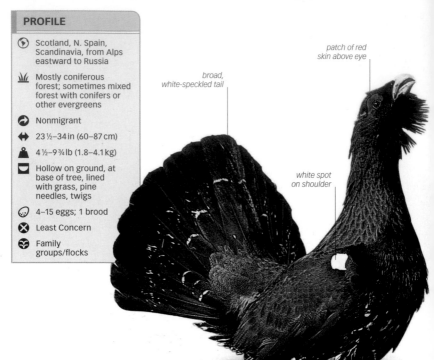

patch of red
skin above eye

broad,
white-speckled tail

white spot
on shoulder

Herbivorous diet
The western capercaillie has a bill with a powerful but precise grip, allowing it to pick up berries or tear pine needles from the branches.

SIMILAR SPECIES

white line outlining
black throat

Spruce grouse Often seen at the edge of forest clearings, or beside forest roads

dark brown back

Sooty grouse Found west of the Rocky Mountains in Canada and the USA

Tetrao urogallus

WESTERN CAPERCAILLIE

The world's largest grouse, the western capercaillie, is a powerful flier. Despite its weight, it speeds between trees, or skims just above the canopy. The male is twice the size of the female and as big as a small turkey. This species feeds mainly on conifer needles, a diet that not many can digest.

The breeding males gather at "leks" to compete for the attention of females. In their courtship dance, they show off their plumage, fan their tails, and engage in mock combat. The male has a strange call that starts with a series of clicks, goes on to sound like a cork being pulled out of a bottle, and ends with a metallic scrape.

Female capercaillie
The female has orange-buff feathers, marked with black. It has a plain rufous chest.

Bearded heavyweight
The male wild turkey weighs about twice as much as the female, with a maximum weight of about 24 lb (11 kg) It has a "beard" growing from the center of its chest.

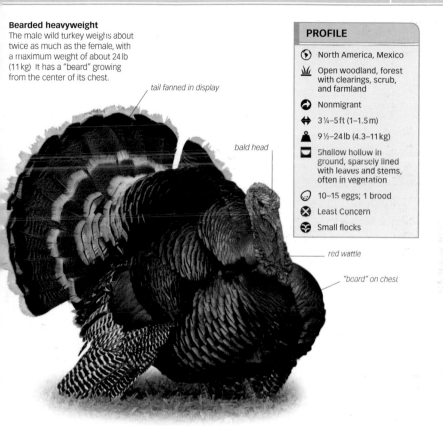

tail fanned in display

bald head

red wattle

"beard" on chest

PROFILE

- North America, Mexico
- Open woodland, forest with clearings, scrub, and farmland
- Nonmigrant
- 3¼–5 ft (1–1.5 m)
- 9½–24 lb (4.3–11 kg)
- Shallow hollow in ground, sparsely lined with leaves and stems, often in vegetation
- 10–15 eggs; 1 brood
- Least Concern
- Small flocks

SIMILAR SPECIES

blue head and neck

Ocellated turkey Found in Central America

Meleagris gallopavo

WILD TURKEY

Found in woods and forests, this bird is the wild ancestor of the farmyard turkey, which was domesticated about 2,000 years ago. Shy and cautious, it frequently lives in small flocks, feeding on seeds, nuts, acorns, and insects. The wild turkey has six recognized subspecies, and its coloration varies across its range. The male generally has a dark bronze body with an iridescent sheen. During the breeding season it has a pronounced red wattle hanging down on one side of its bill. Both sexes have long bodies and strong legs.

Wild turkeys are best known for the male's courtship display, in which it fans its tail and raises its body feathers to look as large as possible. The male also produces a characteristic "gobbling" call, especially during courtship.

Female wild turkey
The female is typically bronze-green, with a less colorful face than the male, and no wattle.

WATERFOWL

Also known as wildfowl, members of this group include ducks, geese, and swans. Found on every continent except Antarctica, most of them dabble or dive for their food—usually in freshwater, but sometimes close to coasts at sea.

With their webbed feet and broad bills, waterfowl are difficult to confuse with any other birds. Their plumage is dense and highly waterproof—a result partly due to its structure, and partly due to a coating of water-repellent oils. Although some species are flightless, waterfowl generally are powerful fliers on fast-flapping wings, and many migrate thousands of miles to breed.

ORDER	ANSERIFORMES
FAMILIES	3
SPECIES	174

FOOD AND BREEDING

Most species of waterfowl eat a mixture of plant and animal food, although some kinds—such as sawbill ducks—specialize in catching fish. Geese are an exception: using their powerful bills and necks, they tear up plants on land, using water as a refuge and often as a place to roost.

Waterfowl usually nest on the ground, close to the water's edge. In swans and geese, both parents help raise the young. In ducks, males (or drakes) are often brightly colored during the breeding season. The female leads the young to water shortly after they have hatched, but the male plays little part in raising the family.

PENGUINS

Confined to Antarctica and the southern oceans, penguins are among the world's most familiar animals. With their well-insulated bodies and flipperlike wings, these flightless birds are superbly adapted to life in some of Earth's coldest habitats.

Penguins spend most of their lives in seawater, where they feed on a wide range of animals, including fish, krill, and squid. To swim, they use their wings as flippers. Their plumage is short, dense, and waterproof, and lies over a thick layer of subcutaneous fat that insulates the body from the surrounding cold. Most penguins come ashore only to breed, often in the same colonies that are occupied year after year. On land, they move with their bodies upright. Some can hop, but most use a slow, waddling gait. The majority breed on cold coasts in the southern oceans—only a handful of species raise their young on Antarctica itself.

ORDER	SPHENISCIFORMES
FAMILIES	1
SPECIES	18

Taking the plunge
Adélie penguins live year-round in Antarctica, leaping into the water directly from the ice. They feed on small fish and krill.

PROFILE

- 🜚 Across Eurasia, apart from N. Russia and N. Siberia; winters as far south as N. Africa, Iran, India, China
- 〰 Mainly in open country
- ↻ Partial migrant
- ↔ 29–33 in (74–84 cm)
- ⚖ 6¾–7¾ lb (3.1–3.5 kg)
- ▭ Shallow, natural depression in ground, lined with leaves and feather down
- ☺ 4–6 eggs; 1 brood
- ✖ Least Concern
- ❀ Pairs/flocks

Farmyard goose
The graylag goose is the ancestor of many breeds of farmyard geese. Domesticated birds vary from gray-brown to pure white.

"ribbed" neck feathers

large, orange-pink bill

large, pale body

gray brown plumage

orange-pink legs

SIMILAR SPECIES

darker head

Bean goose Darker head, orange legs

brown cap

slimmer neck

Swan goose Lesser-known domesticated species

Anser anser

GRAYLAG GOOSE

The largest and heaviest gray wild goose, the graylag has gray-brown plumage with a striking cream-colored rear, orange-pink legs, and a pink bill. It is bulky, thick-necked, and has webbed feet. A good swimmer, it is often seen on rivers and lakes, but it feeds mainly on marshy ground, pulling up plants or excavating roots with its powerful, serrated bill.

The graylag goose is migratory, and breeds farther south than all other gray geese. During the summer, it feeds and nests across Europe and Asia, from Iceland eastward to northern China, while its wintering grounds stretch from Britain to the Middle East, South Asia, and the Far East. During migration flights, these geese often travel in a V-formation, calling loudly as they fly. They nest in groups or isolated pairs close to water, making a simple nest with the minimum of lining. The young, cared for by both parents, are able to swim soon after they hatch. They can fly by the time they are about eight weeks old.

PROFILE

- ⊙ Arctic zone of North America; winters as far south as Mexico
- 🌾 Breeds in low tundra; winters on cultivated land
- ➤ Migrant
- ↔ 26–30 in (65–75 cm)
- ⚖ 5¼–7½ lb (2.4–3.4 kg)

- ▭ Natural hollow in ground, lined with leaves and an inner down cup
- 🥚 3–5 eggs; 1 brood
- ✕ Least Concern
- ✿ Flocks

black patch on pink bill

white plumage

black wing tips

deep pink legs

White form
The snow goose has two color forms, or phases—white and blue. The white form is characterized by brilliant white plumage. Both phases have deep pink legs and bills.

SIMILAR SPECIES

short, deeply furrowed neck

Ross's goose Smaller, with a round head and reddish legs

barred pattern on body

Emperor goose Darker, with a white head and orange legs

Chen caerulescens

SNOW GOOSE

A common North American species, the snow goose is highly gregarious by nature. Long-distance migrants, they breed in Arctic tundra, often close to the sea, and winter mainly in the Gulf states and along the Atlantic seaboard. They arrive at their breeding grounds just as the snow melts, often gathering in flocks of tens of thousands at the same sites they used the year before. Pairs breed just a short distance from each other. They normally lay eggs in June, but if the weather is particularly bad, they may skip breeding entirely until the following year.

Snow geese feed on shoots, roots, and aquatic insects; in winter they often eat berries and cultivated grain.

Immature blue phase
This form is characterized by gray plumage, partly tinged with blue. Mature birds have white heads.

PROFILE

- ⊙ Throughout North America, E. Siberia; winters as far south as New Mexico, E. China, Japan; introduced in N.W. Europe
- 🌾 Tundra, wetland, reservoirs, farmland
- ➤ Partial migrant
- ↔ 2–3 ½ ft (0.6–1.1 m)
- ⚖ 2¾–11 lb (1.2–4.8 kg)
- ▭ Down-lined scrape on the ground, often on a small island
- 🥚 5–6 eggs; 1 brood
- ✖ Least Concern
- ❀ Flocks

Wide range
In their native range, Canada geese breed throughout North America. The smallest forms nest in tundra, north of the Arctic Circle.

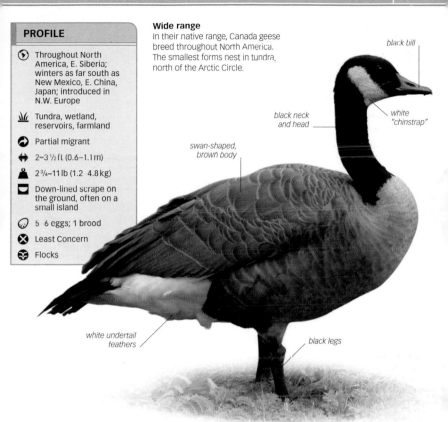

black bill

white "chinstrap"

black neck and head

swan-shaped, brown body

white undertail feathers

black legs

SIMILAR SPECIES

distinct feather grooves on neck

Hawaiian goose Rare brown goose, found on the barren volcanic slopes of the Hawaiian islands

black-and-white bars on back

Barnacle goose Smaller and less widespread

Branta canadensis

CANADA GOOSE

Originally from North America, the Canada goose has become established in several other parts of the world, from Britain to New Zealand. Mainly brownish gray, it has a dark neck and head, with a distinctive white "chinstrap." There are currently seven recognized subspecies, varying not only in their coloration but also in size. In their native range, these geese are migratory, but in other parts of the world, they often remain in one area all year round.

Canada geese feed on land and water, tugging up grass with their powerful bills, or dabbling under the surface to collect small animals. They breed near the waterside. The male courts the female by stretching out its neck parallel to the ground. The female incubates the eggs, but the male usually leads the brood to water. The young can swim immediately, and will dive if danger comes their way. Canada geese usually breed when they are three years old. They show a strong affinity to their nest site, returning there year after year.

PROFILE

- Breeds in Arctic Siberia; winter quarters around shores of the Black, Caspian, and Aral seas

- Breeds by tundra, close to rivers; winters in open steppes among pasture and crops

- Migrant

- 21–21½ in (53–55 cm)

- 2¼–3 lb (1.1–1.4 kg)

- Hollow, lined with down and feathers, on a raised piece of ground

- Endangered

- Flocks

Tundra nester
Red-breasted geese nest in the waterlogged tundra of Russia's Taymyr Peninsula. They overwinter in farmland in southeast Europe.

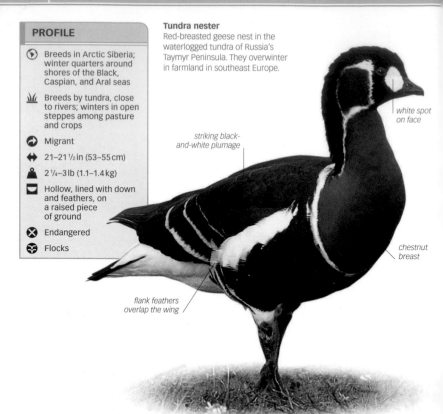

white spot on face

striking black-and-white plumage

chestnut breast

flank feathers overlap the wing

SIMILAR SPECIES

dark gray-brown upperparts

Brant Breeds in the Arctic tundra, wintering farther south on coasts

Branta ruficollis

RED-BREASTED GOOSE

Small but conspicuously marked, this increasingly rare goose breeds in northern Siberia, where it nests on scrub-covered tundra. It is unmistakable when compared to other geese, with a short neck and stubby bill. Its breast and cheeks are chestnut in color, while the rest of its body is largely black and white. The red-breasted goose arrives at the breeding grounds in early summer—much later than migratory birds that breed in warmer parts of the world. It nests in groups of 5–6 pairs, near steep riverbanks or low cliffs.

These geese sometimes breed close to the nests of peregrine falcons, hawks, or large gulls. This protects them, because the more aggressive birds drive predators away. The goslings are ready to fly six weeks after they hatch. At the end of summer, adults and young set off to their winter quarters around the shores of the Black, Caspian and Aral seas. Due to their narrow distribution, red-breasted geese are threatened by global warming and habitat destruction.

PROFILE

- Scattered in areas across Eurasia; introduced in areas of North America, South America, Australia, New Zealand
- Lowland bodies of fresh water, especially man-made; sheltered coastal areas
- Partial migrant
- 4–5 ¼ ft (1.2–1.6 m)

- 21–26 lb (9.5–12 kg)
- Mound of plant material, in reeds on a small island, or on the shore of a lake, river, or stream
- 8 eggs; 1 brood
- Least Concern
- Small flocks

black facial knob

long, S-shaped neck

long, pointed tail

white overall

large, heavy body

Elegance afloat
Adult mute swans have an all-white plumage. Both sexes have a black knob at the base of their bill, but it is more pronounced in males.

SIMILAR SPECIES

yellow wedge on bill

all-white plumage

Whooper swan Second-largest swan in the world

distinctive long neck

Tundra swan Smallest swan in North America

Cygnus olor

MUTE SWAN

Graceful and majestic, the mute swan is one of the world's heaviest waterbirds, and a familiar sight in parks and lakes in Europe, northeast North America, and Australasia. It originally comes from the steppes of Central Asia, where it is still found. Males and females are almost identical, with white plumage. Unlike geese, mute swans feed mainly in water, upending to reach plants and animals in lake mud and riverbeds. They are not completely silent: if threatened, they hiss and snort, raising their wings in defense.

Their weight does not let them take off from a standing start. They typically splash across the water, gaining enough speed to become airborne. Cygnets are tended by both parents and leave the nest soon after they are hatched.

Juvenile mute swan
Cygnets are gray-brown and take four years to reach maturity, with adult plumage and orange bills.

PROFILE

- Australia, New Zealand
- Large shallow lakes, flooded agricultural land, coastal lagoons, sheltered coastal bays
- Partial migrant
- 3½–4½ ft (1.1–1.4 m)
- 11–13 lb (5–6 kg)
- Large mound of reeds, grass, and weeds in shallow water or on islands
- 4–8 eggs
- Least Concern
- Pairs/large flocks

Australian nomad
Native to Australia, the black swan is a nomadic bird, traveling hundreds of miles to places where recent rainfall creates a temporary flush of flood.

sooty black feathers

bright red bill

SIMILAR SPECIES

white stripe behind eye

Black-necked swan Red knob at the base of grayish bill; found in parts of southern South America

Cygnus atratus

BLACK SWAN

The world's only largely black swan can look completely black when swimming, but has conspicuous white flight feathers on the outer half of its wings. These are revealed during flight. Its bill is red with a pronounced hook at the tip.

Black swans are highly social and usually live in pairs or flocks. They are largely vegetarian, eating submerged plants or grazing on the ground. Like most swans, black swans have a single partner, staying together for life. They have no set breeding season, nesting instead when the weather is favorable. Both parents help build the nest, a spreading heap of vegetation in shallow water. A typical clutch has six greenish white eggs, which are incubated for about five weeks. Once fledged, the young swans, called cygnets, need three years to reach maturity. Black swans are often seen in other parts of the world as ornamental birds. In New Zealand, where the species has been introduced, it is now common in the wild.

PROFILE

- W. Europe, C. Asia
- Seacoasts, estuaries, larger inland lakes (particularly saline); gravel and sandpits
- Migrant
- 23–26 in (58–67 cm)
- 2¼ lb (1 kg)
- Hole in the ground, lined with down
- 8–10 eggs; 1 brood
- Least Concern
- Pairs/small flocks

Multicolored duck
The common shelduck is easily recognized by the colorful black, white, and chestnut-brown bands on its body. The male's red bill has a conspicuous knob.

glossy head

red bill with knob

largely white plumage

chestnut-brown breast band

SIMILAR SPECIES

orange-brown body

Ruddy shelduck Widespread species, with paler head

black-and-white body

Radjah shelduck Smaller; with light pink legs, feet, and bill

Tadorna tadorna

COMMON SHELDUCK

This large, colorful bird is one of the most distinctive ducks of western Europe's coasts, although its breeding range also includes lakes across Central Asia, thousands of kilometres from the sea.

Common shelducks feed on water snails and other small animals, sieving them out of the mud or water with side-to-side movements of their bills. They breed away from the water's edge, and like most waterfowl, the adults undergo their post-breeding molt once their young have become independent. This leaves them temporarily flightless, so they congregate beforehand in places that offer security and food. In some places, thousands of flightless adults feed on coastal mudflats, waiting for their new flight feathers to grow.

Female shelduck
The female, duller than the male, has a broken breast band and a bill without a knob.

Wild Muscovy
The Muscovy duck is distinguished by its deep black plumage and large size. The wild form is much sleeker than its domesticated descendants.

prominent knob on bill

black crest

nearly black plumage

PROFILE

- Central and South America
- Lowland lakes, lagoons, marshes, and rivers in forested areas; brackish coastal wetland
- Nonmigrant
- 26–33 in (66–84 cm)
- 4½–6½ lb (2–3 kg)
- Lays eggs in tree cavities or on ground
- 8–10 eggs; 1 brood
- Least Concern
- Small flocks

Cairina moschata

MUSCOVY DUCK

Despite its name, the Muscovy duck comes from Central and South America. It is not known how it got its name; however, it has a long history of domestication, and was raised for food long before Europeans arrived in the Americas. A large, thickset duck the size of a small goose, it has near-black plumage, with eye-catching white forewings in adults. The male has a conspicuous red bill-knob and a domed black crest. Domesticated Muscovy ducks are often piebald, with red facial skin.

Muscovy ducks feed mainly on leaves and seeds obtained by dabbling in shallow water. They also eat worms, aquatic insects, and other small animals. The breeding season varies with the location. The female raises the young on its own, without any help from the male.

Domestic female
The female Muscovy duck is half as heavy as the male, and domestic birds usually have piebald plumage.

PROFILE

- North America to Cuba
- Freshwater ponds, lakes, and slow-flowing rivers in well-wooded places; open areas in winter
- Partial migrant
- 17–20 in (43–51 cm)
- 22–24 oz (625–675 g)
- Tree hole or nest box, lined with down
- 10–15 eggs; 2 broods
- Least Concern
- Small flocks

Breeding male
The male wood duck is brightly colored during the breeding season, but similar to the female at other times of the year.

bare, red eye-ring

slender, drooping crest

white edges on flank feathers

SIMILAR SPECIES

orange "sails"

Mandarin duck Exotic-looking duck of Southeast Asian origin

Aix sponsa

WOOD DUCK

Often kept in captivity, this North American species is one of the world's most attractive ducks—a title it shares with its close relative, the Mandarin duck. In its breeding plumage, the male has a glossy green head with a backswept crest, and a complex pattern of contrasting colors on its body and wings. The female is much more subdued. Adults are fast and agile on the wing. When swimming, it bobs its head back and forth.

Wood ducks usually live in small groups, gathering in larger numbers to spend the winter. They feed mainly by dabbling in shallow water, but also graze on the shore. At the onset of the breeding season, females seek out tree-holes to lay eggs. The ducklings jump to the ground within a day of hatching and make their way to the water.

Female wood duck
The female has a mottled brown underside, a gray head streaked with white, and a gray bill.

Dressed to breed
In spring and summer, the male mallard has a bright green head and a white neck ring. Its upperparts are grayish brown; its breast is chestnut.

green head

bright yellow bill

grayish brown body

short, black curls above white tail

blue wing band

white neck-ring

PROFILE

- North America and Eurasia; winters as far south as Mexico, N. Africa, S.E. Asia
- Freshwater wetland and coastal habitats
- Partial migrant
- 19 ½–26 in (50–65 cm)
- 2 ¾ lb (1.2 kg)
- Hollow in ground or on tree, lined with stems, leaves, and feathers
- 9–13 eggs; 1 brood
- Least Concern
- Flocks

Anas platyrhynchos

MALLARD

The mallard is one of the world's most widespread inland ducks, with a range that stretches across the Northern Hemisphere. Adaptable to human activity, it is at home on rivers, reservoirs, lakes, canals, and urban ponds. The breeding male has a metallic green head, and a speculum—a broad, blue band—that is visible when its wings are outstretched. When the breeding season ends, it loses these colors and develops an "eclipse" plumage that resembles the female's. The female also has a speculum on each wing.

The mallard dabbles at the surface for plants and animals, and nests on the ground. The female tends the eggs and young, leading them to the water after they have hatched. It is the ancestor of all domestic ducks, except the Muscovy's descendants (p.44).

Female mallard
The mottled-brown plumage of the female helps camouflage it during nesting.

PROFILE

- North America, Europe, N. Asia
- Lakes, rivers, and vicinity; freshwater marshes and swamps
- Partial migrant
- 14½ in (37 cm)
- 11½ oz (340 g)
- Depression in dry grass, lined with down, among marsh plants
- 6–9 eggs; 1 brood
- Least Concern
- Flocks

Courtship colors
In the breeding season, the male green-winged teal develops metallic-green eye-patches, outlined with cream stripes, and a cinnamon-colored head.

rufous head

green eye-patch

white stripe on side of breast

intricate pattern on flanks

buff undertail feathers

SIMILAR SPECIES

orangish red eye

Cinnamon teal North American dabbling duck, with a long, spoon-shaped, black bill

Anas crecca

GREEN-WINGED TEAL

Slightly built compared to many other ducks, the green-winged teal is quick to take to the air at the first sign of danger, circling several times before touching down on the water. When breeding, it lives on freshwater pools and lakes, but outside it may be found in reservoirs, estuaries, or tropical swamps. This is when it can form large flocks.

Green-winged teals pair up in their winter quarters. At their breeding grounds, they build nests lined with the female's down, among waterside vegetation. The female incubates the eggs and cares for the young.

The green-winged teal feeds by dabbling or upending in the shallows, collecting plants and small animals. These birds usually migrate southward for winter, although they remain in parts of western Europe all year round.

Female teal
The female, with mottled brown plumage, resembles many other female dabbling ducks.

PROFILE

- Breeds in Eurasia; winters as far south as S. Sudan, N. India, S.E. Asia
- Temperate, lowland bodies of fresh water; occasionally in sheltered marine habitats in winter
- Migrant
- 15 ½–18 ½ in (40–47 cm)
- 1–2 ¼ lb (0.5–1 kg)
- Hollow lined with grass and down, in vegetation close to water
- 8–11 eggs; 1 brood
- Least Concern
- Large flocks

Conspicuous quiff
The crest of the male tufted duck follows the contours of its head. Its plumage is black, apart from white flanks and white wing feathers.

drooping crest

yellow eye

black-tipped bill

black upperparts

SIMILAR SPECIES

smooth, round head

Greater scaup Breeds at high latitudes in tundra wetlands

pointed head

Ring-necked duck White ring behind black bill tip

Aythya fuligula

TUFTED DUCK

With its black-and-white plumage and drooping crest, the tufted duck has a neat and tidy appearance. The male has a strongly contrasted plumage except in midsummer. Unlike most other ducks, it dives for food, sometimes up to 49 ft (15 m) deep. Kicking with its feet, the tufted duck disappears with a forward flop and bobs back to the surface like a cork. It feeds on freshwater lakes and reservoirs, and eats mollusks and insects.

The tufted duck nests close to the waterside, among colonies of gulls or terns, whose aggressive behavior helps defend against intruders. Like many of their relatives, tufted ducks are migratory, breeding across a large swathe of Europe and northern Asia. Once the ducklings fledge, adults and young migrate to their winter quarters.

Female tufted duck
The female is deep rusty brown, with white under-tail coverts. Its crest is smaller than the male duck's.

PROFILE

⊙ North America, Europe, Asia	🏋 2¾–6¼ lb (1.2–2.8 kg)
〰 Low-lying coasts and islands with rocky shores and weedy bays; winters in sandy bays and over mussel beds; very rarely inland	📦 Down-lined hollow on ground, exposed or well hidden
	🥚 4–6 eggs; 1 brood
⊘ Migrant	✕ Least Concern
↔ 19½–28 in (50–71 cm)	🐝 Colonies

black crown

wedge-shaped bill

white upperparts

black underparts

Changing hues
The male common eider has a white body, and black cap and flanks. The body color changes to brownish black after breeding.

SIMILAR SPECIES

blue-gray head

King eider Dives over 82 ft (25 m) when foraging

large, whitish disk around eye

Spectacled eider Arctic species from Siberia and Alaska

Somateria mollissima

COMMON EIDER

The common eider is found on cold-water coasts across the Northern Hemisphere. It is famous for the soft eiderdown that comes from the female bird, which it plucks from its breasts to insulate the nest. Eiderdown provides warmth and helps protect the ducklings in a range that extends far north of the Arctic Circle.

Common eiders have a "Roman nose" profile, but the two sexes look different. Males are mainly black and white; females are mottled brown. Eiders dive from the surface for crabs and mollusks, collecting them with their powerful beaks, often swallowing them whole. They breed inshore in large colonies. The female takes about four weeks to incubate the eggs. Once hatched, broods gather into crèches, with several females taking charge.

Female common eider
The wedge-shaped bill of the female helps distinguish it from most other ducks.

PROFILE

- North America, Europe, Asia
- Breeds by estuaries, rivers, and lakes
- Migrant
- 20–24 in (51–62 cm)
- 1¾–2¾ lb (0.85–1.25 kg)
- In long grass on ground, in tree holes, or among rocks, lined with down
- 8–11 eggs; 1 brood
- Least Concern
- Family groups/flocks

Contrasting colors
The male red-breasted merganser has a green head and a red breast that contrasts with its gray flanks. The bill is deep red.

wispy crest

broad, white line on back

slim, slightly upcurved bill

white collar

SIMILAR SPECIES

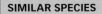

plum-red bill

green-black head

Common merganser Largest sawbill, with a hooked bill and a long tail

Smew Relatively scarce, with a drooping white crest and white plumage

Mergus serrator

RED-BREASTED MERGANSER

This long, streamlined duck belongs to a group known as the sawbills, which dive for fish. Like its relatives, the red-breasted merganser has an unusually slender bill for a duck. The cutting edges of the bill are armed with backward-pointing "teeth," which give it a strong grip on slippery prey. The males resemble females outside of the breeding season, with a brown head and smaller crest.

Red-breasted mergansers spend the summer in the far north and adjacent regions farther south, wintering in warmer climes. The clutch is large, and the female incubates the eggs on its own. Once the young have hatched and left the nest, it sometimes carries them on its back.

Female merganser
The female has gray flanks, and a rusty brown head. Like the male, it has black upper wing tips.

PROFILE

- Antarctic coasts
- Antarctic ice and sea
- Partial migrant
- 3½ ft (1.1 m)
- 66–88 lb (30–40 kg)
- No nest; egg and chick rest on male's feet behind a fold of feathered belly skin
- 1 egg
- Least Concern
- Colonies

Winter warmth
The emperor penguin's plumage and body fat insulate it against winter temperatures as low as −76°F (−60°C).

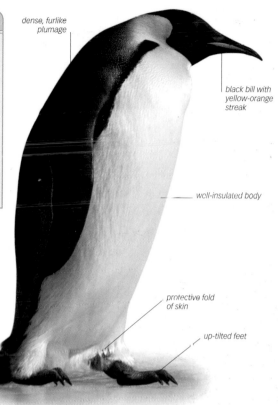

dense, furlike plumage

black bill with yellow-orange streak

well-insulated body

protective fold of skin

up-tilted feet

short, stiff tail

SIMILAR SPECIES

silver-gray back

King penguin Slightly smaller, breeds on sub-Antarctic coasts

Aptenodytes forsteri

EMPEROR PENGUIN

The emperor is the largest and heaviest penguin, and one of the few that breed on mainland Antarctica. Largely black and white, it has orange patches on the neck, flipperlike wings, and short, scaly feet with well-developed claws. It feeds on fish and squid, and is a superb swimmer.

Emperor penguins can dive for 10 minutes and reach depths of up to 820 ft (250 m). Their breeding cycle is remarkable. The male incubates the egg throughout the Antarctic winter, while its partner is away at sea. It rests the egg on its feet, covering it with a fold of skin. Females return in early spring, after the chicks have hatched, letting the males make their way to the sea to feed.

Young emperor
The juvenile emperor penguin has an all-black bill and a black-and-white face, without orange markings.

PROFILE

- ⊙ Coast of Antarctica and nearby islands; winters out at sea
- 〰 Ice-free Antarctic shores, with sandy beaches and accessible rocky areas
- ➦ Migrant
- ↔ 28 in (70 cm)
- 🏋 11 lb (5 kg)
- ▭ Low heap of pebbles, collected by male
- ⊘ 2 eggs; 1 brood
- ✖ Least Concern
- ❀ Colonies

white eye-ring

short bill

dense, waterproof plumage

large, fleshy foot

Black-and-white
The Adélie penguin has a dumpy body, with a black-and-white color scheme, and a prominent white ring around its eyes.

SIMILAR SPECIES

Chinstrap penguin Black bill; white chin with thin black strap

white head patch

Gentoo penguin One of the fastest swimming penguins

Pygoscelis adeliae

ADÉLIE PENGUIN

Thickset and densely feathered, the Adélie is the most abundant species of penguin, and one of the world's most southerly breeding birds. It feeds on young fish and krill found in the icy waters off the Antarctic coast. A rapid swimmer, it gains speed by "porpoising"— repeatedly bursting out of the water before dropping back. It can also leap over 3 ft (1 m) out of the water to land on floating ice. Like other penguins, the Adélie is a social bird, nesting in enormous colonies on Antarctica and its outlying islands. Some of these annual gatherings are over half-a-million birds strong.

The colonies are empty throughout the winter, but adult Adélie penguins begin to arrive in October, when the Southern Hemisphere spring commences. The male arrives first, making a simple nest, and the female then settles on the nest, laying a pair of eggs. Both parents incubate them for about 35 days. The young grow up in crèches, and by March, the colony is deserted once again, as adults and young head out to sea.

PROFILE

- Namibia, South Africa
- Offshore islands; breeds in burrows on rocky ground on African mainland and islands
- Nonmigrant
- 23½–28 in (60–70 cm)
- 4¾–8¼ lb (2.1–3.7 kg)
- Burrows or depressions under boulders and bushes
- 2 eggs; 1 brood
- Endangered
- Colonies

bare, pink skin around eye

narrow, black band around chest

black upperparts

speckled belly

white underparts

clawed feet

African penguin
The jackass is the only penguin that breeds on the African continent. Unlike many Antarctic penguins, their nests are not densely packed.

SIMILAR SPECIES

Humboldt penguin
Raucous, braying call

banded pattern on face

black band around chest

Galapagos penguin Only penguin that breeds on the equator

Spheniscus demersus

JACKASS PENGUIN

Named for its braying call, the jackass penguin has an overall black-and-white body, with a speckled belly surrounded by a conspicuous black band. Like most penguins, the sexes are alike, although the male is larger than the female. Both have a black bill with a vertical bar, and black, strongly clawed feet.

Jackass penguins feed on small fish and squid, and swim low in the water, usually feeding not far from the coast. They come ashore to breed and molt, gathering in small colonies on offshore islands, and in a few locations on the mainland. They nest in burrows and hollows under bushes or boulders, laying a pair of eggs.

Both adults take turns incubate the clutch, which takes about 40 days to hatch. Once the eggs are hatched, the adults guard the young for almost a month, feeding them regurgitated fish. While the parents feed at sea, the young are left in a crèche. They take 2–4 months to fledge. Jackass penguins are listed as an endangered species, and face many threats, from fishing to oil spills.

LOONS

Also known as divers, loons make up a small group of heavy-bodied freshwater and coastal birds. Known for their far-carrying calls, they breed mainly in forested lakes in the far north, diving for fish but moving with difficulty on land.

Spear-shaped bills, habitually held at an upward slant, help distinguish loons from other freshwater birds. Apart from their long necks, loons are also low and streamlined, with striking breeding plumage that is replaced by less colorful patterns once the breeding season comes to an end. Their legs are positioned far back along their bodies, and end in large webbed feet. They can dive to depths of 160ft (50m), staying underwater for five minutes or even more. For their size, loons have very small wings, and need a long run-up over water to take off. Once in the air, they are powerful fliers, capable of migrating considerable distances between

ORDER	GAVIIFORMES
FAMILIES	1
SPECIES	5

freshwater and winter quarters, which are often on sheltered coasts.

BREEDING
Loons make nests out of vegetation, piling it up on islands or near the water's edge. Like grebes (p.62), they frequently carry their young on their backs. Young loons are fed by their parents, and depend on them until they are almost full grown. They have a long lifespan, surviving 20 or more years in the wild.

ALBATROSSES, PETRELS, AND SHEARWATERS

Albatrosses and their relatives are oceanic birds that occur throughout the world, often roaming far from the nearest land.

The birds in this group span a huge range in size, from the world's largest seabirds to some of the smallest. All the members of this order have tubular nostrils and a good sense of smell—a feature that gives them their alternative name of tubenoses.

Most of these birds are adapted to continuous flight, snatching fish and other food from the water's surface. The largest species, including albatrosses, soar over the waves using the power of the wind, while the smallest ones use a combination of wingbeats and glides. Most tubenoses nest on remote coasts and islands, typically laying a single egg each time they breed.

ORDER	PROCELLARIIFORMES
FAMILIES	4
SPECIES	133

Riding the wind
With its wings held out stiffly, a black-browed albatross can soar over the sea for hours on end, watching for prey in the water below.

PROFILE

- Europe, Scandinavia, Russia, Alaska, Canada; winters farther south in Atlantic
- Breeds on islands in freshwater lakes; winters at sea
- Migrant
- 25–30 in (63–75 cm)
- 5½–7¾ lb (2.5–3.5 kg)
- Shallow scrape near water's edge on islands (or raft) in lake, lined with vegetation
- 2 eggs; 1 brood
- Least Concern
- Small summer flocks

Checkerboard markings
The arctic loon has a gray head and dark throat. The white squares on its upperwings are laid out in crisscrossed lines.

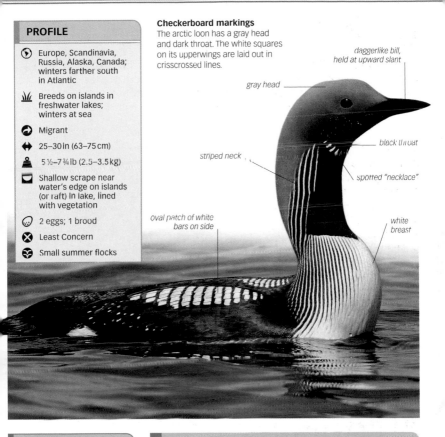

daggerlike bill, held at upward slant

gray head

black throat

striped neck

spotted "necklace"

oval patch of white bars on side

white breast

SIMILAR SPECIES

black "necklace"

Common loon One of the largest loons, with a long, heavy bill

striped gray nape

Red-throated loon Smaller, with an all-brown back and red throat patch

Gavia arctica

ARCTIC LOON

Clumsy on land but elegant on water, this bird lives on cold, freshwater lakes, from northern Europe to the Russian far east. Generally solitary, it gathers in small flocks during summer. Its breeding plumage has precise white squares and spots on black wings. Silent in the winter, it can be recognized by its far-carrying, mournful song when the breeding season begins.

Arctic loons feed on fish and breed close to water. The female lays two eggs and takes charge of incubation, sometimes assisted by the male. The young are fully fledged by the time they are 10 weeks old, and as the summer comes to a close, adults and young migrate to spend the winter on coasts.

Winter plumage
After their post-breeding molt, adults become brown with less noticeable contrasting wing markings.

PROFILE

- Oceans and islands surrounding Antarctica, coasts of the southern continents
- Open ocean on sea; breeds only on bare ground on hillsides and slopes on islands
- Migrant
- 3½–4½ft (1.1–1.4m)
- 14–25lb (6.5–11.5kg)
- Mound of mud and vegetation, on an exposed ridge near sea on remote island
- 1 egg
- Vulnerable
- Colonies

Ocean nomad
The wandering albatross spends most of its life at sea, and can be found in stormy oceans in the Southern Hemisphere.

black markings on upperwings

snowy white plumage

pink bill

SIMILAR SPECIES

black wing tips

Southern royal albatross
Slightly smaller; white plumage, with black-edged wings

Diomedea exulans

WANDERING ALBATROSS

One of the largest flying birds, the wandering albatross has a wingspan of up to 9¾ft (3m). Found in stormy southern oceans, it repeatedly rises and falls on stiff, outstretched wings. This kind of flight, called dynamic soaring, is extremely efficient, and allows it to fly immense distances with very little effort.

Wandering albatrosses nest on slopes where they can easily launch themselves into the wind. They have a slow breeding cycle, raising a single chick every two years. Both parents share the 10-week incubation. Once the chick has hatched, it stays on the nest for a record-breaking 10 months, before it finally takes to the sea.

Juvenile albatross
Brown at first, the young wandering albatross takes seven years to develop adult plumage.

PROFILE

- Southern Ocean, islands in South Atlantic, Pacific, and Indian Ocean
- Open ocean or sea; breeds only on bare, rocky areas and slopes on islands
- Migrant
- 2ft 7in–3ft 2in (80–96cm)
- 6½–10lb (2.9–4.6kg)
- Small mound scraped together out of earth and plant materials, with hollow above
- 1 egg; 1 brood
- Endangered
- Colonies

yellow bill, tipped red

dark upper wings

pure white body

Colors in flight
The adult black-browed albatross is largely white, with dark upper wings. Its white under wings have a thick, dark border.

SIMILAR SPECIES

ash-gray upperparts

Gray-headed albatross
Black bill with yellow ridges; white crescent behind eye

gray-black upperparts

Laysan albatross
Black patch around eye; pink bill with dark tip

Thalassarche melanophris

BLACK-BROWED ALBATROSS

Named for its charcoal-colored "eyebrows," the black-browed albatross is an inhabitant of the southern oceans, soaring over windswept seas as far south as Antarctica. Its dark upper wings and pure white body make it look like an extra-large great black-backed gull (p.142). However, unlike a gull, this albatross spends most of its time on the wing, often roaming hundreds of miles from the coast in search of food. It feeds on fish, krill, jellyfish, and squid, using its hooked bill to snatch up its prey. This bird also snatches baited fishing hooks—one of the reasons why it is now endangered.

The black-browed albatross breeds among tussock grass on exposed islands. The female lays a single egg, and both parents incubate it. Once hatched, the chick remains on the nest for 17 weeks. When fledged, the juvenile has less white on its under wings, and its bill is paler than the adult's, with a black tip.

Gull lookalike
In its gray-white form, the northern fulmar resembles a gull. However, it can be told apart from gulls by its tubular nostrils and its relatively short wings.

hooked bill with tubular nostrils

short, thick neck

gray wings

PROFILE

- N. Atlantic and N. Pacific coasts; disperses out to sea in winter
- Open ocean, sea; breeds in burrows and cliff ledges, on headlands, islands, buildings
- Migrant
- 17–20½ in (43–52 cm)
- 20–23 oz (575–650 g)
- No nest; single egg laid on rock or grass, on exposed ledges, cliff slopes
- 1 egg; 1 brood
- Least Concern
- Flocks/colonies

Fulmarus glacialis

NORTHERN FULMAR

Often mistaken for a gull, this fulmar lives in northern oceans and seas. It divides its time between open water and sea cliffs. There are two color forms of this dark-eyed seabird—one gray and white, and the other bluish gray. A range of intermediates exists between the two color forms. From a distance, the gray-and-white form is the most gull-like. However, it can be told apart by its tubular nostrils and shorter wings.

The northern fulmar feeds on fish, jellyfish, and squid, and often flocks around fishing boats for waste thrown overboard. It uses no nesting material, instead laying a single egg directly on a rock or grass. Both parents help incubate the egg, which hatches after about 52 days. Once the chick is able to fly, parents and young spend the rest of the year at sea.

Dark form
In its dark phase, the bird is entirely gray. This form is generally found in the Pacific Ocean.

Land predator
Feeding on land as well as at sea, the southern giant petrel has two color forms. The more common form has mottled gray plumage.

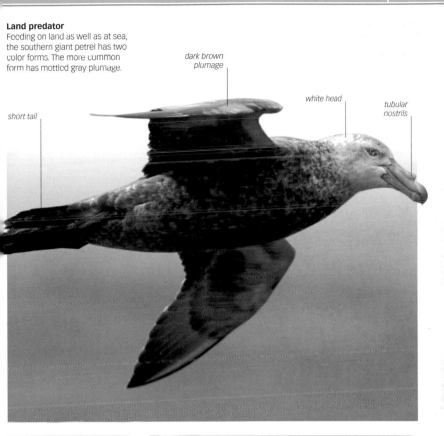

dark brown plumage

white head

tubular nostrils

short tail

PROFILE

- Across the southern oceans, Antarctica
- Open ocean and sea; breeds on exposed beaches, gravel areas, and tussock grass
- Migrant
- 33–39 in (85–100 cm)
- 8½–11 lb (3.8–5 kg)
- Shallow depression in ground, bordered with stone and dry vegetation
- 1 egg; 1 brood
- Least Concern
- Colonies

Macronectes giganteus

SOUTHERN GIANT PETREL

Large and aggressive, the southern giant petrel is a highly opportunistic seabird with a lifestyle that is partly predatory and partly scavenging. It frequently visits colonies of penguins and other birds, feeding on eggs and chicks. It has long, tubular nostrils and an excellent sense of smell, which it uses to track down the remains of whales and seals, ripping them open with its hook-tipped bill.

Southern giant petrels nest on coasts and islands. The female lays a single egg, incubating it for about 60 days. If threatened on the nest, adults and young can squirt out a stream of oily vomit to keep intruders at bay. After fledging, young birds spend their first three years at sea.

White form
This phase is characterized by almost pure white plumage, except for a few scattered dark feathers.

PROFILE

- Antarctic Coast, islands in the Southern Ocean; winters at sea
- Open sea and ocean
- Migrant
- 6–7 ½ in (15–19 cm)
- 1 ¹⁄₁₆–1 ¾ oz (30–50 g)
- Crevices and burrows on islands
- 1 egg; 1 brood
- Least Concern
- Colonies

Walking on water
When it feeds, the Wilson's storm-petrel sometimes looks as if it is walking on waves. This petrel finds its food by sight and smell.

pale bar on upperwing

white rump

long legs

SIMILAR SPECIES

gray bar on wings

Least storm-petrel
Smaller, with blackish brown upperparts

black upperparts

Common diving petrel
Small bill, white underparts

Oceanites oceanicus

WILSON'S STORM-PETREL

There are over 20 species of storm-petrels, and all are rarely seen, except at sea. Small and largely black, they flutter restlessly over water, pattering their legs on the surface as they pick up small animals, or scraps that have been thrown overboard. The petrels usually fly in scattered flocks, sometimes appearing in large numbers where currents create a good supply of food.

The Wilson's storm-petrel is one of the most numerous species, with an enormous range. It breeds in a burrow, on a slope overlooking the coast. The slope is important, because storm-petrels can only move by shuffling on land, and need a drop to help them take off. The female incubates the eggs for six weeks—an extraordinarily long time for such a small bird. After breeding, the birds abandon land, wandering across the equator and reaching as far north as Newfoundland, Canada, and southwestern Europe.

Black and white
The Manx shearwater has black upperparts, while the underparts are largely white. The short bill has tubular nostrils.

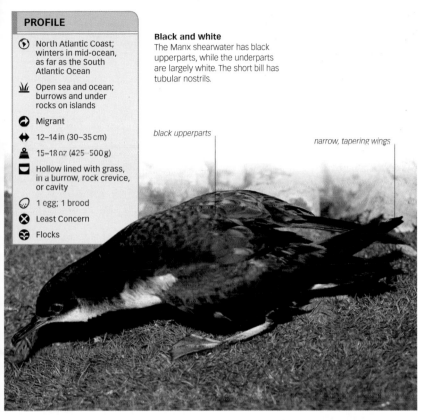

black upperparts

narrow, tapering wings

short neck

Sooty shearwater
Long, slender wings and dark upperparts

sooty brown overall

Short-tailed shearwater
Larger, dark-toned species

Puffinus puffinus

MANX SHEARWATER

Manx shearwaters are usually seen at sea, speeding in small groups over the waves. Pale beneath and sooty black above, this shearwater seems to turn light and dark as it tilts in flight, interspersing rapid wingbeats with long glides. Like other shearwaters, it feeds at the surface or in shallow dives, taking small fish, squid, shrimp, and also waste from fishing boats. Its range includes all of the Atlantic Ocean, but in summer, it is restricted to the north, where it breeds.

This bird nests in colonies on grass-covered offshore islands, laying a single egg. Both parents incubate; one sits while the other goes to sea to feed. To avoid predators such as gulls, the partners change over at night. The sitting bird guides its partner by making a strange wailing sound—even if thousands of birds may be calling, each one manages to find its mate. It takes 10 weeks for the chick to fledge, nourished by supplies of regurgitated oily food. Once the chicks can fly, the birds migrate south until the following year.

GREBES

Relatively few in terms of species, grebes are highly distinctive, fish-eating birds found all over the world. Propelled by their toes and waterproofed by lustrous feathers, they are widespread inhabitants of calm lakes and waterways.

Grebes breed in freshwater in all the world's inhabited continents, sometimes migrating to coasts to avoid winter ice. Unlike ducks, they are rarely gregarious, and tend to live in pairs or loose flocks. Some species—such as the great crested grebe—have a very wide distribution. At the other extreme, this order also includes species that are confined to groups of islands, or even to large, isolated lakes.

ORDER	PODICIPEDIFORMES
FAMILIES	1
SPECIES	22

ANATOMY AND FEEDING
Anatomically, grebes are quite different from other freshwater birds. Most have long necks and slender, pointed bills, and toes that are individually lobed, instead of being connected by webs. Their wings are small, and they have tiny tails, positioned at the rear of their bodies, which gives them an upright waddle when on land. However, in water, grebes have a smooth movement few other birds can match. When they dive, they disappear beneath the surface with barely a ripple, often reappearing many yards away. Fish make up most of their food, but they also catch insect larvae, crustaceans, and small mollusks—the exact mix varying with the grebe's habitat and size.

PLUMAGE AND FLIGHT
Grebe plumage is soft and satinlike, without any marked difference between the sexes, although some species develop eye-catching plumes when they breed. Their wings are small, and are stowed away close to their sides when they are not in use. Most grebes need a run-up to take off, and prefer to dive for safety instead. They can sink by compressing their feathers against their bodies—this reduces the bird's buoyancy until only the top of its head

is visible above the surface. If the threat becomes even more acute, the bird dives and disappears out of sight.

BREEDING
Courtship in grebes often involves elaborate displays, with two partners participating in complex dances that cement their bond. They share the task of nest-building, making a platform of loosely anchored vegetation. Grebe chicks are covered in down when they hatch, and for several weeks the parents carry their young on their backs.

Nesting time
Half-hidden by reeds, a red-necked grebe incubates its eggs. Although its nest is anchored, it floats, reducing the danger from floods.

PROFILE

- Africa, Europe, S. Asia
- Mainly freshwater ponds, vegetated lakes, and reservoirs; also on coastal waters in winter
- Partial migrant
- 10–11½ in (25–29 cm)
- 4–8 oz (125–225 g)
- Floating heap of vegetation, anchored to waterplants or reeds
- 4–6 eggs; 1 brood
- Least Concern
- Small flocks

Breeding colors
In the breeding season, the little grebe's cheeks and neck turn a rich chestnut color, and the base of the bill becomes bright yellow.

blackish cap

reddish brown face

short, stubby bill

rounded body

blunt, fluffy rear

SIMILAR SPECIES

red eye

Black-necked grebe Slim bill, and a peaked crown

black throat patch

Pied-billed grebe Bigger head and a stouter bill

Tachybaptus ruficollis

LITTLE GREBE

Also known as the dabchick, this widespread bird is the smallest grebe in Europe. Its range also includes large parts of Africa and southern Asia. Dumpy in shape, it has a much shorter neck than many other grebes. Rarely seen in flight, it paddles inconspicuously across lakes and ponds, disappearing from time to time as it dives for fish or aquatic insects. Like other grebes, it has an extremely soft plumage, which can be fluffed out or compressed to adjust the amount of air it contains. This alters its buoyancy, letting it sink quietly out of sight in case of any approaching danger.

Little grebes breed on water and the female lays 4–6 eggs. Both parents take care of the eggs and young, frequently carrying them on their backs, and even diving with them held under their wings.

Winter plumage
In winter, adult birds lose their chestnut cheeks, and become dark brown above and light brown below.

PROFILE

- Europe, Africa, Asia, Australia
- Large, open freshwater lakes, fringed with vegetation, and rivers; disperses to coastal waters in winter
- Partial migrant
- 18–20 in (46–51 cm)
- 21–26 oz (600–750 g)
- Heap of plant material, floating in shallow water or among waterplants
- 3–4 eggs; 1 brood
- Least Concern
- Flocks

Breeding adornment
The breeding adult has a ruff of conspicuous plumes on either side of the face, and a small double crest above the head.

white face

black head plumes

daggerlike pink bill

throat ruff

dull, dark back

slender, upright neck

SIMILAR SPECIES

thick, red neck

Red-necked grebe
Thick-necked, with a gray and white face

wispy crest on green-black head

dark gray upperparts

Western grebe Dives often and remains submerged for shorter periods

Podiceps cristatus

GREAT CRESTED GREBE

Few freshwater birds match the elegance of this widespread species. Slow and clumsy on land, it is perfectly at home on lakes and rivers. Propelled by its large, lobed feet, it dives for fish, and remains under water for long periods in search of prey.

Great crested grebes are famous for their elaborate courtship displays on water. A complete display includes several dances. In one, the pair dash across the surface. In another, they dive to the bottom and emerge with weeds in their bills, before facing each other and flicking their heads from side to side. If the dances are performed correctly, the pair bond is formed, and the two grebes mate and build a nest. The young are often carried on their parents' backs until they are fully fledged.

Winter plumage
Adults lose their crest and facial plumes after breeding. They winter on estuaries and coasts.

FLAMINGOS

With their immensely long necks and legs, and pink or white plumage, flamingos are among the world's most recognizable birds. Despite their delicate appearance, they often live in hostile habitats where few other birds can survive.

Flamingos are found mainly in the tropics and subtropics, where some species form flocks that are hundreds of thousands strong. Feeding in shallow water, they sift out microorganisms and small animals with their uniquely structured bills. Their long legs allow them to wade deep into water without soiling their plumage—an important adaptation in the highly saline or alkaline habitats where many of them live.

ORDER	PHOENICOPTERIFORMES
FAMILIES	1
SPECIES	6

Massed ranks
In an East African lake, thousands of lesser flamingos feed in the intense daytime heat. The gray birds are this year's young.

BREEDING
Flamingos make a cone-shaped nest out of mud. The young are covered in down when they hatch, and their bills gradually take on the adult shape.

STORKS, IBISES, AND HERONS

Found mainly in freshwater habitats throughout the world, this group of wading birds also includes some terrestrial species that hunt or scavenge on dry land. With their long legs and powerful bills, most find their food by stealth.

In addition to storks, ibises, and herons, this group of birds also includes egrets and bitterns. Most are tall, long-necked birds that feed on fish or other water animals, showing great patience as they hunt, but using their bills to strike with lightning speed. Storks have bills that are usually straight and long, while herons, egrets, and bitterns have stabbing, spear-shaped bills. Ibises have long, curved bills, while spoonbills have bills that flare out with spoon-shaped tips.

Many of these birds hunt by sight, either by day or after dark. Wading species, such as ibises and spoonbills, have bills with highly sensitive tips, enabling them to fish by touch alone.

ORDER	CICONIIFORMES
FAMILIES	3
SPECIES	121

BREEDING
All birds in this order are monogamous, forming pair-bonds that can involve elaborate courtship displays. Some species—such as bitterns—otherwise lead secretive and solitary lives. However, many herons are gregarious, and ibises and spoonbills roost and breed in colonies, often in waterside trees. In most cases, both parents share the tasks of incubating the eggs and caring for the young.

PROFILE

- ⊙ Scattered locations in S. Europe, Africa, S. Asia

- 🌿 Salt pans, salty lagoons, large shallow inland lakes, mudflats, sandbanks

- ➋ Partial migrant

- ↔ 4–5 ft (1.2–1.5 m)

- ⚖ 5½–7¾ lb (2.5–3.5 kg)

- ▭ Cone of mud with a hollow top, in a dense colony on mudflat or salt lake

- ☺ 1 egg; 1 brood

- ✖ Least Concern

- ❀ Large flocks

Unique bill
The greater flamingo has a remarkable pink bill, with a sharp, downward bend and a black tip.

extremely long neck

whitish to pink plumage

blunt, angled bill

long, pale pink legs

SIMILAR SPECIES

pale pink plumage

darker bill

Lesser flamingo Smallest member of the flamingo family

dark pink plumage

Chilean flamingo Breeds only in South America

Phoenicopterus roseus

GREATER FLAMINGO

Largest of the five species of flamingos, this tall and elegant bird has pale pink plumage and black flight feathers. Like its relatives, it has an immensely long neck and a distinctive bill. It feeds with its bill immersed in the water, filtering out insects, shrimps, and microscopic plants. Its pink color—which varies from bird to bird—is derived from substances in its food.

Greater flamingos are highly sociable and are almost never seen alone. They feed in groups and nest together, building volcano-like nest mounds from wet mud. The female lays a single egg, and both parents help feed and protect the chick. These flamingos are often migratory, and travel between different feeding areas in ribbonlike flocks.

Juvenile flamingos
Young birds initially gather in crèches. Once fledged, they have dark legs and gray-brown plumage.

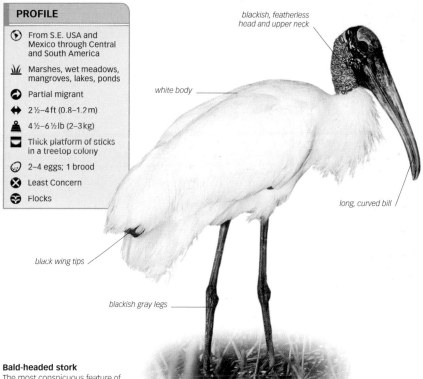

PROFILE

- From S.E. USA and Mexico through Central and South America
- Marshes, wet meadows, mangroves, lakes, ponds
- Partial migrant
- 2½–4 ft (0.8–1.2 m)
- 4½–6½ lb (2–3 kg)
- Thick platform of sticks in a treetop colony
- 2–4 eggs; 1 brood
- Least Concern
- Flocks

blackish, featherless head and upper neck

white body

long, curved bill

black wing tips

blackish gray legs

Bald-headed stork
The most conspicuous feature of the adult bird is its featherless, scaly-looking head.

SIMILAR SPECIES

glossy green upperparts

woolly-necked stork Large, widespread species

black back

Marabou stork Extremely large stork, with bare head and neck

Mycteria americana

WOOD STORK

An inhabitant of swampy ground and coastal shallows, this is the only stork in North America and one of its largest wading birds. Largely white, the adult bird has black flight feathers, a black tail, and a curved bill. Its full range stretches from Florida to as far as Argentina. In most regions, it is a year-round resident, but in some areas it migrates. A graceful flier, it is often seen in small flocks wheeling unhurriedly through the air.

Wood storks feed on fish and other aquatic animals, feeling for prey by moving their bills in shallow water. They breed in colonies, and usually nest on tall trees in water or at the water's edge. The nest is a loose platform of sticks. The female incubates the eggs, but both parents tend the young, which take about eight weeks to fledge.

Juvenile wood stork
The immature bird has a yellow bill and a feathered, grayish brown head. Its plumage is like the adult's.

PROFILE

- Africa, Europe, S. Asia; winters in parts of Africa, Pakistan, India

- Variety of open areas, such as wetland, grassland, pasture, banks of rivers and lakes

- Migrant

- 3¼ ft (1 m)

- 5–9¾ lb (2.3–4.4 kg)

- Large stick platform with central hollow, lined with plants, situated in tree, or on building or utility pole

- 2–4 eggs; 1 brood

- Least Concern

- Flocks

Color scheme
The white stork has a long red bill, black-and-white plumage, and red legs that trail behind the tail when in flight.

white upperparts

long, red bill

broad, rounded wings

red legs

SIMILAR SPECIES

black-green plumage

Black stork Shy species; prefers more wooded areas

blue skin near bill

Abdim's stork Smallest species of the stork family

Ciconia ciconia

WHITE STORK

Throughout its range, in Africa, Europe, and South Asia, the white stork is traditionally associated with good fortune. Much of this comes from its breeding habits: white storks mate for life, and return to the same nesting site year after year. Strongly migratory, they travel separately to their nesting grounds, greeting their partners with a characteristic bill-clattering display.

White storks feed on water and marshy ground, taking any small prey that they find. They fly slowly, with steady wingbeats, but are also accomplished at soaring. During the migration season, hundreds can be seen spiraling upward in columns of warm, rising air, until they are no more than specks in the sky.

In the breeding season, white storks make a large, platformlike nest, built of sticks, and lined with stems and grass. They usually nest in trees, but European white storks also nest on buildings. Both parents incubate the eggs and feed the nestlings. Once independent, the young birds start breeding at the age of four.

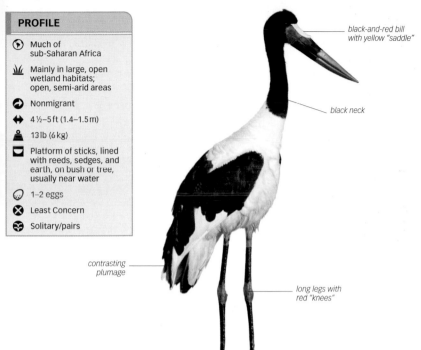

black-and-red bill
with yellow "saddle"

black neck

contrasting
plumage

long legs with
red "knees"

PROFILE

- Much of
  sub-Saharan Africa
- Mainly in large, open
  wetland habitats;
  open, semi-arid areas
- Nonmigrant
- 4½–5 ft (1.4–1.5 m)
- 13 lb (6 kg)
- Platform of sticks, lined
  with reeds, sedges, and
  earth, on bush or tree,
  usually near water
- 1–2 eggs
- Least Concern
- Solitary/pairs

Standing tall
One of the world's tallest storks,
the saddle-billed stork has boldly
marked black-and-white plumage.
The bill is red, with a black bar and
a bright yellow "saddle."

SIMILAR SPECIES

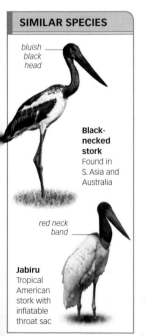

bluish
black
head

**Black-
necked
stork**
Found in
S. Asia and
Australia

red neck
band

Jabiru
Tropical
American
stork with
inflatable
throat sac

Ephippiorhynchus senegalensis

SADDLE-BILLED STORK

A tall and imposing bird, the saddle-billed stork is
found across much of Africa, south of the Sahara desert.
Aptly named, this stork has a conspicuous black-and-red
bill, which has a large, yellow "saddle" in front of the
eyes. The female is slightly smaller than the male, and
has eyes with bright yellow irises. Both sexes have the
same black-and-white plumage, and black legs with
bright red "knees" and feet.

The saddle-billed stork feeds in rivers, streams,
lakes, and flooded grasslands during the rainy season,
pecking on fish, shrimp, snails, and many other water
animals. Unlike some storks, it uses two different feeding
techniques: in clear water, the saddle-billed stork strides
forward and stabs its prey, but where the water is murky,
it hunts by touch, sweeping its bill from side to side.

Although storks typically form breeding colonies, this
species normally nests alone. The eggs take four weeks
to hatch, and the young take up to 14 weeks to fledge
and leave the nest.

PROFILE

- Europe, Africa, Asia
- Shallow water along lakes, rivers, estuaries, and shorelines; also reed marshes and mangroves
- Partial migrant
- 35–39 in (90–98 cm)
- 3 lb (1.4 kg)
- Platform of sticks; more material added each year
- 4–5 eggs; 1 brood
- Least Concern
- Colonies

Solitary hunter
The gray heron typically hunts alone. The bill acts as a dagger with large prey. After being impaled, the catch is swallowed head-first.

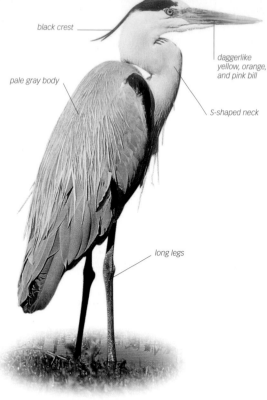

black crest

pale gray body

daggerlike yellow, orange, and pink bill

S-shaped neck

long legs

SIMILAR SPECIES

shaggy plumes on neck

Great blue heron Larger, with gray-blue plumage

bushy crest

Goliath heron World's largest heron; drooping legs in flight

Ardea cinerea

GRAY HERON

Often seen motionless, hunched in shallow water, the gray heron is an expert at hunting by stealth. At the slightest sign of movement, it carefully wades forward, straightens its neck, and drives its bill into its prey. Its diet includes fish and other water animals, but it also hunts on land, catching large insects, mice, and voles. Gray herons fly with slow beats of their large, rounded wings. They are normally silent, but sometimes give a harsh, single-syllable call.

During the breeding season, gray herons nest in colonies. The female makes the nest, which is often reused—and repaired—year after year. Both parents incubate the eggs and feed the young, taking turns to watch over nestlings. The young herons leave the nest after about eight weeks.

Juvenile gray heron
The young bird takes up to three years to develop adult plumage. Until then, it lacks the adult's black crest.

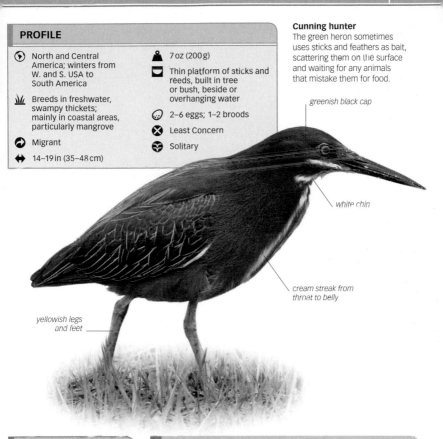

PROFILE

- ⊙ North and Central America; winters from W. and S. USA to South America
- 〽 Breeds in freshwater, swampy thickets; mainly in coastal areas, particularly mangrove
- ⟳ Migrant
- ↔ 14–19 in (35–48 cm)

- ⚖ 7 oz (200 g)
- ⬓ Thin platform of sticks and reeds, built in tree or bush, beside or overhanging water
- 🥚 2–6 eggs; 1–2 broods
- ✖ Least Concern
- ❀ Solitary

Cunning hunter
The green heron sometimes uses sticks and feathers as bait, scattering them on the surface and waiting for any animals that mistake them for food.

greenish black cap

white chin

cream streak from throat to belly

yellowish legs and feet

SIMILAR SPECIES

black cap

Striated heron Small, squat water bird

Butorides virescens

GREEN HERON

A secretive bird of freshwater and coastal wetlands, the green heron lives in Central and North America, wintering in warm parts of its range. Not much bigger than a crow, it has a glossy green cap and chestnut neck, together with green upperparts and a pale underside. Its eyes are large, and they face partly forward, giving it a good view of its prey. The legs are short, with long-toed feet for gripping waterside branches while hunting. The male's legs and feet turn bright orange during breeding.

Green herons hunt mainly at dawn and dusk, foraging on their own, and defending a feeding territory. They eat fish, frogs, and other animals. From a waterside perch, they stare at the water and ambush their prey. Generally silent, they make a loud, abrupt *kyowk* call.

Juvenile green heron
The young bird is browner above, with bars on its wings. Its underside is streaked with brown.

PROFILE

- Europe, N. Asia
- Breeds in extensive reedbeds; winters in a variety of well-vegetated wetland
- Partial migrant
- 26–31 in (65–80 cm)
- 2¾–3¼ lb (1.2–1.5 kg)
- Broad, damp nest of reed stems well out of sight in thick reedbed
- 4–6 eggs; 1 brood
- Least Concern
- Solitary

Perfect disguise
The Eurasian bittern has superbly camouflaged plumage. Its feathers, with light and dark brown streaks, blend with the reeds around it. The bird even sways in the breeze.

mottled brown body

thick neck

blackish crown

daggerlike bill

black stripe on neck

short legs with long toes

SIMILAR SPECIES

rusty brown crown

American bittern Smaller, with black streak on the side of neck

black back and cap

Little bittern Secretive, tiny species with creamy brown underparts

Botaurus stellaris

EURASIAN BITTERN

This large bird of extensive reedbeds breeds across Europe and northern Asia. Cryptically marked, with a long, thickly feathered neck and plumage that remains the same all year round, the bird is an expert at going unseen. If disturbed, it freezes in an upright position. At other times, it often looks much more compact, hunching its body and retracting its long neck.

Eurasian bitterns have dagger-shaped bills and feed on a wide range of reedbed animals, from frogs and water voles to young birds. Like herons—to which they are closely related—they strike by shooting out their necks with explosive speed. They are silent and secretive most of their lives, but during the breeding season males make an extraordinary booming call. Sounding like a foghorn, or someone blowing across the mouth of an empty bottle, it can be heard up to 3 miles (5 km) away. After mating, the female gathers reeds, and uses them to make a large but untidy nest. It takes sole charge of incubation, and looks after the young.

PROFILE

- Most parts of the world, except N. North America, N. Eurasia, and Australasia
- Wetlands, inland waterways to coastal lagoons
- Migrant
- 21½–26 in (55–65 cm)
- 19–29 oz (525–800 g)
- Flimsy stick platform, built in tree, bush, or reedbed
- 3–5 eggs; 1 brood
- Least Concern
- Flocks/colonies

black crown

short, thick bill

buff underparts

yellow legs (red in spring)

Night patrol
The black-crowned night-heron, which generally hunts at night, has large eyes for good nocturnal vision. The adult has a black cap that extends down the back.

SIMILAR SPECIES

yellow eye

Nankeen night-heron
Reddish brown plumage, with buff underparts

gray neck

Yellow-crowned night-heron Black-and-white crown; white stripe under eyes

Nycticorax nycticorax

BLACK-CROWNED NIGHT-HERON

This medium-sized, migratory heron is a compact, stocky bird, with a short neck and short, strong legs. The adult has head plumes at the beginning of the breeding season. This bird hunts at night, and spends the day roosting with its own kind, or in mixed flocks with other wetland birds.

The black-crowned night-heron stealthily climbs logs and branches by the water's edge to find its food. It feeds on a wide range of prey, including fish and snakes, either stabbing or grasping its prey with a lightning strike of the bill. Both parents incubate the eggs and feed the young.

Young night-heron
The juvenile is initially brown, with cream streaks and spots, taking two years to develop adult plumage.

Broad bill
A medium-sized bird, the
boat-billed heron has somber
markings on its body, and an
unusually wide bill.

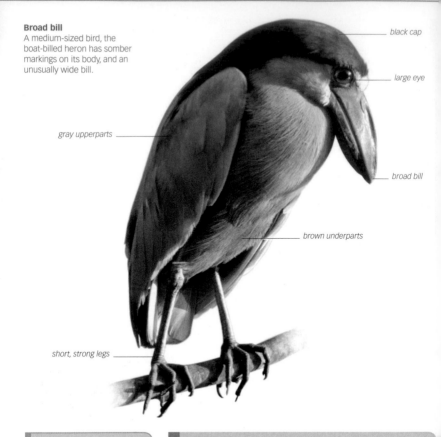

black cap

large eye

gray upperparts

broad bill

brown underparts

short, strong legs

PROFILE

- Mexico to N. Argentina
- Mangroves, densely vegetated wetland
- Nonmigrant
- 17 ½–19 ½ in (45–50 cm)
- 21–25 oz (600–700 g)
- Frail platform made of twigs, placed in a swamp tree or mangrove
- 2–4 eggs; 1 brood
- Least Concern
- Solitary/colonies

Cochlearius cochlearius

BOAT-BILLED HERON

From Central and South America, this reclusive, nocturnal bird is one of the most unusual members of the heron family. The boat-billed heron has a compact body with a short neck, and strong legs that give it a good grip when roosting in trees. The most eye-catching feature of the boat-billed heron is its shovel-shaped bill. Instead of spearing its food, this heron hunts by a strike-and-scoop technique, feeding on fish, frogs, and water snakes— almost anything that it can swallow. Although it often hunts at dusk, it can fish in total darkness, using nerves in its touch-sensitive bill to sense contact with food.

There are a number of subspecies, but all have a characteristic black cap extending down the back, gray upperparts, white or brown underparts, and large eyes—a feature shared by other herons that hunt mainly at night. The boat-billed heron nests alone or in small colonies, making flimsy, platformlike nests from twigs. The female lays 2–4 eggs, and both parents incubate and rear the chicks.

PROFILE

- North and South America, Europe, Africa, S. Asia, Australia
- Grassland and open cultivated country, often far from water
- Partial migrant
- 19–21 in (48–53 cm)
- 11 oz (300 g)
- Shallow cup nest of sticks and reed stems, in tree
- 4–6 eggs; 1 brood
- Least Concern
- Flocks

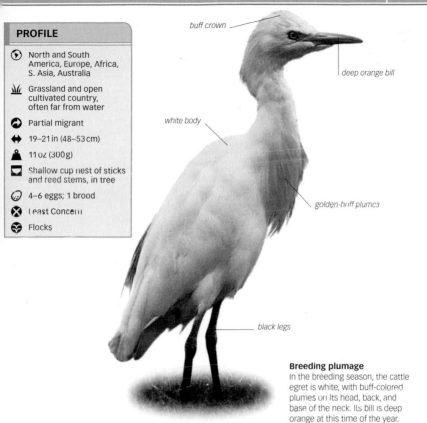

buff crown

deep orange bill

white body

golden-buff plumes

black legs

Breeding plumage
In the breeding season, the cattle egret is white, with buff-colored plumes on its head, back, and base of the neck. Its bill is deep orange at this time of the year.

SIMILAR SPECIES

slim, dark bill

Little egret Most widespread European white heron

slim neck

Great egret Large species with a worldwide range

Bubulcus ibis

CATTLE EGRET

Often seen alongside grazing mammals, this small, white bird is the most widespread member of the heron family. Its original home is in Africa, but it has since spread to many other parts of the world. This is mainly because of the spread of cattle farming, because cattle egrets live in open terrain, and specialize in feeding on insects flushed out by mammal hooves. As well as feeding near cattle, they sometimes fly onto their backs, picking insects off their skin, and using them as traveling perches.

Cattle egrets are highly social birds, roosting and breeding together. Both parents help incubate the eggs and feed the newly hatched chicks. Although they are nonmigratory, some cattle egrets move to warmer parts of their range in cold winters.

Changing colors
After breeding, the cattle egret loses its colored plumes. Its bill, legs, and feet turn yellow.

PROFILE

- N. South America, from Venezuela to S. Brazil
- Mudflats, mangrove swamps, lagoons
- Partial migrant
- 21½–28 in (55–70 cm)
- 21–26 oz (600–750 g)
- Loose, platform-shaped nest in mangroves, waterside trees
- 2–4 eggs
- Least Concern
- Flocks/colonies

Unique tint
The adult scarlet ibis is deep scarlet, apart from a touch of black on its wings. It has long, red legs with partly webbed feet.

intense scarlet body

dull pink bill

long, red legs

SIMILAR SPECIES

white plumage

African sacred ibis
Predominantly white plumage; black head

dark bill

Australian white ibis Black feet; red on underside of wings

Eudocimus ruber

SCARLET IBIS

Native to the northeast coast of South America, including Trinidad and Tobago, the scarlet ibis is one of the world's most spectacular birds. Adults are an intense and uniform scarlet, except for black tips on their wings. They live on mudflats, mangrove swamps, and lagoons, and eat shrimp, crabs, and other small animals, finding their prey with their sensitive, downcurved bills. Like flamingos (p.65), they get their color from pigments in their food, and if deprived of their natural diet, they gradually start to fade.

Scarlet ibises are always seen in flocks—sometimes with their own kind, or intermingled with other wading freshwater birds. They nest in large colonies. Both parents participate in caring for the young, which leave the nest when they are about three weeks old.

Juvenile ibis
The young scarlet ibis has gray-brown upperparts, pale underparts, and pale pink legs and bill.

slim, curved bill

Polished appearance
The breeding adult has colorful, iridescent plumage, with coppery brown upperparts, and metallic green and purple wings.

long neck

purple-green wings

long legs

PROFILE

- North and Central America; S Europe, Africa, Asia, Australia
- Favours freshwater wetland, but also found in some coastal areas
- Migrant
- 19½–26in (50–65cm)
- 17–21oz (475–600g)
- Platform of twigs and reeds, in tree, shrub, or reed, on ground or over water
- 3–4 eggs; 1 brood
- Least Concern
- Flocks/colonies

SIMILAR SPECIES

white cheek mark

Hadada ibis Greenish purple-winged bird with a raucous call

buff neck and breast

Black-faced ibis South American bird with jet-black underparts, brown upperparts, and a rufous cap

Plegadis falcinellus

GLOSSY IBIS

A widespread wetland bird, with a range that includes every continent except South America and Antarctica, the glossy ibis looks grayish black from a distance. Feeding in flooded pastures and marshes, as well as wetlands along coasts, it catches swimming or bottom-dwelling animals with an instantaneous snap of its bill.

Glossy ibises nest in colonies, often with other waterbirds. Both parents help build the nest. The young fledge in four weeks, but may leave the nest well before they can fly. These birds are graceful and powerful fliers and, like other ibises, fly with their necks and legs outstretched. They migrate across much of their range. In Australia, they sometimes behave nomadically, flying far into the interior after heavy rain.

Juvenile glossy ibis
The immature glossy ibis has dull, gray-brown plumage, a white mark on its crown, and a shorter, straighter bill.

PROFILE

- 🜉 Australia, New Zealand
- ⸭ Shallow water (inland and close to coast)
- ⊘ Nonmigrant
- ↔ 29–32 in (74–81 cm)
- ⬦ 3¾ lb (1.7 kg)
- ▱ Bowl-shaped nest of twigs, lined with leaves, usually on tree over water
- ◔ 2–4 eggs; 1 brood
- ✖ Least Concern
- ❀ Colonies

Spoon-shaped bill
The royal spoonbill has a distinctive black bill, which flares out into a flattened spoon shape and is extremely useful in capturing prey.

white plumage

spoon-shaped black bill

SIMILAR SPECIES

all-white body

Eurasian spoonbill Larger, with a yellow-tipped bill

long, white neck

Roseate spoonbill Smaller, with pinkish plumage

Platalea regia

ROYAL SPOONBILL

An unusual waterbird, the royal spoonbill has a remarkable, flattened spoon-shaped bill. Of the six species of spoonbills, it is one of the few with a black bill. The royal spoonbill lives in shallow water, and, like other spoonbills, feeds by striding slowly through the water, scything its open bill from side to side. The bill's "spoon" is highly sensitive. If it touches food, it almost immediately snaps shut. This feeding technique works without the bird having to see its prey, allowing it to feed by night as well as by day.

During the breeding season, royal spoonbills nest in small colonies, often in the company of other waterbirds. The young are tended by both parents until they can feed themselves. At the end of the breeding season adults lose their crests, and their chests turn white.

Breeding plumage
The breeding adult has white plumage, with conspicuous head plumes and a buff chest.

PELICANS AND RELATIVES

This group of web-footed waterbirds includes oceanic species, coastal ones, and also some that live far inland, on lakes and rivers. Almost all of them eat fish, catching their food in a striking variety of different ways.

Pelicans and their relatives are large or medium-sized birds with all four toes joined by webbing, unlike other waterbirds, where only the front three toes are linked. In addition to pelicans, the group includes tropicbirds and frigatebirds from warm water oceans, as well as cormorants, anhingas, gannets, and boobies, which live in a wide variety of habitats, from inland rivers to polar waters.

ORDER	PELECANIFORMES
FAMILIES	8
SPECIES	67

FEEDING

Most pelicans feed from the surface, while gannets, boobies, and tropicbirds plunge-dive from the air. Cormorants and anhingas are surface-divers, swimming low in the water before disappearing in search of prey.

Frigatebirds fish while on the wing, either catching food themselves, or stealing from other seabirds. They return to land every night to roost, but some of the birds in this order spend long periods at sea, particularly once their breeding season is at an end.

AQUATIC ADAPTATIONS

Cormorants and anhingas have surface feathers that absorb water, reducing their buoyancy when they dive. At the other extreme, plunge-divers have water-repellent plumage and bones with substantial air spaces, which help them float back up to the surface with their prey. Many of these birds also have extra air sacs beneath the skin, helping cushion the impact as they hit the water at speeds of up to 60 mph (95 kph).

BREEDING

The birds in this group often nest in colonies, which in the case of gannets and cormorants can be tens of thousands of birds strong. Males and females are sometimes difficult to tell apart, but many males attract partners with spectacular displays. Most species nest on rocks, although some pelicans, anhingas, cormorants, and frigatebirds build their nests in trees. Their young are initially helpless, and are tended by both parents as soon as they hatch.

When raising young, many of these birds swallow food and then regurgitate it back at the nest. This efficient method of food transport allows the parents to hunt for fish a considerable distance away from their hungry brood.

Cliff colony
Northern gannets nest on coasts of the North Atlantic. Each gannetry is packed with breeding birds, spaced just beyond pecking distance of their neighbors.

PROFILE

- 🕙 Tropical Atlantic, Indian, and Pacific oceans, restricted range in W. Pacific
- 〰️ Marine; rocky coastlines
- ↪ Migrant
- ↔ 35–41 in (90–105 cm)
- ⚖ 23–25 oz (650–700 g)
- ▭ Scrape surrounded by stones, shells, twigs, and leaves
- 🥚 1 egg; 1 brood
- ✖ Least Concern
- 🐦 Solitary/colonies

Streamer in flight
The red-billed tropicbird has a ternlike shape, with conspicuous tail streamers, a bright red bill, and yellowish, webbed legs.

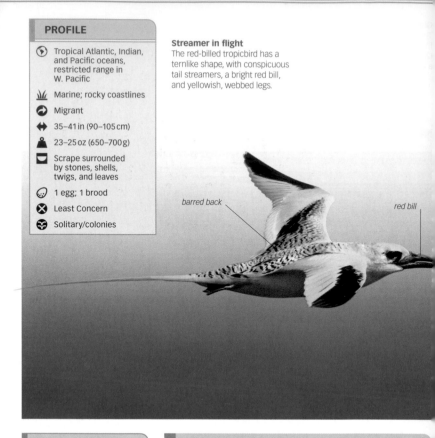

barred back

red bill

SIMILAR SPECIES

White-tailed tropicbird
Yellow bill; larger amount of black on the upperwings

Phaethon aethereus

RED-BILLED TROPICBIRD

Tropicbirds are well named because they rarely wander far from tropical and subtropical seas. The red-billed tropicbird is the largest of three species. It is mostly white and its tail has two long, central streamers that twist and flutter as it flies over the ocean's surface looking for food below.

Red-billed tropicbirds feed by hovering and plunge-diving, and their prey includes fish and squid. After making a catch, they bob to the surface with streamers held high, before taking off again. Like gannets (p.85), these tropicbirds have air-filled cells in their skin, which cushion the impact as they dive. Breeding on rocky coasts, they make no nest, and lay a single egg.

Young tropicbird
Though similar to the adult, the juvenile bird develops tail streamers only when it is old enough to breed.

Giant bill
The storklike shoebill gets its name from its enormous bill, which is 8 in (20 cm) long, and much wider than a true stork's.

large head

small tuft on the crown

large, broad wings

slaty blue plumage

PROFILE	
⊙	Upper Nile Valley, Kenya, Tanzania, and adjacent countries
⩙	Swamp, especially in thick vegetation
⬓	Nonmigrant
↔	4 ft (1.2 m)
⚖	12–14 lb (5.5–6.5 kg)
▭	Bulky platform of rushes, grasses, and leaves, in a dry spot on the ground
⬰	2 eggs; 1 brood
⊗	Vulnerable
⬯	Solitary/pairs

Balaeniceps rex

SHOEBILL

Classified in a family of its own, the shoebill is a unique and highly distinctive bird restricted to Africa. It is instantly recognized by its bill, which looks like an old-fashioned wooden clog with a sharply hooked tip. This extraordinary bill is used for catching lungfish— its favorite food. Shoebills also eat small turtles, crocodiles, and mammals. They attack their prey while wading through the water, and then lunge forward at high speed, with their wings spread. Once they have caught their prey, they toss it into the air before swallowing it head-first.

Despite their top-heavy appearance, shoebills are good fliers, flapping slowly over water and reedbeds. They are territorial, and are usually seen in ones and twos. Each pair claims up to 2 square miles (5 square km) of swamp, defending it against other pairs. They nest on the ground, in a dry spot in the swamp, and lay two chalky white eggs. Generally silent, they occasionally clap their huge bills, making a hollow *klok*.

PROFILE

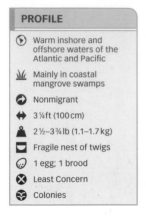

- Warm inshore and offshore waters of the Atlantic and Pacific
- Mainly in coastal mangrove swamps
- Nonmigrant
- 3¼ft (100cm)
- 2½–3¾lb (1.1–1.7kg)
- Fragile nest of twigs
- 1 egg; 1 brood
- Least Concern
- Colonies

long, hooked bill
all-black plumage

Master of the air
The male magnificent frigatebird has all-black plumage, and a bright red gular (throat) pouch. With its small feet, this bird finds it difficult to move on land.

SIMILAR SPECIES

Great frigatebird Found in the Indian Ocean; with deeply forked tail

Fregata magnificens

MAGNIFICENT FRIGATEBIRD

With its remarkably light body and immense, slender wings, the magnificent frigatebird is among the most aerial of all birds. It roosts on land, but spends the daytime soaring and gliding over tropical seas. Unlike most seabirds, it often hangs high overhead.

The magnificent frigatebird feeds by snatching fish from the sea without landing on the surface, but it is also an expert at robbing other birds of their catches in midair. It pursues its victims with extraordinary agility, pecking at their tails until they disgorge their food. When breeding, the male develops a bright red throat sac, which looks like a small balloon. It inflates the throat to court the female, keeping it filled with air for hours.

Female frigatebird
The female also has black plumage, but with a white chest in place of the male's red pouch.

PROFILE

- Breeds in Eurasia from the Adriatic Sea to C. China; winters as far south as Egypt, N. India
- Freshwater marshes and swamps; lakes, rivers, and vicinity
- Migrant
- 5¼–6 ft (1.6–1.8m)
- 21 lb (9.5 kg)
- Platform of grass and twigs on a floating mat of vegetation
- 2–4 eggs; 1 brood
- Vulnerable
- Colonies

Living scoop
The Dalmatian pelican plunges its bill under the water surface, letting the pouch fill up, then lifts its head to sieve food from the water.

small crest

whitish ring around pale eye

white plumage

Pelecanus crispus

DALMATIAN PELICAN

One of the largest pelican species, the Dalmatian pelican is also one of the heaviest flying birds. All six species of pelicans share one outstanding feature: an enormous bill with an elastic pouch. Dalmatian pelicans live on freshwater marshes and shallow coasts, where they feed almost entirely on fish. Paddling forward with their large, webbed feet, these pelicans plunge their bills beneath the water surface, opening them to seize their prey. The upper half of their bills is rigid, but the sides of the lower half spread apart, letting the long, orangish pouch fill up. The Dalmatian pelican then lifts its head above the water surface, draining the water away and swallowing its food.

Dalmatian pelicans often feed in flocks, sometimes joining forces to drive fish toward the shore. They breed in flocks as well, nesting on large piles of reeds and sticks. Both sexes help incubate the eggs and feed the young. Due to gradual loss of habitat, the bird is globally rare and listed as a vulnerable species.

PROFILE

- 🌐 North and South America, along the Pacific, Atlantic, and Caribbean coasts
- 〰️ Coastal and marine habitats
- ↪ Partial migrant
- ↔ 3½ ft (1.1 m)
- ⚖ 7–8¼ lb (3.2–3.7 kg)
- ▭ Hollow in ground, lined with feathers and debris; or mound of mixed materials; or a stick platform in bush or tree
- 🥚 2–3 eggs; 1 brood
- ❌ Least Concern
- 🔰 Colonies

Coastal pelican
Unlike other pelicans, the brown pelican lives on coasts, and is rarely seen inland. The adult brown pelican has a yellow head.

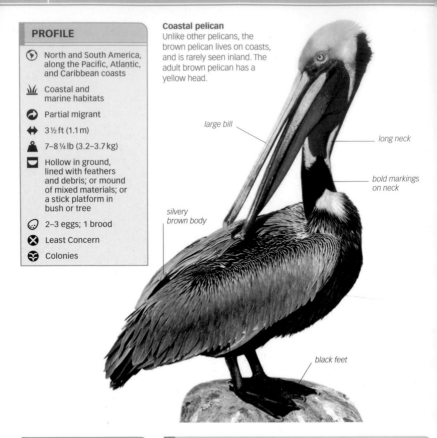

large bill

long neck

bold markings on neck

silvery brown body

black feet

SIMILAR SPECIES

long, tufted feathers on head

Peruvian pelican Larger and heavier, with dark plumage

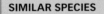
Pelecanus occidentalis

BROWN PELICAN

Unlike most pelicans, which swim at the surface, this coastal species dives to catch its food. Brown pelicans fly up to a height of 33 ft (10 m), before folding back their wings and plunging into the sea to catch fish. In shallow water they also use their bills like scoops. They are often seen flying low over the water in straggling lines, rising and then falling again as they cross the waves.

Brown pelicans live in the Americas, along the Pacific, Atlantic, and Caribbean coasts. Highly gregarious, they are often seen in fishing ports, resting on jetties and docks. During the breeding season, the male selects a nest site. It then displays to attract a mate. Once paired, the male collects the nesting material, while the female constructs the nest.

Juvenile brown pelican
The juvenile takes three years to acquire adult plumage. It is grayish brown, without bold neck markings.

Streamlined appearance
The adult northern gannet has a torpedo-shaped body, a long, tapering bill, and sharply pointed, black-tipped wings. Its feet are large, black, and fully webbed.

buff-yellow on head

daggerlike bill

white plumage

black wing tips

webbed feet

PROFILE

- 🡒 Coasts of N. Atlantic Ocean; winters as far south as E. USA and W. Africa

- 🌾 Temperate marine waters; breeds on inaccessible islands and cliffs

- ⟳ Partial migrant

- ↔ 34–39 in (87–100 cm)

- ⚖ 5¼–8 lb (2.4–3.6 kg)

- ▭ Mound of seaweed and debris, on ground or ledge

- ◔ 1 egg; 1 brood

- ✕ Least Concern

- ✿ Flocks/colonies

SIMILAR SPECIES

pointed bill

Cape gannet Smaller, with a prominent yellow head and hind neck

Morus bassanus

NORTHERN GANNET

Many seabirds plunge-dive to catch their food, but few can rival the northern gannet as it slams near-vertically into the sea. It dives from heights of up to 148 ft (45 m), folding back its wings as it drops, and using the air sacs around its throat and neck to cushion the impact as it hits the waves. Large and powerful, with a highly streamlined body, it looks superficially similar to a gull, but has a distinctive flapping-and-gliding flight, and often travels in single file.

Northern gannets breed in large colonies on small islands or isolated rocks, with some holding thousands of birds. Their nests are placed just beyond pecking distance of their neighbors. Both parents help in incubating the single egg and feeding the young.

Juvenile gannet
The northern gannet takes five years to mature. Initially brown, its plumage gradually becomes white.

Prominent legs
The blue-footed booby gets its name from its striking, bright blue feet. It has pale brown plumage, with white streaks and a pale underside.

long, tapering bill

streaks on body

brown upperwings

blue legs and feet

PROFILE

- Tropical and subtropical western coasts of Central and South America
- Rocky coasts, cliffs, islands
- Nonmigrant
- 30–33 in (76–84 cm)
- 2¾–4 lb (1.3–1.8 kg)
- Eggs are placed on flat ground, usually with no nesting materials
- 1–3 eggs; 1 brood
- Least Concern
- Pairs/colonies

SIMILAR SPECIES

sooty brown plumage

Brown booby Long, pointed, yellowish bill

pale brown underside

Red-footed Booby Pink base to blue bill; striking red or orange feet

Sula nebouxii

BLUE-FOOTED BOOBY

A plunge-diving seabird, the blue-footed booby resembles the gannet (p.85) with sharply pointed wings and a long, tapering bill. However, its lighter build and bright blue feet immediately set it apart.

Blue-footed boobies feed on fish, catching them at sea and in shallows near the shore. Small flocks feed together, climbing to heights of up to 82 ft (25 m) before dropping into the water below. They show off their feet during elaborate pair-bonding displays, such as the "sky pointing" ritual. In this ritual, the two partners face each other, and point their bills vertically, while stretching out their wings. Then they strut with their feet turned out, displaying each foot in turn, while their heads move up and down. These birds nest on coastal rocks, using little or no nesting material.

Juvenile booby
The young bird has bluish gray legs and feet, which turn bright blue once it becomes an adult.

large head with flat forehead

orange-yellow patch of skin near bill

long, black neck

white throat

long body with glossy black upperparts

short, black legs and webbed feet

PROFILE

- E. North America; much of Eurasia; parts of Africa, Asia, Australia
- Coasts, expanses of inland water, including reed marshes and reservoirs
- Partial migrant
- 30–37 in (77–94 cm)
- 4¼–6½ lb (1.9–3 kg)
- Bulky, cup-shaped nest of seaweed and debris, placed on flat rock or cliff ledge; or a stick nest in tree
- 3–4 eggs; 1 brood
- Least Concern
- Flocks

Underwater feeder
The great cormorant has a long body, and large, rear-positioned, webbed feet. It dives up to 33 ft (10 m) deep, twisting and turning after its prey.

SIMILAR SPECIES

brown upperparts with black scales

Double-crested cormorant
Smaller, with white ear tufts and a bare patch of orange-yellow facial skin

tiny, ragged-looking wings

Flightless cormorant
Found only in the Galapagos Islands

Phalacrocorax carbo

GREAT CORMORANT

One of the most widespread birds, the great cormorant is found on every inhabited continent except South America. It has a long neck and dark plumage, with white patches on its cheeks and thighs. The scaly pattern on its wings gives it a reptilian appearance.

Compared to most aquatic birds, the great cormorant swims low in the water, periodically peering under the surface to locate its food. When it spots a fish, it quickly dives in pursuit, holding its wings against its body and propeling itself with powerful kicks of its feet. Unlike most web-footed birds, cormorants do not cover their feathers with waterproofing oil, which reduces buoyancy while diving. In between dives, they often perch on rocks, posts, or buoys, with their wings held open to dry. Great cormorants nest on cliff ledges and in trees. Both parents help make the nest and play an active part in raising the young. At the end of the breeding season, birds in cold regions often disperse to the coast to spend the winter.

Absorbent plumage
The anhinga has greenish black plumage over most of the body, with silvery white feathers on the upperwings. Its plumage is absorbent, and the bird floats with most of its body submerged.

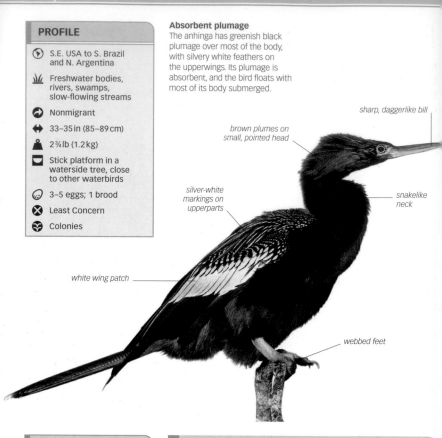

sharp, daggerlike bill

brown plumes on small, pointed head

snakelike neck

silver-white markings on upperparts

white wing patch

webbed feet

SIMILAR SPECIES

buff upperparts

Oriental darter
Waterbird, with a white neck-stripe

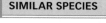

Anhinga anhinga

ANHINGA

A remarkable freshwater bird, the anhinga is also known as the snakebird. Its alternative name is well earned because it usually swims with its body submerged, leaving only its head and snakelike neck exposed. The anhinga has a straight, daggerlike bill, and it hunts fish just below the surface by stabbing and then lifting them into the air. With a quick movement of the neck, the fish is flicked free from the bill, tossed upward, and swallowed head-first.

The anhinga lacks waterproofing oils on its feathers, so it spreads its wings wide to dry when it reaches land. Anhingas nest in trees and once hatched, the young use their bills and feet to climb, but do not stray far until they can fly.

Female anhinga
The female's plumage is slightly paler than the male's, with a light brown neck and upper breast.

BIRDS OF PREY

Many birds hunt live food, but birds of prey are distinguished by their hunting techniques, and often by the size of the animals that they catch. This order includes the world's largest flying carnivores, as well as the fastest birds on Earth.

Also known as raptors, birds of prey are found worldwide in every continent except Antarctica. They are most common in warm habitats, although many are found in cold parts of the world. They range in size from tiny falconets, which are no bigger than a sparrow, to condors, which have a wingspan of up to 10ft (3.2m). Most birds of prey actively kill their food, but this group also includes numerous full- and part-time scavengers, from vultures to eagles and kites. Unlike the nocturnal owls (p.189), nearly all birds of prey are diurnal, hunting during daylight hours and then roosting at the end of each day.

ORDER	FALCONIFORMES
FAMILIES	5
SPECIES	319

ANATOMY

All birds of prey have three key features that make them efficient hunters. The first is high-definition stereoscopic vision, which comes from their large, forward-facing eyes. This makes them extremely good at spotting prey, and also helps them gauge distances with great accuracy as they move in to strike. Birds of prey also have powerful feet with sharp claws, or talons, which they use to make a kill. Unlike most other birds, they often use their feet to carry food aloft, flying away to feed at a nest or a perch. Finally, birds of prey are all equipped with strong hooked bills, which they use to tear apart their food. Most have good hearing, but with the exception of New World vultures, their sense of smell is generally poor.

HUNTING TECHNIQUES

Many eagles and vultures search for food by soaring at great heights, which gives them an uninterrupted view of the ground far below. The smaller birds of prey tend to have a much wider variety of hunting techniques. Falcons often catch their prey in a high-speed aerial pursuit, although some kinds—principally kestrels—find their food by hovering, and then dropping onto the ground. Ospreys and fish eagles swoop on fish in freshwater and on coasts, while specialized feeders tackle many different kinds of prey, from snakes—in the case of the secretary bird (p.96)—to wasps and even snails. Most species in this order hunt alone, but a few, such as the Harris hawk (p.107), operate in pairs or groups, increasing their chances of successfully ambushing their food.

Airborne attack
With its legs lowered, a golden eagle swoops down toward its prey. At the last moment, it will spread its talons to make the kill.

PROFILE

- ⊙ S. Canada to South America, the Falklands
- 〽 Open or semi-open areas, often nesting on open ground with a few other nests
- ➋ Partial migrant
- ↔ 30in (76cm)
- ⚖ 3lb (1.4kg)
- ▭ Cavity on high tree stump, rocky place, and cliff ledge
- ◔ 1–3 eggs; 1 brood
- ✖ Least Concern
- ✿ Flocks

gray-brown plumage

hooked, white bill

black underparts

pink legs

Smell sense
Unusual for a land bird, the turkey vulture has a good sense of smell. This helps it locate food easily.

SIMILAR SPECIES

black plumage

Greater yellow-headed vulture Pinkish white bill and reddish eyes

gray-white legs

Black vulture Grayish black head and a hooked bill

Cathartes aura

TURKEY VULTURE

This bird gets its name from its bare-skinned head, which resembles that of a wild turkey (p.35). Often seen soaring in search of food, the turkey vulture seems black from a distance. A closer look reveals a red face and upper neck, and brown and silvery gray underwings. It flies with its wings in a characteristic shallow "V," and lives in a variety of habitats: from forests to farmland and the outskirts of towns.

The turkey vulture feeds mainly on carrion. It scavenges along roads, but also kills small animals, and steals eggs and young birds. It breeds on high tree stumps, rocky places, and cliff ledges, using little nesting material. Once the eggs have hatched, both parents care for the young, which can fly after about 10 weeks.

Juvenile turkey vulture
The young turkey vulture has a dark head and bill, and gray feet. It takes three years to mature.

PROFILE

- W. South America
- Mountainous areas; also found in lowlands to the west of the Andes
- Nonmigrant
- 4 ft (1.2 m)
- 24–33 lb (11–15 kg)
- No nest; egg laid on inaccessible cliff-ledge
- 1 egg
- Near Threatened
- Solitary

Black condor
The Andean condor is mainly black, with a bald head. The male has a distinctive white ruff at the base of its neck, and a fleshy comb from its bill to the top of its head.

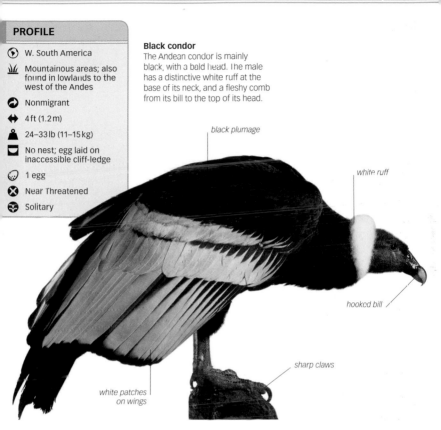

black plumage

white ruff

hooked bill

sharp claws

white patches on wings

SIMILAR SPECIES

bare-skinned head

California condor Larger, with pink head and black neck ruff; critically endangered

Vultur gryphus

ANDEAN CONDOR

A colossal South American vulture, the Andean condor has the greatest wing area of all birds. Instead of flying by flapping, it rides on updrafts from mountains and coastal cliffs, sometimes traveling hundreds of miles a day with barely a flick of its wings. From the ground, condors are unmistakable, with large flight feathers spreading out like the fingers of a hand.

Andean condors have a wide-ranging diet, but feed mainly on carrion. In some places, they also feed at seabird colonies, plundering large numbers of eggs. Exceptionally slow breeders, they produce a single chick every two years. The 5-in (13-cm) egg is deposited directly on bare rock. Both parents share the task of incubation, and help feed the developing chick.

Juvenile Andean condor
The young bird takes six months to fly. During the early years the male lacks the adult's white ruff.

PROFILE

- S. USA, Central and South America to Cape Horn, the Falkland Islands
- Mainly open and semi-open country, such as grassland, bushland, farmland, and ranches
- Nonmigrant
- 20–23½ in (51–60 cm)

- 1¾–2¾ lb (0.8–1.2 kg)
- Large, untidy structure made of twigs and sticks, and placed either in tree or cactus
- 2–4 eggs; 1 brood
- Least Concern
- Solitary

shaggy crest

thick, pale blue bill

white undertail feathers

long legs

Striking predator
The crested caracara is a striking bird of prey, with a red face, black cap, and long toes and claws.

SIMILAR SPECIES

black upperparts

Mountain caracara White underparts, red face

dark brown upperparts

Yellow-headed caracara Buff head and underparts

Caracara cheriway

CRESTED CARACARA

With long legs and strong feet, the crested caracara is an unusual member of the falcon family that walks and hunts on the ground. Found in the Americas, from southern USA to Patagonia, it feeds on carrion as well as living animals, including frogs, lizards, and small birds. It hunts mainly in open grassland and scrub, patrolling roadsides for animals killed by passing traffic. The bird is strong enough to displace vultures from dead remains. At times, it acts like an aerial pirate, pursuing vultures into the air and forcing them to disgorge their food.

Compared to other birds of prey, the crested caracara has relatively flat claws—an adaptation for moving on the ground and for scratching up the soil for insects and worms. It makes stick nests in isolated trees and tall cacti, returning to them year after year. When the breeding season begins, males fight in midair, vying for dominance in an acrobatic display. Pairs take turns to incubate the eggs for 28 days. The young stay in the nest for 10 weeks, until they can fly.

PROFILE

- Eurasia, Africa; winters as far as South Africa, India, China, Japan
- Wide range of areas, including farmland, forest edges, grassland, and suburban places
- Partial migrant
- 10½–14 in (27–35 cm)
- 6–7 oz (175–200 g)
- Natural hollow on ledge of cliff or building, cavity in tree trunk, old nest of a larger bird
- 4–6 eggs; 1 brood
- Least Concern
- Family groups

Hovering colors
The Eurasian kestrel has flecked and barred plumage. The male can be identified by its gray head and upper tail.

short, round, gray head

chestnut back with black flecks

black claws

gray upper tail

slim tail with black band

SIMILAR SPECIES

spotted underparts

American kestrel Two vertical facial lines, gray crown with red cap

blue-gray head

Lesser kestrel Chunkier body and a shorter tail

Falco tinnunculus

EURASIAN KESTREL

Ranging across Europe, Asia, and Africa, the Eurasian kestrel is one of the few birds of prey that hovers to find its food. Often seen over grassland and roadsides, it flutters in the air with rapid downward wingbeats, and its tail widely fanned. Using its sharp eyesight, it watches for signs of movement, and then drops in successive stages before pouncing to make a kill.

The Eurasian kestrel feeds on mice, voles, small birds, beetles, and grasshoppers. It eats small prey on the ground, but larger ones are taken to a favorite perch to be consumed. It nests in a variety of places, including tree holes, cliff ledges, buildings, and old nests of other birds. After the young have fledged, birds in northern regions fly south for winter.

Female Eurasian kestrel
The female is larger than the male, with a paler body, and a brown head and upper tail.

PROFILE

- 🌐 All continents, except Antarctica
- 🌾 Open country from mountains to coasts; large cities along rivers
- ◑ Partial migrant
- ↔ 14–20 in (35–51 cm)
- ⚖ 1–2¾ lb (0.5–1.2 kg)
- ▭ Typically a bare place on a rock ledge
- ◉ 2–4 eggs; 1 brood
- ✕ Least Concern
- ❁ Family groups

Varied color
A large, heavily built falcon, the peregrine falcon is variable in color, but is usually dark gray above and barred brown and white below.

yellow base of bill

blue-gray upperparts

gray bars on flanks and belly

yellow feet

SIMILAR SPECIES

long, tapered wings

Eurasian hobby Smaller, with heavily streaked underparts

short bill

Lanner falcon Paler, with less pointed wings

Falco peregrinus

PEREGRINE FALCON

The world's fastest bird and also one of the most widespread, the peregrine is found on every continent, except Antarctica. It feeds on a wide range of birds, some larger than itself, and attacks them in midair. It spots its prey from high in the sky, and then dive-bombs it in a spectacular plunge known as a "stoop." With its wings folded by its sides, it drops almost vertically, slashing its prey with its talons, and then catching it as it tumbles to the ground. Estimates of its maximum speed vary, but it is able to reach at least 155 mph (250 kph) before it spreads its wings and breaks its fall.

Peregrine falcons live in many different habitats, from rocky coasts to city centers, where pigeons make up a large part of their diet. They nest on rocky ledges and buildings, and raise 2–4 chicks a year, teaching them how to hunt by dropping prey through the air. In many parts of its enormous range, the peregrine falcon is a migrant, heading to warmer regions once the chicks can fly.

PROFILE

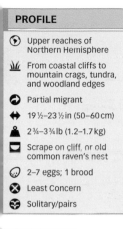

- ⊙ Upper reaches of Northern Hemisphere
- 〰 From coastal cliffs to mountain crags, tundra, and woodland edges
- ➋ Partial migrant
- ↔ 19½–23½ in (50–60 cm)
- ⚖ 2¾–3¾ lb (1.2–1.7 kg)
- ▭ Scrape on cliff, or old common raven's nest
- ◔ 2–7 eggs; 1 brood
- ✕ Least Concern
- ◑ Solitary/pairs

Majestic predator
The gyrfalcon watches its prey from a perch, and then, flying low and fast, catches it by surprise. It may also chase birds in flight, but usually catches them on ground or on water.

yellow patch on skin near bill

dark brown eye

lighter underparts with spots

long, barred tail

Falco rusticolus

GYRFALCON

A bird of the far north, the gyrfalcon is the world's largest falcon. Heavily built, this majestic bird has several different phases, or color forms, including gray, dark, and white barred with black, depending on age and location. This species has sleek, narrowly pointed wings and heavily feathered legs. It has strong feet, and often perches on rocks close to the ground.

The gyrfalcon lives in open tundra and along sea cliffs, where it feeds on mammals and birds. Like several other falcons, including the peregrine falcon (p.94), it is capable of killing prey larger than itself. Gyrfalcons breed on cliffs, laying their eggs directly on the rock. The female usually incubates the eggs, but both parents feed the young. In some regions it is a year-round resident, but in others, it wanders south in the winter, sometimes several hundred miles outside its breeding range. Sought for centuries by the nobility for its power and beauty, it is still a popular bird in falconry, bred in captivity rather than taken from the wild.

White phase
The white gyrfalcon is common in Greenland and other parts of the high Arctic region. In the treeless tundra, it is well camouflaged among snow and rock.

Ground patrol
The secretary bird flies well, but spends most of its life on the ground. Both sexes have black-and-gray plumage and red facial skin.

crest of black feathers

red facial skin

long wings, rarely used in flight

long, wedge-shaped tail

long, strong legs

small feet

PROFILE

- 🌐 Sub-Saharan Africa
- 〽️ Open and bushy grassland, large wheat farms, and semidesert with scrub
- ↩️ Nonmigrant
- ↔️ 3½–5 ft (1.1–1.5 m)
- ⚖️ 8¾ lb (4 kg)
- 🗂️ Flat platform made of sticks, with a central hollow, placed on top of bush or tree, lined with grass, dung, and pellets of the undigested remains of prey
- 🥚 2–3 eggs; 2–3 broods
- ❌ Least Concern
- 😵 Pairs

Sagittarius serpentarius

SECRETARY BIRD

A highly unusual bird of prey, the secretary bird strides on its long legs and is adapted for hunting on the ground. Slim and athletic, it has a storklike body and a crest of black feathers sweeping back from its head. It gets its name from these feathers, which resemble the old-fashioned quill pens that secretaries once used.

Secretary birds feed on a wide variety of small animals, and their hunting technique is highly specialized Since their small feet cannot grasp their prey, they stamp on their victims, pecking with their hooked bills and sometimes using their wings as a shield. They spend most of the day on the move, wandering up to 15 miles (25 km) in search of food. Pairs defend the nest against other pairs in the area, but only the female incubates the eggs.

Walking hunter
The secretary bird spends most of its time hunting in the African grasslands and savanna.

Aerial fisher
The osprey feeds almost entirely on fish. The soles of its feet are covered with spiny scales, and the outer talon can swivel back, giving it a pincerlike grip on slippery fish.

whitish crown

black stripe through eye

curved, black bill

dark brown upperparts

white underparts

large, sharp claws

PROFILE

Pandion haliaetus

OSPREY

- North America, Eurasia, Africa, Australia; winters in South America, Africa, Asia
- Near salt or freshwater lakes, large rivers, estuaries, and coastal lagoons
- Migrant
- 19 ½–26 in (50–66 cm)
- 3 ¼ lb (1.5 kg)
- Mass of sticks, on tree, seashore, crag, or an artificial nest platform
- 2–3 eggs; 1 brood
- Least Concern
- Family groups

Found on every continent except Antarctica, the osprey is one of the world's most widespread birds of prey. It is usually seen on coasts or inland waterways, typically perched on a high tree, or flying over the water in search of prey. A fish-eater, it hunts by skimming close to the water surface, grabbing its prey with one or both feet, and returning to its perch to feed.

The osprey nests in tall trees, often using the same site for many years. The young leave the nest at the age of seven weeks. In many parts of the world, the osprey is a summer visitor, spending the winter in warmer climes. Formerly persecuted, and accidentally poisoned by the insecticide DDT, it is making a gradual comeback to many areas where it had disappeared.

Double catch
The osprey dives to catch fish. It has the strength and skill to catch more than one fish at a time.

PROFILE

- India, Sri Lanka, S. China, Solomon Islands, Australia
- Coastal wetlands, forest, estuaries, farmland, mangrove swamps
- Nonmigrant
- 17 ½–19 ½ in (45–50 cm)
- 11–23 oz (325–650 g)
- Platform made of sticks, in trees or on ground, lined with flotsam, leaves, seaweed, or debris
- 1–4 eggs; 1 brood
- Least Concern
- Solitary/pairs

dark chestnut upperparts

white underparts

Kite colors
The adult Brahminy kite is conspicuously marked, with an all-white head and chest, and a white tip on its tail.

white tail tip

Haliastur indus

BRAHMINY KITE

A distinctive bird of prey, the Brahminy kite is found in India, Southeast Asia, and Australia. It lives in estuaries and mangrove swamps, as well as on the outskirts of coastal towns. The adult has dark chestnut upperparts, with an off-white head, neck, and chest—a coloration that is particularly striking when it is in the air. The Brahminy kite flies on angled wings, searching wetlands for fish, frogs, and insects, and scavenges along the shoreline for dead fish and other remains. It feeds singly or in small groups, but sometimes roosts in parties of a hundred or more.

When breeding, both parents build the nest, but the female solely incubates the eggs. These kites are nonmigratory, and often breed in the same nest year after year.

SIMILAR SPECIES

buff underparts

Whistling kite
Found in Australia; distinctive whistling call when in flight

Young Brahminy kite
Juveniles fledge when they are eight weeks old. They are brown, with gray-brown underwings.

PROFILE

- S.E. USA, Central America, southward to Argentina
- Woodland, forest edges by rivers, wetland areas with trees and bushes
- Partial migrant
- 20½–24 in (52–62 cm)
- 16 oz (450 g)
- Cup nest of small sticks, mostly in tall pine, cypress, and mangrove
- 2 eggs; 1 brood
- Least Concern
- Colonies

Insect-eater
The swallow-tailed kite has a buoyant sailing flight. It uses its slender tail like a rudder as it chases prey on the wing.

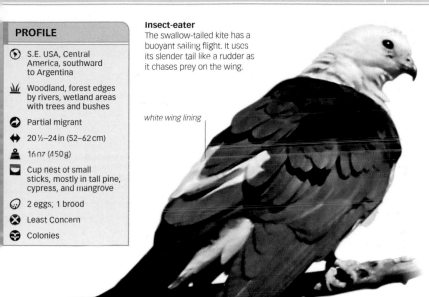

white wing lining

slender tail

black flight feathers

SIMILAR SPECIES

orange eye

White-tailed kite Gray-and-white plumage, with black triangle on shoulder

red eye

Black-winged kite Black upperparts; white underparts

Elanoides forficatus

SWALLOW-TAILED KITE

An elegant and agile flier, the swallow-tailed kite has an unmistakable silhouette, owing to its long and deeply forked tail. A bird of lowland forests and swamps, it has long, pointed wings with black flight feathers, contrasting with its white head and underside.

This kite is a versatile hunter, swooping on snakes, lizards, and small birds. It is also an expert at catching insects on the wing. Unusually for a bird of prey, this kite often eats in flight, and drinks while airborne, skimming the surface of the water like a swallow.

At the onset of the breeding season, the male courts the female by offering food. Once the pair is formed, both birds make a nest of sticks and leaves in a treetop, often building on a nest from the previous year. Both parents take care of the young, which are ready to fly when they are about six weeks old. Swallow-tailed kites breed from the southeastern USA to Argentina. North American birds migrate south in winter, but those in the tropics often remain all year round.

PROFILE

- S. Europe, S. Asia, Africa
- Mountainous areas and high steppes at altitudes of 3,300–14,500 ft (1,000 m–4,500 m)
- Nonmigrant
- 3–4 ft (0.9–1.2 m)
- 11–15 lb (5–7 kg)
- Large platform of branches, central hollow lined with wool hair, skin, and bones
- 1–2 eggs; 1 brood
- Least Concern
- Pairs

Easy to spot
Rusty orange from its chin to the base of its tail, the bearded vulture is conspicuous from below.

feathered head

grayish black wings

black-feathered "beard"

feathered legs

tapering tail

SIMILAR SPECIES

spiky feathers on neck

Egyptian vulture Much smaller; whitish body and tail, with yellow face and thin bill

Gypaetus barbatus

BEARDED VULTURE

Also known as the lammergeier, this very large, mountain-dwelling bird has a distinctive appearance and lifestyle. The bearded vulture feeds at high altitude, mainly on dead remains. It carries bones into the air, drops them onto rocks, and smashes them open to extract the marrow inside. Unlike most vultures, this bird has a fully feathered head, and feathered legs like a bird of prey's. Its wings and face are grayish black, with a "beard" of black feathers on either side of its bill. Compared to most vultures, the bearded vulture has long, narrow wings and a sharply tapering tail.

It nests on cliffs or in the mouths of caves, where it lays a maximum of two eggs. The young are tended for 17 weeks until they fledge.

Juvenile bearded vulture
The young bird has a light brown head and body, with darker wings. It takes 18 months to become an adult.

PROFILE

- Sub-Saharan Africa
- Plains and savanna, but also at altitudes up to 10,000 ft (3,000 m)
- Nonmigrant
- 31–35 in (78–90 cm)
- 12 lb (5.5 kg)
- Platform of sticks, central hollow lined with grass, situated in the crown or fork of a large tree
- 1 egg; 1 brood
- Near Threatened
- Solitary/colonies

Grassland scavenger
The African white-backed vulture uses its hooked bill for tearing off pieces of rotting flesh.

bare head

gray-brown plumage

lightly feathered neck

dark flight feathers

long, sharp claws

SIMILAR SPECIES

bulbous bill

Eurasian griffon
Sand-colored body, with a dull white ruff

heavy bill

Lappet-faced vulture Folds of skin on neck, called lappets

Gyps africanus

AFRICAN WHITE-BACKED VULTURE

Named for the collar of white feathers on its upper back, this bird is the most common of 12 species of vultures that live in Africa. Its plumage is gray-brown, and it has a white leading edge to its underwings that contrasts with its black flight feathers.

An effective scavenger, it spends hours on the wing, looking for signs of food on the ground. It also watches other vultures, following them toward a carcass in a chain reaction that brings birds from far afield. In a few hours, large remains can attract hundreds of birds, pushing and jostling for a share of the food. After eating, the birds rest on the ground before taking to the air again. The African white-backed vulture nests in large trees, making a platform of sticks lined with grass and leaves. The single egg is incubated for about 55 days, and the young bird remains in the nest for 17 weeks, until it is able to follow its parents into the air.

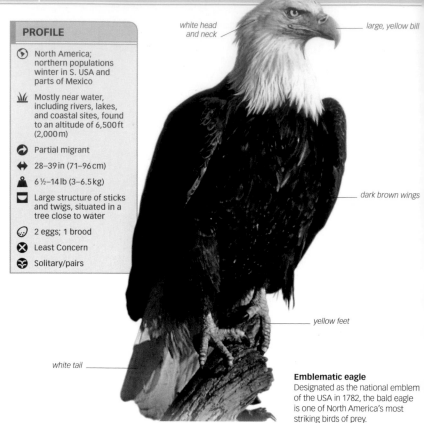

white head and neck

large, yellow bill

dark brown wings

yellow feet

white tail

PROFILE

- 🌐 North America; northern populations winter in S. USA and parts of Mexico

- 〰️ Mostly near water, including rivers, lakes, and coastal sites, found to an altitude of 6,500 ft (2,000 m)

- ➡️ Partial migrant

- ↔️ 28–39 in (71–96 cm)

- ⚖️ 6½–14 lb (3–6.5 kg)

- ✉️ Large structure of sticks and twigs, situated in a tree close to water

- 🥚 2 eggs; 1 brood

- ❌ Least Concern

- 🔁 Solitary/pairs

Emblematic eagle
Designated as the national emblem of the USA in 1782, the bald eagle is one of North America's most striking birds of prey.

SIMILAR SPECIES

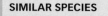

white tail

White-tailed eagle Dark brown, with pale head

dark head

Steller's sea-eagle Larger, with black-and-white body

Haliaeetus leucocephalus

BALD EAGLE

One of North America's largest birds of prey, the bald eagle is heavily built, with a conspicuous white head and strong legs with grasping talons. In summer, it is found as far north as the Canadian Arctic, while it winters on coasts or in southern parts of its range. Bald eagles mainly feed on fish, and every year, they gather in large numbers along salmon rivers, waiting to eat fish that have come upstream to spawn. They also feed on mammals and birds, including ducks and gulls.

Bald eagles mate for life. They build an extremely large stick nest, adding to it year after year, until it may weigh several tons. They usually lay two eggs and raise a single brood. Once hatched, the young birds take up to 14 weeks to become fully fledged.

Juvenile bald eagle
The bald eagle takes up to five years to acquire adult plumage. Juveniles lack yellow bills and are darker.

Voice of Africa

The African fish-eagle has a white head, black wings, and a two-tone yellow-and-black bill. It is a vocal bird, with a far-carrying call.

white head

yellow-and-black bill

white chest

chestnut body

black wings

PROFILE

- 🕐 Sub-Saharan Africa
- 〰 Large rivers, lakes, dams, coastal estuaries
- ⊘ Nonmigrant
- ↔ 25–29 in (63–73 cm)
- 🏋 4½–7¾ lb (2–3.5 kg)
- ▭ A large pile of sticks with a central bowl, lined with grass, placed in tree near water
- ⊙ 1–3 eggs; 1 brood
- ✕ Least Concern
- ❀ Pairs

Haliaeetus vocifer

AFRICAN FISH-EAGLE

A slimmer bird than some of its fish-eating relatives, the African fish-eagle hunts by watching the water below as it sits motionless on a prominent perch. At the sight of a telltale ripple, it launches itself into the air, snatching fish from just beneath the surface with its strong, rough-soled feet. Small fish are taken back to a perch, but large ones may be dragged through the water to the shore. A versatile predator and scavenger, this eagle also eats stranded fish and dead remains, and kills unwary waterbirds.

African fish-eagles normally live in pairs, building a stick nest close to the water's edge. Like many eagles, they use the same nest year after year, adding to it each time they breed. During the breeding season, the two birds carry out acrobatic pair-bonding displays, swooping and diving, and locking their talons as they tumble through the air. The female takes sole charge of the eggs, but both parents feed the young for 10 weeks, until they are able to fly.

PROFILE

- Across North America, Europe, Asia
- Open and deserted areas to an altitude of 18,000 ft (5,500 m) in parts of the range
- Partial migrant
- 30–35 in (75–90 cm)
- 6¼–14 lb (2.8–6.5 kg)
- Large nest of sticks, lined with finer material, on cliff or tree
- 2 eggs; 1 brood
- Least Concern
- Family groups

Mountain monarch
A majestic bird, the golden eagle is often found in high mountains. Adults have golden bronze feathers on their heads and napes, and brown bodies and wings.

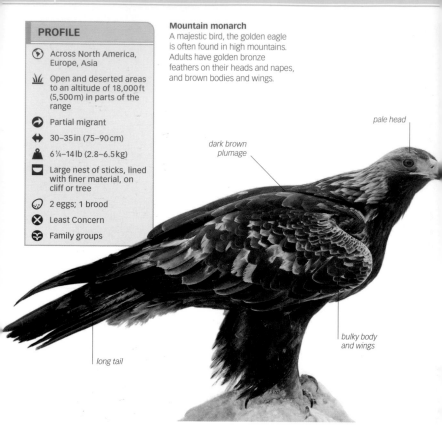

pale head

dark brown plumage

bulky body and wings

long tail

SIMILAR SPECIES

dark plumage

Eastern imperial eagle
Smaller; found mainly in Europe and Asia

dark brown plumage

Wedge-tailed eagle Larger, with a distinctive long, graduated tail

Aquila chrysaetos

GOLDEN EAGLE

This imposing predator is one of the largest land-based eagles in the Northern Hemisphere, and among the most widespread. The golden eagle usually hunts over mountainous regions, where it is relatively free from human disturbance. It soars high up when prospecting for food, but when attacking, it typically flies fast and low, closing in on its prey from behind. Golden eagles have wide-ranging appetites, but usually feed on medium-sized mammals, such as hares, and other mountain birds. If live prey is hard to find, they sometimes feed on carrion.

Golden eagles have extensive breeding territories. Two eggs are laid, but frequently the first chick to hatch kills the other, giving itself exclusive access to all the food that its parents bring to the nest.

Juvenile golden eagle
The young bird is initially chocolate-brown, with white wing patches and a white tail base.

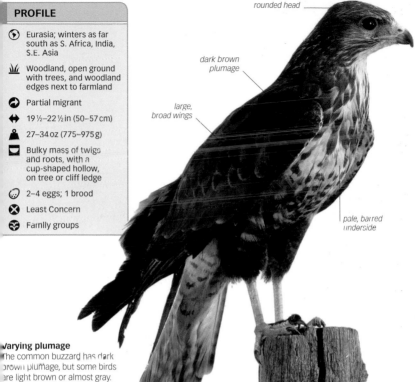

rounded head

dark brown plumage

large, broad wings

pale, barred underside

Varying plumage
The common buzzard has dark brown plumage, but some birds are light brown or almost gray. The female can weigh one-and-a-half times as much as the male.

SIMILAR SPECIES

pale head

Long-legged buzzard
Spends more time on the ground than other buzzards

Rough-legged hawk Darker, with pale feather edges

dark brown wings

Buteo buteo

COMMON BUZZARD

The common buzzard eats an extremely wide range of food. Besides catching small mammals and birds, it eats animals as small as earthworms and beetles, soaring overhead or watching from a fence post before dropping down to make a kill. It also eats berries and scavenges on remains of dead animals. Having successfully adapted to man-made changes in the landscape, it often hunts over pastures and fields.

Plain to look at, it can be extremely agile in the air. During the breeding season, prospective partners carry out highly aerobatic courtship displays, diving and rolling through the air. As nest-building approaches, the two birds pass sticks to each other high above the ground, and make nests in cliff ledges or trees. Both parents help incubate the eggs and tend the chicks for up to 50 days. In many parts of its range, the common buzzard is a year-round resident, but in others it migrates south before winter arrives, traveling as far as southern Africa.

PROFILE

- North and Central America, Caribbean; some populations migrate within this range
- Coniferous and tropical rain forest, prairies, and semi-deserts
- Partial migrant
- 17½–22 in (45–56 cm)
- 2¼–2¾ lb (1–1.2 kg)
- Bulky platform made of sticks on tree, with a cup-shaped hollow lined with twigs and stalks
- 2 eggs; 1 brood
- Least Concern
- Solitary/pairs

reddish brown streaks on head

white spots on back

yellowish legs and toes

Distinct rufous tail
The red-tailed hawk is easily identified by its tail, but some forms lack the distinctive red coloration.

rufous tail

SIMILAR SPECIES

brown upperparts

Broad-winged hawk Rarely hunts on the wing

pointed wing

Swainson's hawk Slender, with pointed wings and a long tail

Buteo jamaicensis

RED-TAILED HAWK

This highly variable predator is one of North America's most common birds of prey, with a range that stretches from Canada to Panama. A hunter of open country, it has a brown head, streaked brown upperparts, and a rusty orange tail. There are numerous subspecies and color phases, or variants, including pale, dark, and rufous forms, and those with a brown or gray tail.

Red-tailed hawks feed mainly on rodents, finding their food while soaring, or watching from a perch. They mate for life, and nest in trees or on ledges. Both parents build the nest and feed the young. During the breeding season, they swoop down on predators or other intruders to keep them away from their nest.

Juvenile bird
The juvenile takes two years to mature. It has a paler head than the adult and lacks the red tail.

Color scheme
The adult Harris's hawk is dark brown, with chestnut shoulder patches, leggings, and the inner edge of the underwings. Its tail is white with a black bar.

yellow eye ring

brown plumage

bright reddish wings

black-and-white tail

yellow legs and feet

PROFILE

🜨 From S. USA through Central America to Chile and Argentina

〽 Dry areas such as prairie and desert

⟳ Nonmigrant

↔ 19½–21½ in (50–55 cm)

⚖ 26–35 oz (0.7–1 kg)

▭ Made of twigs, roots, and stalks, lined with leaves, grass, and bark, in tree or on top of yucca or cactus

🥚 2–4 eggs; 1 brood

✖ Least Concern

🐦 Family groups

Parabuteo unicinctus

HARRIS'S HAWK

Often raised for use in falconry, Harris's hawk is a handsome and unusual bird of prey. In the wild, it is found from southern USA to Argentina and Chile, in a range of dry habitats. A fast-flying hunter, it scouts for food from a perch, speeding after other birds, rabbits, snakes, and lizards.

Sometimes Harris's hawk hunts on its own, but it also shows remarkable cooperation, with three or more birds working together to flush out their prey. After a hunt, the entire team shares the kill. This cooperative behavior also continues in the breeding season. Often the female is partnered by two males. The trio incubate a clutch of 2–4 eggs, and tend the young.

Juvenile hawk
The juvenile has streaked brown underparts, pale underwings, and less evident shoulder patches.

PROFILE

- North America, Eurasia; winters as far as Central America, N. Africa, S.E. Asia
- Moorland, open taiga, steppes, marshes, and dunes in summer; various open areas in winter
- Migrant
- 16½–19½ in (42–50 cm)

- 11–19 oz (300–525 g)
- A mound of small twigs and grass, placed on ground in dense cover
- 4–6 eggs; 1 brood
- Least Concern
- Solitary/pairs/colonies

Plume colors
The male northern harrier is gray with black wing tips, giving it an almost gull-like appearance. Both sexes have yellow legs and feet.

spotted underside

yellow legs

gray tail

SIMILAR SPECIES

black wing tips

Western marsh harrier Biggest and heaviest harrier, with dark underside

white wing panel

Black harrier Black plumage, with a striped tail; yellow legs

Circus cyaneus

NORTHERN HARRIER

Also known as the hen harrier, this long-winged, slender bird has a distinctive way of locating food. Instead of soaring or watching from a perch, it flaps and glides its way low over the ground, with its wings held in a shallow "V." The moment it spots a small bird or a rodent, it swoops down on its target, using its talons and hooked beak to make a kill. Both sexes hunt in the same way, but their different coloration makes it easy to tell them apart.

Unlike most birds of prey, the northern harrier nests on the ground, using sticks, reeds, and grass as building materials. The female incubates the eggs, and does most of the work of raising the chicks. This harrier lives in open habitats, such as grasslands, and migrates south after breeding.

Female northern harrier
Weighing almost twice as much as the male, the female is brown above, with pale, streaked underparts.

PROFILE

- Much of Europe, N.W. Africa, the Middle East
- Open woodland and farmland
- Partial migrant
- 23½–26 in (60–65 cm)
- 1½–2¾ lb (0.9–1.2 kg)
- Large, shallow structure, made of twigs, earth, and wool, placed in tree
- 2–4 eggs; 1 brood
- Near Threatened
- Small flocks

Fork-tailed kite
In most of its range, the red kite is the only bird of prey with a deeply forked tail. Its coloration is a distinctive reddish brown, with black wing tips and yellow legs.

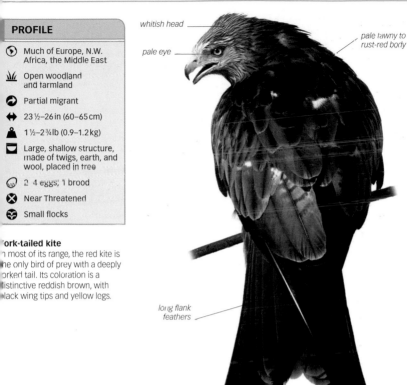

whitish head

pale eye

pale tawny to rust-red body

long flank feathers

SIMILAR SPECIES

dull and dark overall

Black kite Slightly smaller and less angular, with dark brown plumage

Milvus milvus

RED KITE

In medieval times, the red kite was a common scavenger in Europe's towns and cities, when food waste was simply thrown outside. Today, the same bird is seen flying over fields and roadsides, which it patrols for small mammals, worms, and the remains of dead animals. A skillful flier, it is most easily recognized by its narrow wings, which are bent back sharply at the wrist, and by its long, forked tail, which constantly tilts as it steers. It flies at a height of about 33–82 ft (10–25 m)—low enough to drop quickly if it sees any signs of prey.

Red kites breed in trees, making a large nest from sticks and often using an existing nest as the foundation. They raise a single brood, with both parents tending the young. In the south of their range, they are present all year, but in the north, they migrate. The red kite is currently classified as Near Threatened because of a steady decrease in its numbers in mainland Europe. It nearly died out in the British Isles, but a successful reintroduction campaign has led to a steady recovery.

Hidden tail
The bateleur (here, a female) is easy to recognize because its extremely short tail is dwarfed by its broad wings. When the bird is perched, the tail is entirely hidden by the wings.

red facial skin

black bill

rust-red upperparts

lighter secondary flight feathers than those of male

red legs

PROFILE

- Sub-Saharan Africa
- Open woodland and savanna with scattered trees; desert thornbush
- Nonmigrant
- 21 ½–28 in (55–70 cm)
- 4–6 ½ lb (1.8–3 kg)
- Cup nest made of twigs, lined with leaves, placed in canopy of tree
- 1 egg; 1 brood
- Near Threatened
- Solitary/pairs

Terathopius ecaudatus

BATELEUR

Named after the French word for a juggler or an acrobat, the bateleur is renowned for its agility in the air. A type of snake eagle, this bird has a black and rust-red body with conspicuous red legs and face.

Bateleurs spend most of the day searching for their prey, feeding mainly on mammals and birds. Their flight is fast, with an unusual rocking motion as they sway from side to side. During the breeding season, their courtship displays are dramatic, with the male diving at its prospective partner and loudly clapping its wings. Bateleurs nest in trees, making a cup-shaped nest on trees from twigs, which is lined with leaves. The female lays a single egg and incubates alone, while the male brings food, and later helps feed the developing chick.

Male bateleur
The male has a black border on the underwings, and darker secondary feathers on the upperwings.

PROFILE

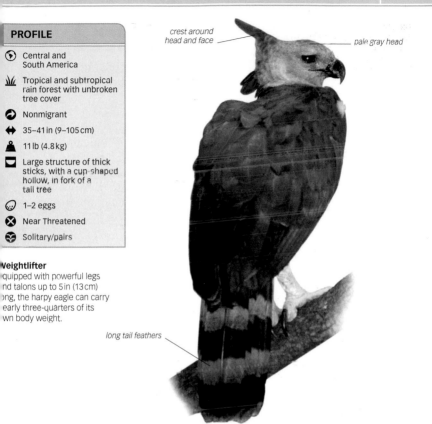

crest around head and face

pale gray head

long tail feathers

- Central and South America
- Tropical and subtropical rain forest with unbroken tree cover
- Nonmigrant
- 35–41 in (9–105 cm)
- 11 lb (4.8 kg)
- Large structure of thick sticks, with a cup-shaped hollow, in fork of a tall tree
- 1–2 eggs
- Near Threatened
- Solitary/pairs

Weightlifter
Equipped with powerful legs and talons up to 5 in (13 cm) long, the harpy eagle can carry nearly three-quarters of its own body weight.

SIMILAR SPECIES

distinctive crest

Philippine eagle Critically endangered species, with brown upperparts

Harpia harpyja

HARPY EAGLE

One of the world's largest and heaviest birds of prey, the harpy eagle is found in the rain forests of Central and South America. Colored in shades of gray, it has a double crest, which is raised if the bird is alarmed. Females can weigh almost twice as much as males.

Harpy eagles have prodigious lifting power, which lets them snatch sloths and monkeys from trees. An acute sense of vision and hearing helps them pinpoint the slow-moving and superbly camouflaged sloths. They also feed on a wide range of other animals, including deer and macaws. Instead of soaring like most other eagles, harpies spend many hours perched on high branches. This gives them a good view through the forest canopy. These eagles have a very slow breeding cycle, nesting only every two or three years. The nest is usually built on a tall tree with spreading branches, and is reused year after year. The female lays one or two eggs, but only one chick survives. It is able to fly when about seven months old.

CRANES AND RAILS

Cranes and their relatives look outwardly very different, some being tall and statuesque, others small, secretive, and barely able to fly. They are united by aspects of their internal anatomy, although they often have very different ways of life.

In addition to cranes themselves, this group of birds includes a wide variety of terrestrial, wetland, and freshwater birds. Among them are the bustards, trumpeters, sunbitterns, and kagus, but by far the largest family is formed by the rails. Cranes and rails are found worldwide, but many other families in this order are much more localized. Throughout the group, a number of species are seriously endangered, often as a result of introduced predators, or from habitat change.

ORDER	GRUIFORMES
FAMILIES	11
SPECIES	228

ANATOMY
Cranes and their relatives generally have long, slender legs, rounded wings, and a slender bill. However, body shape varies greatly depending on their habitat and way of life. Bustards, for example, are broad-bodied, with powerful legs for striding across open ground, while many rails are flattened from side to side so that they can slip easily through reeds. Cranes are the tallest members of the group, while the smallest rails are not much bigger than pocket-sized. As with all birds, their bill shape reflects their food, but their legs and feet are strongly linked to their different lifestyles.

FLIGHT AND MIGRATION
The group includes some species that are powerful fliers, as well as others that fly weakly, or—in a few cases— not at all. Most cranes are long-distance migrants, traveling in large flocks that often touch down at traditional staging posts on their way between their breeding grounds and their winter

quarters. At the other extreme, many members of this group are sedentary birds, staying in the same area all year round. In dry habitats, a few are nomadic, moving on to make use of short-lived sources of food.

BREEDING
Cranes are famous for their courtship rituals, but many other birds in this order perform elegant or drawn-out displays. In addition, some species are highly vocal, drawing attention to themselves with loud and distinctive calls. Most species in this order nest on or near the ground, and their down-covered young leave the nest soon after they have hatched.

Moving on
In North America, migrating sandhill cranes stop off at staging posts to rest and feed. Each year, they can travel over 6,000 miles (10,000 km).

PROFILE

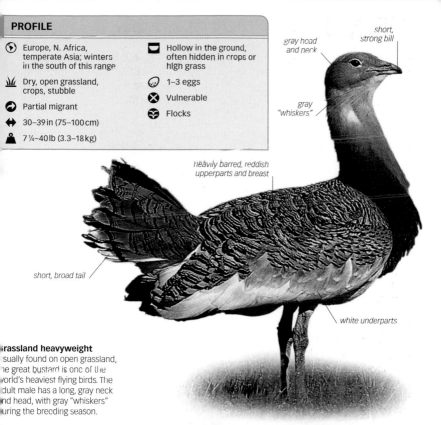

- Europe, N. Africa, temperate Asia; winters in the south of this range
- Dry, open grassland, crops, stubble
- Partial migrant
- 30–39 in (75–100 cm)
- 7 ¼–40 lb (3.3–18 kg)
- Hollow in the ground, often hidden in crops or high grass
- 1–3 eggs
- Vulnerable
- Flocks

short, strong bill

gray head and neck

gray "whiskers"

heavily barred, reddish upperparts and breast

short, broad tail

white underparts

Grassland heavyweight
Usually found on open grassland, the great bustard is one of the world's heaviest flying birds. The adult male has a long, gray neck and head, with gray "whiskers" during the breeding season.

SIMILAR SPECIES

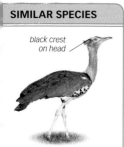

black crest on head

Kori bustard Heaviest of all flying birds

black cap

Australian bustard Larger, with orange-brown wings

Otis tarda

GREAT BUSTARD

An imposing bird with a long neck and head, the adult great bustard can weigh up to 40 lb (18 kg). The female is typically only a third as heavy as the male. It has a slow, measured walk and only occasionally takes to the air.

Great bustards feed on plants, insects, and other small animals. In spring, males gather at special display grounds known as leks, which are used year after year. Here they perform elaborate courtship displays, inflating their throat pouches and folding back their tails and wings. Females gather around to watch, selecting the most impressive performers as their mates. Males take no part in raising the young. Great bustards are partial migrants. In some regions, they winter in the south of their range.

Female great bustard
The female is much smaller and lighter than the male. It does not have "whiskers" or a throat pouch.

Ground dweller
The kagu has fully functioning wings, although it rarely flies. The crest is normally swept back, but can be raised in displays.

back-swept crest

red bill

blue-gray plumage

long legs

PROFILE

- New Caledonia in S.W. Pacific
- Forested areas; occasionally ventures into tall shrubland
- Nonmigrant
- 21½ in (55 cm)
- 32 oz (900 g)
- Loose structure of sticks and leaves, placed on ground
- 1 egg; 1 brood
- Endangered
- Pairs

Rhynochetos jubatus

KAGU

Found only in New Caledonia, the kagu is one of the world's rarest and most endangered birds. It has blue-gray plumage and an elegant, swept-back crest, together with long legs and a probing bill. Practically flightless, it lives on forested mountainsides, and spends almost all its life on the ground. This puts kagus at special risk from introduced predators such as cats and dogs, which eat eggs as well as the adult birds. Their numbers have sharply declined since the 18th century, when European colonists arrived on their island home.

Kagus feed on earthworms and other small animals, and have an unusual hunting technique. Instead of keeping on the move, they repeatedly stop and wait for signs of movement in the soil or among fallen leaves, and snap up their prey with a quick peck. Kagus mate for life, and often build their nests next to a stump or a fallen tree. Both parents help incubate the egg, and protect the young chick.

Hidden away
The clapper rail has camouflaged brown or gray plumage, and long, centrally positioned legs. It flies, but usually only for short distances.

long bill

cinnamon breast

long, thick legs

PROFILE

- E. and W. coast of USA, Mexico to Peru, Brazil, Carribean Islands
- Freshwater, saltwater, and brackish marshes, mangrove forest
- Migrant
- 14½ in (37 cm)
- 10 oz (275 g)
- Bulky cup of grass and plant stems lined with finer material; bends growing plants to form canopy
- 4–14 eggs; 1 brood
- Least Concern
- Solitary

SIMILAR SPECIES

red eye

Water rail Black-and-white barred flanks and brown upperparts with black streaks

brown stripe running down neck

King rail Larger, with short tail, orange breast, and boldly streaked upperparts

Rallus longirostris

CLAPPER RAIL

Heard more often than it is seen, the clapper rail is a secretive waterside bird. It calls at dawn and dusk, making a series of distinctive *kek kek kek* sounds, which carry far through the still air. These help identify it as it moves about unobserved. About the size of a small chicken, it has large feet with slender toes, and a remarkably thin body that lets it slip easily between plant stems along the water's edge. Both sexes have brown or gray plumage.

The clapper rail feeds mainly on shrimp, crabs, snails, and seeds, picking up food with its long, slightly curved bill. It often lives close to coasts, although its habitat includes a range of freshwater and brackish wetlands. During the breeding season, clapper rails make a domed nest above the waterline, using water plants as building material. Both parents incubate the eggs and take part in feeding the chicks. The young birds leave the nest soon after hatching, but it takes 10 weeks for them to become fully fledged.

PROFILE

- Europe, C. Asia; winters in the Mediterranean region and throughout Africa

- Dry to moist meadows, among grain crops

- Migrant

- 10½–12 in (27–30 cm)

- 4–7 oz (125–200 g)

- Shallow cup nest lined with leaves, concealed in grass or isolated tussock

- 8–12 eggs; 1–2 broods

- Least Concern

- Family groups

Camouflage plumage
The corn crake is well camouflaged, with chestnut wings, a gray throat and breast, and a streaked brown body. It has small, strong wings.

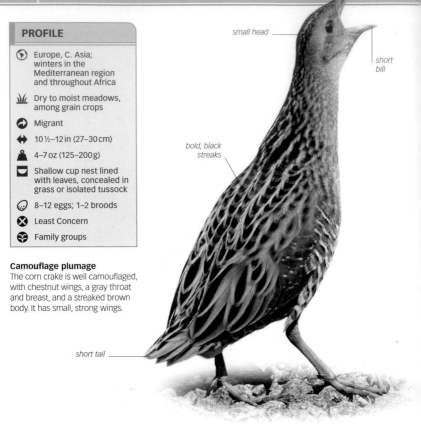

small head

short bill

bold, black streaks

short tail

SIMILAR SPECIES

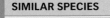

red eye

African crake Streaked, brown upperparts; barred, pale brown underparts

Crex crex

CORN CRAKE

Once a common farmland bird across Europe and temperate Asia, the corn crake lives among damp meadows and cereal crops, where it is heard far more often than it is seen. Corn crakes used to nest in hay meadows, but mechanized hay production has led to destruction of their nests and eggs, making this species increasingly rare.

With its small head and short bill, the corn crake resembles a small gamebird, but when it takes to the air, the bird can be identified by its legs, which trail behind its body in flight. A long-distance migrant from southern Europe and Africa, the corn crake arrives in its breeding grounds in late spring, where the male tries to attract a potential mate. Standing upright, it raises its bill and makes a *krek krek* sound. Once the birds have paired up, the female makes a small, flat nest from grass, where it incubates its clutch of 8–12 eggs. The young leave the nest soon after hatching, but stay by their mother's side for several weeks.

PROFILE

- S.E. USA to South America
- Swamps, marshes, and lagoons
- Migrant
- 10½–14 in (27–36 cm)
- 7–10 oz (200–275 g)
- Hollow raft of plant stems on floating vegetation
- 2–6 eggs; 1 brood
- Least Concern
- Family groups

Long-toed gallinule
The adult Purple gallinule has exceptionally long toes, which allow it to walk over lilypads and soft, waterside mud.

blue shield on forehead

iridescent green back

red bill with yellow tip

purple underparts

bright yellow legs and feet

large toes

SIMILAR SPECIES

large, red bill

Takahe The world's largest living rail

red facial shield

African purple swamphen Large; no yellow tip on bill

Porphyrio martinica

PURPLE GALLINULE

A colorful freshwater bird, the purple gallinule has a bright purple head, neck, and underside. Like other gallinules, it has long legs with slender, spreading toes.

Purple gallinules have an omnivorous diet, feeding on a variety of plant and animal matter, from seeds and leaves to insects and frogs. Highly migratory, they fly north to breed, and sometimes wander far outside their normal range. They nest on floating islands of vegetation, and live in family groups of up to a dozen birds. Nonbreeders in the group help defend the territory and protect the young.

Young gallinule
The juvenile bird has greenish brown plumage, becoming more colorful as it ages.

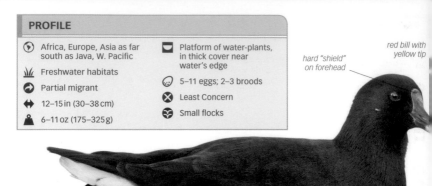

⊙ Africa, Europe, Asia as far south as Java, W. Pacific	▭ Platform of water-plants, in thick cover near water's edge
〰 Freshwater habitats	◓ 5–11 eggs; 2–3 broods
➔ Partial migrant	✖ Least Concern
↔ 12–15 in (30–38 cm)	❀ Small flocks
⚖ 6–11 oz (175–325 g)	

red bill with yellow tip

hard "shield" on forehead

white line along flanks

black underparts

long toes

Old World waterbird
Looking black from a distance, the common moorhen is actually dusky brown above and black beneath, with a white undertail.

SIMILAR SPECIES

Black-tailed native-hen
Found in mainland Australia

yellow bill

Spot-flanked gallinule
South American species with white spots on flanks

Gallinula chloropus

COMMON MOORHEN

This shy but successful waterbird is found on all Old World continents, except Australia, in a wide variety of freshwater habitats. A buoyant swimmer, it feeds on water and land, pecking up insects and other small animals, seeds, grain, and waterweed, and occasionally the young of other birds. Despite its timid nature, it is rarely quiet for long—its common call is a loud *kurruk*, which becomes frequent in the breeding season.

The common moorhen nests by making a platform of water-plants, in thick cover near the water's edge. Both parents incubate the eggs and tend the young, often helped by offspring from an earlier brood. In many parts of its range, this bird is a year-round resident, but it migrates in regions with cold winters.

Juvenile moorhen
The juvenile has a light brown body, and a white undertail that is flicked when the bird moves.

PROFILE

- Europe, Asia, Australia
- Wetlands; prefers large, open freshwater areas
- Partial migrant
- 14–15½ in (36–39 cm)
- 18–32 oz (500–900 g)
- Large bowl of wet vegetation, hidden among reeds
- 6–9 eggs, 1–2 broods
- Least Concern
- Large winter flocks

Subdued colors
The Eurasian coot has grayish
black plumage, a white bill, and
a facial shield. In flight, its wings
show white trailing edges.

red eye

white facial
shield and bill

intensely
black head

slate-black body

SIMILAR SPECIES

top of facial shield
reddish brown

American coot Dark gray
body, with greenish yellow legs

red knob on forehead

Red-knobbed coot Grayish
body, more rounded shape

Fulica atra

EURASIAN COOT

A widespread and assertive freshwater bird, the
Eurasian coot is recognized by the white shield on its
forehead. Apart from its forehead shield and bill, it looks
entirely black, with long, gray legs that trail in flight. Its
feet are large, and each toe has a series of flexible lobes
that act as paddles when it swims.

Eurasian coots are omnivorous, feeding on a wide
variety of plant matter and small animals, as well as the
eggs of other waterbirds. They breed on plant-fringed
lakes and rivers, and sometimes smaller ponds. At all
times of the year, they are noisy and argumentative,
but Eurasian coots become particularly aggressive when
the breeding season begins. Rival birds compete over
breeding territories, facing each other and kicking
furiously with their feet. Unlike some breeding contests,
these fights are real. Serious clashes can end in
permanent injuries or even death. Eurasian coots are
monogamous, and both parents incubate the eggs and
help tend the young.

PROFILE

- From Uganda and Kenya to South Africa
- Mixed grassland and wetland, and cultivated land with irrigation
- Nonmigrant
- 3 ¼ ft (1 m)
- 7 ¾ lb (3.5 kg)
- Large, platform nest of reeds, rushes, and grass, in tree or near ground
- 2–3 eggs; 1 brood
- Vulnerable
- Flocks

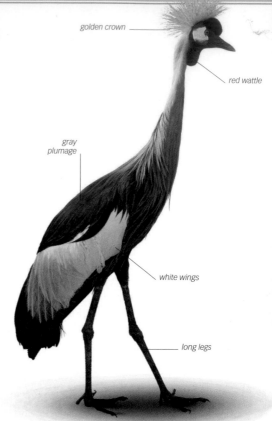

golden crown

red wattle

gray plumage

white wings

long legs

Stately progress
The gray crowned crane has largely gray plumage, with dark gray and white wings. Both sexes have a red wattle, and a characteristic golden crown, giving them a stately air.

SIMILAR SPECIES

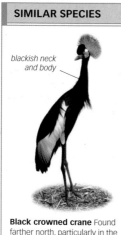

blackish neck and body

Black crowned crane Found farther north, particularly in the swamps of the Upper Nile

Balearica regulorum

GRAY CROWNED CRANE

Like its close relative, the black crowned crane, this elegant bird lives in Africa. The two species differ from other cranes in several ways. Both are able to perch in trees, and they lack the coiled windpipes that other cranes use to make deep bass calls. However, the most obvious difference is in their appearance: crowned cranes have graceful crests of golden bristles that adorn the top of their heads.

The gray crowned crane flies well, but it spends most of the daytime foraging on the ground. It feeds on insects, lizards, frogs, and fish, as well as plant seeds and cultivated crops. This diverse diet helps it survive, although it is still vulnerable to habitat loss and the collection of young birds and eggs. This crane makes a large platform nest, either in trees or near the ground. The young are normally fully fledged by the time they are 12 weeks old.

red crown

straight, sharp bill

long neck

gray plumage

long, black legs

PROFILE

- N.E. Siberia, North America; winters in North America, as far south as Mexico
- Marshes, lake margins, river deltas, from Arctic to tropics
- Partial migrant
- 35–38 in (88–95 cm)
- 7 ¼–13 lb (3.3–6 kg)
- Heap of plant material, large if on wet site, with central hollow
- 1 egg, 1 brood
- Least Concern
- Large flocks

In flight
The sandhill crane has large wings, but its tail is relatively short, leaving its legs trailing when it flies.

SIMILAR SPECIES

white plumage

Whooping crane Larger, with heavy, yellow bill, and black mustache

Grus canadensis

SANDHILL CRANE

One of the smaller species of cranes, the sandhill crane is famous for its migrations, which see tens of thousands of birds on the move. This bird feeds on seeds, (including cultivated grain), buds, leaves, and small animals including insects, young snakes, and mice.

Sandhill cranes arrive at their breeding sites in spring, after a northward journey of up to 3,700 miles (6,000 km). Their courtship involves elaborate dancing displays, with the male bowing, jumping, and throwing sticks into the air. Pairs usually mate for life. Both parents build nests for their eggs on a heap of vegetation, and take turns to incubate the clutch. Once the young chicks fledge, the birds fly south in large flocks to their overwintering grounds.

Young crane
The young sandhill crane has a brown neck and head, with no red crown, until it acquires adult plumage.

PROFILE

- Breeds across Eurasia; winters in S. Eurasia, N.W. and N.E. Africa, India, China
- Grassland, marshes, cultivated land
- Migrant
- 3½–4¼ft (1.1–1.3m)
- 12lb (5.5kg)
- Mound of reeds, grass, with a shallow hollow on top, often in marsh and near or in shallow water
- 2 eggs; 1 brood
- Least Concern
- Large winter flocks

red patch on crown

white patch behind eye

long, black neck

pale chest

thick, dark legs

Black and white
The adult common crane has a gray body, black wings, and a black-and-white neck and head with a small red crown.

SIMILAR SPECIES

striped neck

White-naped crane Only species of crane with pinkish legs and striped neck

black head

Black-necked crane Mostly gray, with black head and neck

Grus grus

COMMON CRANE

This stately bird has the widest distribution of all cranes, stretching across Europe, North Africa, and large parts of Asia. The common crane is a long-distance migrant, traveling in lines that snake across the sky. During these journeys, the birds keep in contact with each other with loud, trumpeting calls, and flocks are often heard long before they are seen. Common cranes feed on seeds and green plants, as well as insects, frogs, and mice. They gather in large numbers where food is plentiful.

In the breeding season, pairs claim a nesting territory, and carry out elaborate displays. These include simultaneous calling with their bills pointed upward, and energetic dances in which the birds leap into the air. Both parents help build the nest and feed the young.

Juvenile crane
The young common crane is largely gray, with a light brown head. Adult plumage develops in up to six years.

- N. Japan, parts of China and Siberia; winters in milder parts of this range
- Reed and sedge marsh, bogs, and wet meadows; rivers and coastal marsh in winter
- Migrant
- 5 ft (1.5 m)
- 15–26 lb (7–12 kg)
- Large mound of reeds and grasses, piled on top of ground
- 2 eggs; 1 brood
- Endangered
- Pairs/winter flocks

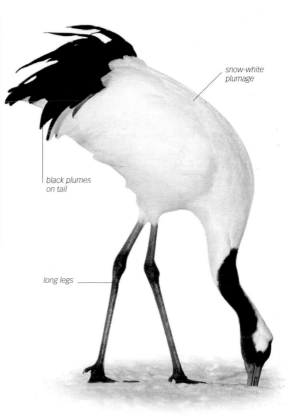

snow-white plumage

black plumes on tail

long legs

Majestic crane
The tall red-crowned crane has striking black-and-white plumage and long, black legs. Its red crown is most evident during breeding.

SIMILAR SPECIES

white plumage

Siberian crane
Large, with red face and black wing tips

Brolga Larger, with red throat pouch and gray-green crown

Grus japonensis

RED-CROWNED CRANE

This imposing bird is the world's tallest crane, as well as one of the rarest. It has spectacular markings on its body. Adults have snowy white bodies, contrasting with black heads and necks, black inner wings, and a collection of black plumes over their tails.

Red-crowned cranes feed in grassland and swampy ground, eating seeds, buds, insects, and small animals. Like other cranes, they mate for life, and perform extraordinary dances to cement the pair bond. They flap their wings and leap high off the ground, sometimes throwing grass or sticks into the air. Nesting among dead reeds, they make a large mound of plant stalks with a central hollow for the eggs. The female lays two eggs, but it is rare for more than one chick to survive.

Juvenile crane
The young bird is initially white with a brown neck and head. It takes three to four years to mature.

WADERS, GULLS, AND AUKS

Waders and their relatives are a common sight on the world's coasts, and often on wetlands and freshwater far inland. Many wade in shallow water, but this group also includes ocean-going species that come ashore only when they breed.

Waders or shorebirds are generally long-legged birds that feed in water, or at the water's edge. They include sandpipers, plovers, avocets, stilts, snipes, curlews, and jacanas—many of which are migrants, traveling great distances to breed. Gulls, which also include terns, jaegers, and skimmers, catch their food on foot or on the wing, while auks are diving birds confined to the seas of the Northern Hemisphere. Auks can look strikingly similar to penguins, but they use their wings to swim and also to fly.

ORDER	CHARADRIIFORMES
FAMILIES	19
SPECIES	379

ANATOMY AND FEEDING
With some exceptions, most of the birds in this group have muted plumage, but this is often offset by colorful legs, bare skin patches, or noticeable bills. Puffins, for example, have vividly colored bills and legs during the breeding season, while some lapwings have eye-catching wattles that hang from their throats. Their legs are highly variable between species: long and slender in most waders, they often have long, weight-spreading toes. In gulls, they are shorter and thickly webbed, while in auks they are stubby and paddlelike, making them ideal for swimming, but less suitable for moving about on land.

Some waders and their relatives have mixed diets, but most of them hunt other animals. Waders probe for invertebrates on coasts, in lagoons, or damp habitats on land. Most gulls are adaptable and opportunistic, catching animals or scavenging whatever they can, while terns plunge-dive for fish. Auks, on the other hand, are more specialized. They paddle on the sea, periodically diving underwater by flapping their stubby but powerful wings.

BREEDING
Most birds in this group nest on bare ground or cliffs, although a small minority nest in trees. Many breed in colonies—incubating murres, for example, have almost no personal space, virtually rubbing shoulders with their neighbors on cliff ledges. If their nests are threatened, some ground-nesting species distract predators with "broken wing" displays, but gulls, jaegers, and terns can be ferocious defenders of their nests and young.

Rich pickings
Adaptable and inquisitive, gulls are quick to exploit any chance of food. Although common on coasts, some species fly far up rivers inland.

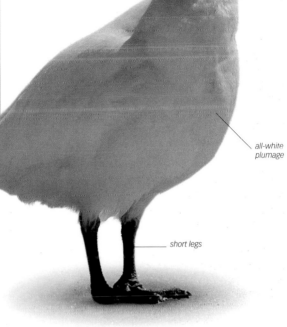

short, strong bill

all-white plumage

short legs

PROFILE

- 🌐 Coast of Antarctica, offshore islands; winters in the Falkland Islands and S. Argentina
- 〰️ Coastal areas
- 🔄 Partial migrant
- ↔️ 15 ½ in (40 cm)
- ⚖️ 22–26 oz (625–725 g)
- 📦 Cup-shaped nests made from seaweed and shoreline debris
- 🥚 2–3 eggs; 1 brood
- ❌ Least Concern
- 🐦 Small flocks

Agile runner
The all-white snowy sheathbill has a short, strong bill, and pink facial skin. Its legs are short, with sturdy toes for clambering over rocky shores.

SIMILAR SPECIES

Black-faced sheathbill
Dark bill, with black tufts; black face with red eye-ring

Chionis albus

SNOWY SHEATHBILL

A chicken-sized bird, with a portly, solid build, the snowy sheathbill lives along shorelines in the far South Atlantic. It is the only bird in Antarctica without webbed feet, and one of the few that feed largely on land. Instead of fishing, the snowy sheathbill walks among colonies of birds and seals, scavenging food scraps, and stealing eggs and newly hatched chicks. It also feeds on dead remains, and harasses penguins into regurgitating food brought for their young. An inquisitive bird, the sheathbill often tries to approach humans, but runs away quickly if alarmed. Despite its dumpy appearance, it flies well.

When breeding, the snowy sheathbill establishes territories among nesting penguins to secure a good supply of food. The female lays a clutch of 2–3 eggs, which are incubated for about 30 days. Once they leave the nest, the young initially forage along the shore. Snowy sheathbills are year-round residents in milder parts of their range, but birds in Antarctica usually fly north before the winter sets in.

Scratching a living
The Magellanic plover has pink legs with strong toes, which are used for scratching up food from the shoreline.

gray-white plumage

red eye

straight, black bill

white underparts

pink legs

PROFILE

- Chile, S. Argentina
- Freshwater or brackish water; winters in coastal areas
- Partial migrant
- 7½–8½ in (19–22 cm)
- 2⅞–3¼ oz (80–90 g)
- Simple scrape lined with gravel
- 2 eggs; 1 brood
- Near Threatened
- Flocks

Pluvianellus socialis

MAGELLANIC PLOVER

The Magellanic plover lives on the southern tip of South America, where it patrols the shoreline for its food. This small bird is a relatively rare species, with a population of less than 10,000 in the wild. In the far south, it is a migrant, but across most of its range, it is present all year round. The Magellanic plover feeds on shrimps, sandhoppers, and other small animals, pecking at them directly, or finding them by turning over stones. It also scratches up food with its feet—a common habit in some birds, but unknown in other shorebirds or waders.

This plover flies strongly and quickly, with rapid flicks of its wings. In early spring, it leaves the coast and heads inland to breed. Nesting on the gravelly shores of lakes and lagoons, the Magellanic plover defends territories against rival pairs. Both parents incubate the eggs, which are laid directly on the ground. When the chicks have hatched, they are fed by regurgitation—provided by both parents—another characteristic that makes them unique among shorebirds as a whole.

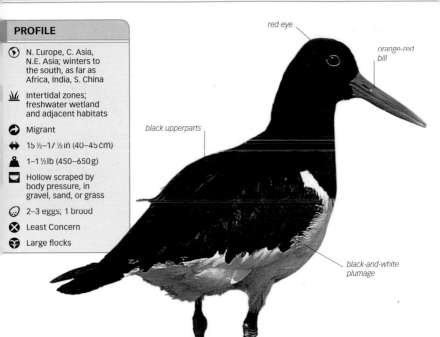

red eye

orange-red bill

black upperparts

black-and-white plumage

Shell smasher
The Eurasian oystercatcher has a laterally flattened bill with a bladelike tip. It is used to hammer open shells, or for slicing through tightly shut muscles.

Haematopus ostralegus

EURASIAN OYSTERCATCHER

A vocal and conspicuous shoreline bird, the Eurasian oystercatcher has strong, wading legs. It periodically moves along the shoreline, making a piercing, *kleep kleep* call on the wing and on the ground. This bird feeds mainly along rocky coasts and mudflats, and specializes in eating mollusks that are exposed by the falling tide. It also feeds inland, probing in mud or damp grass for insects and worms.

During the breeding season, pairs of oystercatchers make a shallow nest scrape on the ground, using little or no lining for the clutch of camouflaged eggs. For the first few weeks, the chicks are also cryptically colored, helping them hide while their parents forage for food.

Juvenile oystercatcher
The immature Eurasian oystercatcher has the same proportions as the adult, but with grayer legs.

PROFILE

- Canadian border through parts of the USA, as far as S. Brazil; northern birds migrate within this range

- Rocky or sandy seashore; freshwater marshes and swamps; lakes, rivers, and vicinity

- Migrant

- 14–15 ½ in (35–39 cm)

- 6 ½ oz (185 g)

- Hollow scrape on open, dry site; or a substantial cup nest of stems and leaves, on tussock

- 3–5 eggs; 1 brood

- Least Concern

- Pairs/colonies

Record legs
Long legs give the black-necked stilt a greater feeding range than other shorebirds. In flight, its legs trail far behind the short tail.

black crown

long, slender bill

white underparts

black, tapering wings

exceptionally long, pink legs

SIMILAR SPECIES

red legs

Black stilt Black plumage; long, thin, black bill

chestnut breast band

Banded stilt White head and underparts; black wings

Himantopus mexicanus

BLACK-NECKED STILT

Adapted to wading through shallow lakes and lagoons, the black-necked stilt's legs are longer in proportion to its body than almost any other bird's. Its bright pink legs contrast with its black-and-white plumage, and dark gray, pencil-thin bill. The black-necked stilt feeds on aquatic insects and other small animals, pecking them off the surface, or catching them with side-to-side movements of its bill. It also probes in soft mud, and strides through the water after fast-moving prey.

The black-necked stilt nests on the ground. Both sexes incubate the eggs, and in hot climates, the parents collect water to cool the eggs and chicks. In winter, northern birds migrate to warmer parts of their range.

Female stilt
Although the female has red legs and a black head like the male, its upperparts are dark brown.

PROFILE

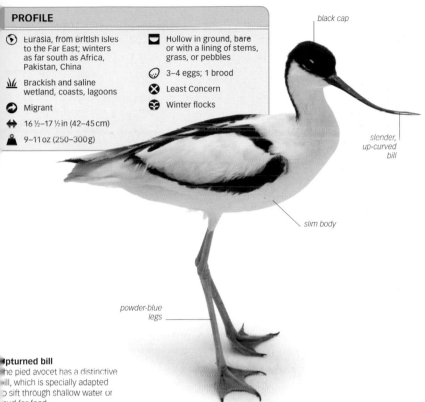

- Eurasia, from British Isles to the Far East; winters as far south as Africa, Pakistan, China
- Brackish and saline wetland, coasts, lagoons
- Migrant
- 16½–17½ in (42–45 cm)
- 9–11 oz (250–300 g)
- Hollow in ground, bare or with a lining of stems, grass, or pebbles
- 3–4 eggs; 1 brood
- Least Concern
- Winter flocks

black cap

slender, up-curved bill

slim body

powder-blue legs

upturned bill
The pied avocet has a distinctive bill, which is specially adapted to sift through shallow water or mud for food.

SIMILAR SPECIES

black-and-white upperparts

bright blue legs

Red-necked avocet Dark, chestnut-red head and neck

less up-turned bill

American avocet Cinnamon head and neck

Recurvirostra avosetta

PIED AVOCET

Remarkable shorebirds, avocets are found in brackish and saline marshes all over the world. There are four species, all of which are similar in size, with long legs and necks, and elegant upturned bills. The pied avocet is the only one with a black-and-white body and conspicuous black cap. Its long, bluish legs trail behind the body in flight.

Like other avocets, pied avocets feed in shallow water, picking out small animals with a side-to-side sweep of their bills. They find their food by touch, halting only an instant to swallow before moving on. Pied avocets nest in large groups, laying their eggs in shallow hollows on mudflats and small islands. Both parents help in incubating the eggs and taking care of the young. Although they look delicate, these birds can be noisy and aggressive when defending their breeding territory. If a crow or a gull approaches the colony, several adults will join forces to dive-bomb the intruder and drive it away.

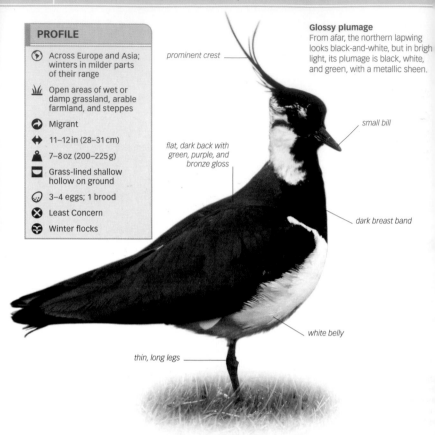

Glossy plumage
From afar, the northern lapwing looks black-and-white, but in bright light, its plumage is black, white, and green, with a metallic sheen.

prominent crest

small bill

flat, dark back with green, purple, and bronze gloss

dark breast band

white belly

thin, long legs

PROFILE

- Across Europe and Asia; winters in milder parts of their range
- Open areas of wet or damp grassland, arable farmland, and steppes
- Migrant
- 11–12 in (28–31 cm)
- 7–8 oz (200–225 g)
- Grass-lined shallow hollow on ground
- 3–4 eggs; 1 brood
- Least Concern
- Winter flocks

SIMILAR SPECIES

bright yellow wattle

Masked lapwing
Black head; long, yellow spurs at bend of wings

bronze wing patch

Southern lapwing Black throat and breast; red spurs at bend of wings

Vanellus vanellus

NORTHERN LAPWING

Also known as the peewit, this aerobatic bird is a common visitor to farmland, where it often follows the plow for insects and worms. Both male and female northern lapwings have slender crests, small bills, and long legs. They have broad wings and a characteristic "flopping" flight. The white underwings are visible when in flight. These birds feed on small animals, finding their food by sight, rather than by touch.

Northern lapwings are noisy and highly gregarious. During the breeding season, males perform a tumbling flight over their nest territory, making a loud *pee wit* cry. If the moon is out, the display can continue long into the night. Northern lapwings breed in a hollow on the ground. Both parents feed and defend the young.

Winter look
The northern lapwing is paler in winter, without the dark markings on the throat and its crest is also smaller.

PROFILE

- Arctic coasts from N.E. Canada to E. Siberia; winters in Africa
- Coasts in Arctic tundra areas and along rivers
- Migrant
- 7–8 in (18–20 cm)
- 2–2⅝ oz (55–75 g)
- Shallow scrape in sand or pebbles on beach, sometimes lined with shells
- 4 eggs; 2–3 broods
- Least Concern
- Small flocks

short, narrow bill

white collar

white underside

orange legs

lack-and-white face
he common ringed plover has haracteristic black-and-white facial narkings and a black neck band. The gs and base of the bill are orange.

SIMILAR SPECIES

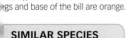

long, tapered wing tips

Little ringed plover Bright yellow eye-ring, stubby bill, and dull pink legs

black bill

Kentish plover Smaller, with incomplete breast band and darker legs

Charadrius hiaticula

COMMON RINGED PLOVER

Superbly camouflaged among pebbles and stones, the common ringed plover lives in small parties. It runs energetically over the shore, keeping just ahead of the breaking waves. If disturbed, it takes off in fast-moving flocks that twist and turn over the sea, before settling down a short distance further on. Compared to many shorebirds, common ringed plovers have short, narrow bills, which are ideal for picking up worms and other small animals from the surface of mud or sand.

Common ringed plovers are highly migratory, wintering as far south as southern Africa and returning to their breeding sites in spring. The female builds the nest, but both parents help in incubating the eggs. If a predator approaches the nest, the incubating parent distracts it by scuttling away, pretending to drag a broken wing. Once the predator is at a safe distance from the nest, the parent "recovers" and flies back to it.

PROFILE

- North, Central, South America; northern birds migrate south in winter
- Inland pools, grassland, fields, car parks, other open areas
- Partial migrant
- 9–10 in (23–26 cm)
- 3⅛–3½ oz (90–100 g)
- Shallow hollow in the ground, lined with pebbles, occasionally on low flat roofs
- 4 eggs; 1 brood (north), 2–3 broods (south)
- Least Concern
- Small flocks

brownish crown

red eye-ring

brown upperparts

small, thin black bill

pinkish legs

Double band
The killdeer is the only North American plover with two breast bands. The young bird has a single band; the second appears on maturity.

SIMILAR SPECIES

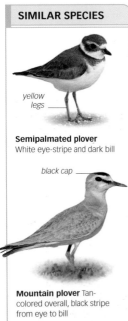

yellow legs

Semipalmated plover
White eye-stripe and dark bill

black cap

Mountain plover Tan-colored overall, black stripe from eye to bill

Charadrius vociferus

KILLDEER

Distinguished by its two breast bands, this American plover can also be identified by its shrill and repeated *kill dee* call. Common in meadows and damp grasslands, it can adapt well to human surroundings, and hence can also be spotted in parking lots, on airport runways, and on farms. It feeds on insects, worms, and other small animals, sometimes pattering on the grass to flush out food before snapping it up in its bill. Despite its camouflaged plumage, feeding in the open makes the killdeer conspicuous, and it takes to the air at the first sign of danger, loudly sounding the alarm.

The male killdeer courts the female with aerial display and scraping movements, to encourage the female to construct a nest. Once the partners have paired up and the nest has been built, both parents incubate the eggs and direct the newly hatched young to places where they can find food. Like many other shorebirds, killdeer perform a "broken wing" distraction display if a predator approaches their nests or chicks.

Walking on water
Also called the lily trotter, the comb-crested jacana typically walks over floating vegetation, pecking on insects and other animal food.

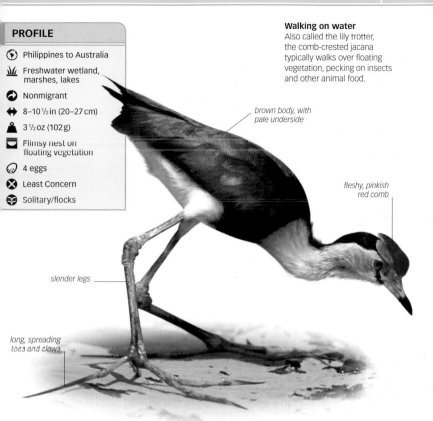

brown body, with pale underside

fleshy, pinkish red comb

slender legs

long, spreading toes and claws

SIMILAR SPECIES

white wings

Pheasant-tailed jacana
Long, narrow tail on both sexes during the breeding season

long legs

Northern jacana From Central America and some islands in the Caribbean

Irediparra gallinacea

COMB-CRESTED JACANA

Found in tropical and subtropical wetlands, jacanas are small to medium-sized shorebirds. Of the eight species of jacanas, the comb-crested jacana is the only one found in Australasia. Like all jacanas, it has exceptionally long toes and claws, and it uses these to spread its weight as it walks on floating water plants.

When breeding, comb-crested jacanas display an unusual sexual role reversal. A single female mates with several males, each of which incubates a clutch of eggs on a separate nest. The young hatch in a well-developed state, with feet that look gigantic for their size.

Juvenile jacana
The newly fledged jacana is browner than the adult, with a chestnut-colored crown. It does not have a comb.

large, black eye
near top of head

long, thin,
pinkish
brown bill

black, gray,
and buff
upperparts

short, rusty tail

rich orange-buff
underparts

PROFILE

- S. Canada to USA, Mexico
- Deciduous woodland, damp fields, marshes
- Partial migrant
- 10–12 in (26–30 cm)
- 6–8 oz (175–225 g)
- Shallow depression lined with leaves, on ground in young, mixed-growth woodland
- 4 eggs; 1 brood
- Least Concern
- Solitary

Woodland camouflage
The American woodcock has a stocky body, short neck, and barred crown. Its mottled brown plumage, makes it almost impossible to spot the bird against fallen leaves.

SIMILAR SPECIES

eye set far
back on head

Eurasian woodcock
Dead-leaf pattern on upperparts, bold black bars on head

Scolopax minor

AMERICAN WOODCOCK

Cryptically colored in shades of brown, the American woodcock spends most of its life unseen. This bird of fields, marshes, and damp woodland feeds on insects and earthworms, probing the ground with its long, pencil-shaped bill. Active mainly after dusk, it hides during the day in dense vegetation. As a defense against predators, its eyes are set very high on its head, giving it an almost panoramic view of its surroundings. If facing danger, it bursts out of cover at close range, flying a short distance before disappearing once again.

When the breeding season begins, the male carries out a spectacular display at special sites in clearings or in fields, and the birds also breed near these areas. The male flies up into the night sky, circling up to 330 ft (100 m) overhead. Suddenly, it zigzags back to the ground, with its wing feathers whistling loudly. Both sexes incubate the eggs and lead the chicks to food.

PROFILE

- Eurasia, Africa
- Tussocky, fresh, and brackish marsh; also damp farmland and other wetlands in winter
- Migrant
- 10–10½ in (25–27 cm)
- 3⅜–4 oz (95–125 g)
- Hollow, scraped with feet and shaped by body pressure, and lined with grass
- 4 eggs; 1–2 broods
- Least Concern
- Small flocks

Drum roll
The common snipe has brown upperparts and the male has two outer tail feathers that are adapted to produce a loud drumming sound to attract the female.

SIMILAR SPECIES

Jack snipe Smaller, with camouflaged plumage but shorter bill

Wilson's snipe American species; with short, russet tail

stripe on head

brown upperparts

long, pointed bill

greenish gray legs

Gallinago gallinago

COMMON SNIPE

A medium-sized bird, with camouflaged brown plumage, the common snipe has a wide range, including Eurasia and Africa.

A bird of damp places, marshes, and agricultural land, the common snipe feeds in muddy and grassy places, using its exceptionally long, finely pointed bill. The tip of the bill is highly sensitive and flexible, letting the snipe feel for worms and pull them to the surface. The common snipe also pecks up insects from the ground, ponds, and pools. If disturbed, it breaks cover with a zigzag flight, dropping out of sight once out of danger's way. In the breeding season, the male plunges through the air with its tail outstretched, producing a bizarre "song" with specially adapted feathers. Attracted by the call, females gather to mate. This bird makes its nest in clumps of plants, usually near water. The chicks are tended by both parents, and leave the nest within hours of hatching. Initially, their parents help them feed. The newly hatched chicks have smaller bills than their parents.

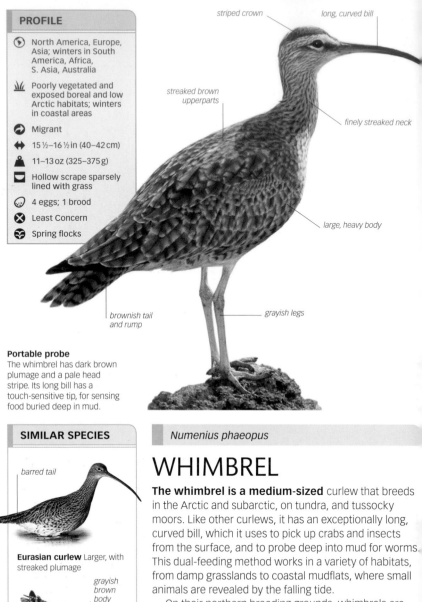

PROFILE

- North America, Europe, Asia; winters in South America, Africa, S. Asia, Australia
- Poorly vegetated and exposed boreal and low Arctic habitats; winters in coastal areas
- Migrant
- 15 ½–16 ½ in (40–42 cm)
- 11–13 oz (325–375 g)
- Hollow scrape sparsely lined with grass
- 4 eggs; 1 brood
- Least Concern
- Spring flocks

striped crown

long, curved bill

streaked brown upperparts

finely streaked neck

large, heavy body

brownish tail and rump

grayish legs

Portable probe
The whimbrel has dark brown plumage and a pale head stripe. Its long bill has a touch-sensitive tip, for sensing food buried deep in mud.

SIMILAR SPECIES

barred tail

Eurasian curlew Larger, with streaked plumage

grayish brown body

Little curlew Smaller, with a shorter, curved bill

Numenius phaeopus

WHIMBREL

The whimbrel is a medium-sized curlew that breeds in the Arctic and subarctic, on tundra, and tussocky moors. Like other curlews, it has an exceptionally long, curved bill, which it uses to pick up crabs and insects from the surface, and to probe deep into mud for worms. This dual-feeding method works in a variety of habitats, from damp grasslands to coastal mudflats, where small animals are revealed by the falling tide.

On their northern breeding grounds, whimbrels are vocal and melodious birds. The males' courtship song is a rich, bubbling sound, delivered on the wing. During the performance, male birds rise to a considerable height, and then glide in circles toward the ground. Both parents help incubate the eggs. The chicks leave the nest within hours of hatching, but cannot fly until they are about six weeks old. Once all the young birds have fledged, adults and young fly south for the winter, to live along coasts. Some travel as far as Australia and South Africa.

PROFILE

- Iceland, across Eurasia from British Isles to E. Asia; winters on coastlines of Eurasia, Africa, India, S.E. Asia
- Variety of wetland habitats
- Migrant
- 10½–11½ in (27–29 cm)
- 4 oz (125 g)
- Hollow scraped with feet, shaped by body pressure, lined, hidden in grass
- 4 eggs; 1 brood
- Least Concern
- Winter flocks

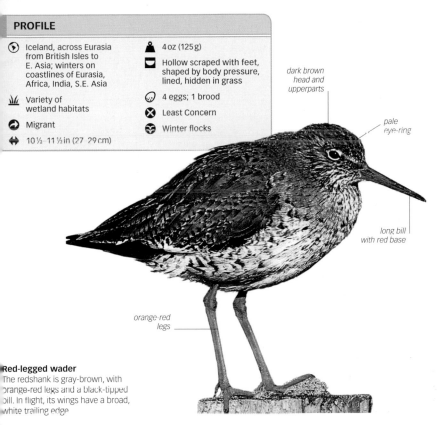

dark brown head and upperparts

pale eye-ring

long bill with red base

orange-red legs

Red-legged wader
The redshank is gray-brown, with orange-red legs and a black-tipped bill. In flight, its wings have a broad, white trailing edge

SIMILAR SPECIES

upturned bill

Common greenshank
Gray-green legs, white underparts

yellow legs

Lesser yellowlegs
Smaller, grayer, with dark bill

Tringa totanus

COMMON REDSHANK

A widespread shorebird of Europe, Africa, and Asia, the common redshank is found on coastlines during winter, but often goes far inland when breeding and raising its young. It gets its name from its orange-red legs, which keep their bright color throughout the year. Armed with a long, straight bill, it pecks food from the surface or probes deep into the mud. It feeds mainly on insects, but also takes small shellfish and worms.

Being social, it often feeds and roosts with other shorebirds. At the first sign of danger, it takes to the air, giving a piping alarm call that alerts the other birds around it. The male also sings during its display flights, vibrating its wings as it circles overhead, or slowly drops back to the ground. The common redshank breeds on coastal and inland wetland, often nesting in large numbers at the most suitable sites. Its nest is a shallow hollow lined with grass, and although both parents take care of the chicks, the female often leaves before the young are fully fledged.

PROFILE

- ⊙ High Arctic; winters on coasts, from British Isles to South America, South Africa, New Zealand
- 🌾 Open landscapes—grassland, tundra, savanna, moorland, and heaths; rocky or sandy seashore; rocky places or cliffs (on coasts and inland)
- ↻ Migrant
- ↔ 8 ½–9 ½ in (21–24 cm)
- ⚖ 2⅞–3⅝ oz (80–110 g)
- ▭ Shallow hollow in ground
- 🥚 4 eggs; 1 brood
- ✖ Least Concern
- ❦ Flocks

Breeding plumage
The ruddy turnstone has a deep chestnut back, and a black-and-white head and chest. Its bill is stout and strong.

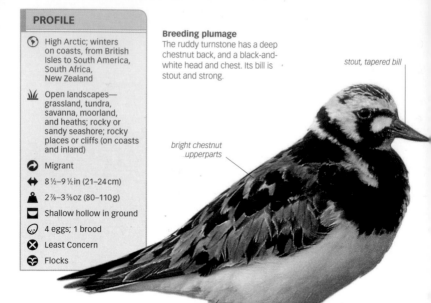

stout, tapered bill

bright chestnut upperparts

white underside

short, orange legs

SIMILAR SPECIES

dark upperparts

Black turnstone Blackish brown legs; white spot between bill and eyes

yellow legs

Surfbird Brown, streaked head, with dark bill; dark spots on white underparts

Arenaria interpres

RUDDY TURNSTONE

Living along most of the world's coasts, except in Antarctica, this small and highly active shorebird has a global distribution. It has a highly specialized feeding method: instead of probing the sand or mud, it walks along the tideline, flipping over seaweed, shells, and small stones. This often reveals small animals, which the turnstone snaps up before moving on. Besides eating live prey, it also scavenges on the remains of dead animals.

The turnstone breeds in the far north, often on the shores of the Arctic Ocean. The female lays a single clutch of four eggs in its nest, which is a simple, shallow hollow. Once hatched, the young leave the nest, and follow their parents as they feed. When the breeding season is over, young and adults fly south to their wintering grounds.

Winter plumage
The ruddy turnstone in winter is duller, without the bright chestnut upperparts. Its head is largely brown.

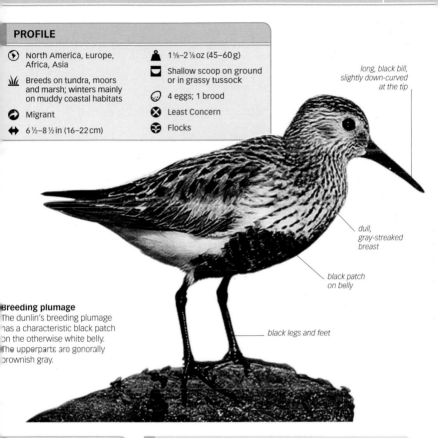

PROFILE

- 🕐 North America, Europe, Africa, Asia
- 〰 Breeds on tundra, moors and marsh; winters mainly on muddy coastal habitats
- ◐ Migrant
- ↔ 6½–8½in (16–22cm)
- 🛍 1⅝–2⅛oz (45–60g)
- 🗔 Shallow scoop on ground or in grassy tussock
- 🥚 4 eggs; 1 brood
- ✖ Least Concern
- 🐦 Flocks

long, black bill, slightly down-curved at the tip

dull, gray-streaked breast

black patch on belly

black legs and feet

Breeding plumage
The dunlin's breeding plumage has a characteristic black patch on the otherwise white belly. The upperparts are generally brownish gray.

SIMILAR SPECIES

short bill

Red knot Among the most social waders; pale coppery head

pale chestnut and black back

white belly

Sanderling Shorebird that breeds in some of the most remote Arctic habitats

Calidris alpina

DUNLIN

An Arctic breeder, the dunlin is more commonly seen in winter, when it feeds on coasts as far south as the equator. This small, compact-bodied wader feeds on coastal mudflats, pecking and probing in a series of rapid bursts, followed by short runs along the water's edge. It eats mainly small crustaceans and worms, which it feels with the sensitive tip of its bill.

Dunlins breed in a variety of Arctic habitats. Females lay a clutch of four eggs. Both sexes incubate and take care of the brood. Once fledged, young birds head southward to winter feeding grounds, where they may form flocks containing tens of thousands of birds. These flocks often look like clouds of smoke, sweeping low over the water and then suddenly changing course before settling on the shore.

Winter plumage
In winter, upperparts are typically light gray and the underparts are largely white, without a black belly patch.

PROFILE

- High Arctic; winters in midocean
- Freshwater bogs and marshes
- Migrant
- 7–7 ½ in (18–19 cm)
- 1 ¼–1 ⁷⁄₁₆ oz (35–40 g)
- Hollow lined with grass
- 4 eggs; 1 brood
- Least Concern
- Winter flocks

Phalarope plumage
The female red-necked phalarope has a compact, buoyant body, with a brown-and-gray head, and a brick-red throat and neck when breeding.

long, fine bill

white chin

buff stripes on gray back

SIMILAR SPECIES

white cheek

Red phalarope Colorful, brick-red breeding plumage

dark eye patch

Wilson's phalarope Largest phalarope; subdued colors in nonbreeding plumage

Phalaropus lobatus

RED-NECKED PHALAROPE

Unlike most shorebirds, the red-necked phalarope is a dedicated swimmer, spending as much time on water as on land. Instead of swimming in straight lines, it often turns in tight circles, creating currents that draw up food from below. It feeds mainly on plankton, but also pecks small insects from the surface of lakes and pools.

The female, which is larger and more colorful than the male, takes the lead role during breeding. It courts several males, and competes with other females for the best nesting territories. Soon after laying eggs, the female phalarope flies south. The male incubates the eggs, raises the young, and migrates only after the chicks have fledged.

Juvenile phalarope
The young red-necked phalarope has paler plumage and lacks the red color seen on the adult.

PROFILE

- Australia, Indonesia, New Guinea; winters in N. Australia, New Guinea, Sulawesi, S.E. Borneo, islands from Timor to Java
- Breeds on arid plains; winters on grassy and flooded plains, mudflats, and beaches
- Partial migrant
- 8 ½ in (22 cm)
- 2 ¼ oz (65 g)
- Small scrape on ground, sometimes surrounded with tiny stones
- 2 eggs; 1 brood
- Least Concern
- Migrates in flocks

short, hook-tipped bill

sandy-brown plumage

long legs

Open country runner
The Australian pratincole has sandy-brown plumage, with narrow black wings. Its hook-tipped bill is unusually short for shorebirds. It has long legs with small feet.

SIMILAR SPECIES

yellowish throat

Collared pratincole Reddish brown underwings; yellowish throat outlined in black

Rock pratincole Found in sub-Saharan Africa

Stiltia isabella

AUSTRALIAN PRATINCOLE

With its long legs and sharply pointed wings, the Australian pratincole is a slim, upright shorebird that spends much of its life inland. It is found in Indonesia and New Guinea, as well as in Australia itself. This bird breeds on stony plains and on the dry edges of swamps, often in the intense summer heat. The Australian pratincole feeds on insects, as well as centipedes and spiders, catching food on the ground and in the air. Like many birds, it gets most of its water from food, but it has special glands that allow it to drink brackish water if freshwater is hard to find.

Instead of having a set breeding season, the Australian pratincole often breeds after it has rained. The female lays a clutch of two eggs, and both parents take care of the young, which are fully fledged after about four weeks. After breeding, these birds winter in northern parts of their range.

PROFILE

🌐 N. Europe to Russia, also eastern coasts of Central and North America

〰️ Coasts, estuaries, large inland waters, and fields

🔄 Partial migrant

↔️ 27–31 in (68–79 cm)

⚖️ 3–5 lb (1.4–2.2 kg)

▭ Shallow grass or weed-lined scrape on cliff, ledge, or pinnacle

😊 3 eggs; 1 brood

❌ Least Concern

🦋 Flocks

yellow bill with red spot

white head and neck

black upperparts

pale pink legs and feet

Coastal predator
The adult great black-backed gull has a white body with gray-black upperwings, and a bill that is used to skin rabbits and seabirds.

SIMILAR SPECIES

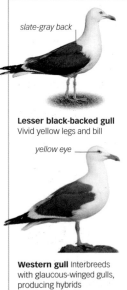

slate-gray back

Lesser black-backed gull
Vivid yellow legs and bill

yellow eye

Western gull Interbreeds with glaucous-winged gulls, producing hybrids

Larus marinus

GREAT BLACK-BACKED GULL

The world's largest gull, the great black-backed gull has a bulky body and head. Armed with a large bill, it scavenges along the shore and at garbage dumps. This aggressive predator is a frequent nest-robber and a skillful aerial pirate, harassing other birds until they regurgitate their catch.

This species breeds on both sides of the Atlantic: from the edges of the Arctic as far south as New York and the British Isles. It nests in small groups. Both parents incubate the eggs, look after the young, and guard against intruders, warning them off with a deep *yowk* call, swooping low overhead to protect their brood.

Juvenile bird
Great black-backed gulls take four years to develop adult plumage. Young birds have a dappled brown back.

PROFILE

- Northern Hemisphere; winters in Central America, N. and N.E. Africa, India, parts of S.E. Asia
- Mainly coastal; inland on large lakes, reservoirs, farmland, and dumps
- Partial migrant
- 21½–26 in (55 67 cm)
- 2¼–3¼ lb (1–1.5 kg)
- Shallow cup nest made of plant material
- 2–4 eggs; 1 brood
- Least Concern
- Colonies

white head

yellow bill with red spot

gray upperparts

white underparts

black wing tips

easide scavenger
he herring gull is one of the rgest gulls, ranging far out to ea, but often feeds on land.

SIMILAR SPECIES

California gull Smaller, with black-ringed, yellow bill

gray back

Iceland gull Heavy-billed; wings extend beyond tail

Larus argentatus

HERRING GULL

The noisy call of the herring gull is a common sound in coastal towns on both sides of the northern Atlantic. It has an extremely varied diet, following boats for fishing waste, and scavenging food from the shore. It also feeds in garbage dumps, and trails after tractors to feed on worms turned up by the plow. The adult herring gull has pale gray, black-tipped wings, with a white patch or "mirror." Its eyes are yellow and the bill has a red spot.

The herring gull breeds in colonies on cliffs, or sometimes on urban rooftops. It builds untidy nests from seaweed and locally available vegetation. Both sexes incubate and take care of the chicks. The young birds take four years to develop their adult plumage.

Juvenile gull
The mottled markings on the dark brown juvenile act as camouflage, growing lighter with age.

PROFILE

⊙ Australia, New Zealand, S. Atlantic

⩊ Rocky coasts, offshore islands

⊘ Nonmigrant

↔ 15 ½–17 ½ in (40–45 cm)

⚖ 10 ¹⁄₁₆ oz (288 g)

▭ Shallow scrape on ground, lined with vegetation

◔ 3 eggs; 1–2 broods

✖ Least Concern

◉ Colonies

Sleek gull
The silver gull has a glossy white body, with pale silvery gray upperparts. Its bill and legs remain scarlet throughout the year.

red bill

gray upperwings

white body

black wing tips

red legs

SIMILAR SPECIES

paler upperparts

Black-billed gull Smaller, with long, thin, black bill and reddish black legs and feet

darker wings

Gray-hooded gull Found in South America and much of Africa

Chroicocephalus novaehollandiae

SILVER GULL

A widespread scavenger, the silver gull is a familiar sight in fishing ports and towns. It also wanders far inland particularly after rain, but seldom ventures far out to sea. Like all scavenging gulls, its diet is extremely varied. Its natural food includes worms, insects, and crustaceans, as well as live and dead fish. An avian opportunist, the silver gull also steals food waste from garbage dumps and follows boats for scraps thrown overboard. Small and sleek, with pale silvery gray wings, it has a harsh *kee-arr* call.

Silver gulls make a nest of seaweed or plant roots on the ground, in low vegetation, among boulders, or in marine debris. Both parents help in incubating the eggs and tending the young. If food is plentiful, two broods may be raised.

Juvenile silver gull
Young birds are mottled with brown, and have duller legs and bills. They take about two years to mature.

PROFILE

- Canada, Europe to Asia
- Coasts, inland wetland, marsh, agricultural land, open areas in towns
- Partial migrant
- 14½–17 in (37–43 cm)
- 10 oz (275 g)
- Pile of vegetation, on marsh
- 3 eggs; 1 brood
- Least Concern
- Large flocks

Changing hood
The black-headed gull has a striking chocolate-brown hood while breeding. However, in winter it has a pale head with a distinct, dark ear spot.

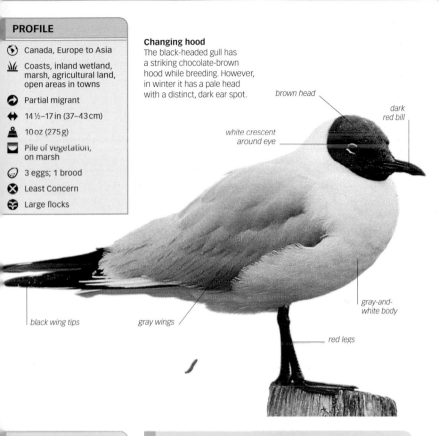

brown head

dark red bill

white crescent around eye

black wing tips

gray wings

gray-and-white body

red legs

Chroicocephalus ridibundus

BLACK-HEADED GULL

Agile in flight, the black-headed gull is a widespread bird, seen on many of the world's coasts and also far inland. It has a dark hood during the breeding season, which contrasts with its dark red bill and legs, and gray plumage.

Black-headed gulls have a wide-ranging diet and usually feed in large flocks, scavenging on the shoreline, on farmland, and in towns. They also steal food from garbage dumps, and rob lapwings and other birds. During the breeding season, they nest in colonies on the ground. Both sexes help in nest-building, incubating the eggs, and tending the young, which fledge at the age of six weeks.

Juvenile gull
The juvenile black-headed gull takes two to three years to mature. It has brown or gray-brown upperwings.

PROFILE

- Arctic coasts, N. Atlantic and N. Pacific oceans; winters at sea as far as the tropics
- Mainly on steep cliffs, increasingly on buildings
- Migrant
- 15–15½ in (38–40 cm)
- 14–15 oz (400–425 g)
- Drum-shaped nest of mud, grass, and seaweed, placed on ledge
- 1–3 eggs; 1 brood
- Least Concern
- Colonies

Seasonal visitor
Often seen near its nesting colonies, the black-legged kittiwake is a summer visitor in many parts of its range.

unmarked yellow bill

gray upperparts

white underpart

black-tipped tail

small, black feet

SIMILAR SPECIES

rounder head

Red-legged kittiwake
Smaller species from the North Pacific, with red legs

Rissa tridactyla

BLACK-LEGGED KITTIWAKE

Named after its loud *kitti-week* call, this small, dainty-looking bird is the world's most abundant species of gull. The gray-and-white gull has sharp claws—an adaptation for clinging to rocky ledges when it breeds. Compared to other gulls, the kittiwake is a highly marine bird, rarely straying far inland. It eats fish and waste thrown from ships and comes ashore only to nest.

The kittiwake breeds in large colonies on cliffs, around the mouths of sea caves, and occasionally on buildings. Both sexes build a tightly trampled nest of seaweed and mud, and tend the chicks. The young birds are ready to fly about 45 days after hatching.

Juvenile kittiwake
The young bird, with a "W" pattern on its upperwings and a black collar, takes three years to mature.

PROFILE

- ⊙ Arctic, sub-Arctic Europe, North America, Antarctica
- ⩗ Nests on gravel beaches, tundra, lakes, and coastal lagoons; usually winters at sea
- ◐ Migrant
- ↔ 13–14 in (33–36 cm)
- ⚖ 3–4 oz (85–125 g)
- ▭ Scrape in sand or gravel, hollow in rock
- ⊛ 2 eggs; 1 brood
- ✪ Least Concern
- ✿ Flocks

Buoyant flight
The Arctic tern has a slender body, with pointed wings, short red legs, and tiny feet. Unlike gulls, it flaps continuously as it flies.

short, red bill (blacker in winter)

round, black cap (with whiter forehead in winter)

gray back

SIMILAR SPECIES

black cap, with white flecks

Caspian tern The world's largest tern

short, black bill

Gull-billed tern Squat tern, with short, forked tail

Sterna paradisaea

ARCTIC TERN

Typically found close to the shore, the Arctic tern watches for food from a height of about 33 ft (10 m), hovering when it sees small fish or crustaceans, and then plunge-dives to make a catch. It has a buoyant flight, steering with its forked tail. It breeds on sandy or gravel beaches, laying its camouflaged eggs directly on the ground. This tern defends its nesting colony fiercely, attacking animals and human intruders by dive-bombing and raking them with its bill.

The Arctic tern is one of the world's greatest migrants. Once the chicks have fledged, adults and young set off on a 25,000 mile- (40,000 km-) journey that takes them to the Southern Ocean and back. As a result, they experience two summers a year, and more daylight than any other animal.

Young tern
The young bird has dark feet and an incomplete cap. It has scalloped plumage on the wings.

PROFILE

- Tropical Pacific, Atlantic, and Indian oceans
- Breeds on tropical and subtropical islands and coral reefs; disperses to sea after breeding
- Migrant
- 15–17 ½ in (38–45 cm)
- 5–10 oz (150–275 g)
- No nest; egg laid directly on ground
- 1 egg; 1 brood
- Least Concern
- Colonies

Dark tern
The brown noddy is dark-colored with a grayish forehead that extends over the top of the eye. The female is smaller and lighter than the male.

pale gray forehead

half eye-ring

long, sharp bill

dark brown plumage

SIMILAR SPECIES

black-and-white plumage

Sooty tern White forehead, deeply forked tail

dark gray plumage

Inca tern Catlike call; feeds by plunge-diving for fish

Anous stolidus

BROWN NODDY

This chocolate-colored tern lives in warm regions of the world's oceans, particularly in the Southern Hemisphere. This slender bird has a long, wedge-shaped tail. It feeds close to the shoreline and also far out at sea. Its diet consists mainly of fish and squid, which it catches by hovering and then swooping down onto the surface. Although it normally feeds alone or in small groups, large flocks sometimes congregate where predatory fish drive smaller ones within reach.

Unlike most terns, brown noddies often settle during flight: they land on the water's surface, on ships' rigs, and even on larger animals' backs. During the breeding season, adult birds move toward tropical islands and coral reefs. Here, the bird courts by nodding to its mate, giving the tern its name. It lays a single egg directly on the ground, and both parents feed the young. Instead of bringing back whole fish, the adults feed their young by regurgitation—a method that lets them fish far away, returning with the catch safely "aboard."

Dressed in white
The white tern has a slender white body including long wings and a long, straight bill. Its tail has a shallow fork.

large eye for night feeding

snow-white plumage

long wings

PROFILE

- Tropical Pacific, Atlantic, Indian oceans
- Coastal areas, coral islands
- Nonmigrant
- 10–12 in (25–30 cm)
- 3 ½ oz (100 g)
- No nest; egg laid on bare branch
- 1 egg; 1 brood
- Least Concern
- Solitary/colonies

Gygis alba

WHITE TERN

The only tern that is pure white in appearance, this bird is also known as the angel tern. Usually seen far from the nearest land, flying lightly and buoyantly over the waves, its appearance often seems to change as it flies past. From a distance, the tern is snowy white, but when it is overhead, its wings look almost transparent in the strong tropical sun.

White terns may seem delicate, but they are completely at home at sea. When feeding, they follow a rising and falling flight-path, dipping to catch small fish and squid, which are then eaten on the wing. Their large, deep black eyes are probably an aid for fishing at night, when many young fish come close to the surface. Normally solitary, white terns gather on remote islands to nest. The single, white egg is laid in a fork in a tree. The parents take turns to incubate the egg, fending off potential predators. After the young bird has fledged, it stays with its parents for several weeks while it is taught how to search for food.

PROFILE

- 🌐 E. USA to Argentina
- 〰️ Inland; coastal wetland in North America
- ↻ Migrant
- ↔️ 16–18 in (41–46 cm)
- ⚖️ 11–13 oz (300–375 g)
- 📧 Unlined hollow in sand, formed by feet and body pressure
- 🥚 1–5 eggs; 1 brood
- ❌ Least Concern
- 🐾 Colonies

Slicing the surface
Like other skimmers, the black skimmer has a remarkable bill, compressed laterally like a knife. It is used to cut through the water's surface to catch fish.

red bill with black tip

black back and crown

long, thick neck

short tail

white underparts

red legs

SIMILAR SPECIES

black upperparts

African skimmer Smaller skimmer, found in Africa

Rynchops niger

BLACK SKIMMER

Skimmers look similar to terns, but they have a unique feature found in no other bird: the lower part of their bills is much longer than the upper part, and is flattened sideways like a blade. Flying low over the surface of lakes and lagoons, they use the lower part of their bills to slice through the water's surface. The instant the bill touches a fish, it snaps shut, and the bird's neck flicks down, securing its catch. There are three species of these distinctive birds—the black skimmer, African skimmer, and Indian skimmer.

The black skimmer is the American representative of the skimmer family. Like its relatives, it has a slim body, with long wings and a short tail. It is especially active at dusk, and during the night. It roosts and breeds in small colonies near the waterside, often with terns and gulls. The female lays a clutch of 1–5 eggs directly on gravel or sand, and the chicks fledge after about 30 days. Their bills have equal upper and lower parts on hatching, but quickly acquire the adult shape.

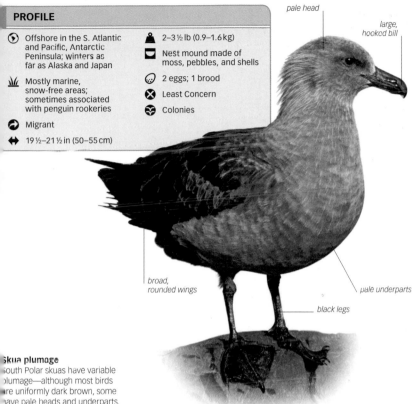

pale head

large, hooked bill

broad, rounded wings

pale underparts

black legs

PROFILE

- ⊙ Offshore in the S. Atlantic and Pacific, Antarctic Peninsula; winters as far as Alaska and Japan
- ⚲ Mostly marine, snow-free areas; sometimes associated with penguin rookeries
- ⊘ Migrant
- ↔ 19½–21½ in (50–55 cm)

- ⚖ 2–3½ lb (0.9–1.6 kg)
- ▭ Nest mound made of moss, pebbles, and shells
- ⊙ 2 eggs; 1 brood
- ⊗ Least Concern
- ❀ Colonies

Skua plumage
South Polar skuas have variable plumage—although most birds are uniformly dark brown, some have pale heads and underparts.

SIMILAR SPECIES

streaked plumage

Great skua Larger species; found in the North Atlantic

longer tail

Brown skua
Found in Antarctica; brown overall, longer tail

Stercorarius maccormicki

SOUTH POLAR SKUA

A powerful bird with a large, hooked bill, the South Polar skua looks like a large, dark brown gull. It spends the southern summer on the shore and sea around Antarctica, migrating northward in the winter as far as Alaska and Japan. Flying fast and well on its broad, angled wings, it fishes at sea, and follows ships for scraps that are thrown overboard. In addition, it is an aggressive predator of young birds, loitering around the edges of penguin colonies, where it steals eggs and chicks. Like other skuas and jaegers, it is also a pirate, robbing other birds of their food on land and at sea.

The South Polar skua breeds on the Antarctic mainland, building a rough nest mound with pebbles, moss, and shells. This bird defends its nest fiercely, flying directly at any intruder that ventures too close. The female lays two eggs, but the parents only rear the first chick that hatches. The juvenile skua resembles the adult, except that it has a blue base on its bill, and blue legs, instead of black ones.

PROFILE

- 🜨 High Arctic, winters in southern oceans
- 〰 Mostly marine; breeds on tundra or coastal grassland
- ↻ Migrant
- ↔ 19–21 in (48–53 cm)
- ⚖ 10–11 oz (275–300 g)
- ▱ Hollow on ground in tundra or on high mountains
- ☺ 2 eggs; 1 brood
- ✖ Least Concern
- ❖ Small flocks

Lightweight
Compared to other jaegers, the long-tailed jaeger has a light body with long wings. Its creamy yellow head is topped with a black cap.

black cap

cream-and-yellow cheek

brownish gray back

long tail streamers when breeding

SIMILAR SPECIES

black cap

Parasitic jaeger Much shorter tail streamers

brown back

Pomarine jaeger Blunt-tipped tail streamers

Stercorarius longicaudus

LONG-TAILED JAEGER

Also known as the long-tailed skua, this is a sleek and elegant seabird, with a light, ternlike flight. It has a small bill and long, narrow wings. Its tail is conspicuous, with two central streamers that twist and turn in the wind.

Less piratical than other jaegers, the long-tailed jaeger feeds mainly on lemmings on land, although it also eats insects and berries, and fish when at sea. These birds breed on Arctic coasts, where they lay their eggs in a hollow in the ground. The eggs are incubated by both parents, and the young are fledged by the age of about four weeks. Once the breeding season is over, the young birds and adults disperse out to sea. They have been spotted in the middle of the Arctic Ocean, and as far south as the tip of South America.

Dark phase juvenile
The young jaeger has mottled plumage, without the adult's tail streamers. It takes 2–3 years to mature.

PROFILE

- Coasts of the Arctic Ocean; winters at sea in the North Atlantic
- Open seas; breeds on scree-slopes of coastal cliffs
- Migrant
- 8½ in (22 cm)
- 6 oz (175 g)
- Unlined burrow
- 1 egg; 1 brood
- Least Concern
- Flocks/colonies

Plankton feeder
The dovekie is a short-necked bird with a short bill. It feeds mainly on fish, crustaceans, and other small planktonic animals.

black cap

short, stubby, black bill

black back

white chest

SIMILAR SPECIES

dark brown head

Marbled murrelet Larger, often nocturnal species from western North America

pale bill tip

Ancient murrelet Breeds mainly in Aleutian Islands, spreading south in winter

Alle alle

DOVEKIE

A bird of cold, **northern waters**, the dovekie, also known as the little auk, is one of the smallest members of the auk family—a group of seabirds that swim underwater with their short, stubby wings. It has a dumpy body, with a black back and white chest, and jet-black legs set far back near its tail.

The dovekie stands upright on land, using its webbed feet to jump over rocks, but when airborne, it flies fast and low, with its wings whirring at high speed. Highly social, this bird breeds in large colonies. It also gathers in flocks, called rafts, that often contain thousands of individual birds. Each year, nesting birds produce a single egg, which is incubated for 29 days. Initially, the chick is fed by both parents, which eventually abandon it, leaving it to fly out to sea alone.

Winter plumage
In winter, the adult has black upperparts, head, and face. Its throat, cheeks, chin, and underparts are whitish.

PROFILE

- ⊙ Atlantic, Pacific; breeds on the coasts of the N. Pacific and N. Atlantic
- 〰 Open seas; breeds on sea cliffs
- ◐ Partial migrant
- ↔ 16½ in (42 cm)
- ▲ 2¼ lb (1 kg)
- ▭ On a bare ledge of a sheer cliff
- ◎ 1 egg; 1 brood
- ✖ Least Concern
- ✿ Small flocks

long neck

sharp, daggerlike bill

white parts rounded against black throat

upright posture

Standing upright
The common murre has legs that are set far back, giving it an upright posture on land. It feeds on fish and crustaceans.

SIMILAR SPECIES

bold, white wing patch

Black guillemot From the far north; has white wing patches and red legs

black head

Razorbill Atlantic species with a laterally compressed bill

Uria aalge

COMMON MURRE

Although common murres spend much of the year out at sea, they become highly visible and vocal when they come to land to breed. Dressed soberly in dark gray and white, with slender, pointed bills, these auks cram onto cliff ledges, where females lay a single egg. They use no nesting material, and their sharply pointed eggs tend to roll in narrow circles instead of falling off. While one parent incubates, the other forages at sea, and the colony resounds with loud, guttural calls as couples keep in touch.

Common murres feed on fish, using their wings as paddles as they dive. Like many other auks, they feed their young until they fledge. Escorted by one or both parents, the chick then flutters down to the sea to complete its development.

Winter pattern
At sea during winter, the adult murre has a white throat and neck, with a black streak behind the eye.

PROFILE

- N.W. Pacific Ocean
- Open ocean and sea; breeds on rocky beaches
- Migrant
- 9 in (23 cm)
- 9⅜ oz (260 g)
- Single egg laid among boulders, or loose scree
- 1 egg; 1 brood
- Least Concern
- Colonies

Deep diver
During the breeding season, the crested auklet has conspicuous orange-red plates on the sides of its bill, and a white plume behind each eye.

white plume behind eye

forward-curving crest

orange-red plate on side of bill

gray underparts

webbed feet

very short tail

SIMILAR SPECIES

thin, black crest

Whiskered auklet Similar species from E. North Pacific

horn at base of upper bill

Rhinoceros auklet Much larger auklet, without a crest

Aethia cristatella

CRESTED AUKLET

A bird of the North Pacific and Bering Sea, the crested auklet is deep black in color, with a crest of plumes that curve forward over its deep orange-red bill. Like other auks, it has a compact body with short, stubby wings, and legs set far back near its tail. Its plumage has a distinctive citruslike odor. The crested auklet is a highly social bird, and often forms mixed flocks with other auks.

Crested auklets feed mainly on small crustaceans. They use their wings as paddles, and dive up to 165 ft (50 m) to find their prey. These auklets are fully at home in water, and rarely venture ashore except to breed. During the breeding season, crested auklets gather in noisy colonies, where each pair raises a single egg among boulders or loose scree. Both parents help to incubate the egg, and bring food to the chick until it is ready to fly. Crested auklets winter out at sea. During this period, their bills are smaller and less bright, and the crests and eye plumes are shorter.

PROFILE

- ⊙ W. and E. coasts of the N. Atlantic Ocean; winters in the same area
- 𝖬 Sea cliffs in summer, oceans and open seas otherwise
- ⊘ Migrant
- ↔ 10–14 in (26–36 cm)

- ⚖ 16 oz (450 g)
- ⌂ Burrows, or under boulders, lined with vegetation
- ◔ 1 egg; 1 brood
- ✕ Least Concern
- ⊗ Flocks

Summer colors
The Atlantic puffin has black-and-white plumage. In spring and summer, its bill is covered with brightly colored plates.

white face

bright orange bill in summer

black upperparts

black collar

SIMILAR SPECIES

black horn

Horned puffin
Northern Pacific species, with yellow bill

colorful sheath (lost in winter)

Tufted puffin Pacific species, with head tufts when breeding

Fratercula arctica

ATLANTIC PUFFIN

With its multicolored bill and brilliant orange-red feet, this puffin is one of the most familiar birds of North Atlantic coasts. A member of the auk family, the Atlantic puffin flies low over the sea on rapidly whirring wings. It can dive to 66 ft (20 m) beneath the surface, flapping its wings to swim. This gregarious bird, often seen in floating flocks or rafts, feeds on fish—particularly sand eels. At the beginning of the breeding season, it comes ashore on rocky coasts with cliff-top turf.

This bird nests in burrows or under boulders, lined with vegetation. The female lays a single egg and the chick is fed by both parents for about six weeks. Then, the parents desert their offspring, which hides underground. After days without food, it crawls out after dark, and flutters down to the sea.

Winter colors
After the breeding season, the outer plates of the bill fall off, revealing a small, less colorful bill beneath.

SANDGROUSE

Resembling both grouse and pigeons, sandgrouse are fast-flying birds from arid parts of Europe, Africa, and Asia. Many species have long tail feathers, and intricately patterned plumage that helps conceal them as they forage on the ground.

Once classified with pigeons and doves (below), sandgrouse share the same powerful flight, with fast-beating wings. However, they differ from pigeons in several important ways. Some birds in this order have a raised hind toe, or no hind toe at all, and they lack the fleshy band, called a cere, that pigeons have at the base of the upper bill. Also, sandgrouse do not produce "pigeon's milk," even though they do have a crop for storing their food. The sexes differ in color, with the females usually being more subdued than the males. Sandgrouse feed mainly on seeds, often flying in low-level flocks to locate their food.

ORDER	PTEROCLIDIFORMES
FAMILIES	1
SPECIES	16

COLLECTING WATER
Sandgrouse nest on the ground, among rocks and stones, and they produce down-covered young. Both adults and young need a daily supply of water, which some species collect by flying to distant waterholes. The adults wade chest-deep into the water, ensuring that their belly feathers are soaking wet. The young birds can then drink this moisture when the adults return to the nest.

PIGEONS AND DOVES

Small-headed birds with plump bodies, pigeons and doves are found in many different habitats, from semi-deserts to tropical forests. Almost exclusively vegetarian, they have powerful, fast-flapping wings, and feed their young on a form of milk.

The familiar urban pigeons are just one species in this large and diverse group of birds. Pigeons and doves are often easy to recognize, from their overall shape and their habit of bobbing their heads when they walk. Many species feed on the ground, often eating seeds, but the order also includes an enormous range of tropical fruit-eating species, which spend their lives in trees.

ORDER	COLUMBIFORMES
FAMILIES	2
SPECIES	321

BREEDING
Pigeons and doves almost always lay two eggs. For their first few days, the young are fed on a milklike secretion from the parents' crops. This is rich in fats and proteins, helping fuel early growth.

Show time
Perched on a branch, a mourning dove fans its tail. Like most pigeons and doves, it seeks safety in trees, even though it feeds on the ground.

PROFILE

- S. Europe, N. Africa, Middle East
- Semi-desert, treeless steppes, dry mudflats, arable farmland
- Partial migrant
- 12–15 ½ in (31–39 cm)
- 7–14 oz (200–400 g)
- Simple depression in bare ground
- 3 eggs; 1 brood
- Least Concern
- Flocks

Ground-dweller
The male pin-tailed sandgrouse has short legs and small feet. It normally runs away from danger, but is extremely fast on the wing.

small, downcurved bill

small head

brown and chestnut patterns on body

pointed tail

chestnut breast band

short legs

SIMILAR SPECIES

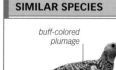

buff-colored plumage

Pallas's sandgrouse
Central Asian species with needlelike tail

Chestnut-bellied sandgrouse Species from Africa and southern Asia

Pterocles alchata

PIN-TAILED SANDGROUSE

Named for its long, slender tail, the pin-tailed sandgrouse is found in dry places in Europe, Africa, and the Middle East. Like other sandgrouse, it has a plump body and pointed wings. The complex pattern of brown and chestnut on its body makes superb camouflage when seen against baked earth, or sand with scattered stones.

The pin-tailed sandgrouse lives in flocks, and feeds entirely on shoots and seeds. Its flight is fast and direct, letting it travel long distances to find food. Both parents incubate the eggs, and tend to the young. In summer, males wade into lakes and waterholes until their breasts are soaked. Then they fly back to their nests with water for their young.

Female sandgrouse
The female has two bands on its throat, while the male has only one.

PROFILE

- 🌐 Africa, Europe, Asia
- 🌿 Wild, rocky regions (wild populations); cities (feral birds)
- ↻ Nonmigrant
- ↔ 12–13 ½ in (31–34 cm)
- ⚖ 6–12 oz (175–350 g)
- ▭ Loose, untidy, sparse nest on ledge, in cavity
- 🥚 2 eggs; 3 broods
- ✕ Least Concern
- 🦅 Flocks

Ancestral pigeon
The rock pigeon has light gray plumage, black wing-bars, and a black tail. It is the ancestor of all feral pigeons.

two black wing-bars

dark underside

dark tail

SIMILAR SPECIES

bifurcated neck collar

Speckled pigeon African species with speckled wings and red eye-patches

Stock dove Similar to the rock pigeon, but without black wing-bars

Columba livia

ROCK PIGEON

Ranging across Europe, Africa, and Asia, the rock pigeon is the ancestor of feral pigeons, which are among the world's most widespread birds. Found mainly in towns and cities, feral pigeons are fully adapted to urban life, breeding in buildings and eating leftover food. Compared to them, pure-bred rock pigeons are much shier birds, living on rocky coasts, mountains, and in deserts, and feed mostly on seeds.

Rock pigeons nest on cliff ledges and in caves, building flimsy nests from plant stems and seaweed. Both parents incubate the eggs, and help feed the young on "pigeon's milk," a nutritious fluid produced by the crop lining. Once a common species, rock pigeons are becoming increasingly rare due to interbreeding with feral birds.

Feral pigeon
The feral or city pigeon, with its many colors and patterns, is more varied than the wild rock pigeon.

PROFILE

- Europe, N. Africa, Middle East
- Woodland, especially in arable farmland; parks and gardens, including urban areas
- Partial migrant
- 15½–16½ in (40–42 cm)
- 17–19 oz (480–550 g)
- Thin platform of twigs or sticks in tree or bush
- 2 eggs; 2 broods
- Least Concern
- Large flocks

Boldly marked pigeon
Wood pigeons can be identified by their white neck patches, and the white bands on their wings, which are visible in flight.

bold white patch on sides of neck

brownish gray back

white bars on wing

SIMILAR SPECIES

iridescent head and neck

Japanese wood pigeon
A solitary bird of mature forests

Columba palumbus

WOOD PIGEON

A plump woodland bird, the wood pigeon has a brownish gray back, pink breast and legs, a gray head, and prominent neck patches. Its soft cooing is a familiar sound in many parts of Europe, N. Africa, and the Middle East, where it lives and breeds. The wood pigeon flies fast and well. It is constantly on the watch for danger, and if disturbed, bursts out of cover on loudly clapping wings.

Like most pigeons, the wood pigeon feeds on the ground, and eats seeds, green shoots, and young plants, particularly in cultivated fields. In winter, it descends on its food in large flocks. These can create significant damage on farmland, where its population is difficult to control. Wood pigeons breed in any month of the year, raising a minimum of two broods. The nest is usually above the ground in thick cover, and is a flimsy latticework of sticks and twigs. Both parents help incubate the young, and tend the chicks, which are ready to fly when about one month old.

PROFILE

- Europe to C. Asia; winters in Africa
- Mainly in woodland, but also in open country with some trees; avoids dense forest
- Migrant
- 10½–11½ in (27–29 cm)
- 3½–6 oz (100–175 g)
- Loose platform of twigs, situated in a low tree or bush
- 2 eggs; 2–3 broods
- Least Concern
- Small flocks

Patterned plumage
The European turtle dove has a gray-brown body and a checkered pattern on its upperwings. It has an area of pink skin around each eye.

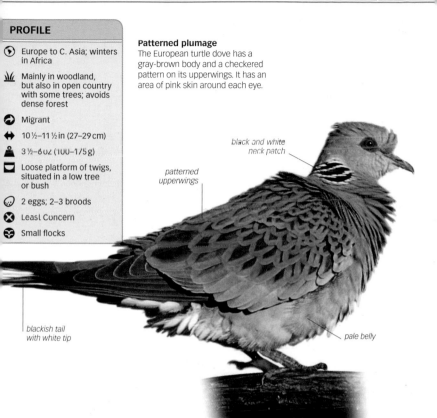

black and white neck patch

patterned upperwings

blackish tail with white tip

pale belly

SIMILAR SPECIES

blue-gray wings

Laughing dove
Smaller African species, does not migrate

black collar

Eurasian collared dove
Larger Eurasian species with pale gray-brown body

Streptopelia turtur

EUROPEAN TURTLE DOVE

This small dove is a summer visitor to Europe and Asia, wintering in sub-Saharan Africa. Its soft purring is often heard in the warmth of a summer's day, when male birds call to attract potential mates. European turtle doves also display in the air, climbing high into the sky, and then gliding down on stiffly outstretched wings.

European turtle doves feed on seeds and leaves. Adult birds prepare to breed soon after migration. They nest in trees or shrubs, and both parents help incubate the eggs and tend the young. If their young are threatened, a parent bird will often feign an injury, while moving away from the nest. This distraction display helps lure a predator away from the young birds. The young fledge after about 20 days, and once they have left the nest, the parents often raise a second brood. European turtle doves are not endangered, but many thousands are shot on migration every year.

PROFILE

- Drier areas of Australia, north of the Tropic of Capricorn
- Dry grassland dominated by tussock-forming spinifex; open woodland with rocky ridges
- Nonmigrant
- 8–9½ in (20–24 cm)
- 3½ oz (100 g)
- Slight hollow lined with twigs, often under clump of spinifex grass
- 2 eggs
- Least Concern
- Pairs/small flocks

Upright crest
The spinifex pigeon has a compact body, and a long wispy crest that is permanently raised. It has a white chinstrap and red facial skin.

red facial skin

black and pale gray bands on body

short tail

SIMILAR SPECIES

grayish plumage

Crested pigeon Only other Australian pigeon with an upright crest

iridescent wings

Common bronzewing Larger, widespread pigeon of the Australian interior

Geophaps plumifera

SPINIFEX PIGEON

One of Australia's most characteristic inland birds, the spinifex pigeon has two different color forms. One has white underparts, but both are rusty brown above, with black barring on the head, red facial skin, a white "chinstrap," and a permanently raised crest.

Spinifex pigeons live mainly on the ground. Their plumage camouflages them against dry grass and bare earth. When threatened, they either run away on their short legs, or burst into the air with a whirr of their rounded wings. They feed on seeds, particularly from drought-resistant clumps of spinifex grass, and stay within reach of seasonal creeks and springs for water. Rain prompts them to breed. Incubation takes about 18 days, and the young birds leave the nest before they are two weeks old.

Juvenile pigeon
The immature bird is plain. It has a crest, but lacks the conspicuous facial marking of the adult.

PROFILE

- Semi-arid, desert areas of N.W. and interior Australia
- Lightly wooded, semi-arid, or arid grassland near water
- Nonmigrant
- 7 ½–9 ½ in (19–24 cm)
- 1 ¹⁄₁₆ oz (30 g)
- Small platform made of very fine twigs, placed low in tree or bush
- 2 eggs
- Least Concern
- Pairs/small flocks

Conspicuous eye-rings
The diamond dove has prominent, red eye-rings, which are slightly larger in the male than in the female. Both sexes have long tails and pink legs and feet.

red eye-ring

diamondlike spots on wings

long tail

SIMILAR SPECIES

black and white bars on body

Zebra dove Native to S.E. Asia; barred body

blue-gray head

Bar-shouldered dove Larger Australian dove, with scalloped back and neck

Geopelia cuneata

DIAMOND DOVE

Often kept in captivity, the diamond dove is native to Australia, where it lives in scattered woodland and scrub. A tiny, long-tailed dove, it is blue-gray above, with white, diamondlike spots on its wings. It has a gray neck and head, with distinctive red rings around its eyes.

Usually seen in pairs or small flocks, diamond doves feed on the ground, eating seeds, green shoots, and small buds. Like most dryland pigeons and doves, they need access to water, and often gather at springs and creeks. They run rapidly, despite their small legs, but if alarmed, they take to the air on rapidly whirring wings. They have a strong and direct flight, but rarely fly far before returning to the ground.

Diamond doves breed after rain, at any time of the year. They make an insubstantial platform of twigs low in a bush or tree. The female lays two eggs, which take 14 days to hatch. The young birds lack the colored eye-rings and diamondlike spots on the wings. They take about two weeks to fledge and leave the nest.

PROFILE

- 🔄 From US–Canadian border area as far south as Panama, N. Caribbean, and the Bahamas; northern populations migrate south within this range

- 〽️ Wide range of open and semi-open habitats, including urban areas

- ↪️ Partial migrant

- ↔️ 9–13 ½ in (23–34 cm)

- ⚖️ 4 oz (125 g)

- ▭ Scanty platform of thin twigs, sometimes lined with finer stems, usually in tree or shrub

- 😊 2 eggs; 2–6 broods

- ❌ Least Concern

- 💬 Pairs/winter flocks

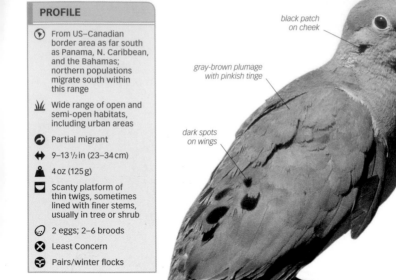

black patch on cheek

gray-brown plumage with pinkish tinge

dark spots on wings

pink legs and toes

long, pointed tail

Tapering tail
The slender-bodied mourning dove has a long, sharply tapering tail, with outer tail feathers tipped with white. The sexes look similar.

Zenaida macroura

MOURNING DOVE

Common throughout North and Central America, the mourning dove gets its name from its call—a mournful, multisyllable cooing. This bird has a rapid, direct fight, and lands with a characteristic upward flick of its tail. It feeds almost entirely on the ground, eating seeds and green shoots, and also waste grain from cultivated fields. At the beginning of the breeding season, the male courts the female with a display flight, spiraling upward with noisy flapping, and then gliding back to the ground.

Like most doves, mourning doves are monogamous. Both parents share the work of building the nest and feeding the young. The young are helpless on hatching, and are initially fed on crop "milk" before being given seeds. In warm parts of its range, this bird can raise 5–6 broods a year—a record for any North American bird.

SIMILAR SPECIES

black mark on cheek

White-winged dove
Shorter-tailed species with large, white wing patches

Juvenile mourning dove
The young has a shorter tail. Heavily spotted with brown, it lacks the adult's pinkish head and underparts.

PROFILE

- N. New Guinea
- Swamp, sago palm, and dry forests
- Nonmigrant
- 26–29 in (66–74 cm)
- 5 ½ lb (2.5 kg)
- Large, solid platformlike mass of stems and twigs, placed in tree
- 1 egg; 1 brood
- Vulnerable
- Flocks

Dressed in blue
Adult Victoria crowned pigeons are largely blue, with dark eye-stripes. Both sexes have a crest, which is flattened from side to side.

lacy crest with fan-shaped tips

red eye

powder-blue plumage

pale white wing patch

pale spots on tail

SIMILAR SPECIES

bluish gray plumage

Southern crowned pigeon
Deep maroon breast with a prominent white wing patch

Goura victoria

VICTORIA CROWNED PIGEON

Found only in the forests of northern New Guinea, this eye-catching bird is one of the world's largest pigeons. It has strong feet, for a life spent mainly on the ground, and a permanently raised crest that bobs back and forth as the bird walks.

Victoria crowned pigeons live in small groups of 2–10 birds, which search the forest floor for fruit and seeds. If threatened, they either slip away among the trees, or take off noisily into the branches overhead. They also roost off the ground for safety. Unusual for a pigeon, this species makes substantial nests, where each pair raises its single young. Once the chick has hatched, it takes four weeks to fledge and leave the nest. In New Guinea, Victoria crowned pigeons are prized for food and their plumage. This, combined with deforestation, has brought about a sharp decline in their numbers in recent years.

PROFILE

- Sub-Saharan Africa
- Various types of forest and woodland, forest edges, and mangroves
- Nonmigrant
- 10–12 in (25–30 cm)
- 6–8 oz (175–225 g)
- Platform of twigs and leaves
- 1–2 eggs; 1 brood
- Least Concern
- Flocks

Shades of green
African green pigeons are largely green above, with pale underparts and yellow thighs. The leg color varies across their range.

red bill with white tip

thickset green body

bright red legs

SIMILAR SPECIES

grayish green plumage

Large green pigeon
Fruit-eating species from the forests of Indonesia

Treron calvus

AFRICAN GREEN PIGEON

Found across most of sub-Saharan Africa, the African green pigeon spends its life in trees. Its feet are strong, and it uses them much like a parrot for clambering up high branches and rarely coming down to the ground. African green pigeons feed on fruit. They are normally found in small parties, but can gather in large numbers where food is easily found. With such a wide range, their breeding season varies, but it usually coincides with the peak fruiting period, particularly of wild fig trees.

The African green pigeon's nest is a platform of twigs and leaves, which the female builds using materials gathered by her mate. The eggs are incubated by both parents for about 14 days. On hatching, the chicks are initially fed on pigeon's "milk," before switching to the adult diet. They remain in the nest for about 12 days, leaving it before they are fully fledged.

PROFILE

- E. Australia
- Lowland tropical rain forest; eucalyptus forest and farmland in winter
- Nonmigrant
- 11 ½–17 ½ in (29–45 cm)
- 6–7 oz 1 (75–200 g)
- Fragile-looking nest on palm frond or branch
- 1 egg; 1 brood
- Least Concern
- Flocks

Splash of color
The wompoo fruit-dove has an ash-gray head, with a green back and a plum-colored breast. The rear underparts and underwings are bright yellow.

red and yellow bill

green back

yellow wing markings

long tail

SIMILAR SPECIES

gray throat

Superb fruit-dove
Smaller Australian species; male has purple crown

Ptilinopus magnificus

WOMPOO FRUIT-DOVE

Fruit-doves live in Southeast Asia and Australasia, where they feed in the treetops, only occasionally descending to the ground. There are over 50 species of these sumptuously colored birds, including the wompoo fruit-dove, which live in the coastal forests of Australia's east. A large, beautiful pigeon, the wompoo fruit dove gets its name from its *wompoo* call. Like its relatives, this bird is eye-catching in flight, with its bright yellow underparts, but can be difficult to spot in the treetops unless it moves.

The wompoo fruit-dove feeds on fruit, particularly wild figs, and the fruit of some palms. It clambers around in the branches, swallowing its food whole, and often dislodges a shower of fruit as it feeds. This bird breeds during the summer rainy season. The female lays a single egg, which is incubated by both parents for about 21 days. The parents also take turns to tend the chick, which fledges in about three weeks.

PARROTS AND COCKATOOS

Parrots are—with a few exceptions—found mainly in warm parts of the world. Colorful, noisy, and often gregarious, they feed on a wide variety of plant-based food, using their hooked bills and grasping feet.

Parrots and cockatoos are readily recognized by their large heads, short necks, and stout hooked beaks. Their feet are fleshy, and are used for climbing, for perching, and often for holding food. Some are largely green, while others are black or gray, but they also include many of the world's most flamboyant birds. A number are solitary, but parrots typically live in flocks, often calling loudly to each other as they fly between sources of food and the places where they roost. These daily excursions can cover a considerable distance, but very few species migrate.

ORDER	PSITTACIFORMES
FAMILIES	1
SPECIES	375

Prized pets
Many parrots—such as macaws—have seen a sharp decline in their numbers as a result of the caged-bird trade. They are also affected by deforestation.

CUCKOOS, HOATZIN, AND TURACOS

Found mainly in woodland and forests, this order includes cuckoos and African turacos, as well as the aberrant hoatzin.

With some notable exceptions—such as the roadrunner (p.188)—most cuckoos are small or medium-sized birds that typically live in trees. They often feed on insects, but in spite of their reputation, not all lay their eggs in other birds' nests. Most ground-living cuckoos build nests and raise their own young, but many tree-dwelling species are brood parasites, tricking other birds into raising their young. In temperate regions these cuckoos are usually migratory, arriving when the hosts' breeding season begins.

TURACOS AND HOATZIN
Turacos, thought to be distantly related to cuckoos, are found only in Africa.

ORDER	CUCULIFORMES
FAMILIES	3
SPECIES	170

Generally plump and mainly tree-dwelling, they are vegetarians with short, chickenlike bills. Their exceptional colors are due to pigments found in no other birds. They build flimsy nests from twigs, and their young often clamber out of their nests before they can fly.

The hoatzin is a unique bird from the forests of South America. Its exact affinities are uncertain, but it differs from cuckoos and turacos not only in its bizarre appearance, but also in its diet.

Mountain parrot
A large, stocky bird, the kea is
a unique parrot adapted to life
in cold climates. It has a hooked
bill and spends its life foraging
on the ground.

long, hooked bill

dark-edged
feathers

olive-green
plumage

PROFILE

🎯 South Island,
New Zealand

🌿 Upland scrub and
grassland in summer;
wooded valleys in winter

↔ Nonmigrant

↔ 19 in (48 cm)

⚖ 28–34 oz (800–950 g)

📇 Crevice or cavity under
rocks, among tree roots,
or in logs; lined with
moss, lichen, leaves,
twigs, and chewed wood

🥚 2–5 eggs

✖ Vulnerable

🐦 Family groups

Nestor notabilis

KEA

Found in exposed alpine pastures in New Zealand's
South Island, the kea is among the few parrots that
thrives in cold, mountainous regions. Large and solidly
built, it has powerful legs and feet for foraging on
the ground. The kea has olive-green plumage, with
bright orange underwings, and it flies well, even in
strong mountain winds.

For a parrot, the kea's bill is very unusual, with a
long and slender upper half, or mandible, that can be
used like a lever to extract food. Using its bill, the kea
probes the soil for insects and grubs, and also tears
open remains of dead animals. Gregarious and highly
inquisitive, it also investigates picnic sites and cars,
damaging backpacks and even windshield wipers
in its search for new sources of food. Keas nest in
rock crevices, where the female lays 2–5 eggs. The
incubation period is about 21 days, but it can take a
further 12 weeks before the young birds are ready
to leave the nest.

Owl-parrot
The kakapo's rounded face has led to its alternative name—the "owl-parrot." Its bill is surrounded by whiskerlike feathers, which act like sensors and help in moving after dark.

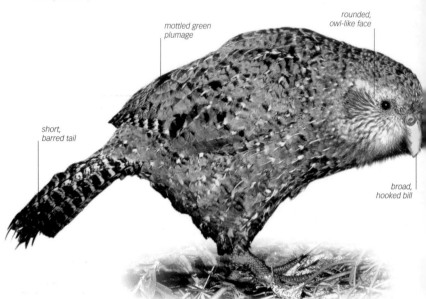

rounded, owl-like face

mottled green plumage

short, barred tail

broad, hooked bill

PROFILE

- 🜚 Codfish and Anchor islands, New Zealand
- 🌿 Forests on offshore islands
- ◑ Nonmigrant
- ↔ 25 in (64 cm)
- ⬥ 3¼–6½ lb (1.5–3 kg)
- ▭ Cavity in burrow, low or fallen tree trunk, or crevice
- ☺ 2–3 eggs
- ✖ Critically Endangered
- ❀ Solitary

Strigops habroptila

KAKAPO

The critically endangered kakapo is the world's rarest and heaviest parrot, and the only one that cannot fly. The size of a large chicken, it has mottled green plumage, powerful feet, and a rounded face with a broad, hooked bill. Its wings are small and weak, although it can make short downhill glides.

Kakapos are nocturnal, roosting by day. They emerge at dusk, tramping along well-worn paths to feed on plant juices, leaves, and stems. In years when food is plentiful, males gather at mating grounds, where they make a loud booming sound to attract females. After mating, the female bird lays 2–3 eggs. The chicks remain with their mother for several months; the male takes no part in raising the young. At one time, kakapos were widespread across New Zealand, but they were decimated by introduced predators, such as rats and stoats. The surviving birds—now numbering over 130—have been relocated to predator-free offshore islands, which has saved the species from extinction.

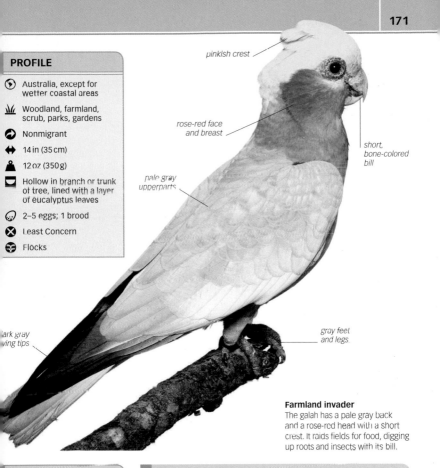

pinkish crest

rose-red face
and breast

short,
bone-colored
bill

pale gray
upperparts

ark gray
ving tips

gray feet
and legs

PROFILE

- Australia, except for wetter coastal areas
- Woodland, farmland, scrub, parks, gardens
- Nonmigrant
- 14 in (35 cm)
- 12 oz (350 g)
- Hollow in branch or trunk of tree, lined with a layer of eucalyptus leaves
- 2–5 eggs; 1 brood
- Least Concern
- Flocks

Farmland invader
The galah has a pale gray back
and a rose-red head with a short
crest. It raids fields for food, digging
up roots and insects with its bill.

SIMILAR SPECIES

short bill

Little corella
Found in inland
Australia; bare,
blue skin
around eye

pale yellow
underparts

**Western
corella**
Small, all-white
cockatoo from
W. Australia

Eolophus roseicapilla

GALAH

A gray and pink cockatoo with a small, folding crest
that varies in color, the galah is one of Australia's most
widespread parrots. The sexes are similar, differing only
in eye color: brown in the male and red in the female.
A highly social bird, the galah is often seen in large,
screeching flocks, which sometimes speed haphazardly
through the sky.

Galahs are originally birds of open country with
scattered trees, but they have greatly benefited from
the spread of farming. In grassy places, particularly parks
and playing fields, they can be seen digging roots and
insects with their bills. Galahs feed on the ground, but they
also perch on trees and on wires—hanging upside-down
to drink rainwater. Toward dusk, noisy flocks gather at
plantations to roost, wheeling around trees before settling
down for the night. Galahs nest in tree hollows, lining
them with leaves and twigs. Females incubate the
eggs for 25 days. Both parents feed the young during
the seven weeks that they are in the nest.

PROFILE

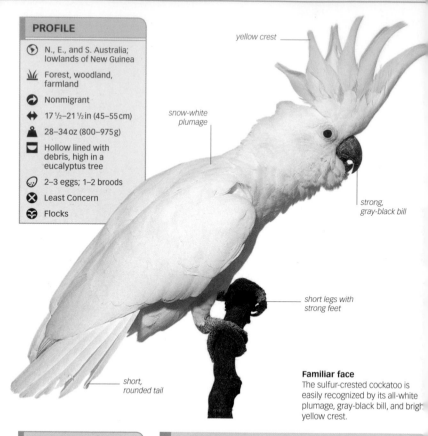

◉ N., E., and S. Australia; lowlands of New Guinea

〰 Forest, woodland, farmland

➔ Nonmigrant

↔ 17 ½–21 ½ in (45–55 cm)

⚖ 28–34 oz (800–975 g)

▭ Hollow lined with debris, high in a eucalyptus tree

🥚 2–3 eggs; 1–2 broods

✖ Least Concern

❤ Flocks

yellow crest

snow-white plumage

strong, gray-black bill

short legs with strong feet

short, rounded tail

Familiar face
The sulfur-crested cockatoo is easily recognized by its all-white plumage, gray-black bill, and bright yellow crest.

SIMILAR SPECIES

pink head and breast

Major Mitchell's cockatoo
C. Australian species, with pink-and-yellow crest

Cacatua galerita

SULFUR-CRESTED COCKATOO

A medium-sized bird with a raucous screeching call, the sulfur-crested cockatoo is a common sight across much of its range. It has distinct, all-white plumage, and a vivid yellow crest. The crest is normally held flat like a folded fan, but is raised when the bird is alarmed, or carrying out a display.

Also known as white cockatoos, these flock-forming parrots roost and breed in trees, but feed mainly on the ground. Their bills are multipurpose tools, used to collect seeds, dig up roots and tubers, and to climb. These are also used to tear off strips of wood—a habit that makes these birds problematic visitors in cities and towns. Like most parrots, sulfur-crested cockatoos are cavity-nesters. They lay their eggs in hollows lined with debris, high in eucalyptus trees. The parents share the task of incubation, and both bring food to the chicks. The young fledge after about 12 weeks.

yellow, upswept crest

range ear spot

yellow throat
and face

white wing bar

PROFILE

- Australia, except for wetter coastal areas
- Dry, open country close to water, including open woodland, grassland, and farmland
- Nonmigrant
- 13 in (33 cm)
- 2⅞–3½ oz (80–100 g)
- Hollow in tree, often near or standing in water
- 4–7 eggs; 1 brood
- Least Concern
- Pairs/small flocks

Foldaway crest
The male cockatiel has a yellow head and a long crest, which it usually holds upright when it is perched, but folds back during flight.

Nymphicus hollandicus

COCKATIEL

Widely kept as a caged bird, the cockatiel is the smallest of Australia's cockatoos. Slender and graceful, it has a gray body with a long, tapering tail. This bird travels in flocks, small groups, or pairs. It flies rapidly with backswept wings, making a loud, two-syllable call to keep in touch.

Cockatiels feed on the seed of wild shrubs and grasses, as well as spilled grain. When alarmed, they often perch on dead trees, settling lengthwise along the branches, which makes it harder to spot them. These birds are year-round residents in some parts of their range, but in many, they are nomadic, staying on the move in search of food. Cockatiels lay up to seven eggs. Incubation lasts 22 days, and the young birds are fledged in five weeks.

Female cockatiel
The female's head and crest are grayer than the male's. The flight feathers are also lightly chequered with white.

PROFILE

- 🜚 Indonesia to S. Australia
- 🌱 Woodland, rain forest, open country with trees, mangroves, parks, gardens
- ➋ Partial migrant
- ↔ 10–12 in (25–30 cm)
- ⚖ 3–4 oz (85–125 g)
- ▭ Cavity in a hollow limb or tree trunk
- 🥚 2–3 eggs
- ❌ Least Concern
- ❀ Flocks

bright red eye

deep blue head

bright orange bill

orange-red chest

thin, pointed wings

Nectar feeder
The rainbow lorikeet has a brush-tipped tongue that helps it collect nectar and pollen from trees and shrubs.

Trichoglossus haematodus

RAINBOW LORIKEET

One of the most colorful and variable species in the parrot family, the rainbow lorikeet is a slim, sleek bird with a long, tapering tail, a streamlined shape, and sharply pointed wings. It typically has a deep blue head, and a bright orange bill, while its back and wings are green. One widespread form has an orange-red chest, but there are a dozen subspecies with their own distinct coloration and range. Unlike seed-eating parrots, rainbow lorikeets feed mainly on nectar and pollen, along with fruits and blossoms, and also some insects and small animals.

During the breeding season, rainbow lorikeets nest in hollows high up in trees. Females incubate alone, and once the eggs hatch, take sole charge of the young.

Color variant
This variant is mainly green with bars of red and blue running down from the chin to the chest.

PROFILE

- 🜨 Australia
- 🌾 Arid grassland, open woodland, but usually close to water
- 🔄 Nonmigrant
- ↔ 7–8 in (18–20 cm)
- ⚖ 1 1/16 oz (30 g)
- 📦 Unlined hole or hollow in tree trunk, rotten stump, or fence post
- 🥚 4–8 eggs
- ❌ Least Concern
- 🐦 Flocks

Natural colors
The wild budgerigar is always green with a yellow head and throat. The male has blue skin round its nostrils—In the female, it is brown.

yellow face

black-striped plumage on back, neck, and head

blue-green tail

Melopsittacus undulatus

BUDGERIGAR

This small Australian parrot is familiar the world over as a caged bird, with several artificially bred color forms. In its natural habitat, the budgerigar lives in nomadic flocks, moving on in search of seeds. Where food is plentiful, budgerigars may congregate in the thousands before flying on again. Although they live in dry places, they are vulnerable to prolonged drought and will flock around creeks and waterholes early and late in the day.

Like most nomadic birds, budgerigars are opportunistic breeders, nesting whenever rain produces a flush of food. Eggs are incubated for 21 days. The chicks fledge a month after hatching, at which point the flock often moves on once more.

Color variant
Domesticated budgerigars are found in various colors, which are derived through selective breeding.

bright green plumage

pale yellow bill

blue tail

Male eclectus parrot
Largely green, the male parrot
has red-and-blue underwings
and a blue tail, which are
visible in flight.

PROFILE

- Islands of E. Indonesia, New Guinea, the Solomon Islands, extreme northeast tip of Australia
- Woodland canopy
- Nonmigrant
- 14–16 ½ in (35–42 cm)
- 12–21 oz (350–600 g)
- Hole in the trunk of a tall tree, often situated close to forest edge
- 2 eggs; 1 brood
- Least Concern
- Flocks

Eclectus roratus

ECLECTUS PARROT

This rain forest parrot shows a remarkable difference between the sexes, which is rare among parrots. Males are bright green with a pale yellow bill, while females are scarlet, with a black bill and a blue band across the chest and back. At one time, they were thought to be different species, until the two sexes were found to breed.

Eclectus parrots feed on fruit, seeds, and flowers, mainly high up in trees. They forage in pairs or small flocks, but gather in larger groups to roost. Their breeding system is also unusual: females nest in tree holes, pairing up with several males. They remain at the nest, while the males bring food for them and the young. The eggs are incubated for up to 30 days, and the young parrots fledge at about 12 weeks.

Female eclectus parrot
The female parrot is more colorful than the male, with red plumage and a conspicuous blue band.

PROFILE

- Tropical Africa; S. Asia, China; feral populations scattered worldwide
- Mainly deciduous woodland and forest; also farmland
- Nonmigrant
- 14½–17 in (37–43 cm)
- 3½–5 oz (100–150 g)
- Hole in trunk of tree, usually unlined
- 2–6 eggs; 1 brood
- Least Concern
- Flocks

pink neck ring

red bill

long tail

Urban parrot
Usually green-colored, the rose-ringed parakeet often lives in parks and gardens, frequently visiting birdfeeders during winter months.

SIMILAR SPECIES

purple shoulder patch

Plum-headed parakeet
S. Asian species with plum-colored head

reddish brown shoulder patch

Alexandrine parakeet
Large species from S. and S.E. Asia

Psittacula krameri

ROSE-RINGED PARAKEET

Also known as the ring-necked parakeet, this common parrot is native to Africa and South Asia, but has become established as a feral species in many other parts of the world. Highly gregarious, with a raucous screech, it is usually green, but caged varieties can be turquoise, gray, or bright yellow.

In the wild, rose-ringed parakeets feed on seeds and fruit, sometimes raiding crops from fields. In areas where they have been introduced, they live and feed in parks and in gardens. They nest in tree holes, and raise a single brood each year. Females incubate the eggs, and the young fledge by the time they are seven weeks old.

Female parakeet
Female birds—shown here in a caged variety—do not have neck-rings. Males are similar until they become adults.

PROFILE

- ⊙ Tanzanian Highlands; introduced in coastal Tanzania, S. Kenya
- ⋀ Bushland and thorned shrubs
- ➔ Nonmigrant
- ↔ 5½ in (14 cm)
- ⚖ 1¾–2 oz (50–55 g)
- ▭ Bulky, domed nest of thin twigs and bark strips, in hole in tree or building
- ⊘ 4–5 eggs; 1 brood
- ✕ Least Concern
- ❀ Pairs/small flocks

Faithful partner
Named for the unusually close pair bonds that they form, yellow-collared lovebirds are bright green, with a yellow chest.

golden yellow neck and chest

white eye-rir

short, rounded wings

SIMILAR SPECIES

Rosy-faced lovebird
S.W. African species, with rose-pink face

bright blue rump

red face

Red-headed lovebird
African species, with mostly green plumage and red bill

Agapornis personatus

YELLOW-COLLARED LOVEBIRD

Well known as caged birds, the yellow-collared lovebirds are bright green with dark brown heads. Lovebirds get their name from their habit of perching side by side for long periods, signifying their strong pair bond. There are nine species of these small, short-tailed parrots. Native to the Tanzania Highlands, the yellow-collared lovebird has also been introduced to adjacent parts of Africa.

Yellow-collared lovebirds live in well-wooded grassland and feed on seeds, buds, and leaves. Traveling in small flocks, they have a fast, direct flight, often screeching noisily while on the wing. They breed in small colonies, with each pair building a nest in a tree hole, or sometimes on a building. The females incubate the eggs, and the young are ready to fly after about six weeks. Like all lovebirds, the partners mate for life, building another nest the following year.

African parrot
Found exclusively in Africa, the gray parrot is thickset, with a short, red tail and uniformly gray plumage. It has a white face, yellow eyes, and a strong, black bill.

white face and forehead

strong, black bill

dark gray wings

uniformly gray plumage

red tail

backward-pointing toes

PROFILE

- 🜨 Tropical Africa
- 🌿 Mature forest, isolated clumps of palms
- 🔄 Nonmigrant
- ↔ 11–15 ½ in (28–39 cm)
- 🟰 14–18 oz (400–500 g)
- ▢ Tree holes
- 🥚 3–5 eggs; 1 brood
- ✖ Near Threatened
- 🔗 Flocks

Psittacus erithacus

AFRICAN GRAY PARROT

A forest-dweller, the African gray parrot is one of the most distinctive members of the parrot family, and also among the most intelligent. No other parrot looks like it, and few can match its remarkable ability to mimic human speech and other sounds, making it a prized caged bird. Although this has had a harmful effect on the species, this bird is still locally common in some parts of its range.

In the wild, African gray parrots spend most of their lives in trees, favoring mature forest and isolated clumps of palms. They feed on nuts and fruit, also raiding fields for corn. Flying high over treetops on fast-flapping wings, they make a variety of screeching and whistling sounds to keep in touch with each other. Like most parrots, African gray parrots mate for life. They incubate the eggs for about 30 days. The young make their first flights at the age of about 14 weeks. Once fledged, they have a potential lifespan of over 50 years.

Parrot in danger
Although locally common in some areas, the cobalt-blue hyacinth macaw is endangered by collection for the pet trade and deforestation.

large, downcurved bill

yellow band at base of bill

cobalt-blue plumage

long tail

PROFILE

🜨	Bolivia, Brazil
🌾	Tropical lowland forest, gallery forest, palm groves
↻	Nonmigrant
↔	39 in (1 m)
🏋	3¼ lb (1.5 kg)
▭	Large, unlined cavity in tree trunk
⊙	2–3 eggs
✖	Endangered
✿	Small flocks

SIMILAR SPECIES

blue body

Lear's macaw
Smaller; from E. Brazil; also endangered

Anodorhynchus hyacinthinus

HYACINTH MACAW

The largest parrot in South America, the hyacinth macaw is the second largest in the world, after the flightless kakapo (p.170). Its plumage is an intense cobalt-blue, contrasting with brilliant yellow eye-rings and a band of yellow skin at the base of the lower bill. The bill itself is huge and strongly curved—an adaptation for cracking open palm nuts and other hard-shelled seeds. With their outsized bills, they eat unripe nuts growing on trees, as well as ripe ones that lie scattered on the ground.

Hyacinth macaws are social birds, living in small flocks of up to a dozen birds. Their natural habitat is palm-studded savanna and dry, thorny forest in South America's tropical belt. Nesting in tree cavities, they usually lay a pair of eggs, although often only one chick survives. The female incubates the eggs for about 28 days and the chicks fledge at approximately three months. The parents continue to feed the chicks even after they can fly.

rainbow colours
The scarlet macaw has a rich medley of blue, green, and yellow plumage. Its head, chest, and central tail feathers are scarlet.

white bill with black tip

blue flight feathers

long tail

PROFILE

- Central and N. South America
- Humid evergreen forest and gallery woodland; occasionally pine forest and mangrove
- Nonmigrant
- 33–35 in (84–89 cm)
- 2–3¼ lb (0.9–1.5 kg)
- Cavity in trunk of forest tree
- 1–4 eggs
- Least Concern
- Flocks

SIMILAR SPECIES

black bill

Blue-and-yellow macaw Bicolored species from central South America

gray-black bill

Military macaw Red, blue, and green species from Central and South America

Ara macao

SCARLET MACAW

With its brilliant colors and strident calls, the scarlet macaw is one of the world's most striking tropical birds. It has blue flight feathers and a patch of bright yellow, edged with green, on each wing. Its face has a large patch of bare skin. It lives in forests and open woodland, and has the widest range of any macaw, stretching from Mexico as far south as Bolivia.

Like other macaws, this bird lives mainly on fruit, nuts, and seeds, cracking open hard shells and seed cases to get at the edible parts. Scarlet macaws are usually seen in flocks, which fly high over the forest canopy, heading toward their roosts or feeding areas. Normally silent when feeding, they screech loudly on the wing. Each flock consists of several adult pairs, which seek out high tree cavities in the breeding season. The female lays 1–4 eggs, which hatch after 28 days. The fledging period is about 14 weeks, after which the young are ready to fly with the adult birds.

Raised crest
The hoatzin is colored in shades
of brown, with a bare, blue face
and red eyes. Its spiky crest is
permanently raised.

spiky crest

brown plumage

long tail

PROFILE

- 🔄 Venezuela to
  Bolivia, Brazil
- 🌾 Well-vegetated
  riverbanks; edges
  of swamps and lakes
- ⟳ Nonmigrant
- ↔ 24–26 in (61–66 cm)
- ⚖ 25 oz (700 g)
- ◻ Frail platform of sticks in
  tree overhanging water
- 🥚 2–3 eggs
- ❌ Least Concern
- 🔁 Small flocks

Opisthocomus hoazin

HOATZIN

One of South America's strangest birds, the
hoatzin has no equivalent in any other part of the world.
About the size of a pheasant, it has a bulky body and
a long neck, but a small head. It lives in forest edges
bordering rivers and lakes, and spends much of the
daytime clambering about in branches, where it feeds
on green leaves. The leaves take a long time to digest
and the hoatzin breaks them down with the help of
microorganisms. This process is known as "microbial
digestion," the same system used by grazing mammals.

Hoatzins live in small parties, near the water's edge.
They nest above the water, making a loose platform
of sticks when the rainy season begins. The female
incubates the eggs for about 30 days. The newly born
chicks have claws on their wings. If the nest is disturbed,
or threatened, the chicks drop into the water below.
Once the danger has passed, they use their claws to
climb their way back into the nest. These claws are
lost when the chicks become adults.

PROFILE

- Sub-Saharan Africa
- Tall tropical forest and forest edge, savanna
- Nonmigrant
- 15 ½ in (40 cm)
- 8 oz (225 g)
- Platform made of sticks, placed high in tree
- 2–3 eggs; 1 brood
- Least Concern
- Small flocks

Rich colors
Native to Africa, south of the Sahara, the red-crested turaco is a richly colored bird. Its swiveling outer toe can point forward or backward.

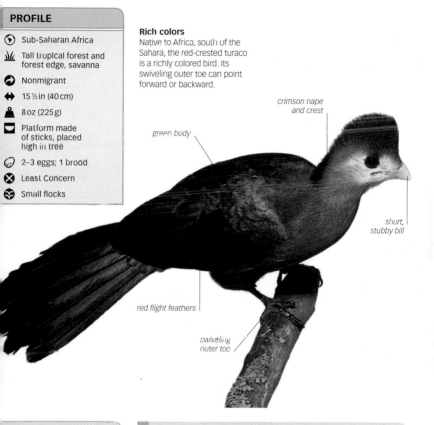

crimson nape and crest

green body

short, stubby bill

red flight feathers

swiveling outer toe

SIMILAR SPECIES

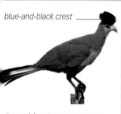

blue-and-black crest

Great blue turaco Largest turaco from central and western Africa

green crest

Green turaco West African species with a long tail

Tauraco erythrolophus

RED-CRESTED TURACO

This eye-catching African species has a crimson crest and nape, which contrasts with its off-white face. Plump-bodied, with soft, silky, green plumage, the red-crested turaco has a long tail and bright crimson flight feathers. Like most of its relatives, this bird reveals a flash of color when it flies from tree to tree. It can be difficult to spot high in the canopy, where it feeds quietly, hidden by the leaves. Despite its heavy shape, the turaco is a good climber, and can run nimbly along branches as it reaches for its food. It eats mostly fruit, leaves, and invertebrates.

Red-crested turacos live in small groups, keeping in touch with loud, barking calls. They make large, loose nest platforms from sticks and twigs, high up in trees. The female lays 2–3 eggs, which are incubated by both parents. The young leave the nest about 10 days after hatching, and climb onto nearby branches before starting to fly. The parents feed the young on regurgitated fruit until they are able to feed themselves.

PROFILE

- ⊕ Two populations: one in S. Europe, winters in W. Africa, the other in S. Africa, winters in tropical Africa
- ⫝ Mainly semi-dry areas of woodland and scrub, but also rocky hillsides
- ↻ Migrant
- ↔ 14–15½ in (35–39 cm)
- ⚖ 4 oz (125 g)
- ▭ Single egg laid in nest of magpie, crow, or one of several species of starlings (in South Africa)
- ◔ 1–2 eggs
- ✕ Least Concern
- ❀ Solitary

Avian interloper
The great spotted cuckoo has a gray crest and conspicuous white spots on its dark gray wings. It does not make a nest, instead laying its eggs in other birds' nests.

silver-gray crest

white-spotted upperparts

SIMILAR SPECIES

prominent crest

long tail

Jacobin cuckoo
Black-and-white species from Africa and South Asia

Clamator glandarius

GREAT SPOTTED CUCKOO

A sleek-looking bird, the great spotted cuckoo is a summer visitor to southern Europe, the Middle East, and southern Africa, wintering in the African tropics. It is a specialist predator of hairy caterpillars, which most other insect-eaters avoid. It also feeds on lizards and other small animals, often catching its prey on the ground. Unlike the common cuckoo (p.185), it has a harsh, chattering call, heard when it arrives at its breeding grounds.

The young cuckoo grows in the foster bird's nest, and hatches earlier than other nestlings. It receives the largest share of food, but continues to beg for more until it migrates.

Juvenile cuckoo
The juvenile great spotted cuckoo has a black head, with little or no crest, and chestnut wing patches.

gray head and chest

dark gray
upperparts

gray bars on
white underside

short feet

PROFILE

- W. Europe to E. and N. Asia; winters in S. Africa, India, S.E. Asia
- Wide variety of habitats from woodland to reedbeds and open country to 6,500 ft (2,000 m)
- Migrant
- 13 in (33 cm)
- 4 oz (125 g)
- Single egg laid in nest of insect-eating bird which rears the young cuckoo
- 1–25 eggs
- Least Concern
- Solitary

Sound of spring
The two-note call of the common cuckoo is a sign that spring is well underway. A medium-sized, dark gray bird, it is more often heard than seen

SIMILAR SPECIES

dark bars on
white underside

Himalayan cuckoo Breeds in C. and E. Asia

gray plumage

Pallid cuckoo Australian species, with a whistling call

Cuculus canorus

COMMON CUCKOO

The familiar call of this long-distance migrant anounces spring throughout Europe and northern Asia. Hawklike in shape, the common cuckoo has sharply pointed wings

The common cuckoo is a classic brood parasite, tricking other birds into raising its young. The process begins after mating, when the female cuckoo searches for the nests of smaller birds. Waiting until the owners are absent, it removes an egg and replaces it with one of its own. Hatching first, the young cuckoo sets about ejecting the other eggs from the nest. The young bird soon outgrows its home, and becomes so big that the foster parents may perch on it to put food in its mouth. Once fledged, it migrates alone, guided by instinct to its winter range.

Female common cuckoo
Usually similar to the male, the female can sometimes be brownish red or rufous, above, instead of gray.

Giant bill
Named for its large, grooved bill, the adult channel-billed cuckoo has dark and light gray plumage, with black wing tips. It also has an area of red skin around the eyes.

large, grooved bill

long, pointed wings

gray plumage

long, barred tail

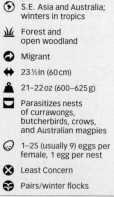

Scythrops novaehollandiae

CHANNEL-BILLED CUCKOO

Its distinctive appearance makes the channel-billed cuckoo one of the most remarkable members of its family. Besides feeding on fruit—particularly figs—it also eats small animals, including the nestlings of other birds.

The channel-billed cuckoo is a brood parasite, laying its eggs in the nests of other birds. When breeding, the male and female often work in pairs: the male attracts potential hosts, which fly up to chase it away; meanwhile, the female lays her eggs in their unguarded nests. The cuckoo's chicks grow up rapidly, taking the largest share of the food. Their foster parents continue feeding them even after they have fledged.

PROFILE

- S.E. Asia and Australia; winters in tropics
- Forest and open woodland
- Migrant
- 23½in (60cm)
- 21–22oz (600–625g)
- Parasitizes nests of currawongs, butcherbirds, crows, and Australian magpies
- 1–25 (usually 9) eggs per female, 1 egg per nest
- Least Concern
- Pairs/winter flocks

Juvenile cuckoo
The young channel-billed cuckoo is paler than the adult, with a smaller bill and plain facial skin.

yellow bill

gray-brown body

long tail

Rapid developer
Yellow-billed cuckoos, unlike many
other cuckoos, are gray-brown
above, with a yellow bill. They are
known to develop very quickly.

PROFILE

- USA; winters in C. South America
- Found primarily in open forests with a mix of openings and thick understory cover, especially those near water
- Migrant
- 10–12 in (26–30 cm)
- 2–2¼ oz (55–65 g)
- Flimsy oval-shaped platform of small sticks, lined with leaves and strips of plants
- 2–4 eggs; 1–2 broods
- Least Concern
- Small winter flocks

SIMILAR SPECIES

bare red skin around eye

Black-billed cuckoo
Summer migrant to northeast
North America

black mask around eye

Mangrove cuckoo Found in mangrove swamps from Florida, USA, to Brazil

Coccyzus americanus

YELLOW-BILLED CUCKOO

A summer visitor to North America, the yellow-billed cuckoo winters as far south as Argentina. The bird has a yellow eye-ring, gray-brown upperparts, and off-white underparts. It has a typical cuckoo shape, with broad wings and a long, tapering tail, the underside of which is black with white spots. The lower part of its bill is yellow, distinguishing it from the black-billed cuckoo, which overlaps its range. Common in forests and woodland edges, particularly along streams, this bird can be difficult to see, but gives itself away by its staccato call.

Yellow-billed cuckoos feed on insects, particularly hairy caterpillars. They also eat lizards, frogs, and fruit. Unlike many cuckoos, they usually raise their own young, only occasionally laying eggs in the nests of other birds, including their own kind. The young develop remarkably quickly. When 10 days old, they can clamber out of the nest and fly soon afterward.

PROFILE

- S. USA, Mexico
- Arid areas, including scrub and more open areas, to an altitude of 8,200 ft (2,500 m)
- Nonmigrant
- 22 in (56 cm)
- 11–12 oz (300–325 g)
- Cup nest of sticks, placed in cactus or thorn bush
- 3–5 eggs; 2 broods
- Least Concern
- Solitary/pairs

Desert sprinter
The greater roadrunner has a long tail that is used for balance when running. It also has brown plumage and a shaggy crest.

long, thick, powerful bill

large crest

light brown body

long, dark tail with white-edged tip

SIMILAR SPECIES

longer legs

Lesser roadrunner Smaller species from Mexico and Central America

Geococcyx californianus

GREATER ROADRUNNER

With its strong legs and upright stance, this celebrated terrestrial cuckoo is very different from species that spend their lives in trees. An opportunistic predator, it hunts a wide range of animals, including spiders, small birds, lizards, and venomous snakes. Flying only rarely, it can sprint at speeds up to 18 mph (30 kph), swerving around obstacles to avoid danger or to find food.

Roadrunners hunt on their own, although two birds may cooperate to kill a large snake. Small animals are pecked and battered to make sure they are dead, but large ones are beaten against rocks before being swallowed head-first. If water is available, roadrunners will drink, but their diet usually provides them with all the moisture they need. Greater roadrunners raise their own young. The eggs are incubated by both parents for up to 20 days, and the young can fly when they are less than three weeks old.

OWLS

With their highly developed eyes and acute sense of hearing, owls are the bird world's most efficient nocturnal predators. Found in every continent except Antarctica, they prey mainly on small animals, usually swallowing their prey whole.

Divided into two families—barn owls and typical owls—all owls share many adaptations for a similar way of life. All are raptorial birds, attacking their prey with their sharp talons rather than their bills. Most have fringed edges on their leading wing feathers, which gives them an almost silent flight. Even more importantly, their senses are exceptionally sharp. They have cylindrical eyes that flare out inside their heads, giving them a huge light-gathering potential even when the ambient light is extremely faint. When it is completely dark, some species—such as barn owls—can hunt by their hearing alone.

Owls' internal ears (not to be confused with feathery ear tufts) are unusually large and sensitive, and also

ORDER	STRIGIFORMES
FAMILIES	2
SPECIES	202

asymmetrically positioned, giving them an exact fix on their prey. To help with gathering sound, many owls have round or oval faces—these facial disks channel sound toward the ear openings, which are hidden beneath feathers on the sides of the head. Owls have large bills, but they are normally hidden beneath tufts of bristles. Food remains that they cannot digest, such as fur and feathers, are regurgitated in the form of pellets, which often litter the ground beneath owl roosts.

COLORS AND CAMOUFLAGE
The majority of owls hunt by night and roost by day, hiding until sunset when they take to the wing. To reduce the chances of being discovered, almost all owls are cryptically colored, typically in a mixture of browns and grays. With their eyes fixed in their heads, they are unable to follow movement without turning their heads, but they can swivel their necks by up to 270 degrees, allowing them to look behind them without moving their bodies as they sit on a perch.

BREEDING
Owls rarely make nests of their own, instead breeding in natural cavities or in old nests made by other birds. They lay round, chalky white eggs and often feed their young for several weeks. The eggs are laid and hatch in sequence, producing young that are covered with a grayish down. The oldest and strongest nestlings are sometimes the only ones that survive the rivalry for food.

Cavity nest
Like many owls, this great gray owl nests in cavities in trees. Both parents deliver food to the young.

large, blunt head

speckled and spotted upperwings and back

white underside coloration

feathered legs

PROFILE

- ⊙ Much of North and South America, Europe, Africa, through S. and S.E. Asia to Australia
- ⩙ Widespread, but favors lowland areas with some cover
- ⊘ Nonmigrant
- ↔ 12–17½in (30–45cm)
- ⚖ 10–21oz (275–600g)
- ▭ Underlined scrape or cavity in tree-hole or building
- ⊘ 4–7 eggs; 1–2 broods
- ✕ Least Concern
- ⊛ Solitary/pairs

Color forms
Barn owls have large, blunt heads with a heart-shaped facial disk. One common phase or color form has a ghostly white underside.

SIMILAR SPECIES

gray and white spots on upperparts

Australian masked-owl
Variable species typically from wooded habitats

Tyto alba

BARN OWL

A secretive, nocturnal hunter, the barn owl is among the world's most widespread land birds, and one of the few that can locate its prey in pitch darkness, using sound alone. It feeds on rodents, insects, and birds. This species can be recognized by its heart-shaped face, which channels sound toward its ears, and by its low, flapping flight, which reveals the pale undersides of its wings. The barn owl's call is a loud *screech*, often heard while on the wing.

Barn owls are cavity-nesters, setting up home in a variety of places, from ruined buildings to hollow trees. They do not use any nesting material. The female alone incubates the eggs, and the chicks fledge at about eight weeks. If food is plentiful, pairs raise a second brood.

Dark form
The barn owl has several color forms. One common form is brownish yellow, with dark spots.

PROFILE

- From S. Canada through E., C., and S. USA to N.E. Mexico
- Woodland, parks, gardens
- Nonmigrant
- 6½–10 in (16–25 cm)
- 6–7 oz (175–200 g)
- Lined cavity in tree, rotten stump
- 2–6 eggs; 1 brood
- Least Concern
- Solitary

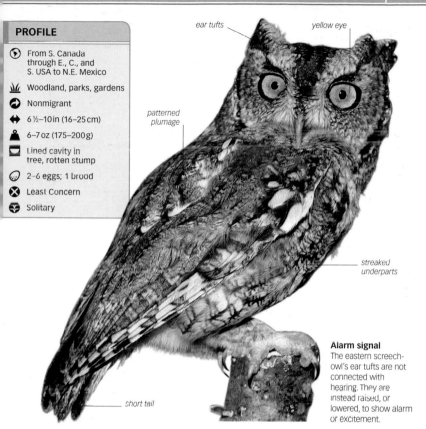

ear tufts

yellow eye

patterned plumage

streaked underparts

short tail

Alarm signal
The eastern screech-owl's ear tufts are not connected with hearing. They are instead raised, or lowered, to show alarm or excitement.

SIMILAR SPECIES

yellow eye

Western screech owl
Very similar species from western North America

gray-brown plumage

Eurasian scops owl Found in open woodland in Africa, Asia, and Europe

Megascops asio

EASTERN SCREECH-OWL

Like many owls, this small North American species is heard more often than it is seen. It has a variety of calls, including the screech that gives it its name, as well as a series of descending whistles, and a long, drawn-out trill. Squat and short-necked, the eastern screech-owl has a round head and a black-edged facial disk. The plumage is either gray or a rich rufous brown, depending on the phase or color form.

The eastern screech-owl lives in a wide variety of wooded habitats, including forests and plantations, where it hunts insects, birds, and small mammals. It occasionally catches fish as well. At the onset of the breeding season, the male courts the female on a perch, bowing and raising its wings, and also presenting the female with gifts of food. The female incubates a clutch of 2–6 pure-white eggs, and the pair raises a single brood each year.

Northern hunter
The snowy owl spots some of its prey on the wing, but more often sits in a prominent perch, waiting for signs of movement before swooping on its food.

large, round head

yellow eye

large, thickset body

PROFILE

- N. tundra, including N. North America, Greenland, N. Eurasia; migrates south in winter if food becomes scarce
- Open tundra with terrestrial perches and sparse, low vegetation, usually in lowland
- Migrant
- 21½–28 in (55–70 cm)
- 4–5 lb (1.8–2.3 kg)
- Shallow hollow in ground, on a slightly raised site
- 3–12 eggs; 1 brood
- Least Concern
- Solitary

Bubo scandiaca

SNOWY OWL

An imposing predator, the snowy owl is beautifully insulated and superbly camouflaged. Its thick plumage covers its entire body, including its nostrils and toes, and its white color makes it very difficult to spot against a background of rocks and snow. The male is almost entirely white, apart from dark flecks. The immature bird of both sexes is similar, although the male becomes whiter as it ages. Unlike some tundra birds, this species keeps its white plumage all year round. The snowy owl feeds mainly on small mammals, but can catch prey as large as ptarmigans and hares.

In late spring, female snowy owls lay a clutch of eggs in a hollow on the ground. The young chicks take seven weeks to fledge.

Female snowy owl
Larger than the male, the female is heavily barred and has a speckled crown, which helps in camouflage.

PROFILE

- 🜨 North, Central, and South America
- 〰 Coniferous woodland, deserts, parks
- ➋ Partial migrant
- ↔ 20–23 ½ in (51–60 cm)
- ⚖ 2–3 ¼ lb (0.9–1.5 kg)
- 🗆 Old nest of a large bird of prey, in tree or on cliff
- 🥚 1–5 eggs; 1 brood
- ✖ Least Concern
- 🜋 Solitary

Adaptable predator
The great horned owl has richly patterned plumage. It can be dark or pale, depending on the location, keeping it camouflaged.

large ear tufts

richly patterned upperparts

barred chest

barred undertail

SIMILAR SPECIES

orange eye

Eurasian eagle-owl World's largest owl, also with prominent ear tufts

pink eyelid

Verreaux's eagle-owl Large-eared, white-throated owl from E. and S. Africa

Bubo virginianus

GREAT HORNED OWL

Named for its ear tufts or "horns," the bulky-bodied great horned owl is one of the largest owls in the Americas, with an exceptionally wide range stretching from Alaska to Patagonia. It lives in many different habitats, from coniferous woodland and deserts to city-center parks. Despite its size, it is seldom seen at its daytime roosts—instead, it is most often pinpointed after dark, by its deep, hooting call.

The great horned owl uses a "sit-and-wait" strategy to hunt, watching for signs of prey from a high perch. Its diet includes anything that it can overpower: mammals up to the size of hares, lizards, frogs, and a large variety of birds. It hides, or caches, surplus prey. In the far north, when low temperatures freeze the prey solid, it sometimes thaws this stored food with its own body heat. During the breeding season, the great horned owl nests in trees, among rocks, or on the ground. The eggs are incubated for up to 35 days, and the chicks take the same amount of time to fledge.

streaked plumage

large talon

PROFILE

- S.E. Asia; Myanmar and Borneo to Java
- Forest, woodland, mountainous areas
- Nonmigrant
- 16½ in (42 cm)
- 2¾ lb (1.3 kg)
- Unlined cavity in a large tree, or an old nest of another large, tree-nesting bird
- 1 egg; 1 brood
- Least Concern
- Solitary

Airborne angler
The buffy fish-owl has brown, streaked plumage, conspicuous ear tufts, and bare legs and toes. Its eyes are bright yellow and it has a powerful, hooked bill for fishing.

SIMILAR SPECIES

pale underside

Pel's fishing-owl One of the largest fishing owls, from tropical and S. Africa

round head with no ear tufts

Vermiculated fishing-owl Smaller species from the forests of W. Africa

Ketupa ketupu

BUFFY FISH-OWL

From the forested waterways of Southeast Asia, this nocturnal predator is one of the small number of owls that specialize in catching fish. With its large ear tufts, it looks similar to species that hunt mammals and birds, but it is specially adapted for its unusual diet. Its legs are unfeathered, and its toes have spiky, nonslippery scales. Its talons are also larger than those of other owls of its size, and give it a secure grip on its slippery prey.

During the day, these owls roost in waterside trees, where their streaked plumage makes them hard to spot. From dusk onward, they watch for signs of movement on the water's surface, swooping low to catch their food. In addition to fish, their diet includes frogs and crayfish, and also bats, birds, and beetles, which they catch on the wing. Buffy fish-owls nest in tree cavities, or take over the abandoned nests of other birds. The female often lays a single egg, which is incubated for about 30 days. Fed by both parents, the chick takes up to seven weeks to leave the nest.

PROFILE

- Europe and N. Africa, east to China, Korea
- Deciduous and mixed woodland, urban parks, gardens
- Nonmigrant
- 14½–15½ in (37–39 cm)
- 15–19 oz (425–525 g)
- Hollow in tree or rock
- 2–5 eggs; 1 brood
- Least Concern
- Family groups

Sharp hooter
The plump, round-headed tawny owl is known for its hooting calls. Both sexes also make a *kee-wick* sound to keep in touch.

prominent facial disk

large, black eye

feathered toes

short tail

SIMILAR SPECIES

horizontal bars on chest

Barred owl
Larger North American forest species

Spotted owl
Western North American species, no ear tufts

fluffy, brown image

Strix aluco

TAWNY OWL

This plump-bodied nocturnal bird has short legs and a round head with two prominent facial disks, separated by the bristles that lead down to its bill. Its wings are short and broad, and characteristically curve downward when it glides. It preys chiefly on mice and voles, although its pellets—regurgitated after a meal—often include the undigested remains of other food, from birds to beetles and frogs. It locates most of these animals from a perch, and then catches them in a swift, silent swoop toward the ground.

Like most owls, the tawny owl nests in cavities, laying its eggs in tree-holes or old buildings without any attempt at making a nest. The female incubates the eggs, and both parents feed the young, which can fly after about 35 days.

Gray form
The tawny owl has several color forms, ranging from reddish brown and dark brown to gray.

Sitting and waiting
With its barred gray plumage, the great gray owl resembles a piece of wood. It stays perched for long intervals, moving its head to track sounds.

gray and white facial disks

mottled gray upperparts

thickset body

heavily streaked underparts

Strix nebulosa

GREAT GRAY OWL

A bird of cold northern forests, from North America to Siberia, the great gray owl is instantly recognizable by its size and by its exceptionally large facial disks, which surround two staring yellow eyes. In terms of length, it is one of the world's largest owls, but has a relatively small body. Most of its bulk is made up of thick gray plumage, which keeps it warm. It hunts by day or night, using its facial disks to gather sound—its hearing is acute enough to pinpoint voles and lemmings under 2 ft (60 cm) of snow. When it hears movement, it swoops down on the source, plunging feet-first to seize its food.

The female incubates the eggs, and both parents feed the chicks. Fledging at about 28 days, they remain with their parents for several months after starting to fly.

PROFILE

- 🌐 North America to Siberia; some populations move south in winter
- 🌿 Coniferous forest
- ↻ Partial migrant
- ↔ 23–27 in (59–69 cm)
- ⚖ 1¾–3¾ lb (0.8–1.7 kg)
- 🗀 Old nest of another large bird in tree, particularly conifer; or hollow in tree stump
- 🥚 2–5 eggs; 1 brood
- ✖ Least Concern
- ✿ Solitary

Snow swoop
Its acute hearing allows great gray owl to catc[...]
hidden beneath the s[...]

PROFILE

- From Mexico south as far as N. Argentina, Paraguay, S. Brazil
- Old-growth tropical and subtropical forests; plantations
- Nonmigrant
- 16–19 in (41–48 cm)
- 27–32 oz (775–900 g)
- Large hole or cavity in tree
- 2 eggs; 1 brood;
- Least Concern
- Solitary

black face mask

yellow iris

incomplete breast band

off-white underside

ain forest owl
tropical forest bird, the
pectacled owl has a large
ead, an off-white belly, and
dark breast band.

strong feet

SIMILAR SPECIES

black eye

Band-bellied owl Spectacled species from N. South America

Pulsatrix perspicillata

SPECTACLED OWL

Named for the white "spectacles" around its yellow eyes, this owl is found in the American tropics. The adult spectacled owl has a dark brown back, head, and face, with highly contrasting eye-rings. Its head is large and lacks ear tufts. Like most strictly nocturnal owls, it spends the daytime in well-hidden roosts, and is rarely seen. It hunts by watching for prey from a perch, swooping down to snatch it from the foliage, or more often, from the ground.

Apart from small mammals, the spectacled owl's diet includes insects, tree frogs, bats, crayfish, and crabs. It nests in tree hollows. Incubation lasts for up to 35 days, and the young fledge after about six weeks.

Juvenile spectacled owl
The young has a white body and a contrasting black mask. It takes several years to mature into an adult.

Round head
The elf owl has a round head, without ear tufts, and conspicuous facial markings. Its folded wings are almost as long as its tail.

prominent facial disks

large yellow eye

long wings

brown, streaked plumage

short tail

PROFILE

⊙ S.W. USA, Mexico

〰 Desert containing cacti or dry woodland up to 6,000 ft (2,000 m)

↱ Partial migrant

↔ 5½ in (14 cm)

⚖ 1 ⁷⁄₁₆ oz (40 g)

▭ Abandoned woodpecker holes in cacti

◔ 2–3 eggs; 1 brood

✕ Least Concern

❀ Solitary

Micrathene whitneyi

ELF OWL

About the same size as a sparrow, this tiny predator is the world's smallest owl. Roosting during the day, the elf owl hunts mostly at dusk and after dark, preying on animals on the ground, among plants, and in midair. It swoops acrobatically on flying beetles and moths, using its talons in the same way as much bigger owls. It also feeds on insects, young lizards, and snakes.

For their size, elf owls are extremely vocal. As the sun sets, they exchange loud, chattering and chuckling calls. Breeding males make a series of high-pitched *yips*. These owls often nest in old woodpecker holes and defend them aggressively. The female takes charge of incubating the eggs. The owlets fledge when they are one month old.

Prominent "eyebrows"
The elf owl has conspicuous slanting "eyebrows" that form a "V" on its face, and bright yellow eyes.

small, rounded head

large, yellow eyes

brown plumage

streaked or spotted breast

PROFILE

- 🜨 Australia and islands to the north, including New Guinea and Timor
- ⑊ Wide range of habitats from forest to farmland, up to 7,500 ft (2,300 m)
- ➷ Nonmigrant
- ⇔ 10–14 in (25–36 cm)
- ⚖ 9–11 oz (250–300 g)
- ▭ Tree cavity with little or no lining
- 🥚 2–3 eggs; 1 brood
- ✖ Least Concern
- ⊛ Solitary/pairs

Hawklike profile
The southern boobook has a hawklike appearance, with a relatively small, rounded head and spectacle-like markings around its eyes.

SIMILAR SPECIES

gray-brown plumage

Powerful owl Largest owl found in Australia

white spots on wings

Barking owl Bigger; distinctive barking call

Ninox novaeseelandiae

SOUTHERN BOOBOOK

Also known as the mopoke or morepork, the southern boobook is the smallest and most widespread Australian owl, absent only from some parts of the continent's interior. The exact shade of its brown plumage varies in different regions. It lives in a wide variety of habitats, from rain forests to grasslands with scattered trees, and is equally at home in urban environments, from parks to leafy streets.

Difficult to spot when roosting, it gives itself away after dark by its distinctive *boobook* call. Consisting of two notes, the call is repeated rapidly—sometimes over a long period of time.

Southern boobooks feed on small mammals and birds, swooping on them from a perch. Using their talons, they also catch insects on the wing, and transfer them to their bills in midair. Like most owls, they nest in tree cavities, using little or no lining material. The eggs hatch after about 35 days and the young leave the nest when they are six weeks old.

NIGHTJARS AND FROGMOUTHS

Rarely spotted except at dusk, nightjars and their relatives are mainly insect-eating birds with exceptional daytime camouflage.

Nightjars and their relatives are found mainly in the tropics or subtropics, with some species migrating in late spring to temperate parts of the world. Nightjars themselves make up most of the species in this order, although the group also includes frogmouths, owlet-nightjars, potoos, and oilbirds. All are active at dusk or throughout the night, spending the day roosting while other birds are on the move.

These birds all have long, pointed wings, and cryptically colored plumage in shades of brown, black, and gray. By mimicking dead leaves and branches, they are able to hide on the ground or in trees. During the daytime, they stay completely immobile—a predator has to be almost within touching distance before a nightjar will betray its presence by flying away.

FOOD AND FEEDING

Nightjars feed on moths and other flying insects, typically "trawling" for them a few yards above the ground. They have small bills but very wide mouths, often fringed by bristles that help funnel in their catch. The bristles also help protect their eyes, which are unusually large, giving them nocturnal vision second only to an owl's. Owlet-nightjars use a variation of the trawling technique, while potoos perch on branches, chasing individual insects as they fly past, and then returning with their prey. Frogmouths feed mainly on the ground, watching from a branch or fence post where they can drop on suitable food. Only the oilbird is a vegetarian: roosting in caves, it flies out at dusk to feed on the fruit of palms and other trees. Remarkable for a bird, it finds its way underground by echolocation.

ORDER	CAPRIMULGIFORMES
FAMILIES	5
SPECIES	125

BREEDING

Many birds in this order have repetitive and sometimes eerie cries, which announce that their breeding season is underway. In addition to calling, males sometimes carry out display flights in the fading light of dusk, trailing specialized courtship plumes or clapping their wings. Females typically lay their eggs on the ground, on tree stumps, or on ledges, with little or no nesting material. The young are covered in down on hatching, and are fed by both parents until they can feed themselves.

Open wide
The tawny frogmouth's huge mouth enables it to swallow small animals whole. By day, its camouflage makes it very difficult to see.

Hidden in the open
The tawny frogmouth has remarkable daytime camouflage because of its mottled plumage. Instead of roosting in thick cover, it perches in the open, imitating the stump of a broken branch.

yellow eye

tuft of feathers on wide bill

silvery gray plumage

PROFILE

🌐	Australia, Tasmania, New Guinea
🌾	All types of wooded habitats, from rain forests to roadsides, also perches on fenceposts in open ground
⟳	Nonmigrant
↔	13½–21 in (34–53 cm)
⚖	10–12 oz (275–350 g)
▭	Rudimentary nests in tree-forks
🥚	2–3 eggs; 1 brood
✖	Least Concern
🐦	Pairs

Podargus strigoides

TAWNY FROGMOUTH

A nocturnal predator from Australia, the tawny frogmouth has varying plumage—silver-gray to russet brown—across its range, which helps it camouflage during the day. It often imitates the stump of a broken branch. Its mottled markings mimic wood and lichen-covered bark. When approached, it assumes an upright posture that makes the similarity even more complete. Remaining motionless all day, the tawny frogmouth becomes active at dusk, when its large eyes scan the ground for moving prey. If disturbed when roosting, it slants its head upward and closes its eyes to narrow slits.

The tawny frogmouth feeds mainly on insects, although it also eats snails, frogs, lizards, and small birds. Instead of catching its prey with its feet, it swoops down and scoops it up in its extra-wide bill. These birds hunt in all kinds of wooded habitats. They make a flimsy nest of sticks or take over an old nest made by other birds. The female incubates for about 30 days, and the young leave the nest when about a month old.

SIMILAR SPECIES

red eye

Papuan frogmouth Larger frogmouth from Australia and New Guinea

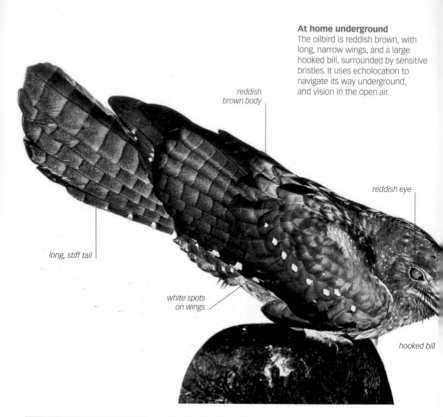

At home underground
The oilbird is reddish brown, with long, narrow wings, and a large hooked bill, surrounded by sensitive bristles. It uses echolocation to navigate its way underground, and vision in the open air.

reddish brown body

reddish eye

long, stiff tail

white spots on wings

hooked bill

PROFILE

- N. South America, Trinidad
- Nests in caves and deep rocky clefts; feeds in undisturbed forest
- Nonmigrant
- 15½–19½ in (40–50cm)
- 12–17 oz (350–475 g)
- Mound of plant fibers, own droppings, and regurgitated seeds on cave ledges
- 2–4 eggs; 1 brood
- Least Concern
- Colonies

Steatornis caripensis

OILBIRD

This nocturnal bird is so unusual that it is classified in a family of its own. Unlike nightjars and their relatives, oilbirds roost in large colonies, deep in caves. Adults are lean and well camouflaged, but the young are squat and fat, and were harvested for their oil in the past. This is how the bird got its name.

Oilbirds feed on the fruit of palm trees, sometimes traveling over 30 miles (50 km) to find their food. Instead of landing on trees, they hover close to the foliage, snatching the fruit with their bills. Before daybreak, they head back to their roosts, navigating their way through the twisting passages deep underground. They accomplish this feat by echolocation—the clicks that they use to do this are just audible beneath their eerie screams and wails.

Oilbirds nest on cave ledges, laying the eggs on a nest of their own droppings, mixed with plant fibers. Their young take about 32 days to hatch, but grow slowly, staying in the nest until they are four months old.

PROFILE

- 🜨 Central to N. South America
- 🌾 Forest, mangroves, scrub, savanna, and other open habitats with trees
- ↻ Nonmigrant
- ↔ 13–15 in (33–38 cm)
- ⚖ 5–6 oz (150–175 g)
- ▭ Hare depression of knothole on branch, at the top end of broken branch, or on broken stump
- 🥚 1 egg; 1 brood
- ✖ Least Concern
- ✦ Solitary

Perfect disguise
The common potoo has gray-and-white plumage with a fine black and buff pattern, which provides an effective camouflage against tree bark.

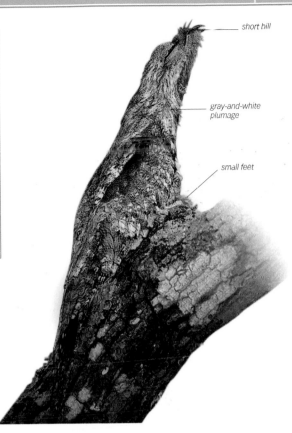

short bill

gray-and-white plumage

small feet

Nyctibius griseus

COMMON POTOO

A nocturnal forest-dweller, the common potoo is a large relative of nightjars found in the American tropics. It uses a survival technique similar to the tawny frogmouth (p.201), disguising itself as the stump of a broken branch. Its plumage is gray and mottled, and it assumes a bolt-upright posture if approached, making it look uncannily like a piece of wood. Its mouth has an exceptionally large gape that is almost as wide as its head. Its eyelids are also unusual, with small slits that allow the bird to see danger, even when its eyes are completely closed.

Common potoos feed on flying insects, catching them by flying out from their perch. They sometimes snatch insects from nearby foliage, but unlike frogmouths, they do not hunt on the ground. Common potoos lay a single egg directly in a depression on a branch, and the parents share the incubation duties. The egg hatches after 30 days, and the chick remains in its precarious "nest" for about eight weeks.

PROFILE

- 🌐 North and Central America; winters in South America to N. Argentina
- 🌾 Open, dry country, grassland, farmland, and human-modified landscapes
- ⟳ Migrant
- ↔ 8½–10 in (22–25 cm)
- ⚖ 1⁹⁄₁₆–3½ oz (45–100 g)
- ▭ Any bare, flat surface
- 🥚 2 eggs; 1 brood
- ⊗ Least Concern
- ❄ Solitary/flocks

Rooftop nester
The common nighthawk has long, pointed wings, a notched tail, and a white undertail band. It roosts on the ground and on roofs.

large eye

tiny bill

mottled plumage

SIMILAR SPECIES

pale upperwings

Lesser nighthawk Smaller species, reaching southwestern USA in summer

black upperwings

Antillean nighthawk Breeds in the Bahamas and the Florida Keys, USA

Chordeiles minor

COMMON NIGHTHAWK

A summer visitor to North America, the common nighthawk is a widespread, nocturnal insect-eater. Sleek and compact, it has mottled brown, white, and black plumage, with a bold, white bar on its underwings. This bird can be recognized by its call—a low, nasal *beep*. When breeding, the male makes a booming sound, which is produced when it dives and the air rushes through its wings.

The common nighthawk has adapted well to urbanization. It feeds on flying insects, catching them near streetlights that attract its prey. The female lays its eggs on sandy soil or flat gravel roofs, and incubates them for 20 days. The young fledge when they are three weeks old.

Female nighthawk
Although similar, the female lacks the male's white undertail band and is sometimes darker below.

PROFILE

- W. Canada, USA; winters as far as central Mexico
- Arid and semi-arid country, woodland, and forest clearings
- Migrant
- 7–8 in (18–20 cm)
- 1 1/16–2 1/8 oz (30–60 g)
- Slight depression on ground
- 2 eggs; 2 broods
- Least Concern
- Solitary

Plume colors
The plumage of the common poorwill is mostly gray, patterned with black on the upperparts. The male has bolder, white tail tips.

fringe of bristles

black and gray upperparts

camouflage plumage

SIMILAR SPECIES

buff-brown plumage

Chuck-will's-widow Largest North American nightjar, with a loud, whistling call

Phalaenoptilus nuttallii

COMMON POORWILL

Named after its *poor-will* call, this well-camouflaged bird is the smallest nightjar in North America. The common poorwill has a compact body, with a short tail and rounded wings. Its bill is small, although—like all nightjars—it has a large gape, and a fringe of bristles that help funnel insects into its open mouth. Remarkably for a bird, it can become torpid for extended periods—a form of hibernation that helps it survive cold periods when food is hard to find. When torpid, the common poorwill's body temperature can drop to as low as 41° F (5° C), and it may stay at that level for weeks.

The common poorwill breeds in the mountainous west of North America, from Canada to Mexico, and overwinters in the southern part of its range. A bird of dry, open habitats, it lays its eggs directly on gravel or flat rocks, often using the same spot in successive years. The female performs distraction displays to lure predators away from its eggs. Both parents incubate, and the young fledge in three weeks.

PROFILE

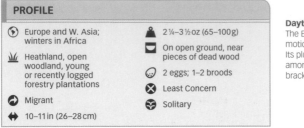

- Europe and W. Asia; winters in Africa
- Heathland, open woodland, young or recently logged forestry plantations
- Migrant
- 10–11 in (26–28 cm)
- 2¼–3½ oz (65–100 g)
- On open ground, near pieces of dead wood
- 2 eggs; 1–2 broods
- Least Concern
- Solitary

Daytime hideout
The European nightjar stays motionless in the daytime. Its plumage camouflages it among fallen branches, dry bracken, and dead leaves.

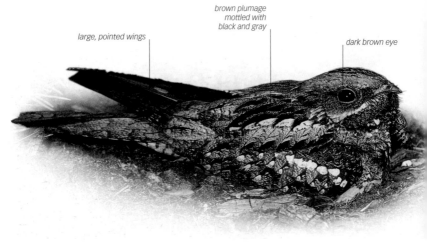

large, pointed wings

brown plumage mottled with black and gray

dark brown eye

SIMILAR SPECIES

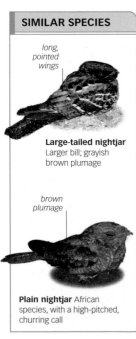

long, pointed wings

Large-tailed nightjar
Larger bill; grayish brown plumage

brown plumage

Plain nightjar African species, with a high-pitched, churring call

Caprimulgus europaeus

EUROPEAN NIGHTJAR

Rarely seen, except at dusk, the European nightjar can be identified by its distinctive courtship call. Males make a sustained churring call, which sounds like a piece of distant machinery. It is hard to locate, but rhythmically rises and falls as the bird turns its head from side to side. Courting males also clap their wings.

European nightjars spend the day roosting on the ground or along fallen branches, where they are almost invisible among dead leaves. As the sun sinks, they take to the air, scooping up moths and other insects with their open mouths. They breed in Europe and western Asia, where they are often the last spring migrants to arrive. They nest on the ground, using the same site year after year. The young can fly after about 17 days, and the parents often raise two broods before the end of summer.

Female nightjar
The female does not have white spots on its wings or tail. It is also slightly darker than the male.

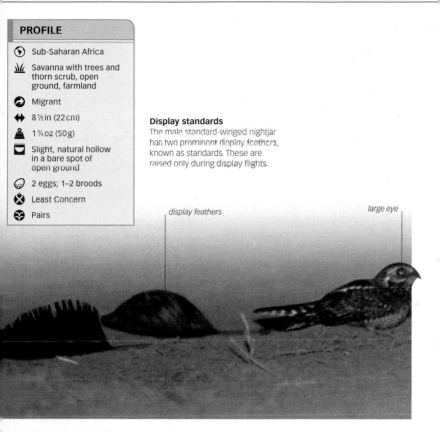

Display standards
The male standard-winged nightjar has two prominent display feathers, known as standards. These are raised only during display flights.

display feathers

large eye

Pennant-winged nightjar
Slightly smaller African species with narrow display feathers

Macrodipteryx longipennis

STANDARD-WINGED NIGHTJAR

In many nightjars, males and females differ only slightly, and are hard to tell apart. There is no difficulty with this African species, because the breeding male has two giant display feathers known as standards, which are absent in the female. Each standard is an enormously elongated primary flight feather, near the center of the wing. Nearly twice as long as the body of the bird, it is largely bare, except for a bladelike vane at its tip. During display flights, the male slowly circles the female, with the two standards raised like flags. Once the breeding season is over, the male molts the standards, and becomes much more like the female.

Standard-winged nightjars feed on night-flying insects, such as moths and beetles. They roost and nest on the ground, hidden by their camouflaged plumage, and often return to the same nest site the following year. They migrate within Africa.

HUMMINGBIRDS AND SWIFTS

Hovering in the air or speeding after insects, hummingbirds and swifts include many of the world's fastest and most agile birds.

Swifts are found worldwide, often as migrants, but hummingbirds are confined to the Americas. Despite their outward differences, they share two key features that unite them as a group: their feet are tiny, and their wings are structured in a unique way. The inner wing bone is unusually short, and the "elbow" is close to the body—a feature that gives their wing muscles greater leverage as they speed through the air. Swifts' bills are small, but with a wide gape. Most hummingbirds have long bills that work like drinking straws. In some species, such as the sword-billed hummingbird (p.214), this adaptation has evolved to an amazing extreme, with the bill making up a large part of the bird's total length.

ORDER	APODIFORMES
FAMILIES	3
SPECIES	447

PLUMAGE AND COLORS
Swifts have somber plumage, while most hummingbirds—particularly males—have vivid metallic colors. Produced by the structure of their feathers, these depend on the angle of view, so that hummingbirds sometimes seem to change color as they move.

FLIGHT AND FEEDING
Swifts and hummingbirds both eat insects, although for swifts, this makes up the whole of their diet, rather than just a part. Swifts pursue their food to great heights, unlike swallows, which usually hunt closer to the ground. Many swifts even sleep while they are on the wing. Insects are also important for young hummingbirds because they need animal protein to grow, but adults feed mainly on nectar, which they collect by visiting flowers. Hovering in front of blooms, their wings beat dozens of times a second, while their long tongues flick in and out to lap up their food. In energy terms, this feeding method is costly but efficient, and only a handful of hummingbird species perch when they feed.

BREEDING
Most swifts make rudimentary nests, using their own saliva to glue together building materials, such as feathers snatched up in midair. By comparison, hummingbird nests are superbly crafted constructions, often not much bigger than a thimble and usually perched on top of a branch. Like swifts, their young are slow to develop, but fly almost as well as the adults as soon as they leave the nest.

In-flight maneuver
Hummingbirds, such as this sparkling violet-ear, can fly with extraordinary precision, hovering or even reversing to catch insects and feed at flowers.

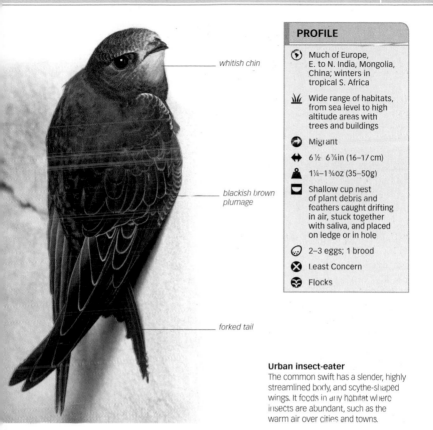

whitish chin

blackish brown
plumage

forked tail

PROFILE

Much of Europe,
E. to N. India, Mongolia,
China; winters in
tropical S. Africa

Wide range of habitats,
from sea level to high
altitude areas with
trees and buildings

Migrant

6½–6¾in (16–17 cm)

1¼–1¾oz (35–50g)

Shallow cup nest
of plant debris and
feathers caught drifting
in air, stuck together
with saliva, and placed
on ledge or in hole

2–3 eggs; 1 brood

Least Concern

Flocks

Urban insect-eater
The common swift has a slender, highly
streamlined body, and scythe-shaped
wings. It feeds in any habitat where
insects are abundant, such as the
warm air over cities and towns.

SIMILAR SPECIES

long wings

Fork-tailed swift
White-rumped
Asian species;
winters south
to Australia

dark undertail

Alpine swift
One of the largest
swifts, with
a distinctive,
white belly

Apus apus

COMMON SWIFT

This fast-flying insect-eater is one of the most aerial
of all birds, spending several years on the wing until it
eventually lands to breed. The common swift eats and
sleeps on the wing. Like other swifts, it has a slender,
streamlined body, and short legs with tiny feet. Its tail
is deeply forked, and its long wings flutter stiffly as it
speeds through the air. Wintering in southern Africa, this
swift flies north to Europe and Asia in late spring, where
its time in its breeding range may be as little as 12 weeks.

The common swift's natural nesting site includes
holes among rocks, but in today's urbanized landscapes
it more often uses roof spaces or holes in walls. Its nest
is a collection of feathers and debris, gathered on the
wing. The young are fed on insects, which the parents
store in a pouch beneath their tongues. If the weather
is warm, and food plentiful, young swifts leave the nest
after about five weeks, but their development can be
delayed by cold periods, particularly in the far north
of the bird's range.

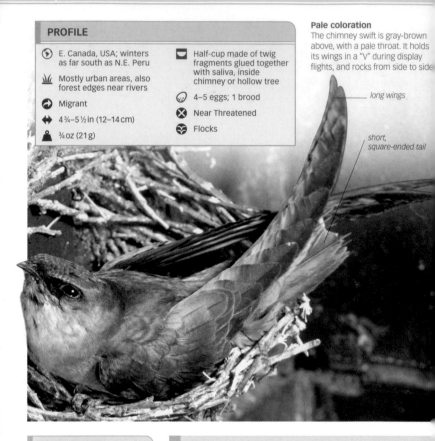

PROFILE

- E. Canada, USA; winters as far south as N.E. Peru
- Mostly urban areas, also forest edges near rivers
- Migrant
- 4¾–5½ in (12–14 cm)
- ¾ oz (21 g)
- Half-cup made of twig fragments glued together with saliva, inside chimney or hollow tree
- 4–5 eggs; 1 brood
- Near Threatened
- Flocks

Pale coloration
The chimney swift is gray-brown above, with a pale throat. It holds its wings in a "V" during display flights, and rocks from side to side

long wings

short, square-ended tail

SIMILAR SPECIES

Vaux's swift
Paler throat, shorter wings and tail

white patch

White-throated swift
Whitish throat patch, which extends down to belly

Chaetura pelagica

CHIMNEY SWIFT

A common summer visitor to eastern North America, the chimney swift winters as far south as northeast Peru. Small and sleek, this insect-eating bird is the only swift in most of its breeding range. Like many swifts, it originally nested in hollow trees, but with the spread of towns and cities, it now favors man-made structures instead. With its tiny feet, it clings to the inner walls of chimneys and barns, using these places to roost and raise its young.

Chimney swifts hunt aerial insects in small flocks, and they nest in colonies of a few pairs. They feed on the wing, usually at heights, feeding close to the ground only when it is cold and cloudy. They take up to a month to build their nests, although the eggs are often laid before it is complete. Both parents take part in incubation. The chicks fledge at about four weeks, but the young often leave the nest before they can fly, crawling with their claws. Once the breeding season is over, thousands of chimney swifts may roost together before beginning the annual migration south.

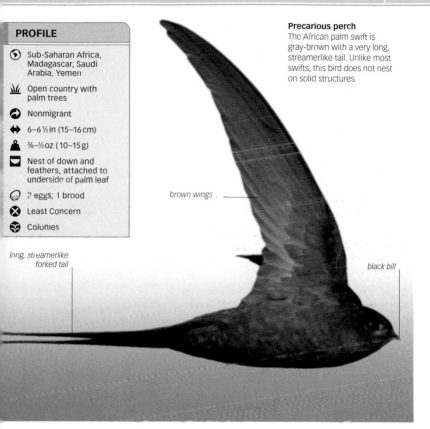

Precarious perch
The African palm swift is gray-brown with a very long, streamerlike tail. Unlike most swifts, this bird does not nest on solid structures.

brown wings

long, streamerlike forked tail

black bill

Asian palm swift Pale brown in color; once classified as the same species

Cypsiurus parvus

AFRICAN PALM SWIFT

Originally from the forests of tropical Africa, the African palm swift is common across most of the continent south of the Sahara. This expansion in its range is due to the planting of palms in farms and towns.

Most swifts make their nests on solid structures, where there is some shelter from the rain and wind. But the African palm swift nests out in the open, on the drooping leaves of palms. It usually breeds in colonies of up to 100 pairs. When breeding, this swift gathers feathers in midair and fastens them to palm fronds, using its gluelike saliva to create a nest. When completed, each nest forms a small, oval pad. The female crouches over it to lay the eggs, which are glued to the nest with its saliva. Perched precariously, the sexes incubate the eggs for 22 days. The newly hatched chicks already have well-developed feet. They stay in place even if the palm frond is tossed about by the wind.

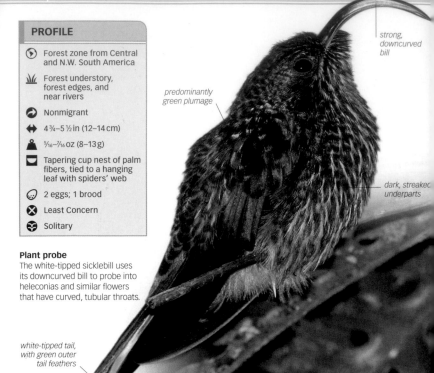

strong, downcurved bill

predominantly green plumage

dark, streaked underparts

PROFILE

- Forest zone from Central and N.W. South America
- Forest understory, forest edges, and near rivers
- Nonmigrant
- 4¾–5½ in (12–14 cm)
- ⁵⁄₁₆–⁷⁄₁₆ oz (8–13 g)
- Tapering cup nest of palm fibers, tied to a hanging leaf with spiders' web
- 2 eggs; 1 brood
- Least Concern
- Solitary

Plant probe
The white-tipped sicklebill uses its downcurved bill to probe into heleconias and similar flowers that have curved, tubular throats.

white-tipped tail, with green outer tail feathers

SIMILAR SPECIES

dull greenish upperparts

Buff-tailed sicklebill
Found in N.E. South America; buff-edged tail

Eutoxeres aquila

WHITE-TIPPED SICKLEBILL

From Central and South America, the white-tipped sicklebill is among the few hummingbirds that can be identified solely by its bill. The bill is bent like an old-fashioned sickle, and has evolved for probing into the flowers of the tropical heliconia plants. This is the only hummingbird that can reach the nectar inside, giving it a monopoly over this food. Unusually for a hummingbird, it perches while it drinks nectar, instead of hovering in front of the blooms.

White-tipped sicklebills live in rain forests, usually where open spaces of rivers let light reach the ground. Using a technique called "traplining," they visit plants in a set sequence instead of foraging at random. This gives each plant a chance to "recharge" with nectar before the bird returns. Intruding hummingbirds are fought off in ferocious skirmishes, given the size of these birds. Females incubate two tiny eggs that hatch after about 17 days.

PROFILE

- ⊙ Andes from Peru to Argentina, Chile
- 〰 High-altitude scrub and heathland on Andean plateau
- ⊘ Nonmigrant
- ↔ 5½ in (14 cm)
- ⚖ ⁹⁄₃₂ oz (8 g)
- ▢ Thick-walled cup nest of moss, plant fiber, and lichens, suspended under cliff overhang, in cave, or under house eaves
- ◔ 2 eggs
- ✕ Least Concern
- ⊗ Solitary/small flocks

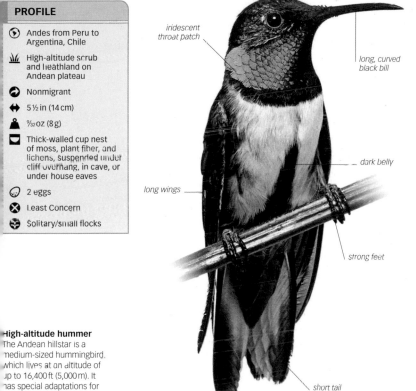

iridescent throat patch

long, curved black bill

dark belly

long wings

strong feet

short tail

High-altitude hummer
The Andean hillstar is a medium-sized hummingbird, which lives at an altitude of up to 16,400 ft (5,000 m). It has special adaptations for surviving cold nights.

SIMILAR SPECIES

bluish purple head

Ecuadorian hillstar
Close relative, found as high as the snowline

Oreotrochilus estella

ANDEAN HILLSTAR

Despite its delicate appearance, this medium-sized hummingbird lives at very high altitudes in the central plateau of the Andes. The male Andean hillstar has an iridescent throat patch that looks black or green, depending on the angle of view. The female is much plainer, and is shades of gray and brown in color.

Slender-winged, with strong feet, the Andean hillstar drinks nectar from bromeliads and other mountain flowers. Since hovering is a challenge in the thin mountain air, it usually clings to flowers as it feeds. Like other hillstars, it also has special adaptations for surviving cold nights. As the temperature falls, it lets its own body cool, entering a state similar to overnight hibernation. When the sun rises, its body warms up, and it sets off to find food. Andean hillstars make well-insulated nests, suspended from overhanging rocks or in caves. The female holds breeding territories, and raises the family on its own—in typical hummingbird style. The young birds are fully fledged at about five weeks old.

Record reach
The long bill of the sword-billed hummingbird helps it extract nectar from flowers. It has the largest bill of any bird in comparison with its overall size.

slightly upcurved bill

greenish gold plumage

brown belly and underparts

PROFILE

- 🜨 Andes, from Venezuela south to Bolivia
- 🌱 Montane forest and its edges; patches of shrubs
- ↻ Nonmigrant
- ↔ 6¾–9 in (17–23 cm)
- ⚖ ⁷⁄₁₆–½ oz (12–15 g)
- 🛏 Cup nest on a twig in forests, or among the roots of epiphytic plants
- 🥚 2 eggs; 1 brood
- ❌ Least Concern
- 🔀 Solitary

Ensifera ensifera

SWORD-BILLED HUMMINGBIRD

Measuring nearly half the bird's length, the bill of this South American hummingbird allows it to feed at hanging flowers with tubular corollas up to 6 in (15 cm) deep. The sword-billed hummingbird hovers beneath the bloom and flicks out its extra-long tongue to reach the nectar glands, which provide it with a high-energy meal.

When perching and flying, this hummingbird keeps its bill at a steep angle to reduce the strain on its head and neck—hence it can groom itself only with its feet. Sword-billed hummingbirds can catch insects in midair, and are remarkably nimble at delivering food to their young. The female incubates and cares for the young alone.

Female hummingbird
The female bird has white patches on its throat and underparts, and more white behind the eye than the male.

long bill

cinnamon-and-brown plumage

white rump patch

long, pointed wings

Hummingbird heavyweight
The giant hummingbird is about the size of a starling, although it is much lighter. It dwarfs most other species in the hummingbird family.

Patagona gigas

GIANT HUMMINGBIRD

The largest hummingbird, this species from the Andes lives in open scrub at altitudes of up to 14,760 ft (4,500 m). Even from a distance, it is visibly different from other hummingbirds in the way it flies. Its wings beat in quick bursts, mixed with glides—a pattern that makes it look like a long-billed swift. It is capable of hovering, although compared to small hummingbirds, it spends more time perched, both resting and when it feeds.

Giant hummingbirds feed on insects as well as nectar—the protein from animal food is particularly important when the breeding season begins. For their size, they make relatively small cup nests. Females take care of the developing chicks.

PROFILE

- Andes, from Ecuador to Chile; lowlands of W. Argentina
- Arid open and semi-open areas with a few trees at higher altitudes
- Partial migrant
- 8–8 ½ in (20–22 cm)
- ⅝–¹¹⁄₁₆ oz (18–20 g)
- Small cup nest made of moss and lichens, placed on top of level branch or on cactus stem
- 2 eggs; 1 brood
- Least Concern
- Solitary/small flocks

Female hummingbird
The sexes have similar plumage, but the female has a smaller white rump patch than the male.

reddish markings on head

bright red throat

grayish white underparts

Miniature male
The male bee hummingbird, weighing just under ¹⁄₁₆ oz (2 g) is the world's smallest bird, with a relatively short bill, and tiny feet.

SIMILAR SPECIES

greenish back

Vervain hummingbird
World's second-smallest bird; from the Caribbean

Mellisuga helenae

BEE HUMMINGBIRD

The world's smallest bird, this Cuban hummingbird weighs more than the bee, but far less than many large beetles and moths. The female is larger, but has the same insectlike flight, abruptly stopping in midair, or speeding past plants on whirring wings.

Bee hummingbirds live in forests and on forest edges, where they feed on a wide range of plants. They also eat small insects, particularly in the breeding season. They feed with their bodies held horizontally, unlike many hummingbirds that have a vertical stance. When perched, their short tails give a stubby look to their bodies. As with most hummingbirds, females make the nests and raise the young. The nests are smaller than walnut shells and the eggs barely the size of peas. The chicks are ready to leave the nest after about 19 days.

Female hummingbird
The female does not have red head markings. Its body is bluish green above and off-white below.

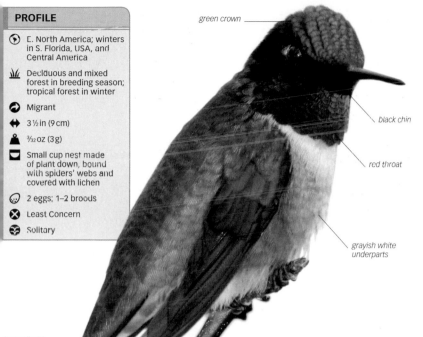

green crown

black chin

red throat

grayish white underparts

long tail with deep notch

PROFILE

- E. North America; winters in S. Florida, USA, and Central America
- Deciduous and mixed forest in breeding season; tropical forest in winter
- Migrant
- 3½ in (9 cm)
- ³⁄₃₂ oz (3 g)
- Small cup nest made of plant down, bound with spiders' webs and covered with lichen
- 2 eggs; 1–2 broods
- Least Concern
- Solitary

Distinct patch
The male ruby-throated hummingbird has an iridescent red throat patch. It also has green upperparts, a green crown, and grayish white underparts.

SIMILAR SPECIES

red head and throat

Anna's hummingbird
Red-headed species from western North America

beardlike throat patch

short, square tail

Calliope hummingbird
Smallest North American bird

Archilochus colubris

RUBY-THROATED HUMMINGBIRD

This hummingbird is the only species that breeds across the eastern half of Canada and the USA. It lives in forests and forest edges, frequents hummingbird feeders in gardens, and drinks the nectar of wildflowers.

The males arrive at the breeding grounds first, and court females with high-speed display flights. They often mate with several partners in a season, and take no part in building the nest or raising the young. Incubation lasts about 16 days, and the young fledge after about 20 days. In the weeks after, they fatten up rapidly—essential preparation for their migration across the Gulf of Mexico, a nonstop sea crossing of over 500 miles (800 km).

Female hummingbird
The female is plainer, larger, and has a slightly longer bill. It raises the young on its own.

MOUSEBIRDS

Named after their scurrying, rodentlike movements, mousebirds are found only in sub-Saharan Africa. Although they fly well, they are even more agile in shrubs and trees, clinging on vertically or even upside-down.

Also known as colies, mousebirds are slim and highly gregarious birds with short, downcurved bills. Their tails are slender, and can be twice as long as their bodies. Invariably seen in groups, which often fly in single file, mousebirds feed mainly on fruit, berries, and buds, as well as on small insects such as aphids. They also steal eggs and the nestlings of other birds—one of the reasons why they are frequently mobbed by smaller birds.

ORDER	COLIIFORMES
FAMILIES	1
SPECIES	6

UNIQUE ANATOMY
Mousebirds are classified in a group of their own because they have some features found in no other birds. Chief among these features are their two outer toes, which can swivel to point forward or backward, creating a foot that is divided in two. With all four toes pointing forward, a mousebird can hang from a twig; with the toes facing in opposite directions, it can grasp and perch. The position of the toes can change very rapidly, which accounts for some of the strange movements that only mousebirds can make.

TROGONS

Some of the most brilliantly colored of all birds, trogons are fruit-eaters from the tropical forests of the Americas, Southeast Asia, and sub-Saharan Africa. Unhurried and sedate, they often go unnoticed high above the forest floor.

Trogons have long tails, wide bills, and soft plumage loosely attached to a remarkably thin epidermis (outer skin). Their colors are often iridescent, with marked differences between the two sexes. They have small feet, with two toes pointing forward and two behind, and they typically spend long periods sitting quietly on a perch. Some trogons feed entirely on fruit, but many also take insects.

Trogons nest in cavities, using preexisting holes in tree trunks or digging their own in rotting wood. They use no lining material, laying eggs directly in the bottom of the nest

ORDER	TROGONIFORMES
FAMILIES	1
SPECIES	40

Secret splendor
Sitting on a branch, a female resplendent quetzal shows off its rich colors, which are even more magnificent in males.

backyard bird
The speckled mousebird is one of the largest birds within its family. It creeps through the vegetation to find food, and often visits gardens and backyards to plunder fruiting trees.

short crest

brown plumage

powerful, curved bill

PROFILE

- Sub-Saharan Africa, Nigeria east to Ethiopia; south to South Africa
- Open woodland and forest edges; secondary growth, abandoned cultivation, and scrub
- Nonmigrant
- 12–14 in (30–36 cm)
- 1 1/4–2 7/8 oz (35–80 g)
- Large, cup-shaped nest of twigs and grass
- 2–4 eggs; 1 brood
- Least Concern
- Flocks

very long, tapering tail

SIMILAR SPECIES

red feet

White-backed mousebird
Paler species found in southern and southwestern Africa

red ring around eye

Red-faced mousebird
Pale southern African species with a red face

Colius striatus

SPECKLED MOUSEBIRD

This African bird has a scurrying movement that gives mousebirds their name. Drably colored in shades of brown and gray, the speckled mousebird has a long tail, which is held out stiffly when it flies. Largely vegetarian, this species feeds on buds, flowers, and fruit, although it also eats some insects. Instead of perching on branches, it is frequently seen hanging vertically or upside down—a characteristic habit that most mousebirds share.

Speckled mousebirds live in tightly knit flocks, which break up at the beginning of the breeding season and re-form once the young have fledged. Incubation takes about 14 days, and the young fledge by the time they are 17 days old. They often leave the nest during the daytime well before they can fly.

red eye-ring

yellow bill

red belly

long tail

PROFILE

- S. USA, Mexico, Central America
- Canopy of woodland, including pine-oak forest, from lowland to highland
- Nonmigrant
- 11–12 in (28–30 cm)
- 2 ¼–2 ½ oz (65–70 g)
- Natural tree cavity; abandoned woodpecker hole
- 2–4 eggs; 1 brood
- Least Concern
- Pairs

Tropical touch
The male elegant trogon is adorned in bright, tropical colors. It has metallic, coppery green upperparts, and a bright red belly.

SIMILAR SPECIES

red plumage

Red-headed trogon
Red-breasted species, from S. and S.E. Asia

olive-yellow head

Orange-breasted trogon Smaller species, with orange breast

Trogon elegans

ELEGANT TROGON

Fittingly named, the elegant trogon is one of North America's most striking birds. The male is flamboyantly colored, and both sexes have long, square-ended tails, which are conspicuously barred below. It is among the few trogons whose range extends well outside the tropics including northern Mexico and the extreme south of the USA. Like all trogons, it is primarily a forest species, often found in thickly wooded canyons, where its secretive habits make it difficult to spot.

Elegant trogons eat insects and fruit, using the typical family feeding technique of flying out to collect food and returning to a perch to feed. Little is known about their breeding biology, although there is a close pair bond, with couples roosting together in trees, and cooperating to bring up the young.

Female trogon
The female is grayish brown above, with a distinctive white spot behind each eye. It has paler underparts.

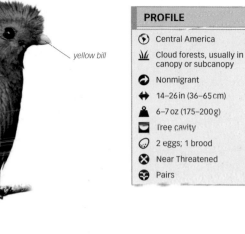

bushy crest

yellow bill

emerald-green
plumage

short tail

long tail
streamers

PROFILE

- 🜨 Central America
- 〰 Cloud forests, usually in canopy or subcanopy
- ➔ Nonmigrant
- ↔ 14–26 in (36–65 cm)
- ⚖ 6–7 oz (175–200 g)
- ▭ Tree cavity
- ☺ 2 eggs; 1 brood
- ✖ Near Threatened
- ✿ Pairs

Breeding splendor
In the breeding season, the male resplendent quetzal has extra-long middle wing coverts, and a collection of streamers over its tail.

Pharomachrus mocinno

RESPLENDENT QUETZAL

With its lustrous, green upper tail streamers, the male resplendent quetzal is among the world's most spectacular birds. The streamers can be more than 23 ½ in (60 cm) long, and are the highlight of its breeding plumage.

The resplendant quetzal feeds on wild avocados and other oily fruit. It rarely comes to the ground, and instead perches motionless among high branch, fluttering out from time to time, to snatch a fruit before swallowing it whole. Both parents help incubate the eggs. The female sits on the eggs without difficulty, but the male has to double its streamers over its back to fit into the nest.

Female quetzal
The female has a dark green head without a crest. It has a shorter tail, without elongated streamers.

KINGFISHERS AND RELATIVES

Kingfishers and their relatives are found worldwide, sometimes far from water. Most dig cavity nests in banks or trees.

Despite being familiar birds, kingfishers make up only three of the 13 families in this large and diverse order, commonly known as coraciiforms. It also includes rollers, bee-eaters, and hornbills, as well as a number of other mainly tropical families, such as motmots and todies. Many kingfishers live and hunt by water, but most other coraciiforms are not waterside birds.

ORDER	CORACIIFORMES
FAMILIES	13
SPECIES	218

ANATOMY
Coraciiforms vary in size from tiny todies to huge hornbills, up to 5ft (1.5m) long. Most of them have a large head, long bill, and relatively compact body with short and sometimes weak feet. They include some superb fliers—such as the bee-eaters—and also some species that rarely leave the ground.

FEEDING
Birds in this group are typically carnivorous, and use a sit-and-wait feeding strategy, catching their prey in the air, in water, or on the ground. Once caught, prey is often stunned or killed with a succession of blows, before being swallowed head-first.

WOODPECKERS AND TOUCANS

Toucans and their close relatives are mainly tropical birds, but woodpeckers are also widespread in temperate regions.

In addition to woodpeckers and toucans, this group of birds includes jacamars, puffbirds, and barbets, and other species such as honeyguides. Almost all of them nest in cavities, and most spend their lives in trees. Despite their outward differences—a key one being the shape of their bills—they are linked by a shared foot structure, with two toes pointing forward and two backward, helping them climb easily.

Toucans take over existing nest holes, but woodpeckers make them by hammering into the wood with their bills. They play a key role in avian ecology because their old nests are often used by many different species of birds.

ORDER	PICIFORMES
FAMILIES	9
SPECIES	411

Cavity nest
All the birds in this order have well-developed bills. The woodpeckers also have thicker skulls to absorb the shock of pecking several thousand times per day.

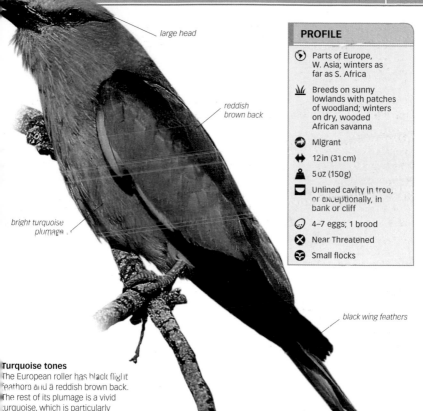

large head

reddish brown back

bright turquoise plumage

black wing feathers

PROFILE

- Parts of Europe, W. Asia; winters as far as S. Africa
- Breeds on sunny lowlands with patches of woodland; winters on dry, wooded African savanna
- Migrant
- 12 in (31 cm)
- 5 oz (150 g)
- Unlined cavity in tree, or exceptionally, in bank or cliff
- 4–7 eggs; 1 brood
- Near Threatened
- Small flocks

Turquoise tones
The European roller has black flight feathers and a reddish brown back. The rest of its plumage is a vivid turquoise, which is particularly eye-catching when it flies.

SIMILAR SPECIES

pale purple plumage

Rufous-crowned roller
Largest roller, with purple wings and tail

long tail with streamers

Blue-bellied roller
African roller with slender tail-streamers

Coracias garrulus

EUROPEAN ROLLER

Named for its aerobatic display flights, the European roller is one of the most northerly species, spending the winter in tropical and southern Africa, and migrating to Europe and western Asia to breed. In Africa, it lives in wooded savanna, while its summer habitat includes warm, sunny lowlands with patches of woodlands, and dry, grassy roadsides with overhead power lines.

Like forest kingfishers and their relatives, European rollers feed on beetles, lizards, scorpions, and frogs. They watch for prey from a perch and swoop down on it. They eat small animals on the ground, but take the larger ones to their perch, and beat them many times before swallowing them. European rollers incubate their eggs for about 18 days, and the young fledge before they are one month old.

Perched to prey
The juvenile European roller spends much of its time perched in a prominent spot, watching for prey.

Stylish tail
The male and female racket-tailed rollers look identical, with dark blue underwings and long tail-streamers. They get their name from these outer tail feathers with racket-shaped tips.

black bill

purple upperwings

brown back

long tail with streamers

PROFILE

- S. Angola, S.E. Zaire, through Zimbabwe to N.E. South Africa
- Undisturbed, mature woodland and well-wooded savanna
- Nonmigrant
- 14 in (36 cm)
- 3½ oz (100 g)
- Unlined tree cavity, often abandoned woodpecker holes
- 2–4 eggs; 1 brood
- Least Concern
- Solitary/pairs/small flocks

Coracias spatulatus

RACKET-TAILED ROLLER

Found year-round in southern Africa, the racket-tailed roller is the smallest and lightest of its kind. It is named for its two tail-streamers, which have spoon- or racket-shaped tips. Difficult to see as it perches among the trees, it is conspicuous in flight, due to its elegant tail and intensely blue underwings.

Racket-tailed rollers usually hunt on their own. They scan the ground for insects, scorpions, and lizards, and swoop down on them from the woodland canopy. Like other rollers, they beat larger prey before swallowing it, usually on a perch rather than on the ground. Highly territorial, they claim an area of woodland by flying high above the treetops before diving with noisy screeching to regain their perch.

The female lays 2–4 eggs, but the exact incubation period is unknown. It is speculated to be 18–20 days. The young fledge in about one month.

SIMILAR SPECIES

violet upperparts

Lilac-breasted roller
Common long-tailed roller from E. and S. Africa

dark crown

striped face

brown back
and wings

heavy,
powerful bill

barred tail

PROFILE

- E. and S.W. Australia
- Eucalyptus forest and woodland, often along watercourses; parks and farmland
- Nonmigrant
- 15½ in (40 cm)
- 11–12 oz (325–350 g)
- Unlined cavity in trunk or branch of tree
- 2–4 eggs; 1 brood
- Least Concern
- Family groups

Familiar cry
Male and female laughing kookaburras are almost identical. Their distinctive calls are mainly heard at dawn and at dusk.

SIMILAR SPECIES

long,
broad bill

Blue-winged kookaburra
Smaller Australian species from tropical and subtropical woodlands

Dacelo novaeguineae

LAUGHING KOOKABURRA

Famous for its humanlike laughing call, this thickset bird is the world's largest kingfisher, and one of Australia's best-known birds. Unlike aquatic kingfishers, it lives in varied wooded habitats, often far from water, where, perched on branches, it keeps a watchful eye on the ground below.

The laughing kookaburra eats anything it can swoop on and overpower. Its diet includes insects, snakes, small birds, and even food stolen from picnic tables, and fish from garden ponds. This species lives in family groups, where each group has its own territory. A group consists of a breeding pair, and young "helpers" raised in the previous years. The dominant female lays eggs and both parents and helpers assist in incubation and in feeding the young. Young birds take more than a month to fledge and they stay with their parents for a year or more, helping feed and raise the next generation.

PROFILE

- 🌀 Red Sea to Australia and Polynesia
- 〰️ Mangrove and other coastal vegetation, sometimes penetrating inland to open areas
- ↪ Partial migrant
- ↔ 9½ in (24 cm)
- ⚖ 2–2⅞ oz (55–80 g)
- ▭ Burrow in bank, tree-hole, or termite nest
- 🥚 2–5 eggs
- ❌ Least Concern
- 🐦 Solitary/pairs

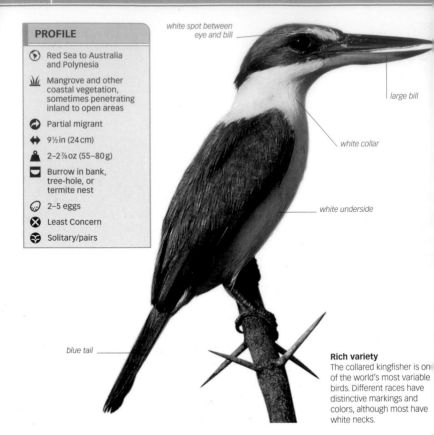

white spot between eye and bill

large bill

white collar

white underside

blue tail

Rich variety
The collared kingfisher is one of the world's most variable birds. Different races have distinctive markings and colors, although most have white necks.

SIMILAR SPECIES

black eye mask

Sacred kingfisher
Smaller species from S.E. Asia and Australasia

blue-green and white wings

Red-backed kingfisher
Smaller; found in forests in Australia

Todiramphus chloris

COLLARED KINGFISHER

This common coastal bird, also known as the mangrove kingfisher, shows a great variety of colors and markings throughout its range. Altogether, nearly 50 races have been described, some more widespread than others. Despite these differences, all collared kingfishers have a similar shape, with blue or blue-green upperparts and a distinctive white collar that gives them their name. They also have a large bill, which is black above and yellowish brown near the chin.

Collared kingfishers are found in mangrove swamps and tidal creeks, or sometimes in cultivated ground farther inland. Using a selection of favorite perches, they watch patiently before swooping down on prey. On coasts, they feed mainly on small crabs, shrimp, and fish, but those living farther inland eat a wide range of animals, such as insects, frogs, lizards, and snakes.

Pairs breed in burrows, and in holes in trees. The female lays 2–5 eggs and the young fledge after about 3 days in the nest.

PROFILE

- 🜨 Eurasia, N. Africa eastward to Japan, south to Indonesia, S.W. Pacific; northern birds migrate south within this range
- 〜 Streams, small rivers, canals, small lakes, and ponds
- ⟳ Partial migrant
- ↔ 6½ in (16 cm)
- ⚖ ⅞–1¼ oz (25–35 g)
- ▭ Upward-sloping tunnel in bank near water
- ◔ 5–7 eggs; 2 broods
- ✖ Least Concern
- ❧ Pairs

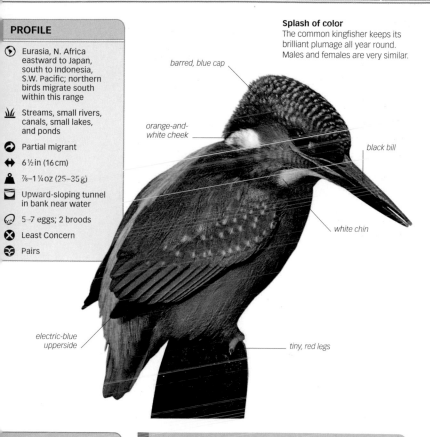

Splash of color
The common kingfisher keeps its brilliant plumage all year round. Males and females are very similar.

barred, blue cap

orange-and-white cheek

black bill

white chin

electric-blue upperside

white chin

tiny, red legs

SIMILAR SPECIES

white underparts

Little kingfisher Smaller species from the coasts of N. Australia and New Guinea

white-tipped bill

Azure kingfisher
Deep blue upperparts; orange underparts

Alcedo atthis

COMMON KINGFISHER

One of Europe's most vividly colored birds, the common kingfisher is easy to spot as it speeds down rivers and streams, but hard to view when it watches for food from a shady perch. Appearing blue from a distance, this bird has bright orange underparts and a stripe beneath the eyes. It has a relatively short tail, and a large, daggerlike bill that is nearly a third of its total length.

The common kingfisher hunts along slow-flowing waterways, using a sit-and-wait strategy to find its prey. On spotting a fish, the common kingfisher plunges vertically into the water, folding back its wings as it slices through the surface. When diving, its eyes are covered by transparent membranes, which let it see its prey. Once the kingfisher has made a catch, it carries its prey back to a perch, often beating it several times before swallowing it head-first. Both parents incubate and feed the young, which leave the burrow when they are about 27 days old. Northern common kingfishers migrate south to avoid winter ice.

PROFILE

- North America; winters as far south as N. South America
- Stretches of clear water, from streams to garden ponds and tidal creeks; lowlands to highlands
- Partial migrant
- 11–14 in (28–35 cm)
- 4–5 oz (125–150 g)
- Upward-slanting burrow in bank beside water, up to 16 ½ ft (5 m) long
- 6–7 eggs; 1 brood
- Least Concern
- Solitary

short, shaggy crest

long, thick bill

dark band across breast

white belly

slate-blue back

Plunge-diver
The blue-and-white belted kingfisher normally swoops directly from its lookout, hovering briefly to pinpoint its prey before diving down to make a catch.

SIMILAR SPECIES

shaggy crest

Ringed kingfisher Similar but larger species from Texas to southern parts of South America

long, heavy bill

speckled breast

Giant kingfisher One of the largest crested kingfishers from Africa

Megaceryle alcyon

BELTED KINGFISHER

North America is home to three species of kingfishers, of which the belted kingfisher is by far the most widespread. With its ragged crest and slate-blue belt, it is easy to identify at the water's edge. A bird of all kinds of waterways, from estuaries and lakes to streams and ponds, it breeds across most of the continent, reaching as far north as the Arctic Circle. Belted kingfishers have strong feet. They perch and watch for food, which includes not only fish, but also insects, crustaceans, and small animals caught on land.

Belted kingfishers excavate nest burrows in vertical banks, where the female incubates a hatch of 6–7 eggs for 24 days. After breeding, northern birds migrate southward to avoid winter ice, or toward ice-free coasts.

Female belted kingfisher
The female kingfisher has rust-colored sides, which merge with a rusty band running across the breast.

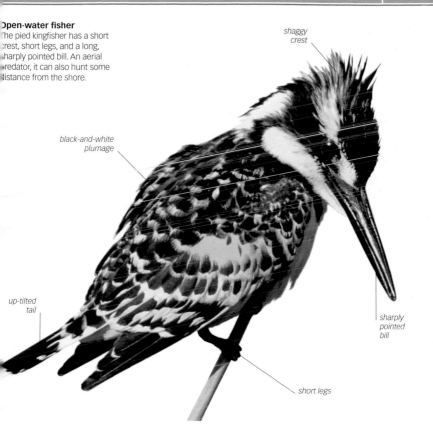

Open-water fisher
The pied kingfisher has a short crest, short legs, and a long, sharply pointed bill. An aerial predator, it can also hunt some distance from the shore.

shaggy crest

black-and-white plumage

up-tilted tail

sharply pointed bill

short legs

PROFILE

- Much of Africa, Middle East, India, S.E. Asia
- Lakes, rivers, estuaries, mangroves, ditches, marshes, reservoirs
- Nonmigrant
- 10 in (25 cm)
- 2 ½–3 ½ oz (70–100 g)
- Burrow in sandy bank with layer of regurgitated fish scales and bones
- 5–7 eggs
- Least Concern
- Pairs/flocks

Ceryle rudis

PIED KINGFISHER

Noisy and gregarious, pied kingfishers live in Africa and tropical Asia, where they are a common sight on bodies of water and waterways. Both sexes have black-and-white plumage, but males can be identified by their double breast bands.

Like other kingfishers, this bird often hunts by flying out from a perch, but its real specialty lies in hovering, which gives it access to open water and more food. It takes large fish back to land, beating them against its perch, but eats small ones on the wing. Pied kingfishers live in pairs or family groups. Parent birds excavate nest tunnels in waterside banks, digging with their bills and kicking out the soil with their feet. The incubation lasts for 18 days. "Helpers," the birds of the earlier brood, assist at the nest when the young hatch.

Female pied kingfisher
The female has a single breast band, with a break in the midline. Like the male, it calls frequently on the wing.

PROFILE

- Jamaica in West Indies
- All forest types, except plantations and the highest areas inland
- Nonmigrant
- 4¼ in (11 cm)
- ¼ oz (7 g)
- Small burrow up to 12 in (30 cm) into a low bank
- 2–3 eggs
- Least Concern
- Solitary/pairs

Island inhabitant
A small, plump-bodied bird, the Jamaican tody is found only in Jamaica. It has a red throat and a pale yellow chest.

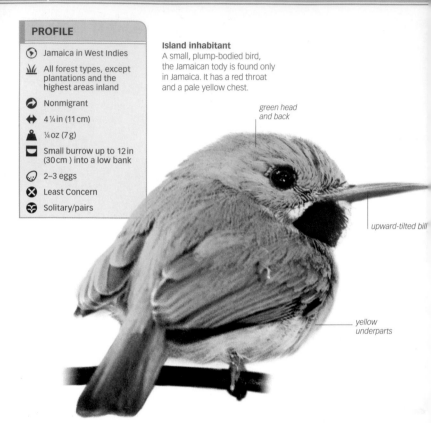

green head and back

upward-tilted bill

yellow underparts

SIMILAR SPECIES

pink flanks

Cuban tody Found in Cuba and adjacent islands; has a striking pattern on its body

long bill

Puerto Rican tody Endemic to the forests of Puerto Rico

Todus todus

JAMAICAN TODY

Tiny forest-dwelling relatives of kingfishers, todies are found only in the West Indies. The Jamaican tody is one of the five species belonging to this small family. They all have colorful plumage with emerald-green head and backs, and paler underparts.

Jamaican todies feed by catching insects, which they spot from a perch. Most of their prey is caught in midair, but they also snatch insects from leaves and from the ground. Like kingfishers, they bring their prey back to a perch to feed. Although they rarely venture out more than 3 ft (1 m) at a time, todies feed voraciously, consuming hundreds of small insects a day.

The breeding season brings bouts of intense activity, with males pursuing prospective partners, or defending their territories against rival males. Jamaican todies nest in burrows, using their bills to dig. The female lays exceptionally large eggs for her size. They hatch after about 21 days, and the young spend the same amount time in the burrow before emerging on the ground.

red eye

long, slender bill

PROFILE

- S. Europe, N.W. Africa to N. India, South Africa; winters in much of tropical Africa, S. Asia
- River valleys, pastures, and cultivated land with bushes, as well as open wooded areas
- Migrant
- 9½ in (24 cm)
- 1⁹⁄₁₆–2⁷⁄₈ oz (45–80 g)
- Unlined chamber at the end of burrow up to 5 ft (1.5 m) long
- 4–7 eggs; 1 brood
- Least Concern
- Flocks

small feet used for perching

two long central feathers on tail

Colorful migrant
In addition to dark yellow upperparts and a blue underside, the European bee-eater has a yellow throat and dark eye-stripe.

Merops apiaster

EUROPEAN BEE-EATER

Brilliantly colored, elegant, and highly social, this long-distance migrant is a specialist hunter of flying insects, which it catches on the wing. True to its name, the European bee-eater often eats bees, among a variety of other insects. Snapping its bill like a pair of forceps, it grabs its prey in midflight, before returning to the perch to feed. Here, stinging insects are "processed" by rubbing their abdomens—this squeezes out the venom, making the insects safe to eat. Flocks on the move are often first detected by their loud, liquid calls.

European bee-eaters breed in colonies, digging nesting tunnels in steep banks of sand or clay. The eggs are incubated for 31 days. After the breeding season, flocks migrate to Africa and southern Asia, where they spend the winter.

Immature bee-eater
The young European bee-eater is paler than the adult, and has brown eyes.

Fanned crest
The common hoopoe raises its fan-shaped crest when it has settled, and sometimes also in flight.

fan-shaped crest

pink-beige head and body

slender, slightly curved bill

barred wings

black tail with white band

PROFILE

- 🌐 Eurasia, Africa, Madagascar; northern populations winter in tropical Africa, India, S.E. Asia
- 🌾 Open country and parkland; treeless steppes, if there are walls in which to nest
- ↔ Partial migrant
- ↔ 10–12 ½ in (26–32 cm)
- ⚖ 1 ¾–3 ⅛ oz (50–90 g)
- 📦 Hole in tree, termite mound, or wall
- 🥚 5–8 eggs; 2 broods
- ❌ Least Concern
- 🐦 Family groups

Upupa epops

COMMON HOOPOE

The hoopoe family has just one species, in which both sexes have crests and make *hoop-hoop-hoop* calls. Often seen on the ground, the bird takes off suddenly when disturbed, revealing zebralike stripes on its wings. On landing, it briefly fans its crest, resuming its search for food. Hoopoes forage in grassy ground, probing with their bill. They feed on insects, lizards, and small snakes, eating their prey on the spot, but beat larger animals against a stone before swallowing them.

Hoopoes raise two broods a year. Females incubate the eggs and produce a foul-smelling secretion, which gives the nest a bad odor but defends the young from predators. In the temperate regions of their range, common hoopoes are migratory.

Flash coloration
The common hoopoe's salmon-pink body contrasts with boldly marked black-and-white wings.

PROFILE

- From S. Sahara through E. Africa to South Africa
- Dry woodland and savanna, usually with little ground vegetation
- Nonmigrant
- 15 ½–19 in (40–48 cm)
- 7–11 oz (200–325 g)
- Tree hole sparsely lined with plants; entrance is plastered with mud and droppings, leaving a narrow slit for feeding
- 3–6 eggs; 1 brood
- Least Concern
- Pairs/family groups

gray, white, and black plumage

long, red bill

long tail

Ground feeder
The red-billed hornbill gets most of its food on the ground. The male has a long red bill, with a black patch on the lower half.

Tockus erythrorhynchus

RED-BILLED HORNBILL

Found in savanna and open woodland, the red-billed hornbill is one of about 30 species of hornbills living in Africa. A middleweight member of its family, it has a slender body and strong legs, and gets most of its food on the ground. An opportunistic omnivore, it snaps up insects, small lizards, and snakes, and also probes for animals and seeds hidden in the soil. Among its regular haunts are paths made by large mammals, where it hunts beetles that feed on animal dung. Usually found in pairs or small family groups, it may gather in groups of several hundred birds during the dry season.

During the breeding season, pairs of these hornbills select a tree hole, which they line with plants. The female plasters the entrance with mud and droppings, leaving only a small hole for the male to pass it food. In this secure environment, the female lays 3–6 eggs, which take about 25 days to hatch. The female leaves the nest when the young are half-grown, resealing the nest until they are fully fledged.

SIMILAR SPECIES

long tail

Southern yellow-billed hornbill Smaller, with a yellow bill

PROFILE

- 🌐 Forests in India, S.E. Asia
- 🌾 Tropical evergreen forest up to 6,500 ft (2,000 m)
- ➤ Nonmigrant
- ↔ 37–41 in (95–105 cm)
- ⚖ 5 lb (2.2 kg)
- 📭 Hole in tree, lined with dry leaves
- 🥚 2 eggs
- ✖ Vulnerable
- 🐦 Flocks

Colossal casque
The male great hornbill, as well as the female, has a large helmet, or casque, divided into two ridges over its giant yellow bill.

large, divided casque

black-and-white plumage

SIMILAR SPECIES

upturned casque

Rhinoceros hornbill S.E. Asian species

brown-black plumage

Rufous hornbill Species from Philippines, with flat, red casque

Buceros bicornis

GREAT HORNBILL

One of the largest members of the hornbill family, this impressive bird gets its scientific name from its head shield, or casque, which is drawn into two points over its giant yellow bill. The great hornbill has strong, partly feathered legs and a long, heavily barred tail.

This bird spends most of its life in treetops, feeding mainly on fruit. It also eats small mammals and birds, tossing its food into the air before swallowing it whole. With its 5 ft (1.5 m) wingspan, the great hornbill is not as maneuverable as smaller forest birds, but once airborne, it is able to fly strongly. Beating its wings with deep flaps interspersed with glides, it makes a loud whooshing sound that can be heard hundreds of yards away. Like its smaller relatives, this hornbill nests in tree cavities, with the female being sealed in the nest by a wall of its own excrement. The male feeds it through a small slit during the 40-day incubation period. The female later breaks out and reseals the nest, helping feed the young from outside.

PROFILE

 Parts of sub-Saharan Africa

Woodland and savanna up to an altitude of 10,000 ft (3,000 m)

Nonmigrant

35–39 in (90–100 cm)

5 lb (2.2 kg)

Hole in tree, lined with dry leaves

2 eggs; 1 brood

Vulnerable

Flocks

Ground force

The southern ground hornbill is a large, heavy bird. It spends most of its life foraging on the ground. The sexes are similar.

black plumage

strong, black bill with casque

red throat wattle

long legs adapted to hunting

SIMILAR SPECIES

blue throat pouch

Northern ground hornbill
Blue-faced females, with a prominent head shield, or casque

Bucorvus leadbeateri

SOUTHERN GROUND HORNBILL

Its bright red facial skin and black body make the southern ground hornbill one of Africa's most distinctive birds. The female has a smaller patch of red on its throat. These birds forage in family parties, which consist of a breeding pair and one or more young from the previous season's brood. They make loud booming calls at sunrise.

These hornbills feed on a variety of animals, including small mammals and the young of ground-nesting birds. The female lays two eggs, several days apart, in a tree cavity. Since the elder chick gets more food, the younger one usually does not survive for more than a week.

Juvenile hornbill
The juvenile has a yellowish face and throat. It helps the breeding pair raise the current year's brood.

bright blue
lower face

yellow-and-
black bill

emerald-green
plumage

Emerald hue
This small-sized toucan is largely
green, with varying bill colors.
The most common race has
a yellow upper mandible and
a black lower mandible.

rust-colored
tail tip

Aulacorhynchus prasinus

EMERALD TOUCANET

An inhabitant of mountain forests and clearings,
the emerald toucanet is a widespread member of the
toucan family. Its range stretches from central Mexico
to as far south as Bolivia, with several different races
varying in the colors of their bills. All emerald toucanets
have brilliant green plumage, which makes them difficult
to spot when they perch on treetops—like other toucans,
they only occasionally come to the ground.

Emerald toucanets live in small flocks of up to 10
birds, feeding on fruit, as well as insects and other
small animals. They follow each other through the
forest canopy, flapping their wings in short bursts,
which gives them a dipping flight. Noisy and excitable,
they call to each other frequently when feeding, and
when on the move. Emerald toucanets nest in abandoned
woodpecker holes, or in natural cavities in trees. The
eggs are incubated by both parents. The incubation
period is about 16 days and the chicks fledge after
about six weeks.

SIMILAR SPECIES

pale green
around eye

Spot-billed toucanet
South American toucanet
with spotted bill

PROFILE

- ⊙ Tropical South America
- ⋌ Wet forest around rivers and lakes
- ⊘ Nonmigrant
- ↔ 17–18 ½ in (43–47 cm)
- ⚖ 8–11 oz (225–300 g)
- ⬚ Unlined cavity in tree, old woodpecker holes
- ◔ 3–4 eggs; 1 brood
- ⊗ Least Concern
- ⊜ Small flocks

Striking face
This species is named for the chestnut color behind its eyes. The sexes are almost identical, but the female has a slightly shorter bill.

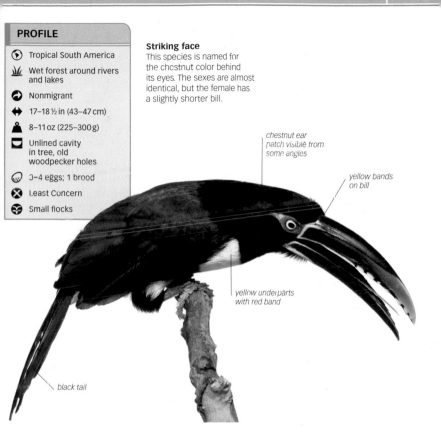

chestnut ear patch visible from some angles

yellow bands on bill

yellow underparts with red band

black tail

SIMILAR SPECIES

orange around eye

Collared araçari Found in Central and South America, with paler upper mandible

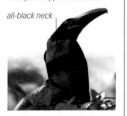

all-black neck

Black-necked araçari Smaller araçari found in South America

Pteroglossus castanotis

CHESTNUT-EARED ARAÇARI

Close relatives of toucans, araçaris have a lighter build and slightly smaller bills. There are over a dozen different species, often with similar lifestyles, but with varying ranges and colors that help distinguish them from each other. The chestnut-eared araçari has yellow underparts with a contrasting red band, while its bill is black and yellow, with a jagged pattern that looks like a row of teeth. A highly arboreal bird, it bounds along slender branches, or flies in a single file across gaps in the forest canopy.

Chestnut-eared araçaris live in groups of up to a dozen birds that forage and roost together. They feed mainly on fruit, but also have a carnivorous streak, eating insects and raiding the nests of other birds. They breed in tree holes, where the female lays a clutch of 3–4 eggs. The young hatch after about 16 days, and are able to fly by the age of six weeks.

PROFILE

- 🎯 Mexico to Colombia, Venezuela
- 〰️ Wet lowland forest, usually below 2,600 ft (800 m), but up to 5,200 ft (1,600 m) in some areas
- 🔄 Nonmigrant
- ↔️ 18–20 in (46–51 cm)
- ⚖️ 10–19 oz (275–550 g)
- 🕳️ Tree cavity
- 🥚 2–4 eggs; 1 brood
- ❌ Least Concern
- 🐦 Flocks

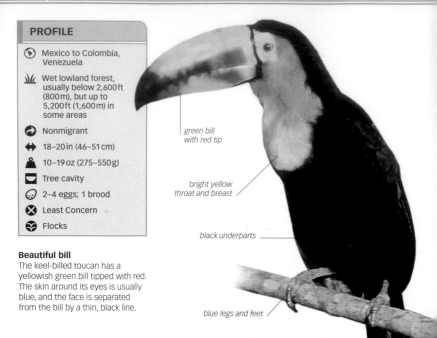

green bill with red tip

bright yellow throat and breast

black underparts

Beautiful bill
The keel-billed toucan has a yellowish green bill tipped with red. The skin around its eyes is usually blue, and the face is separated from the bill by a thin, black line.

blue legs and feet

black tail

SIMILAR SPECIES

blue around eye

Channel-billed toucan Highly variable species from tropical South America

blue legs

Black-mandibled toucan Larger species, found in Central and South America

Ramphastos sulfuratus

KEEL-BILLED TOUCAN

Instantly recognizable by their gigantic bills, toucans are among world's most spectacular tropical birds. This colorful species from Central and South America is typically showy, with mainly black-and-yellow plumage, and a multicolored bill almost half its body length. Its face is green, while its legs and feet are blue. Like all toucans, two of its toes face forward and two face backward, giving it a firm grip on a perch.

Keel-billed toucans are a gregarious species, living in flocks of up to 12 birds. They feed largely on fruit, reaching out to pick it with the tips of their bills, and then throwing it into the air before swallowing. They also prey on small animals, and occasionally steal eggs from the nests of other birds. At dusk, the flock roosts together, with the birds crowding in tree cavities. During the breeding season, the female lays 2–4 eggs, and both parents share the 20-day incubation. The young remain in the nest for up to eight weeks before venturing outside.

PROFILE

- From Venezuela south through Brazil to N.W. Argentina
- Riverine and forest edges, orchards, and rarely, in urban areas up to 5,750 ft (1,750 m)
- Nonmigrant
- 21½–24 in (55–61 cm)
- 18–30 oz (500–850 g)
- Hollow in tree
- 2–4 eggs; 1 brood
- Least Concern
- Small flocks

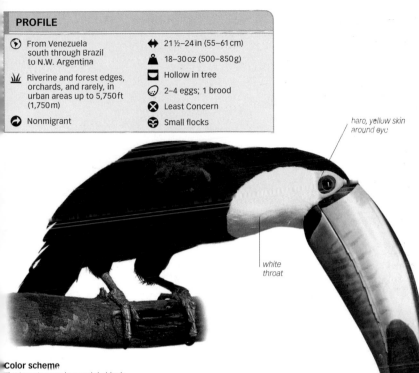

haro, yellow skin around eye

white throat

Color scheme
The toco toucan has mainly black plumage, and a white rump. Its bill is orange-yellow, with a black area near the tip.

black tipped bill

SIMILAR SPECIES

blue patch around eye

White-throated toucan
Dark-billed species from N.E. South America

green bill

Red-breasted toucan
Small toucan, from E. South America

Ramphastos toco

TOCO TOUCAN

With its gigantic orange-yellow bill, this remarkable bird is the largest toucan, and is familiar far beyond its rain forest home. Its bill looks unwieldy, but is actually a precision instrument, with a system of internal struts that makes it surprisingly light for its size. Toco toucans use their bills to pick fruit—leaning out from a branch, they can reach food growing on the thinnest twigs, as well as small animals in the trees and occasionally on the ground. In the air, they have the characteristic dipping flight of all toucans, while they move along branches in a series of bounds. Toco toucans live in tropical South America, avoiding the densest forests, preferring forest edges and stretches of secondary forest, which have regrown after being cut down.

Toco toucans breed in tree holes, where females lay 2–4 eggs. Both parents take turns incubating, with the eggs hatching after about 18 days. The chicks have very small bills, and it takes several months for their bills to reach adult size.

PROFILE

- S.W. Colombia, W. Ecuador
- Mountain forest
- Nonmigrant
- 7½ in (19 cm)
- 3½ oz (98 g)
- Unlined cavity in tree hole
- 2–3 eggs; 1 brood
- Near Threatened
- Family groups

Fruit feeder
The toucan barbet is a colorful, fruit-eating bird. Like toucans, its toes are arranged in forward- and backward-facing pairs.

thick, yellow bill

white patch on head

bristlelike feathers on face

SIMILAR SPECIES

grayish yellow back

Prong-billed barbet Found in Central America; does not form family groups

Semnornis ramphastinus

TOUCAN BARBET

A short-necked, stocky bird, the toucan barbet is a distant relative of the toucans, despite its far shorter bill and much smaller size. Its bill has a broad base, and its face has bristly feathers, although much shorter than in most true barbets (p.241). This colorful bird has a black-and-gray head, and a bright orange breast.

Toucan barbets feed mainly on fruit, and forage at all levels of the forest, hopping along branches to reach their food. Their call is a loud honk, and adult pairs often sing in duets, keeping up their performance for several minutes at a time. Unusual for fruit-eating birds, toucan barbets often live in family groups, with two breeding adults and several young from previous years. They nest in holes in dead trees. Only the dominant pair breed; the rest of the family group act as helpers at the nest. The female lays 2–3 eggs, which are incubated for about 15 days—a task shared by all the members of the group. The young leave the nest when about six weeks old.

Facial bristles
The bearded barbet gets its name from the dense tuft of bristles sprouting from underneath the bill. Its body is dark above, and red and creamy white below.

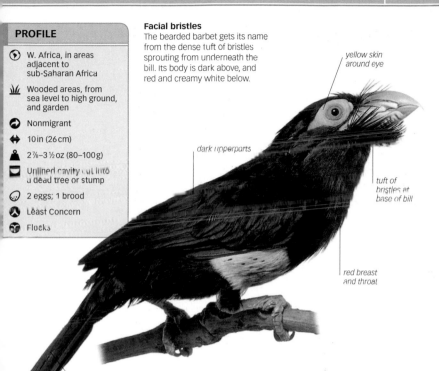

yellow skin around eye

dark upperparts

tuft of bristles at base of bill

red breast and throat

short, black tail

Lybius dubius

BEARDED BARBET

Barbets are distinguished by the tuft of bristles at the base of their bills. In some species, the tuft is thin, but in this West African species, it is more like a stubbly beard, giving the bird its common name.

Found in woodland and wooded grassland south of the Sahara, bearded barbets spend their time hopping along the branches of wild fig and other fruiting trees, feeding mainly on fruit. Colored black, red, and white, they have a patch of yellow skin around their eyes, and strong bills, with deep grooves. This gives their bills a jagged edge, making them useful for feeding and for excavating holes in dead trees. Some of these holes are used as roosting sites, while others are places to nest. Females lay a clutch of two eggs, which hatch after about 16 days. Like many fruit-eating birds, their young are fed partly on insects to fuel their early growth. Despite this, the development of the chicks is quite slow, and they take about six weeks to fledge and leave the nest.

Follow me
The greater honeyguide has white spots on its tail, which it uses to lure mammals and humans toward the bee's nest.

white ear patch

pinkish bill

streaked wings

white underparts

PROFILE

- Parts of Africa, from Senegal to South Africa
- Open woodland, wooded edges, bushland, plantations, gardens, and riparian woodland
- Nonmigrant
- 8 in (20 cm)
- 1¾ oz (50 g)
- Parasitizes nests of other species; single egg is laid in nest of insect-eating bird
- 1 egg
- Least Concern
- Mixed flocks

Indicator indicator

GREATER HONEYGUIDE

A long-bodied bird with sparrowlike markings, the greater honeyguide is remarkable for its behavior, and for its ability to digest wax. It feeds mainly on insects, catching them on the ground or on the wing. But upon locating a bee's nest, it lures animals toward it, flicking its white-spotted tail. Once the animal or human has broken open the nest and removed the honey, this bird gets the pupae and wax.

The honeyguide lays a single egg in another bird's nest. The chick has a lethal hook at its bill tip, used for killing other birds in the nest. With access to all the incoming food, it develops quickly, soon outgrowing its foster parents.

Juvenile honeyguide
The juvenile has a yellowish underside, a white rump, and a black bill. Its tail is shorter than the adult's.

red crown

black bill

white iris

black-and-white plumage

PROFILE

- 🌐 W. North America to Colombia
- 🌿 Oak and pine woodland, Douglas fir and redwood stands, in open areas on migration
- 🔄 Partial migrant
- ↔ 9 in (23 cm)
- ⚖ 2⅞ oz (80 g)
- 🕳 Hole cut in trunk
- 🥚 4–5 eggs; 1 brood
- ❌ Least Concern
- 🐦 Flocks

Winter storage
This woodpecker is largely black-and-white and feeds on stored acorns in winter. It guards its stores against rivals.

SIMILAR SPECIES

red patch on nape

Downy woodpecker
Smaller North American species; does not store acorns

small black cap

Hairy woodpecker
Widespread North American species

Melanerpes formicivorus

ACORN WOODPECKER

Most woodpeckers live alone, but this species from western North America is a highly social bird, living and feeding in communal groups. During summer, acorn woodpeckers feed on insects, but in fall they store acorns by boring holes in dead "granary" trees and utility poles. For small birds, their work is phenomenal: by the time winter arrives, a granary tree may contain thousands of acorns, each placed in a snug-fitting hole drilled into the wood. Groups of woodpeckers often use the same granary tree year after year.

    These birds nest in large tree holes, with several males competing to mate with a small number of females. The eggs are incubated for about 14 days, and the young birds leave the nest after a month, remaining with the group and often returning to the nest at night.

Female acorn woodpecker
The female has a smaller red cap on its head than the male.

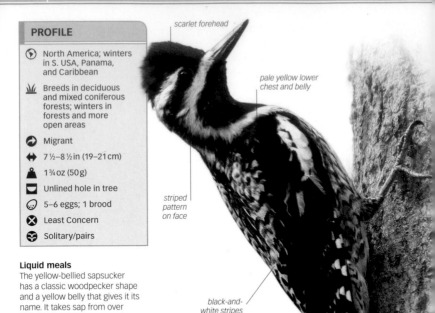

scarlet forehead

pale yellow lower chest and belly

striped pattern on face

black-and-white stripes on back

PROFILE

- North America; winters in S. USA, Panama, and Caribbean
- Breeds in deciduous and mixed coniferous forests; winters in forests and more open areas
- Migrant
- 7½–8½ in (19–21 cm)
- 1¾ oz (50 g)
- Unlined hole in tree
- 5–6 eggs; 1 brood
- Least Concern
- Solitary/pairs

Liquid meals
The yellow-bellied sapsucker has a classic woodpecker shape and a yellow belly that gives it its name. It takes sap from over 100 different trees.

SIMILAR SPECIES

red throat patch

Red-naped sapsucker
Western species; migrates to Mexico in winter

black back with white bars

Red-breasted sapsucker
Prominent species, with bright red head and breast

Sphyrapicus varius

YELLOW-BELLIED SAPSUCKER

Unlike typical woodpeckers, sapsuckers drill lines of shallow holes in trees, which make sap ooze out of the wounds. At intervals, sapsuckers return to their holes, feeding not only on the sap itself, but also on the insects that it attracts. They also guard their holes from other birds. The yellow-bellied sapsucker is among the most widespread of the four species of these specialized woodpeckers in North America.

These birds breed in mixed and coniferous forests. The young leave the nest after a month, and are taught sap-sucking by their parents, after which they fend for themselves.

Female sapsucker
The female has paler underparts and a white chin, unlike the male's red chin. It is in sole charge of incubating the eggs.

red patch on nape

black stripe on face

white shoulder patch

Steady grip
The great spotted woodpecker's strong feet provide anchorage while it hammers into trees. Its drumming call—heard in the breeding season—is one of the fastest among European woodpeckers.

PROFILE

⊙	From Europe to Japan, S. to N. Africa, N.E. India, China
〰	All types of woodland and forest; parks and gardens
↻	Partial migrant
↔	8–9 ½ in (20–24 cm)
⚖	2½–2⅞ oz (70–80 g)
▭	Unlined hole excavated in tree
🥚	4–7 eggs; 1 brood
✕	Least Concern
❀	Solitary

white bars on wings

tail used for support

SIMILAR SPECIES

red crown

White-backed woodpecker
Larger species with a heavily barred back

broad white bars on wings

Lesser-spotted woodpecker
Much smaller; red cap on male

Dendrocopos major

GREAT SPOTTED WOODPECKER

One of the most common woodpecker species, the great spotted woodpecker is found across most of Europe and as far eastward as Japan. Several other species, including the black woodpecker (p.248), exceed it in size. Like other woodpeckers, these birds forage their way up on tree trunks and branches, with their heads up and their tails braced for support. The bills are used to lever up bark, probing underneath with long, sticky tongues. They also hack into wood to dig out insect grubs, and occasionally steal young birds from their nests.

During the breeding season, both sexes help excavate a hole in a tree, where the female lays and incubates the eggs.

Female woodpecker
The female resembles the male but lacks a red patch on its nape.

black "mustache"

red nape

black barring
on back

yellow edges on
tail feathers

PROFILE

- North America, West Indies, C. America; northern populations winter south within this range
- Mostly forest edges and other open areas
- Partial migrant
- 12–14 in (30–35 cm)
- 4–5 oz (125–150 g)
- Cavity excavated in a dead tree or branch
- 6–8 eggs; 1 brood
- Least Concern
- Solitary

On and off the ground
The northern flicker perches vertically on trees, but spends much of its time on the ground. It stands upright, like a thrush, watching for ants and worms, and probing with its long, sticky tongue.

SIMILAR SPECIES

black
crown and
forehead

Campo flicker Ground woodpecker from the grasslands of South America

Colaptes auratus

NORTHERN FLICKER

This handsomely spotted bird feeds primarily on the ground, instead of in trees. The northern flicker specializes in feeding on ants, which it collects with its sticky tongue. It also feeds on worms, seeds, and acorns. When it takes off, this flicker flies in typical woodpecker fashion, with a strongly dipping flight.

Throughout North America, there are several forms of the northern flicker—eastern birds have yellow-shafted wing linings, while in western birds, they are red. Gilded flickers, from the Southwest, are yellow beneath. All forms are easily distinguished when in flight. Northern flickers are partial migrants, spending the winter in the southern part of their range. To nest, they excavate cavities in dead tree trunks. The female lays up to 6–8 eggs. Both parents tend the young.

Female flicker
The sexes are similar, but the female lacks the male's black or red "mustache" stripe.

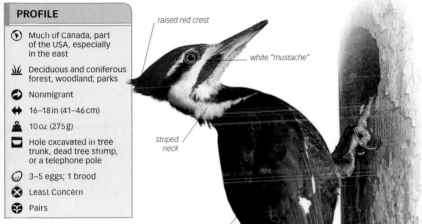

raised red crest

white "mustache"

striped neck

black body

strong, stiff tail used for balance

PROFILE

- Much of Canada, part of the USA, especially in the east
- Deciduous and coniferous forest, woodland; parks
- Nonmigrant
- 16–18 in (41–46 cm)
- 10 oz (275 g)
- Hole excavated in tree trunk, dead tree stump, or a telephone pole
- 3–5 eggs; 1 brood
- Least Concern
- Pairs

Conspicuous crest
The pileated woodpecker has a prominent bushy crest that is permanently raised. The plumage is mainly black, but the head and neck have bold stripes.

SIMILAR SPECIES

white stripe on shoulder

Lineated woodpecker
Found in Central and South America

Dryocopus pileatus

PILEATED WOODPECKER

With its black plumage, striped face, and prominent black crest, the pileated woodpecker is hard to confuse with any other bird. At one time, it was the second-largest woodpecker in North America, but with the extinction of the ivory-billed woodpecker in the 20th century, it became the largest.

Pileated woodpeckers feed on insects that bore into dead wood, and their hammering sound is audible at a considerable distance as they excavate their food. Females incubate the eggs by day, and the males take over at night. Once the eggs have hatched, both parents participate in the month-long period that it takes to raise their young.

Female bird
The sexes are very similar, but the female has a black forehead and a black "mustache."

PROFILE

- Europe to Asia
- Coniferous forest
- Partial migrant
- 17 ½–21 ½ in (45–55 cm)
- 11 oz (325 g)
- Large, oval hole in big tree
- 4–6 eggs; 1 brood
- Least Concern
- Solitary

Upright stance
The black woodpecker braces itself with its stiff tail, which acts as a prop. Unlike other woodpeckers, it flies horizontally, rather than following a dipping flight-path.

white eye

bright red crown

black plumage

SIMILAR SPECIES

white underside

White-bellied woodpecker
Similar red-headed species from forests of Asia

Dryocopus martius

BLACK WOODPECKER

Europe's largest woodpecker, this crow-sized bird has a slender neck and pale ivory-colored bill. The black woodpecker can hack fist-sized holes in trees to get at its food. It feeds low down on tree trunks, and on branches on the ground, using its very long tongue to reach insects buried deep in the wood. When breeding, the male calls by drumming its bill against a dead tree. Hitting 10 times a second, it produces an extraordinarily loud sound that can carry up to ½ mile (1 km).

After breeding, these birds abandon their nest holes, which are later taken over by other hole-nesting birds.

Female woodpecker
The female is all black, like the male, with a smaller red cap. It helps the male excavate the nest hole.

PROFILE

- 🜨 Europe, from Britain to Russia, parts of S.W. Asia to N. Iran
- 🌿 Semi-open areas such as woodland edges, heaths, and parks
- ◐ Nonmigrant
- ↔ 12–13 in (31–33 cm)
- ⚖ 6 oz (175 g)
- ▭ Hole excavated in trunk of a free-standing tree, sometimes as low as 3¼ ft (1 m) above the ground
- 🥚 5–6 eggs; 1 brood
- ✕ Least Concern
- ❋ Solitary

black around white eye-ring

red crown

bright green upperside

Ant eater
The green woodpecker specializes in eating ants, collecting them by probing anthills with its sticky, 4-in (10-cm)-long tongue. It collects huge amounts of ants both for itself, and for feeding its young.

SIMILAR SPECIES

red forehead patch

Gray-headed woodpecker
Smaller European species with gray body and green wings

greenish yellow rump

Japanese woodpecker
Close relative of the green woodpecker from Japan

Picus viridis

GREEN WOODPECKER

A bright green, well-camouflaged bird, the green woodpecker looks very different from most European species, both on the ground, and on the wing. It is common in rough-pastured farmland, with scattered woodland and trees. Like the northern flicker (p.246), this bird divides its time between trees, where it seeks refuge and breeds, and the ground, where it feeds.

Often the only sign of its presence is its ringing laugh, or "yaffle," which it makes when caught by surprise. Both parents take turns to feed the young, which fledge after 24 days but continue to beg for food for several weeks.

Female woodpecker
The female is similar to the male, but has slightly different markings on its head, and a softer call.

PROFILE

- Central and South America

- Wooded areas, scattered trees along creek, rarely in deep forest

- Nonmigrant

- 7 ½–10 in (19–25 cm)

- ⅝–1 ¹⁄₁₆ oz (18–30 g)

- Unlined burrow, in bank or upturned tree root

- 3–4 eggs; 1–2 broods

- Least Concern

- Solitary/pairs

long, narrow bill

bright markings on throat

orange underside

long tail

Stunning plumage
A vividly colored bird, the rufous-tailed jacamar has glossy green and rufous-bronze plumage, with an iridescent sheen.

SIMILAR SPECIES

thicker bill

Chestnut jacamar
Found in the swamp forests of c. South America

red underparts

Great jacamar
Largest jacamar; found in Central and South America

Galbula ruficauda

RUFOUS-TAILED JACAMAR

Found only in the American tropics, jacamars are supremely elegant birds, with plumage colors that rival hummingbirds for their vivid and iridescent sheen. There are about 18 species—the rufous-tailed jacamar is one of the most graceful, with plumage that is glossy green above, and rufous below. However, the female lacks the bright throat markings seen on the male. Like its relatives, the rufous-tailed jacamar has a narrow bill, long tail, and a slender body, with small and weak legs. It spends most of its time on a perch, waiting for insect prey to come its way.

Rufous-tailed jacamars feed on butterflies and other large insects, which they can catch in their narrow bills. Both parents paticipate in building the nest and incubating the clutch of eggs that hatch in 21 days. The young stay in the nest for a further three weeks, until they are fully fledged.

hook-tipped bill

white neck

contrasting black and white plumage

PROFILE

- 🌐 Central America and N.W. South America
- 🌲 Woodland, woodland edges, high treetops
- ↩ Nonmigrant
- ↔ 10 in (25 cm)
- ⚖ 2⅞–3½ oz (80–100 g)
- ▭ Tree cavity, termite mound, hole in ground
- 🥚 2–3 eggs; 1 brood
- ✖ Least Concern
- 🐦 Pairs

Waiting game
The white-necked puffbird waits for butterflies and other large flying insects to fly within range before it feeds on them. The broad bill also helps it catch food on the ground.

narrow tail

SIMILAR SPECIES

dark bluish gray feathers on wings

Black-breasted puffbird
Thicket puffbird from the forests of Central and N. South America

orange bill

White-eared puffbird Found in Brazil; plump body, orange bill, distinctive white "ears"

Notharchus hyperrhynchus

WHITE-NECKED PUFFBIRD

Puffbirds are found in Central and South America, with the Amazon Basin being their principal home. Closely related to jacamars, puffbirds lack their elegant plumage. Most species are colored earth-brown and gray-black, except for one or two, including the white-necked puffbird. These birds have a black breast band, strong feet, and large, hook-tipped bills.

Like jacamars (p.250), white-necked puffbirds sit quietly on a prominent perch, waiting for prey to come their way. They also feed on the ground, always returning to the same vantage point after collecting their food. Like many woodpecker relatives, the puffbirds often nest on the ground, making small burrows in earthern banks, or inside abandoned termite mounds. Both parents share the task of digging the nest. The females incubate the clutch of 2–3 eggs, for a period of about 15 days. The young leave the nest after about two weeks.

PASSERINES

Passerines make up just over half the world's known birds. Ranging from tiny finches to crows and birds-of-paradise, they share many specialized features, including a unique type of foot that can lock onto the slimmest perch.

With nearly 100 families, passerine birds vary enormously in habitat, lifestyle, and size. Many species—such as warblers—migrate thousands of miles each year, making use of seasonal sources of food. At the other extreme, some kinds—such as Hawaiian and Galapagos finches—have evolved on remote oceanic islands and are found nowhere else in the world. Passerines can form enormous flocks numbering hundreds of thousands of birds. Conversely, many—including male European robins—are highly aggressive and will not permit rivals to intrude anywhere within their territory.

All these birds share the same perching feet, but their bill anatomy varies widely, depending on their food. Seed-eaters usually have conical bills for cracking open their food, while insect-eaters have much narrower bills for picking insects from leaves, bark, or

ORDER	PASSERIFORMES
FAMILIES	96
SPECIES	5,962

for snatching them in midair. Crows have all-purpose bills for dealing with many kinds of food. With the exception of dippers (p.303), almost all passerines collect their food on the ground, on trees and shrubs, or on the wing.

SONGBIRDS

Unlike other birds, most passerines have a highly complex syrinx (voicebox) that can produce remarkably rapid and complex songs. Most of the singers are males, and they typically use their songs in the breeding season to attract females and to deter competing males.

Singing is instinctive, but young birds refine their performance as they grow up, often acquiring a local "accent" that distinguishes them from individuals from farther away. Passerines also use a wide range of much simpler contact calls. Often heard with flocking birds, these keep the flock together as they feed.

BREEDING

Most passerines hatch in a very poorly developed state—blind, without feathers, and unable to regulate their body temperature. They depend entirely on one or both of their parents for warmth and food. However, once hatched, passerines can develop with phenomenal speed. Some can be fully fledged and ready to leave the nest in as little as two weeks, giving their parents a chance for additional broods.

On the wing
Like most passerines, this Bohemian waxwing has short, broad wings that give it an almost instant takeoff, and good maneuverability once it is in the air.

PROFILE

- ⊙ Lowland and subtropical zones of S.E. Brazil, E. Paraguay, N.E. Argentina
- ⥊ Humid forest; secondary growth in Atlantic forest, usually in lowland and on slopes
- ⊘ Nonmigrant
- ⬌ 6 in (15 cm)
- ⚖ ⅞ oz (25 g)
- ▭ Small cup nest of grass and plant fibers, placed in fork of bush
- ◔ 2 eggs
- ✕ Least Concern
- ❦ Small flocks

Colorful male
Male blue manakins have evolved highly colorful plumage to attract females at their showgrounds, or leks. The most eye-catching male wins the most mates.

bright red cap

intense blue plumage

black wing feathers

short tail

SIMILAR SPECIES

black plumage

Golden-headed manakin
Found in Central and South America; tiny, bright yellow-headed species

striped underside

Striped manakin
Found in E. and W. South America; lek-forming species

Chiroxiphia caudata

BLUE MANAKIN

Despite their small size, manakins are some of the most noticeable birds in American tropical forests, due to their ceaseless activity and their extraordinary courtship displays. There are nearly 60 species, all with comparatively large heads, short tails, and slender feet, feeding on a mixture of insects and fruit. The male blue manakin is one of the most colorful species.

When breeding, rival males parade at showgrounds, or leks, to compete for the females' attention. As with many lekking species, mated females promptly leave the lek, building a cup-shaped nest unaided by the male. The female blue manakin incubates the eggs for about 21 days. Fed entirely by their mother, the young are fledged after about two weeks.

Female blue manakin
The female looks very different from the male, with camouflaged plumage that hides it on the nest.

PROFILE

⊙ Andes, from Venezuela to Bolivia, at altitudes where the climate is subtropical

〰 Montane forest, especially in ravines

↻ Nonmigrant

↔ 12–12½ in (30–32 cm)

⚖ 7–10 oz (200–275 g)

◻ Cup-shaped nest made of mud and stuck to rock face in sheltered hollow

🥚 2 eggs; 1 brood

✖ Least Concern

✪ Solitary

Forest display
The male Andean cock-of-the-rock displays on low branches and on the ground. It has a semicircular crest that opens out during the display.

semicircular crest

round, staring eye

white wings

SIMILAR SPECIES

Guianan cock-of-the-rock
Found in N.E. South America; silky, orange filaments

Rupicola peruvianus

ANDEAN COCK-OF-THE-ROCK

A prize find for birdwatchers, the Andean cock-of-the-rock is one of South America's most beautiful and remarkable birds. The male has a vivid, red breast and back, and a semicircular crest that folds forward over the head, almost concealing the bird's bill.

Andean cocks-of-the-rock feed on fruit and small animals, and can be surprisingly difficult to spot. Males compete for females at traditional showgrounds or leks. Females visit the lek, watch the participants, and then select a mate. While females incubate the clutch, males take no part in building the nest, or raising the family. Instead, they mate with as many females as they can.

Female cock-of-the-rock
Cinnamon-brown overall, the female is muted in comparison to the male, and has a smaller crest.

PROFILE

- 🜨 From the USA to Argentina, Galapagos Islands; southern populations winter in the Amazon, northern ones in Central America
- ⩲ Variety of open areas, often near water, with scrub, bushes, or trees
- ↻ Migrant
- ↔ 5½ in (14 cm)
- ⚖ ½ oz (14 g)
- ▭ Shallow cup nest made of twigs, grass, and spiders' webs, in tree fork
- ◔ 2–3 eggs; 1–2 broods
- ✖ Least Concern
- ❂ Small flocks

Multicolored migrant
The adult male vermilion flycatcher has intense, red-and-brown plumage. It lives in damp woodland and stream-side vegetation.

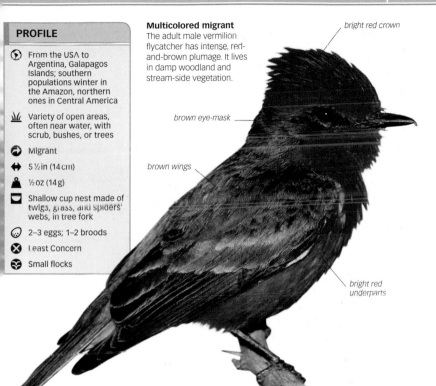

bright red crown

brown eye-mask

brown wings

bright red underparts

SIMILAR SPECIES

brownish legs

Great crested flycatcher
Large, yellow-bellied flycatcher found in E. North America

white wing-bars

Eastern wood-pewee Small eastern flycatcher; distinct by its *pee-a-wee* call

Pyrocephalus rubinus

VERMILION FLYCATCHER

This small bird belongs to the tyrant flycatcher family, a collection of insect-eating birds that is restricted to the Americas. Of over 400 species, just 30 of them, including the vermilion flycatcher, migrate out of the tropics to breed. Compared to most of its relatives, the male vermilion flycatcher is a sumptuously colored bird.

The female lays 2–3 eggs, in a cup-shaped nest made of twigs, grass, and spiders' webs, and incubates them for about 15 days. The young fledge about two weeks later, and in a good year, the female may raise two broods. Once the young are fully independent, they fly south, returning the following spring.

Female flycatcher
The female has grey-brown upperparts and a white underside. Its head is brown, with pale "eyebrows."

PROFILE

🏵 Australia	⬛ Domed nest made of grass and spiders' webs, with side entrance, placed in thicket or spinifex plant
🌾 Undergrowth of eucalyptus forest, woodland, clearings, and mallee scrub	🥚 2–4 eggs; 1 brood
↪ Nonmigrant	❌ Least Concern
↔ 5 ½ in (14 cm)	🐦 Groups
⚖ ⁵⁄₁₆–³⁄₈ oz (9–11 g)	

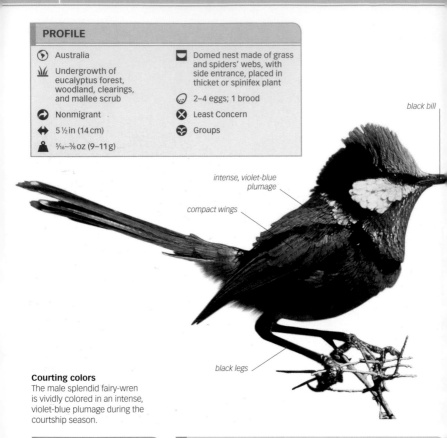

black bill

intense, violet-blue plumage

compact wings

black legs

Courting colors
The male splendid fairy-wren is vividly colored in an intense, violet-blue plumage during the courtship season.

SIMILAR SPECIES

blue eye-patch

Variegated fairy-wren
One of the most widespread fairy-wrens found in Australia

Red-backed fairy-wren
Smallest fairy-wren; red back, black head and underside

Malurus splendens

SPLENDID FAIRY-WREN

Despite its name, this bird is not a true wren, but a member of an Australian family of wrenlike birds. The tiny splendid fairy-wren has a short body, white cheeks, and a wrenlike habit of holding its tail cocked high over the back. There are several regional subspecies of this bird, varying slightly in color and markings. The male is vividly colored, except after the breeding season, when it assumes dull "eclipse" plumage.

The fairy-wren feeds on insects and seeds. When breeding, the male offers the female colored flower petals. The female builds the nest and incubates the eggs for up to 15 days.

Female fairy-wren
The female splendid fairy-wren has brownish gray upperparts and a pale, dull blue tail.

PROFILE

- E. Australia
- Rain forest, wet eucalyptus, woodland
- Nonmigrant
- 11–12½in (28–32cm)
- 6oz (175g)
- Shallow cup nest of twigs and dry leaves, built in twig fork or mistletoe clump, in tree
- 1–3 eggs
- Least Concern
- Solitary

Show-off
The mature male satin bowerbird has glossy blue-black plumage, and a strong, blue bill. It spends much of its time making bowers to attract females.

glossy blue-black plumage

striking blue eye

SIMILAR SPECIES

green wings

Green catbird Similar to the female satin bowerbird; does not build bowers

yellow underparts

Golden bowerbird From Australia; builds the largest bowers, up to 10ft (3m) high

Ptilonorhynchus violaceus

SATIN BOWERBIRD

Bowerbirds have a unique way of attracting partners, by constructing complex "bowers" made of sticks, which are often decorated with flowers, petals, or empty shells. Females arrive at these courtship arenas, where they pair up and mate. After moving on to build their nests, they may never see the males again.

The satin bowerbird is one typical example. The male makes an avenue-style bower, scattered with all kinds of blue objects, such as feathers and bottle tops. When a female approaches, it seizes an object in its bill—the female often finds the display irresistible, especially when it is accompanied by the male's wheezing song. Once mated, the female makes a nest that holds 1–3 eggs, and the chicks are fledged when they are about three weeks old.

Juvenile bowerbird
Females and juvenile satin bowerbirds are olive-green, with brown wings.

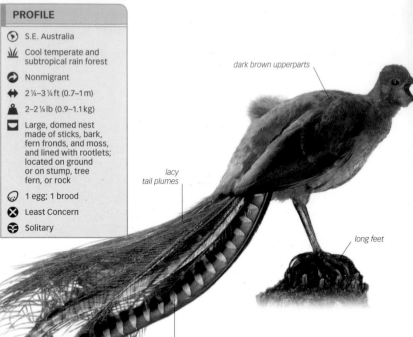

PROFILE

- S.E. Australia
- Cool temperate and subtropical rain forest
- Nonmigrant
- 2¼–3¼ft (0.7–1 m)
- 2–2¼lb (0.9–1.1kg)
- Large, domed nest made of sticks, bark, fern fronds, and moss, and lined with rootlets; located on ground or on stump, tree fern, or rock
- 1 egg; 1 brood
- Least Concern
- Solitary

dark brown upperparts

lacy tail plumes

long feet

lyre-shaped feathers

Irresistible attraction
The superb lyrebird gets its name from the two lyre-shaped feathers on either side of its tail. These help complete the male's display during courtship.

Menura novaehollandiae

SUPERB LYREBIRD

Famous as a national symbol, Australia's superb lyrebird is about the size of a chicken. It has long, powerful feet, and is one of the world's largest songbirds, with a total length of up to 3¼ft (1 m), including the male's elaborate tail. Normally, the tail is carried horizontally, but the male folds it over its head during courtship displays.

Superb lyrebirds are known for their astonishing powers of mimicry. They imitate the sounds of other birds as well as all kinds of inanimate objects or other animals, from mobile phones to barking dogs. They feed on small animals, scratching up the leaf litter with their feet. Males mate with many females, attracting them with their calls and displays. Females lay a single egg and they take sole charge of incubation and raising the chick.

SIMILAR SPECIES

chestnut plumage

Albert's lyrebird Smaller species restricted to the border of Queensland and New South Wales

Female superb lyrebird
The female is similar in appearance to the male. It has a long tail, but lacks elaborate tail plumes.

PROFILE

- S.E. South America
- Open habitats, from city parks to agricultural areas and scrub, mainly in lowlands
- Nonmigrant
- 6½–9 in (16–23 cm)
- 1 1/16–2 3/8 oz (30–65 g)
- Domed mud nest on top of branch or pole
- 3–4 eggs; 1 brood
- Least Concern
- Pairs

Ground feeder
The rufous hornero has a long, strong, slightly curved bill, which it uses to probe the ground for insects and their larvae, and also other small animals and seeds.

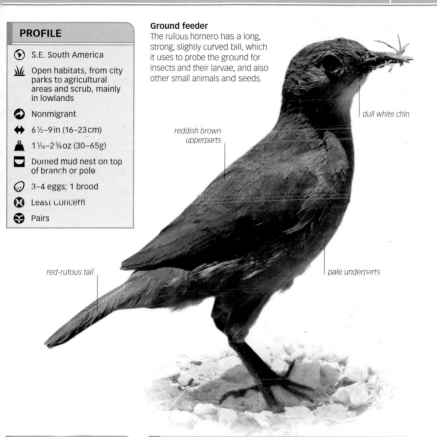

dull white chin

reddish brown upperparts

red-rufous tail

pale underparts

SIMILAR SPECIES

brown upperparts

White-eyed foliage-gleaner Chunky ovenbird; striking white throat

slender bill

Common miner Smaller, tunnel-nesting ovenbird; variable coloration

Furnarius rufus

RUFOUS HORNERO

Unremarkable to look at, this plain brown bird is common in parks and gardens, as well as farmland and scrub. It has a jaunty gait, and strides across the ground feeding on insects and other small animals.

Named after the Spanish word for baker, the rufous hornero builds a football-sized nest from sunbaked mud, which resembles an old-fashioned baker's oven. Pairs start work in the rainy season, making a domed nest about 12 in (30 cm) wide. Often placed on a fence post or bare branch, the nest has an entrance near the base, which is connected to the interior by a winding corridor, with an upright threshold. This keeps most predators out. By the time the female lays the eggs, the nest dries out and is rock-hard, making a secure home for a growing family. The eggs are incubated for about 18 days and the nest is abandoned at the end of the breeding season. The empty nests often last for several years, and other birds frequently take them over to raise their own young.

PROFILE

- S.E. and W. Australia
- Woodland, scrub, parks, gardens, heaths
- Nonmigrant
- 7 in (18 cm)
- 11/16 oz (20 g)
- Cup nest of twigs and grass, bound with spider webs, with a softer lining, placed in bush or tree
- 2 eggs; 2–3 broods
- Least Concern
- Small flocks

Feeding at flowers
The New Holland honeyeater extracts nectar from flowers. It often feeds on banksia and eucalyptus, which have long flowering seasons.

black-and-white plumage

long, narrow bill

SIMILAR SPECIES

blue patch around eye

Blue-faced honeyeater Larger; from northern and eastern Australia

olive-gray plumage

Lewin's honeyeater Slightly larger; found in Australia's eastern forests

Phylidonyris novaehollandiae

NEW HOLLAND HONEYEATER

Found only in Australia and the southwest Pacific, honeyeaters are a large family of birds that live and feed on plants. Despite their name, they do not eat honey—instead, most of their food comes from nectar, and sometimes from fruit. With over 170 species, the New Holland honeyeater is a typical example. Like its relatives, it has a long, narrow bill, and a brush-tipped tongue that protrudes to collect nectar from flowers. Noisy, active, and inquisitive, it is sometimes seen jostling for food among flowering trees. It has a slender body, with bright yellow panels on its wings and tail.

New Holland honeyeaters live in a variety of wooded habitats, and also feed in cities and gardens. During the breeding season, they make cup-shaped nests where females lay eggs and incubate them for 18 days. If there is a plentiful supply of food, 2–3 broods may be raised in a year.

PROFILE

- New Zealand
- Forest, woodland, suburban areas
- Nonmigrant
- 12 in (30 cm)
- 3 ⅛–5 oz (90–150 g)
- Made of twigs, leaves, moss, and lichen; lined with grass and feathers
- 2–4 eggs
- Least Concern
- Pairs/family groups

curved bill

white ruff

Hidden color
The tui appears completely black from a distance, except for its white ruff. However, on close inspection, a green and purple sheen can be seen on its feathers.

SIMILAR SPECIES

green plumage

New Zealand bellbird
Smaller honeyeater, with no ruff around its throat

Prosthemadera novaeseelandiae

TUI

Common throughout New Zealand, the tui has successfully adapted to manmade changes in its habitat. A medium-sized member of the honeyeater family, it looks entirely black from a distance, but is actually iridescent, with a distinctive white ruff on its throat. Like other honeyeaters, it has a brush-tipped tongue, and feeds mainly on nectar, although it also eats pollen and insects when climbing about in blooms. Its probing bill is an exact fit for many of New Zealand's native flowers, as well as for ones that have been introduced from Australia and beyond.

Tuis are vocal and melodious birds, making a wide variety of sounds, from bell-like ringing to clicks and wheezes. Loud and assertive when defending their favorite flowering trees, they join together to chase away birds much larger than themselves. During the breeding season, females build the nest and incubate the eggs for about 14 days. The young take about 21 days to fledge.

PROFILE

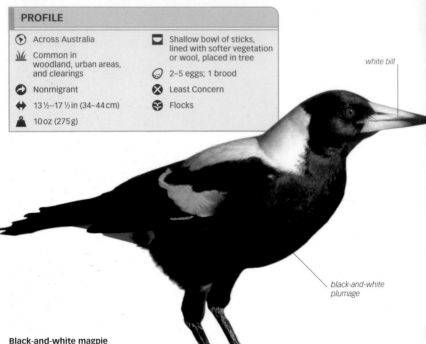

⊕ Across Australia	▭ Shallow bowl of sticks, lined with softer vegetation or wool, placed in tree
☷ Common in woodland, urban areas, and clearings	
	⬭ 2–5 eggs; 1 brood
➡ Nonmigrant	✖ Least Concern
↔ 13½–17½in (34–44cm)	✿ Flocks
⚖ 10oz (275g)	

white bill

black-and-white plumage

Black-and-white magpie
The Australian magpie exists in a wide array of forms, but the basic color scheme is black and white. Each form has varying amounts of white on its back and wings.

SIMILAR SPECIES

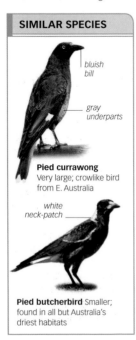

bluish bill

gray underparts

Pied currawong Very large; crowlike bird from E. Australia

white neck-patch

Pied butcherbird Smaller; found in all but Australia's driest habitats

Gymnorhina tibicen

AUSTRALIAN MAGPIE

This large, crowlike bird belongs to the butcherbird family—a group of about a dozen species that are found only in Australia. Its basic color scheme is black and white, but it exists in an array of forms, each with its own variation in the amount of white on its back and wings. Once considered separate species, these forms are now classified as subspecies of the Australian magpie. They all share the same habits and omnivorous lifestyles, roosting in areas with scattered trees and soft ground that they can probe for food. Unlike many Australian birds, which make noisy squawks, they are gifted songsters.

Australian magpies generally nest high in trees, where the female produces a clutch of 2–5 eggs. Incubation takes about 20 days. At this stage, some males become highly defensive of the nest. They will fearlessly swoop on animals and passersby, sometimes causing injuries with their determined attacks. Recently fledged birds may form large, nomadic flocks.

PROFILE

- E. and C. North America
- Woods, parks, gardens
- Nonmigrant
- 10–11 in (25–28 cm)
- 3 ⅛ oz (90 g)
- Cup nest of twigs and moss, lined with small roots, placed in tree
- 4–5 eggs; 1 brood
- Least Concern
- Small flocks

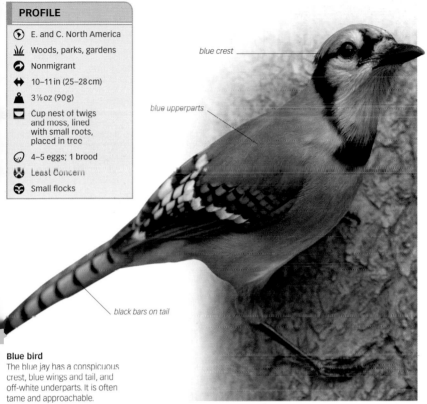

blue crest

blue upperparts

black bars on tail

Blue bird
The blue jay has a conspicuous crest, blue wings and tail, and off-white underparts. It is often tame and approachable.

SIMILAR SPECIES

black crest

Steller's jay Larger; from W. North America

Pinyon jay Flock-forming jay from S.W. North America

duller plumage

Cyanocitta cristata

BLUE JAY

Like many members of the crow family, the blue jay is an intelligent, adaptable bird, equally at home in parks and backyards as it is in its natural woodland habitat. The most common jay in North America, this handsome bird has blue upperparts and white wing spots. Its range extends northward to Canada in summer, and east of the Rockies at all times of the year.

Blue jays usually feed on acorns and other seeds, but they also eat insects and other small animals, as well as the remains of dead animals. They are also committed nest-robbers: gifted mimics of other birds' calls, they scare away parent birds by imitating the cries of birds of prey and then feed on the young birds and unhatched eggs in the nests. In fall, when food is abundant, they bury or "cache" it for use in times of scarcity. Blue jays nest in trees, making their nests out of twigs, moss, and even string, and lined with small roots. The female lays a clutch of 4–5 eggs, which hatch after an incubation period of 18 days.

PROFILE

- Europe, N. Africa, Asia, Greenland, Iceland, North America
- Rugged mountains, coastal cliffs, steppes, semi-desert
- Nonmigrant
- 23–27 in (58–69 cm)
- 2–3½ lb (0.9–1.6 kg)
- Large nest of thick sticks, wool, grass, and heather, under overhang on cliff, or in tree
- 4–6 eggs; 1 brood
- Least Concern
- Solitary/pairs/ small flocks

thick bill

black plumage

long, tapering tail

Remarkable raven
The common raven is among the largest members of the crow family. It has a massive bill and a tapering tail.

SIMILAR SPECIES

black plumage

Carrion crow Widespread Eurasian crow with two distinct color forms

gray-black bill

Rook Among the most social crows, usually seen in large flocks

Corvus corax

COMMON RAVEN

One of the world's largest songbirds, the common raven is found across the Northern Hemisphere, particularly in mountainous regions. A strong flier, with wing tips splayed out like hands, it is highly aerobatic, dodging flocks of small birds that instinctively mob it as it passes overhead. Less social than other crows, it typically flies in twos or threes, periodically uttering a raucous call on the wing.

Powerful scavengers, common ravens rival many birds of prey of the same size. They fly at a great range of altitudes: common at sea level on remote, rocky coasts, they can reach heights of over 16,250 ft (5,000 m) while patrolling mountainsides for food. Their diet is wide-ranging and includes rabbits, birds, and the remains of dead animals. In spring, they sometimes eat grain from fields, but rarely in large flocks like other crows. Common ravens build large nests, which are often used year after year. The chicks leave the nest when they are about 40 days old.

PROFILE

- 🧭 Europe, N.W. Africa, parts of the Middle East, much of C. and E. Asia
- 🌾 Woodland, open ground with bushes and hedges, and urban gardens
- 🔄 Nonmigrant
- ↔ 17 ½ in (45 cm)

- ⚖ 8 oz (225 g)
- 🪹 Bowl of twigs, with loose dome of branches, placed high in tree
- 🥚 5–7 eggs; 1 brood
- ✖ Least Concern
- 🐦 Small flocks

thick, black bill

black back and head

blue-green sheen to wings and tail

white belly

Elegant omnivore
Male Eurasian magpies have longer tails than the females. These magpies are often seen feeding in farmland and suburban settings.

SIMILAR SPECIES

glossy black head

Azure-winged magpie
Shy species from Spain, Portugal, and eastern Asia

red bill

blue plumage

Red-billed blue magpie
From the Far East; exceptionally long tail

Pica pica

EURASIAN MAGPIE

A widespread and eye-catching bird, the Eurasian magpie is originally from woodland and open, scrubby ground. However, it has adapted well to human changes in the landscape, and is now just as common in parks and urban gardens. Like many other crows, it is an opportunistic omnivore. It feeds on insects, seeds, and worms, as well as leftover food. However, during spring, it turns to nest-robbing—a habit that makes it an unwelcome visitor for many bird enthusiasts. Small birds attempt to defend their brood, but once a magpie has spotted the nest, the eggs and young have little chance of survival.

Magpies build highly elaborate nests, which are repaired and reused every year. Consisting of a bowl of twigs, roofed with a dome of small branches, the nests are often placed high in trees. Females lay a clutch of 5–7 eggs, which hatch after about 18 days. The young are fed by both parents, and are ready to leave the nest within four weeks.

Striking wings
The Eurasian jay has electric-blue and white patches on its otherwise black and brown wings. These are especially prominent in flight.

striped crown

pale pinkish brown body

electric-blue wing patch

black tail

PROFILE

- From Europe, N.W. Africa through C. Asia to E. and S.E. Asia
- Woodland, parks, gardens
- Nonmigrant
- 14 in (35 cm)
- 6 oz (175 g)
- Cup-shaped nest, lined with twigs and roots, placed in a tall tree
- 4–6 eggs; 1 brood
- Least Concern
- Small flocks

Garrulus glandarius

EURASIAN JAY

Although it has a noisy call, the Eurasian jay is a shy bird, often seen flying away from its perch. Compared to many other members of the crow family, it is slow and erratic in the air, fluttering on its broad wings before regaining the safety of trees. Its color varies across its wide range, but all birds have electric-blue wing patches that are particularly visible in flight.

Eurasian jays are omnivorous, eating insects, fruit, and young birds, but they specialize in feeding on acorns, which they collect during fall. Most of these are buried and then retrieved as winter wears on, but jays invariably overlook some of their caches, helping oak trees to spread. These jays breed in woodland and both parents incubate the eggs. The young birds leave the nest when they are three weeks old.

Color variant
The Eurasian jay has various color forms. This variant is darker, with a brownish crown and throat.

gray head

Masked raider
The male red-backed shrike has a conspicuous black mask along its eyes. It has a hooked bill and powerful feet for tackling large prey.

hooked bill

chestnut back

PROFILE

- Eurasia from S.E. Britain to W. Siberia; migrates southward, some birds reaching S. Africa
- Open areas of scrubland, heath, farmland; winters mainly in arid savanna
- Migrant
- 7 in (18 cm)
- 1 ¼ oz (30 g)
- Deep cup nest of grass and rootlets, placed in dense bush
- 5–6 eggs; 1 brood
- Least Concern
- Solitary

SIMILAR SPECIES

black back

Southern fiscal Widespread nonmigratory African shrike

gray-and-black plumage

Northern shrike Europe's largest shrike, typically a summer visitor

Lanius collurio

RED-BACKED SHRIKE

With their hooked bills and sharp claws, red-backed shrikes are predatory songbirds that specialize in catching small mammals and reptiles, as well as beetles, grasshoppers, and other insects. When food is plentiful, they impale the bodies of surplus prey on thorns and barbed wire; these "shrike larders" soon dry out in the air, so the food remains edible for a long period of time.

Red-backed shrikes winter in southern Africa, and breed in scrubland and heath in Europe and western Asia. Like many shrikes, the sexes differ in appearance. The males court the females with elaborate displays, and arrive at the breeding site in advance. Both parents help build the nest. The eggs take around 16 days to incubate. The young take about two weeks to fledge.

Female shrike
Duller than the male, the female has a scalloped underside. It lacks the male's black mask.

PROFILE

- ⊙ Europe, C. Asia; winters in Africa
- 〰 Deciduous lowland woodland, parks, gardens
- ➜ Migrant
- ↔ 9½ in (24 cm)
- ⚖ 2⅞ oz (80 g)
- ▭ Cup nest slung in twig fork; made of grass, wool, and strips of bark, finely lined, and situated high in outer twigs of tree
- ⊘ 3–4 eggs; 1 brood
- ⊗ Least Concern
- ⊛ Solitary

Brilliant colors
The Eurasian golden oriole has an intense yellow body, a red bill, and black wings. However, it is rarely seen since it perches in high treetops.

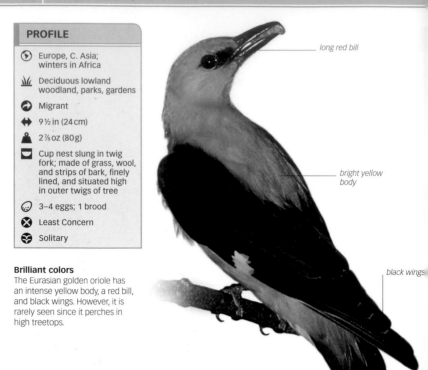

long red bill

bright yellow body

black wings

long tail

Oriolus oriolus

EURASIAN GOLDEN ORIOLE

Arriving late in the European spring, the golden oriole is one of the most colorful migrants from Africa. The adult male has an intense yellow body, with a red bill and black wings. The Eurasian golden oriole has an undulating flight similar to a woodpecker's.

This bird feeds on insects and fruit, which it consumes in great quantities when ripe. It has a distinctive, fluting song, and a raucous call similar to a jay's. During the short breeding season, the female lays 3–4 eggs, which it incubates for about 15 days. The young are fledged in a fortnight, and ready to leave the nest.

Female golden oriole
The female has green upperparts and is faintly striped below. Like the male it has a long, red bill.

PROFILE

- 🌐 N. North America, as far as Arctic Circle
- 〰 Woodland and forest, particularly deciduous and mixed; parks and gardens
- 🔄 Nonmigrant
- ↔ 5 in (13 cm)
- ⚖ ³/₈ oz (11 g)
- ▭ Cup nest lined with moss, feathers, and hair, placed in tree cavity
- 🥚 8 eggs; 1 brood
- ✖ Least Concern
- 🐦 Mixed flocks

short, black bill

black bib

pale buff flanks

Perching on trees
The black-capped chickadee spends most of its life in trees and shrubs, where it feeds on seeds, as well as caterpillars and insect eggs.

SIMILAR SPECIES

white "eyebrow"

Mountain chickadee
Species found in American West; striking white "eyebrow" and buff-tinged flanks

brown cap

Boreal chickadee Species found as far north as Alaska and Hudson Bay; distinct brown cap and flanks

Poecile atricapillus

BLACK-CAPPED CHICKADEE

Named for its *chick-a-dee-dee* call, this bird belongs to the same family as the blue tit (p.270), and has a similar way of life. The black-capped chickadee rarely sets foot on the ground, and spends its life in trees and shrubs, where it feeds on caterpillars, insect eggs, and seeds from conifers and other trees. Most insect-eating birds migrate south in the fall, but the chickadee typically remains in the far north all year round. Its range extends as far as the Arctic Circle including Alaska, and Canada's Northern Territories and Newfoundland.

The black-capped chickadee feeds all through the hours of daylight to generate enough body heat to keep warm. In winter, it frequently forages and roosts together, which helps conserve vital warmth. The eggs hatch after 13 days and the young are fledged in a little over two weeks. The chicks stay with the parents for up to a month, and then disperse to find feeding areas of their own.

PROFILE

- Europe, parts of N. Africa, Middle East
- Wide range of habitats, including woodland, scrub, parks, gardens
- Partial migrant
- 4¾ in (12 cm)
- ⅜ oz (10 g)
- Cup lined with moss and animal hair; hole in tree or wall; nest box
- 7–16 eggs; 1 brood
- Least Concern
- Loose flocks

Garden visitor
Thin legs with large toes let the blue tit cling to slender branches and garden birdfeeders, sometimes hanging upside down as it feeds.

thin eye-stripe

greenish blue upperparts

yellow underside

blue tail

SIMILAR SPECIES

black cap

Coal tit Slightly smaller; black bib

Cyanistes caeruleus

BLUE TIT

Small and highly active, the blue tit is one of Europe's most familiar birds, although it also lives in North Africa and the Middle East. Its coloration varies across its range, but it is typically greenish blue above, with yellow underparts, white cheeks, and a blue cap. During daylight hours, blue tits are always on the move, calling to maintain contact as they seek food. Their small and sharply pointed bills are ideal for gleaning small insects from leaves and twigs. Although they rarely venture down to the ground, they are agile on their feet, often hanging upside down as they feed.

Blue tits are hole-nesters, readily taking up residence in nest boxes. They make a cup-shaped nest lined with moss and animal hair, where the female incubates her brood. Once the eggs have hatched, both parents help feed the young—together, they can make over a thousand excursions a day to collect food. Once the young have fledged and left the nest, blue tits often form mixed flocks with other birds.

PROFILE

- ⊙ Europe, N.W. Africa, parts of Siberia, E. Asia, parts of C. Asia, Indian subcontinent, S.E. Asia

- 〰 Woodland, farmland, parks, gardens

- ◐ Nonmigrant

- ↔ 5½ in (14 cm)

- ⚖ ⁹⁄₁₆–¾ oz (16–21 g)

- ▭ Cup nest made of moss, animal hair, or feathers, lined with fine grass; placed in a hole in a tree or wall

- ◔ 5–11 eggs; 1 brood

- ✖ Least Concern

- ❧ Loose flocks

Colorful tit
The great tit is among the most brightly colored tits, with green and bluish gray upperparts and a bright yellow underside.

shiny black head

white cheek patch

green back

black band on yellow underside

gray tail with white sides

SIMILAR SPECIES

plain gray-brown upperparts

Marsh tit Glossy black cap and gray-brown wings

dull brown back

Willow tit Large-headed, with a dull, gray-buff underside

Parus major

GREAT TIT

Larger and more assertive than most other tits, the great tit is a common visitor to European gardens. Its range is extensive, running from Western Europe eastward to Japan, and as far south as Indonesia. It lives in deciduous or mixed woodland, as well as in farmland and parks. It advertises its presence with an extremely wide repertoire of calls, including a rasping *teacher-teacher-teacher*, which is often broadcast from the low branches of a bush or tree.

The great tit feeds on insects, seeds, and fruit. It frequents birdfeeders during winter, driving other tits into second place. The female incubates the eggs for 13 days, and the fast-growing young, fed by both parents, are ready to fly by the time they are three weeks old.

Female great tit
The female has a narrower band on the underside, but is otherwise very similar to the male.

Southern form
In the southern part of its range, the long-tailed tit has a black head, upperside, and tail. The underside is white, suffused with pink.

dull black-and-pink back

black band behind eye

dull white head

long, slim, black tail with white sides

dull white underside

PROFILE

⊙	From W. Europe eastward to Japan
⩆	Deciduous woodland, wetland reedbeds
⟳	Nonmigrant
↔	5½ in (14 cm)
⚖	¼–⁵⁄₁₆ oz (7–9 g)
⬚	Domed nest made of moss, hair, and spiders' webs, placed in hedge or tree
⊙	8–12 eggs; 1 brood
✕	Least Concern
❀	Flocks

Aegithalos caudatus

LONG-TAILED TIT

This energetic little bird is the most widespread member of its family— a group of tiny songbirds found mainly in Europe and Asia, with just one species in North America. Collectively known as bushtits, they have long tails, rounded bodies not much bigger than a ping-pong ball, and tiny bills for gleaning insects from twigs and leaves. Long-tailed tits are social birds, and are usually seen in small flocks, flitting through woodlands and hedgerows, calling constantly to maintain contact.

They breed in trees or hedges, making remarkably intricate domed nests from feathers and spiders' webs. Both parents help build the nest and feed the young once they have hatched. In winter, adults and young often form mixed flocks with other tits.

Northern form
In the north of its range, this tit often has an all-white head. At times, the bird moves south in winter.

silvery white
crown

maroon-brown
body

Prize performance
The male has a silvery white
crown, a maroon-brown body,
and stunningly beautiful display
plumes that are used to attract
potential mates.

PROFILE

⊙ Indonesia, New Guinea

〽 Forest

● Nonmigrant

↔ 5 ½–6 ¾ in (14–17 cm)

▲ 6 oz (170 g)

▭ Cup-shaped nest made
of leaves and vines

◔ 2–3 eggs

✕ Least Concern

♻ Flocks

lacy plumes

SIMILAR SPECIES

green
throat

**Raggiana
bird-of-
paradise**
Smaller species
found in New
Guinea; lacks
yellow plumes

**Magnificent
riflebird**
Species from
New Guinea
and Australia;
iridescent
throat

Paradisaea apoda

GREATER
BIRD-OF-PARADISE

Found in the forests of New Guinea and Indonesia,
the greater bird-of-paradise ranks as one of the most
beautiful species in the entire animal kingdom. The male
greater bird-of-paradise is polygynous, attracting several
females during the breeding season, but forming no
lasting pairs. The female is smaller than the male, and
is relatively drab in appearance, a common pattern in
birds-of-paradise. The greater bird-of-paradise is one
of the largest members of its family, with the male
measuring over 15 ½ in (40 cm) in length. This species
feeds mainly on fruit, seeds, and small insects. Highly
sedentary, it rarely travels more than a few hundred
metres from its home range.

During the breeding season, the male greater
bird-of-paradise shows off its finery to visiting females,
but its participation ends with mating. It plays no part
in building the nest, or in raising its young.

Smooth as silk
Pinkish brown in color, the Bohemian waxwing has silky plumage, a backswept crest, and a conspicuous yellow tip on its tail.

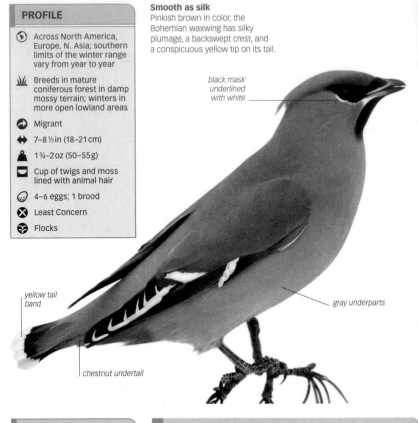

black mask underlined with white

yellow tail band

gray underparts

chestnut undertail

SIMILAR SPECIES

red tips on wing feathers

Cedar waxwing Nomadic bird, moves around for food

red tail tip

Japanese waxwing Unlike other waxwings, lacks the waxy red spots on wings

Bombycilla garrulus

BOHEMIAN WAXWING

Sleek and portly, waxwings get their name from the beadlike tips on their inner flight feathers, which look like tiny drops of sealing wax. Of the three species, the Bohemian waxwing is the most widespread. A fruit-eating songbird, it devours berries of trees and shrubs, supplementing its diet with insects.

Bohemian waxwings usually raise a single brood. After the female has incubated the eggs, both parents feed and look after the young. All three waxwing species are known for their unusual migratory behavior. If their winter food is in short supply, they fly south on journeys called "irruptions," which are unpredictable and occur several years apart.

Juvenile waxwing
The young bird is duller and browner than the adult, but also has a crest.

PROFILE

- New Guinea and Australia, except far south of Tasmania
- Almost anywhere, except dense forest
- Nonmigrant
- 7½–8½ in (19–21 cm)
- ⅝–⅞ oz (17–25 g)
- Cup nest of bark, grass, spiders' webs, and finer lining, often on branches overhanging water; also in buildings, street lamps, and phone masts
- 2–4 eggs; 1 brood
- Least Concern
- Solitary/pairs

Clean sweep
This widespread fantail from Australia has a tail-sweeping motion, characteristic of the species. When hunting on the ground, it also flares its wings.

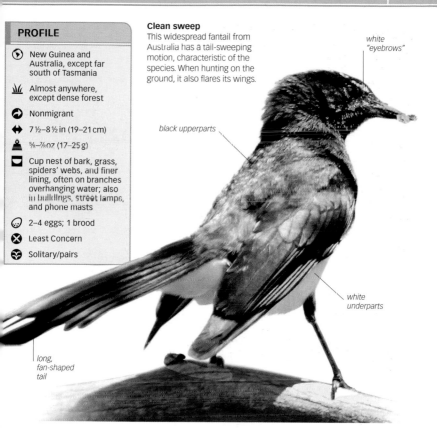

white "eyebrows"

black upperparts

white underparts

long, fan-shaped tail

SIMILAR SPECIES

gray upperparts

Gray fantail Slimmest wagtail; also has longest tail

gray-brown wings

Rufous fantail Colorful species from East Australia; with speckled breast

Rhipidura leucophrys

WILLY WAGTAIL

This small, energetic insect-eater is one of Australia's best-known and widespread birds. It hunts for food from low branches and fences, hawking insects in the air, or catching them on the ground. It gets its name from its habit of sweeping its tail from side to side—behavior that is thought to disturb small animals, making them easier to catch. Once the wagtail has caught its prey, it often carries it to a perch to remove its legs and wings, making the catch easier to eat.

This bird lives in a variety of habitats from woodlands to farms and suburbs, showing very little fear of people, although it can be aggressive during the breeding season. The willy wagtail nests on branches overhanging water, but is equally at home in buildings, street lamps, and mobile phone masts, where it defends its nests vigorously against intruders. During the breeding season, the female lays 2–4 eggs, which are incubated for about 14 days. Two weeks later, the young are fledged and ready to leave the nest.

Conspicuous features
The male African paradise-flycatcher has a conspicuous eye-ring and crest. Its tail is almost as long as the rest of its body.

prominent crest

rufous upperparts

black throat

PROFILE

- Sub-Saharan Africa
- Forest, woodland, plantations, gardens
- Partial migrant
- 7 in (18 cm)
- ⁷⁄₁₆–½ oz (12–14 g)
- Cup-shaped nest lined with grass and animal hair, in tree
- 2–5 eggs; 1 brood
- Least Concern
- Solitary/pairs

long central tail feathers

SIMILAR SPECIES

Red-bellied paradise-flycatcher Red-bodied species from C. and W. Africa

black throat

Asian paradise-flycatcher Widespread in Asia; blue eye-ring

Tersiphone viridis

AFRICAN PARADISE-FLYCATCHER

Despite its name, this handsome bird is not a typica flycatcher, but a member of the monarch family, which consists of small, insect-eating birds with long, elegant tails. Monarchs range from Africa and Asia to Australia and the Far East, but this species is found exclusively south of the Sahara.

African paradise-flycatchers have variable colors, ranging from brown to white. They feed on flying insects, termites, and ants, dashing out after them from a prominent perch. They also glean insects from the undersides of leaves. The eggs hatch in 15 days and the young leave the nest after about two weeks.

Female flycatcher The female has a shorter tail and duller plumage. It lacks the male's prominent eye-ring and crest.

Striking appearance
The white face of the female magpie-lark gives it an open-faced look. The male has a black forehead, with thin white eyebrows. The sexes are otherwise very similar.

white forehead and throat

black-and-white plumage

PROFILE

- Australia, parts of S. New Guinea
- Widespread, except for very dry areas
- Nonmigrant
- 10–12 in (26–30 cm)
- 2⅞ oz (80 g)
- Mud bowl lined with fine grass and feathers, built on branch
- 3–5 eggs; 1 brood
- Least Concern
- Solitary/pairs

Grallina cyanoleuca

MAGPIE-LARK

Also known as the mudlark, this black-and-white bird is a common sight throughout Australia, wherever it can find trees and mud to build a nest. A highly active ground-feeder, the magpie-lark eats worms, and insects and their larvae. It can be remarkably tame, and is as widespread in urban areas as it is in waterside woodlands and farms. Assertive and self-confident, it frequently scuffles with neighboring pairs, and is quick to chase off crows and larger predators. Despite its name, the magpie-lark is not related to larks or magpies. It belongs to the same family as the African paradise flycatcher (p.276).

Like many Australian birds, magpie-larks are sedentary, but also nomadic—during droughts, they may fly hundreds of miles in search of more suitable breeding grounds. They typically build a beautifully crafted bowl-shaped nest with grass and mud, which is attached to a branch. The females lay a clutch of 3–5 eggs, which hatch after about 19 days. Once the young have fledged, they frequently join large flocks to disperse.

PROFILE

- ⊙ Grasslands across Eurasia, N. Africa; northern populations migrate southward in winter
- ⋓ Mainly farmlands, but also occupies heaths, moors, meadows, and steppes, even forest clearings
- ⮌ Partial migrant

- ↔ 6 ½–7 ½ in (16–19 cm)
- ⚖ ⅞–1 ¾ oz (25–50 g)
- ▭ Deep cup nest in hollow, well concealed by grass
- ◔ 3–5 eggs; 2–3 broods
- ✖ Least Concern
- ✦ Flocks

Singing on the wing
The skylark has unremarkable plumage, but a powerful and melodious voice. It broadcasts its song on the wing as part of a territorial display.

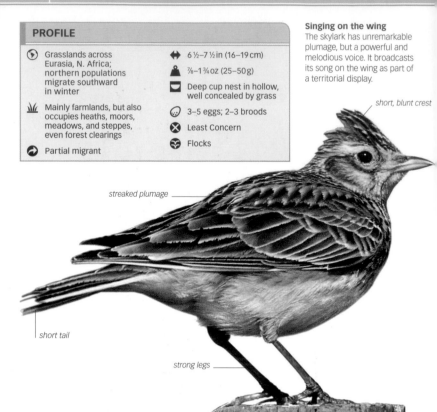

short, blunt crest

streaked plumage

short tail

strong legs

SIMILAR SPECIES

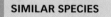
broad wings

Woodlark Smaller woodland species; sometimes singing at night

streaked plumage

Short-toed lark Small lark of dry places, found in southern Europe

Alauda arvensis

SKYLARK

Celebrated by poets over the centuries, skylarks are tireless singers, typically heard high over fields and grasslands, where they look like small, fluttering shapes framed by the open sky. Energetic and melodious, the skylark is primarily a bird of farmland and pasture, although changes in farming practices mean that this fine singer is no longer as common as it was.

The skylark's singing territorial display may go on for hours. From time to time, the bird descends in midsong, seeming to vanish into the grass. Within a few minutes, it often reappears, and the song begins again.

Like all members of the lark family, skylarks are ground dwellers, making a deep cup nest—well concealed by grass. Both parents help in taking care of the young. In former times, the skylark's breeding cycle was complete by the time fields were cut for hay, giving their young brood time to mature. However, modern farming methods cut grass much earlier, making it harder for this traditional farmland bird to thrive.

PROFILE

- Parts of India, China, S.E. Asia; introduced in USA, Australia
- Lightly wooded areas, scrub, farmland
- Nonmigrant
- 8 in (20 cm)
- 1 1/16 oz (30 g)
- Shallow, neat cup nest of twigs and dead leaves, with finer lining, bound with spiders' webs placed in tree
- 2–3 eggs; 2–3 broods
- Least Concern
- Flocks

Conspicuous crest
The tall, pointed crest of the red-whiskered bulbul Is permanently raised. The sexes have identical crests and plumage.

red patch behind eye

dark brown upperparts

white throat

pale brown underparts

SIMILAR SPECIES

pale brown underparts

Common bulbul Widepread species throughout Africa, north and south of the Sahara

orangish red bill

Black bulbul Lives in the forests of E. and S.E. Asia

Pycnonotus jocosus

RED-WHISKERED BULBUL

Introduced into parts of Australia and the USA, the red-whiskered bulbul originally comes from southern and Southeast Asia, where its natural range stretches from India to China and Vietnam. An active and vocal bird, it gets its name from its red facial patch, although its raised crest is just as much a distinguishing feature.

The red-whiskered bulbul lives in all kinds of open wooded habitats, including farms and gardens. It feeds mainly on insects, fruit, and buds, sometimes raiding orchard trees. Red-whiskered bulbuls make shallow, neat cup nests from twigs and dead leaves, using spiders' webs as a binding material. The female red-whiskered bulbul typically lays 2–3 eggs, which take about 12 days to hatch. Both parents take part in incubating and raising the young. Its song and vivacious nature make this species a popular caged bird, but it is not currently listed as threatened.

PROFILE

- North America, Eurasia; winters in S. Africa, South America, and S. Asia
- Open farmland and savanna, especially near water; also urban areas
- Migrant
- 7 in (18 cm)
- ½–⅞ oz (14–25 g)
- Mud bowl built on small support on wall or roof of building or cave
- 4–6 eggs; 2–3 broods
- Least Concern
- Migrant flocks

Sign of spring
These migrant songbirds often return to the place they bred the previous year. They utter a chuckling twitter when flying.

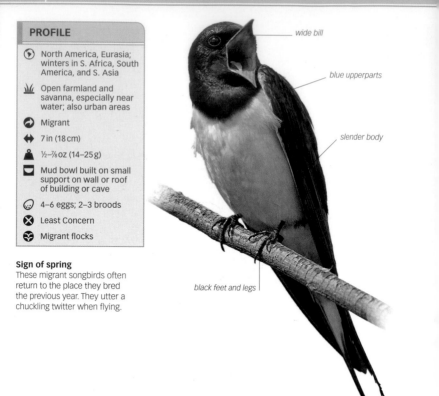

wide bill

blue upperparts

slender body

black feet and legs

forked tail

SIMILAR SPECIES

red facial markings

Welcome swallow
Smaller Australian species

streaked chest

Greater striped swallow
Long-tailed swallow; migratory within southern Africa

Hirundo rustica

BARN SWALLOW

A long-distance migrant, the barn swallow undertakes some of the longest journeys of any migrating songbird, sometimes reaching beyond the Arctic Circle. In many parts of the Northern Hemisphere, its arrival confirms the advent of spring.

Barn swallows are superbly streamlined, with a wide gape for catching insects in flight. Compared to swifts, they generally feed close to the ground, picking off insects flushed by grazing animals, or flying over pools. They nest in barns and other open-sided buildings, making cups of mud fastened to rafters or beams. Females lay 4–6 eggs, which are incubated for up to 16 days. Once the young are fully independent, they set off on the return journey to their winter home with the adults.

Juvenile barn swallow
The young bird has a shorter tail than the adult. It takes about six months to acquire adult plumage.

PROFILE

- E. and W. North America; winters in South America
- Open or semi-open areas, mostly near water
- Migrant
- 7 ½ in (19 cm)
- 1 ¾–2 ¼ oz (50–65 g)
- Tree hole lined with mud and grass; birdhouses
- 4–6 eggs; 1 brood
- Least Concern
- Large flocks/colonies

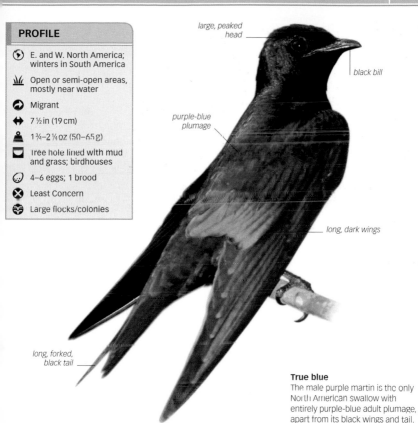

large, peaked head

black bill

purple-blue plumage

long, dark wings

long, forked, black tail

True blue
The male purple martin is the only North American swallow with entirely purple-blue adult plumage, apart from its black wings and tail.

SIMILAR SPECIES

grayish throat

Gray-breasted martin Found in Central and South America; paler underparts

blue back

Common house martin
Smaller migratory swallow; winters in Africa

Progne subis

PURPLE MARTIN

The largest swallow found in North America, the purple martin is originally from the west of the continent, where it nests in old woodpecker holes. However, its population is now firmly established in the east as well, due to custom-made birdhouses, where several dozen pairs may nest in separate compartments under the same roof. It migrates north each spring.

Like all swallows, purple martins are aerial insect-eaters. They feed on a variety of flying insects, relatively high in the sky compared to some swallows that hunt near the ground. Parent birds cooperate to make the nest, but the female incubates the clutch of eggs. The young swallows remain in the nest for about a month. They are fed by their parents, even after they start to fly.

Female purple martin
The female bird is similar in shape and size to the male, but is duller and has a gray underside.

PROFILE

- 🜚 North America, Eurasia; winters in South America, Africa, N. India, S.E. Asia

- 〰 Lowland habitats near water

- ◑ Migrant

- ↔ 4¾ in (12 cm)

- 🜛 ⅜–¹¹⁄₁₆ oz (11–20 g)

- ▭ Cup nest of plant matter lined with feathers in tunnel in bank or cliff

- ◔ 4–5 eggs; 2 broods

- ✖ Least Concern

- ⬡ Small flocks

Social swallow
The small, compact bank swallows typically feed, nest, and migrate in groups. They return to the same breeding sites year after year.

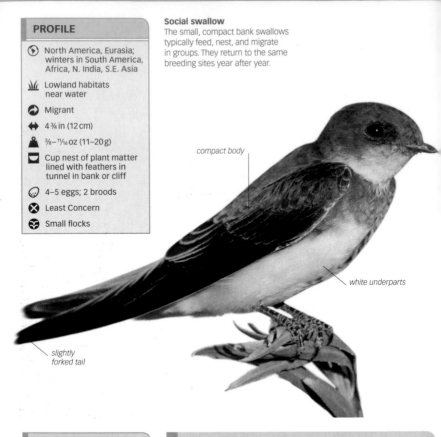

compact body

white underparts

slightly forked tail

SIMILAR SPECIES

white throat

Banded martin Large brown martin found in Africa south of the Sahara

brown upperparts

Crag martin Brown mountain swallow from Europe, Africa, and Asia

Riparia riparia

BANK SWALLOW

This small, light brown bird is one of the most widespread members of the swallow family, present on every inhabited continent except Australia. It is a summer visitor in the Northern Hemisphere, where it breeds in colonies, making nesting holes in sandy waterside banks. The bank swallow is one of the smallest swallows in North America, and in many other parts of its range. Its voice is a quiet twitter, usually made when on the wing. This bird feeds over water, scooping up insects flying close to the surface.

Bank swallows used to nest exclusively in natural sites, particularly along riverbanks. However, modern sand works and gravel pits provide them with extra nesting opportunities. The nesting tunnels—made by both parents—can be up to 3 ft (1 m) deep, and are lined with feathers. The female lays 4–5 eggs, and often raises two broods a year.

white stripe
over eye

mottled brown
plumage

stiff tail
for support

PROFILE

- Parts of W. Europe; E. Europe through central Asia to Japan

- Deciduous, coniferous, and mixed woodland that contains trees with loose, rough bark

- Partial migrant

- 5 in (13 cm)

- ⁵⁄₁₆ oz (9 g)

- Pocket-shaped nest of plant fibers, tucked behind loose bark, in split tree, or behind heavy growth of ivy

- 5–6 eggs; 1–2 broods

- Least Concern

- Mixed flocks

One-way journey
The Eurasian treecreeper has short legs, but its long, sharp toes give it a good grip as it climbs the tree. It only climbs upward, never downward.

SIMILAR SPECIES

downcurved
bill

long,
forked tail

Brown creeper
Partial migrant, and the only treecreeper in North America

Certhia familiaris

EURASIAN TREECREEPER

Among the most widespread members of the treecreeper family, which has fewer than 10 species, the Eurasian treecreeper is found as far eastward as Japan. Like its relatives, it is a small woodland bird with a thin, downcurved bill. Instead of foraging on twigs and branches, it spirals its way up tree trunks, picking out insects and spiders from crevices in the bark. It inspects the tree minutely as it makes its halting progress in search of animal food. Nearing the top of one tree, it makes a short flight to the base of a neighboring one, and begins the whole process again. Its mottled brown back merges well against tree trunks.

Like other treecreepers, the Eurasian treecreeper makes a pocketlike nest from plant fibers, tucked behind a piece of loose bark. The female lays 5–6 eggs, which hatch after about 15 days. It may raise a second brood in years when food is in good supply.

PROFILE

- 🌐 Australia
- 〰️ Open plains, grassland, and savanna with few trees, farmland
- ➤ Nonmigrant
- ↔ 7½–10in (19–25cm)
- ⚖ 1¹⁄₁₆–2⅝oz (30–75g)
- ▭ Simple hollow in ground, lined with grass
- ◔ 2–5 eggs; 1 brood
- ✖ Least Concern
- ❀ Pairs/small flocks

Size matters
The male brown songlark uses its superior size to set up breeding territories in open grassland. Large males are more attractive to females.

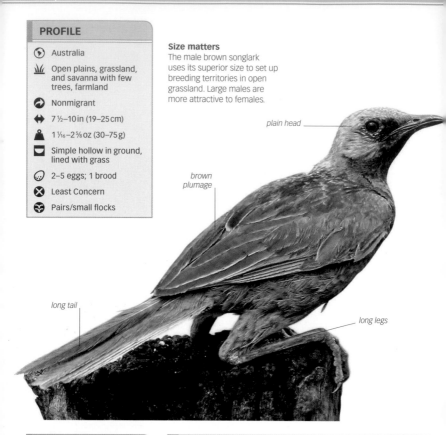

plain head

brown plumage

long tail

long legs

SIMILAR SPECIES

Little grassbird Smaller species found in wet habitats; streaked brown back

Spinifexbird Smaller species; rich brown cap and golden brown streaked wings

Cincloramphus cruralis

BROWN SONGLARK

Visually unremarkable, the brown songlark is a plain bird, with light brown plumage and very long, larklike legs. However, it is not a true lark, but a member of the Old World warbler family. While many warblers are migrants, the brown songlark is a typical Australian nomad, congregating wherever recent rains provide a good supply of food. It feeds mainly on insects and seeds collected from the ground. Found in open plains, grassland, and savanna with scattered trees, it is also a familiar bird in farmland, particularly during harvest time.

This species shows a huge difference in size that is exceptional in any songbird. Males can be over 50 percent heavier than females, and they use their size during the breeding season to set up territories, where they install a number of partners. Females build the nest, which is a simple hollow on the ground, and lay 2–5 eggs. They are largely responsible for raising the young.

PROFILE

- Europe, Asia; winters in Africa
- Wetland areas, mainly reedbeds
- Migrant
- 5 in (13 cm)
- ⅜–½ oz (10–15 g)
- Deep cup of grass slung from reed stems
- 3–5 eggs; 2 broods
- Least Concern
- Solitary

Hidden singer
Identifying a Eurasian reed warbler can be difficult: its inconspicuous plain, brown plumage and slender bill resemble that of many other warblers. The only sure diagnostic sign is its voice.

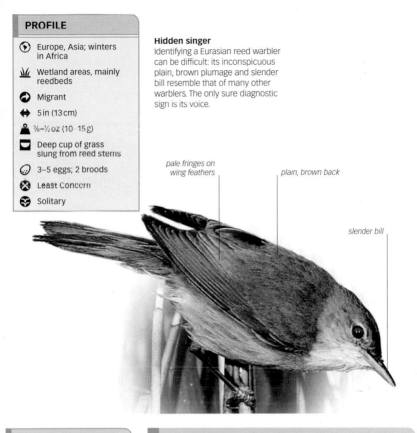

pale fringes on wing feathers

plain, brown back

slender bill

SIMILAR SPECIES

"eyebrow" stripe

Sedge warbler Breeds in Europe and C. Asia, in reedbeds and wetlands

cocked tail

Paddyfield warbler Breeds in tall grasses, reeds, and other concealing vegetation

Acrocephalus scirpaceus

EURASIAN REED WARBLER

Arriving in Europe and Asia each spring, this long-distance migrant is far more often heard than seen. True to its name, it breeds and feeds in dense reedbeds, rarely coming into view. Eurasian reed warblers call from among the reeds, making a wide variety of churring sounds and whistles, mixed in with mimicked songs of many other birds. Unlike most songbirds, they call while on the move, instead of singing from a perch. In common with almost all warblers, they feed on insects, and migrate south when cold weather reduces their food supply.

Eurasian reed warblers make exquisitely crafted nests that are just large enough to hold a clutch of five eggs. The young grow up rapidly, leaving the nest before they are two weeks old. However, this species is often parasitized by cuckoos (p.185)—when this happens, none of the original nestlings survive.

PROFILE

- Europe, C. Asia, Siberia, N. Africa; winters in Africa, south of the equator, India
- Wooded areas, but more open places outside breeding season
- Partial migrant
- 4 ¼ in (11 cm)
- ⁷⁄₃₂–⁵⁄₁₆ oz (6–9 g)
- Almost spherical nest of leaves, moss, stems, lined with feathers, on or near ground
- 5–6 eggs; 1–2 broods
- Least Concern
- Solitary

Significant song
The common chiffchaff resembles many other Old World warblers, but it can be told apart by its characteristi[c] song, often sung high up in trees.

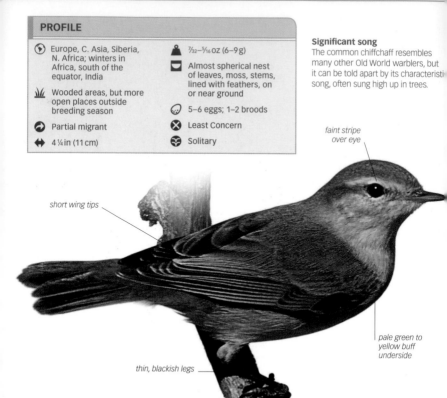

faint stripe over eye

short wing tips

pale green to yellow buff underside

thin, blackish legs

SIMILAR SPECIES

long wing tips

Wood warbler Lives in similar habitat but has a different song

olive-green back

pale yellow legs

Arctic warbler Breeds north of the Arctic Circle in Russia, Scandinavia, and Alaska, USA.

Phylloscopus collybita

COMMON CHIFFCHAFF

Small, unobtrusive, and tricky to spot, the common chiffchaff can be identified by its insistent *chip-chap-chip-chap* call. The first part of its scientific name literally means "leaf examiner," describing how it lives. It typically feeds on treetops as they come into leaf, restlessly searching for caterpillars and insect eggs, which make up most of its diet. Together, the chiffchaff and its warbler relatives eat huge quantities of this food, particularly in spring.

The common chiffchaff nests close to the ground, making an almost spherical nest of leaves and moss, lined with feathers. The average clutch size is 5–6 eggs, and the female sometimes raises two broods a year. The male plays almost no role in family life, leaving the female to incubate the eggs, and only occasionally providing food for the young. In many parts of Europe and Asia, the common chiffchaff is the first migrant bird to arrive in spring, after a journey that takes it across the Sahara from its winter quarters in Africa.

PROFILE

- ⊕ Japan, China, South Korea; winters in S.E. Asia
- ☖ Well-wooded areas, including gardens, parks, cultivated land
- ⟳ Partial migrant
- ↔ 4–4¾ in (10–12 cm)
- ⚖ ⅜ oz (11 g)
- ▭ Cup-shaped nest of spiders' webs, moss, lichen, animal hair
- ⬤ 2–4 eggs
- ✖ Least Concern
- ✿ Flocks

broad white ring around eye

yellow chin and throat

olive-green tail

White eye-ring
The most striking feature of the Japanese white-eye is its very obvious white eye-ring, which gives it its name.

SIMILAR SPECIES

white underparts

Cape white-eye Common throughout well-wooded habitats in southern Africa

olive-green plumage

Oriental white-eye One of the smallest white-eye species from southern Asia

Zosterops japonicus

JAPANESE WHITE-EYE

The Japanese white-eye belongs to a family of small songbirds that are remarkably similar in appearance, despite their very wide distribution. There are more than 90 species, and nearly all, including the Japanese white-eye, can be recognized by the characteristic white ring around their dark eyes.

Extending all the way from southern Africa and southern Asia to the Pacific and Japan, this species has a very large range that includes most of the Asian mainland. Although some birds are year-round residents, others migrate to Southeast Asia, returning in spring.

Japanese white-eyes are active, gregarious, and are often found in fast-moving flocks. They eat a range of foods, including insects and nectar, lapping it up with their brush-tipped tongues. Since nectar is a seasonal food in Japan, these birds eat seeds, fruits, and berries when the flowering season comes to an end. The clutch of 2–4 eggs takes about 12 days to hatch. The young birds leave the nest in as little as two weeks.

bright red eye

stout bill

iridescent plumage

dark blue wings

Hidden finery
Male Asian fairy-bluebirds are a stunning combination of dark and light blue, which catches the light with an iridescent sheen. They have bright red eyes.

Irena puella

ASIAN FAIRY-BLUEBIRD

With its stunning combination of dark and light blue plumage, the Asian fairy-bluebird is one of the most beautiful songbirds. It feeds on fruit, and nectar from tree blossoms, and like many fruit-eating birds, catches insects to feed its young. Because it spends a large part of its life in the forest canopy, its full splendor is rarely seen. With just two species, the fairy-bluebirds make up one of the smallest families of songbirds. The other species lives in the Philippines. Given its secretive habitats, relatively very little is known about its life cycle.

The female incubates the eggs for about 14 days and both parents feed the chicks. The young stay in the nest for about two weeks before they make their first independent forays for food.

Female fairy-bluebird
Turquoise or blue-green all over, the female also has bright red eyes.

PROFILE

- Europe, parts of N. Africa, C. Asia to Japan; northern populations winter in the south of this range
- Coniferous woodland, parks, gardens
- Partial migrant
- 3½ in (9 cm)
- ³/₁₆–¼ oz (5–7 g)
- Hammocklike nest of moss and grass, under a conifer bough
- 7–8 eggs; 2 broods
- Least Concern
- Solitary

Feature stripe
The male goldcrest has a distinctive orange-yellow crest, which is normally flat, but is raised during courtship and in displays to rivals.

orange-yellow crest

round body

SIMILAR SPECIES

bronze-yellow neck

Firecrest European species; white underparts and fiery orange crown stripe

yellow crown patch in female

Golden-crowned kinglet North American species, with orange crown patch in male

Regulus regulus

GOLDCREST

Found across a wide swathe of Europe and temperate Asia, the goldcrest is one of the smallest birds in many parts of its range. Adults weigh less than a sugar cube, yet they are amazingly robust and energetic. They are insect-eaters, living in coniferous forests and places with scattered trees. They are ceaselessly active, picking their food from bark crevices and even small twigs. As they feed, they give out high-pitched calls, which keep them in contact with their flock.

In spring, males often engage in courtship battles. Once paired, both partners collect moss and spiders' webs, and use them to make a cup-shaped nest suspended by handles to a branch. In a good year, they can raise two families, making a total of up to 16 young. The fledglings fly when three weeks old.

Female goldcrest
The female's crest is yellow, flanked by black stripes. Its markings are like the male's.

PROFILE

- North America
- Breeds in coniferous forest; in winter, also in deciduous and mixed woods, parks, and gardens
- Migrant
- 4¾ in (12 cm)
- ⅜ oz (10 g)
- Cavity in pine tree, with sticky pine resin applied to entrance
- 5–7 eggs; 1 brood
- Least Concern
- Solitary/pairs

Talented climber
Using its powerful claws, the red-breasted nuthatch can climb in any direction on tree trunks, even feeding upside down.

pointed bill

black eye-stripe

blue-gray upperparts

white cheek

short, grayish tail

rusty underparts

SIMILAR SPECIES

black eye-stripe

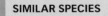

Eurasian nuthatch Most common nuthatch in Europe and Asia

blue-gray upperparts

Pygmy nuthatch Small, brown-headed species from western North America

Sitta canadensis

RED-BREASTED NUTHATCH

A typical nuthatch species, the red-breasted nuthatch is a short-tailed bird, with a large head and powerful climbing feet. There are about 25 species in the nuthatch family, and nearly all of them live in forests, although some climb rocks instead. The red-breasted nuthatch is a forest example. It feeds on seeds, on insects gleaned from bark crevices, and also hoards nuts. Using its bill like a hammer, it cracks open nuts. This hammering sound, together with its sharp call, is a sure sign that the nuthatch is overhead.

Nuthatches excavate nest holes; some European species plaster the entrance with mud. Red-breasted nuthatches nest in pine trees. Their eggs hatch after about 12 days.

Female nuthatch
The female bird is similar to the male, but has dull gray upperparts and paler underparts.

Crimson wings
The wallcreeper is mainly gray, with bright red wings. Its wing color is not obvious at long range, giving it excellent camouflage.

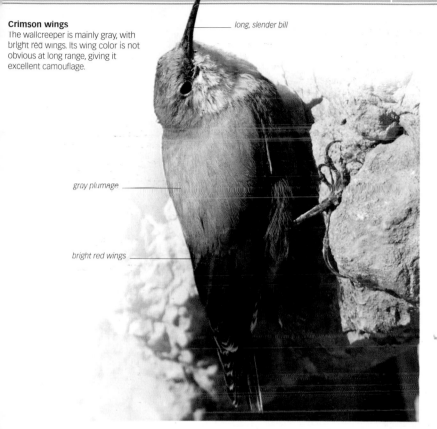

long, slender bill

gray plumage

bright red wings

PROFILE

- 🜨 Europe to E. Asia
- 🌿 Cliffs and rocky slopes in mountainous regions; winters in quarries, riverbeds, and towns
- ↻ Migrant
- ↔ 6½ in (16 cm)
- ⚖ ⅝ oz (18 g)
- ▱ Nest built with roots, grass, and moss, lined with wool and hair, placed in a rock crevice
- 🥚 4 eggs; 1 brood
- ✖ Least Concern
- ❖ Family groups

Tichodroma muraria

WALLCREEPER

An inhabitant of exposed cliffs from Europe to the Himalayas, the wallcreeper has evolved a way of life paralleled by few other birds. It scales sheer rock faces with its tenacious claws, climbing in short hops, and flicking with its wings. It flutters its wings as it moves, creating butterfly-like flashes of color as it probes rocks for insects. As well as being a skilled climber, the wallcreeper is perfectly equipped to get at its food: its bill is very long and slender—an ideal instrument for extracting prey from tiny cracks.

The young hatch after 19 days and leave the nest after about three weeks, already able to fly and to climb. Despite living in high mountains, wallcreepers do not migrate long distances, although they do move to lower altitudes during the winter months.

Winter plumage
In winter, the wallcreeper's gray chin and throat turn white, while the head becomes brownish.

PROFILE

- Europe, N. Africa, Asia
- Forest, woodland, parks, gardens, heaths
- Partial migrant
- 4 in (10 cm)
- $^{7}/_{32}$–$^{7}/_{16}$ oz (6–12 g)
- Untidy, domed nest lined with feathers, built in dense vegetation
- 4–6 eggs; 3–4 broods
- Least Concern
- Solitary/family groups

pale stripe above eye

thin, pointed bill

striped plumage on wings and tail

pale buff underside

thin, strong legs and feet

Conditional polygamist
The male Eurasian wren is pale brown above, with a long stripe over the eye. When food is plentiful the male helps raise young with several partners.

SIMILAR SPECIES

House wren Slightly larger than the Eurasian wren, with longer tail

pinkish legs and toes

Carolina wren Larger, with loud and tuneful song

Troglodytes troglodytes

EURASIAN WREN

There are nearly 80 species in the wren family, and this tiny bird with striped plumage on the wings and tail is the only one that lives across Eurasia. Feeding mainly on the ground, it scurries mouselike among plants, picking up small insects and worms. However, its behavior is very different when it sings: climbing to a high branch, it cocks its tail and spreads its wings, delivering a series of powerful musical trills that seem completely out of proportion for a bird of its size. Unlike many songbirds, it sings throughout the year, instead of just in spring.

Eurasian wrens live in habitats that give them thick cover when they feed. They build domed nests lined with feathers in dense vegetation and the female lays 4–6 eggs. The males may mate with several females, fathering 3–4 separate broods a year. Eurasian wrens are partial migrants, and in some regions, several dozen may crowd together in tree holes on cold winter nights to conserve vital body heat.

PROFILE

- Parts of S.W. USA, Mexico
- Desert, semi-desert with cacti
- Nonmigrant
- 7 in (18 cm)
- 1¼–1⁹⁄₁₆ oz (35–45 g)
- Spherical, large, untidy, in cactus or thorny bush
- 3–5 eggs; 1–2 broods
- Least concern
- Family groups

Home security
The cactus wren sometimes breeds in nest holes, but it more often nests in mature cactus plants. The sharp spines deter most potential predators.

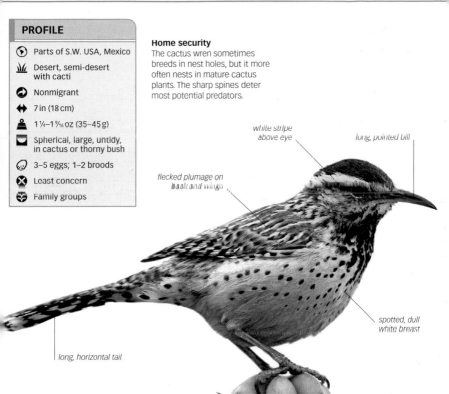

white stripe above eye

long, pointed bill

flecked plumage on back and wings

spotted, dull white breast

long, horizontal tail

SIMILAR SPECIES

buff tips on tail feathers

Rock wren Smaller species; found in North America's arid Southwest

Canyon wren North American species, commonly found in canyons and cliffs

Campylorhynchus brunneicapillus

CACTUS WREN

A comparative giant of the wren family, the cactus wren dwarfs many of the smaller species that live in North America. Measuring about 7 in (18 cm) long, it has a long, pointed bill and a pattern of intricate flecks on its back and wings. For a wren, its tail is unusually long and held horizontally, not cocked like many of its relatives. Cactus wrens live in the deserts and semi-deserts of southwestern USA and Mexico, where they feed on a variety of insects and other small animals. They catch their food on the ground, making short flights before returning to a perch, which is typically on a cactus. In the desert habitat, the well-protected cacti serve as lookout posts for this bird, and also as places to nest.

Cactus wren nests are large, untidy, and spherical, with an entrance at one side, leading into the inner chamber. This chamber is lined with feathers and grass. The female usually lays four eggs, and often raises two broods a year. Old nests are used for roosting, particularly in the winter.

Under cover
The gray catbird feeds in thickets and deep vegetation, making it difficult to spot. It makes migration flights after dark.

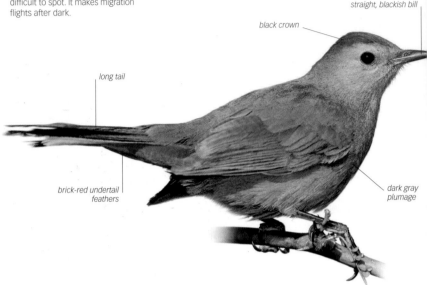

straight, blackish bill

black crown

long tail

brick-red undertail feathers

dark gray plumage

Dumetella carolinensis

GRAY CATBIRD

A common North American migrant, the gray catbird is named for its catlike, mewing call. Like its relative, the northern mockingbird (p.295), it is a gifted and versatile mimic. One of the smallest members of the mimic-thrush family, it is predominantly dark gray, with a long tail that is held at an upward tilt. A widespread species, it is found in a broad range of habitats, from woodlands to gardens and parks. However, its furtive habits make it less evident than many other birds.

Gray catbirds feed mainly on the ground, tossing aside dead leaves to reveal small animals underneath. They also peck on berries and seeds. These birds nest soon after their arrival on migration, with the female building a low, cup-shaped nest from twigs, lined with rootlets and placed in dense undergrowth. The average clutch size is four eggs, which hatch after an incubation period of about 13 days. Two broods are often raised before the return migration to Central America and the Caribbean.

PROFILE

- North America and most of Mexico; northern populations migrate south within this range in winter
- Low, scrubby, and open vegetation, including suburban gardens
- Partial migrant
- 10 in (26 cm)
- 1 ¾ oz (50 g)
- Cup nests in shrubs and trees
- 3–5 eggs; 1–3 broods
- Least Concern
- Pairs

Accomplished performer
Despite its dull appearance, the northern mockingbird is a very well-known bird. It sings all year round, most frequently in spring and summer.

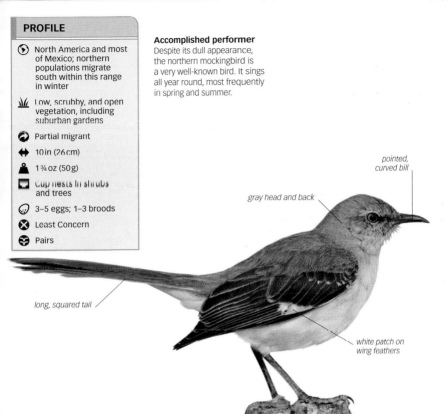

pointed, curved bill

gray head and back

long, squared tail

white patch on wing feathers

SIMILAR SPECIES

yellow eye

Tropical mockingbird
Year-round resident from Central and South America

Mimus polyglottos

NORTHERN MOCKINGBIRD

A versatile mimic, the northern mockingbird is one of North America's best-known birds. Its repertoire includes all kinds of natural and inanimate sounds, from the calls of other birds to barking dogs, ringing phones, and even slamming doors. A peculiarity of its mimicry is that it repeats each phrase several times. The northern mockingbird is undistinguished in looks, with drab plumage and a long, square-ended tail—typical of the mimic-thrush family.

Found in thickets, woodland edges, and suburbs, it feeds on the ground. The young are fed by both parents, and fledge about 13 days after hatching. Some birds migrate to southern parts of their range in winter.

Juvenile mockingbird
The juvenile has a speckled underside, whereas the adult's is plain pale gray. Its back is also lighter.

PROFILE

- Europe, N. Africa, Asia; introduced in North America, South Africa, Australia, New Zealand
- Damp grassland with scattered trees
- Migrant
- 8½–9½ in (21–22 cm)
- 2⅛–3⅛ oz (60–90 g)
- Cup-shaped grass nest in tree hole, among rocks, or inside building or nest-box
- 4–6 eggs; 1–2 broods
- Least Concern
- Flocks

Spotted mimic
Adult European starlings have dark, iridescent plumage, more heavily spotted in winter. Gifted mimics, these starlings copy many other birdsongs.

iridescent plumage

yellow bill

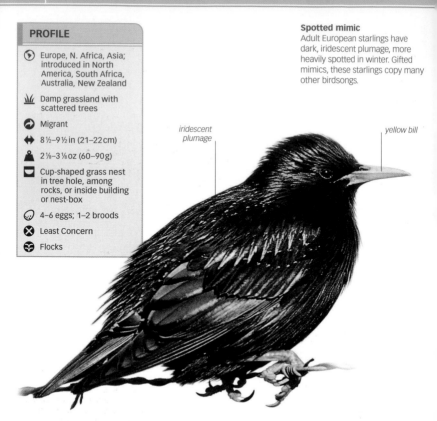

SIMILAR SPECIES

Spotless starling From Iberia and North Africa; summer plumage lacks spots

Sturnus vulgaris

EUROPEAN STARLING

In many parts of the world, the European starling is a highly successful and omnipresent bird. Originally from Europe, North Africa, and Asia, it has been introduced to North America, South Africa, Australia, and New Zealand, where it has been quick to establish itself as a breeding species. Its natural habitat is damp grassland with scattered trees, where it feeds on worms and small insects, but it is also a successful urban bird, roosting in parks on winter nights, and feeding on leftover food. In the wild, these birds are hole-nesters. However, they also nest in buildings and nest boxes. They sometimes drive out the native species when competing for nesting sites.

Out of the breeding season, starlings form immense aerobatic flocks—some contain over a million birds.

Juvenile starling
Initially mousy gray, the juvenile starling acquires its black spotted plumage in the first year.

PROFILE

- ⊙ Forest zone of W. and C. Africa
- 〰 Forest
- ⬳ Partial migrant
- ↔ 12 in (30 cm)
- ⚖ 4 oz (125 g)
- ▭ Tree hole lined with dry grasses, often high above ground
- ☺ 2–4 eggs; 1 brood
- ⊗ Least Concern
- ✿ Flocks

iridescent plumage

strong, curved bill

bronze neck patch

strong legs

long tail

Starling on show
The male splendid glossy starling looks blue-green from a distance, but a closer look reveals its rich palette of brilliant colors.

SIMILAR SPECIES

green wings

Superb starling Intensely colored N.E. African starling, with orange underside

blue-green plumage

Cape glossy starling Uniformly blue-green starling from S. and S.W. Africa

Lamprotornis splendidus

SPLENDID GLOSSY STARLING

A spectacular bird with iridescent plumage, the splendid glossy starling is among more than 50 species of starlings that are found in Africa. Medium-sized, it is mainly amethyst-blue above and deep bronze below, with conspicuous, pale yellow eyes. Its striking color makes it remarkably distinct from the European starling (p.296). Except for its flamboyant colors, the splendid glossy starling has very much a classic starling's body, with strong legs, a short tail, and a springlike bill that opens as powerfully as it closes.

The splendid glossy starling comes from the equatorial belt of central Africa, where it lives in rain forests, plantations, and gardens. Noisy and gregarious, it often roosts in large numbers at night. It is very fond of wild figs, and fruiting trees attract large numbers of feeding birds. The female lays about 2–4 eggs, which take about 13 days to hatch.

PROFILE

- Scattered areas in the Indian subcontinent, from the Himalayas east into S. China, S. India, and much of S.E. Asia
- Broadleaved evergreen and deciduous forest, usually below 2,000 ft (600 m)
- Nonmigrant
- 10½–12 in (27–31 cm)
- 7 oz (200 g)
- Cup nest placed deep in hole in a tall tree
- 2–4 eggs; 2–3 broods
- Least Concern
- Pairs/small flocks

Natural mimic
In captivity, hill mynas mimic all kinds of sounds, from musical instruments and machinery to human speech. Birds learn from an early age.

bright yellow wattle

orangish yellow bill

short tail

short, strong perching legs

SIMILAR SPECIES

yellow neck

Golden myna Spectacular yellow-and-black species from New Guinea

black hood

Common myna Urban starling from southern Asia; introduced in several other parts of the world

Gracula religiosa

HILL MYNA

An engaging, noisy caged bird, the hill myna has few rivals—apart from parrots—that can match its ability to mimic human speech, accounting for its widespread popularity. Curiously, it does not mimic other birds in the wild, although it has a huge repertoire of chattering and wheezing calls. Found mostly in trees, the hill myna has strong perching legs, a short tail, glossy black plumage, and a characteristic yellow wattle around the face and the nape of the neck, which makes this species easy to recognize. Juvenile birds lack the yellow wattle of their parents, and their plumage is initially brown. Hill mynas live in forests and plantations, from south India to Southeast Asia. They feed on fruit, berries, and insects, also visiting flowers to drink their nectar. In captivity, they are adept at mimicking a variety of sounds.

Hill mynas nest in tree cavities, lining them to form an untidy nest. Females lay 2–4 eggs, which take up to 17 days to hatch. Young birds leave the nest at the age of about one month.

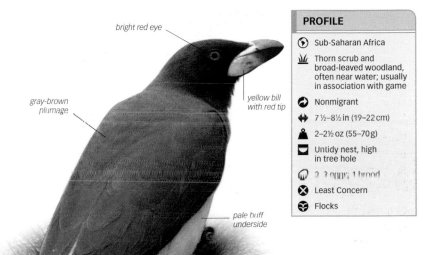

bright red eye

gray-brown
plumage

yellow bill
with red tip

pale buff
underside

Striking bill
The yellow-billed oxpecker is recognized by its striking yellow bill, with a flame-red tip. It has bright red eyes.

Buphagus africanus

YELLOW-BILLED OXPECKER

Named after its distinctive bill, the yellow-billed oxpecker is found only in sub-Saharan Africa. It has evolved an unusual way of life, rarely feeding on the ground and instead scaling the backs of large animals such as buffalo, cattle, and giraffes. It has shorter legs than typical starlings (p.296), and its bill is compressed sideways, helping it lever tenacious ticks and other external parasites from its hosts' skin. It can feed on hundreds of these in a day.

Most host mammals willingly tolerate these avian guests, but the relationship is not as simple as it seems. For oxpeckers, large animals provide a vantage point and a place to roost. They alert these animals to signs of danger, but they also feed on blood and their sharp bills keep wounds open when they feed. However, oxpeckers behave more like typical starlings during breeding. Their chicks leave the nest after about four weeks.

SIMILAR SPECIES

Red-billed oxpecker
Found in eastern and southern Africa; striking red bill

small, black bill

olive-brown wings

squared tail

High alert
The male European robin is very aggressive toward rivals. It uses its orange-red breast in threat display when defending its territory.

SIMILAR SPECIES

round head

Japanese robin Prized songbird from the Far East

Erithacus rubecula

EUROPEAN ROBIN

With its approachable manner and attractive orange-red breast, the European robin is a firm favorite with birdwatchers—including those who have never seen this little bird in real life. The European robin has lent its name to over a dozen other red-breasted birds, many of whom are unrelated to the true robin, which belongs to the chat and flycatcher family.

This bird feeds on insects such as beetles, ants, and other small animals, arriving as soon as the soil is turned over by the spade. Although male and female European robins seem identical, males are territorial and very aggressive, attacking anything that resembles a rival male's orange-red breast. In a good year, the female can raise up to three broods.

Juvenile robin
The juvenile robin has a speckled, brown body. It lacks the orange-red breast of the adult.

PROFILE

- Europe, Africa, Asia
- Open, often barren habitats, such as heathland
- Partial migrant
- 5 in (13 cm)
- ⅜–½ oz (11–15 g)
- Loose cup nest of plant materials, lined and tucked into vegetation on or near ground
- 5–6 eggs; 2 broods
- Least Concern
- Family groups

Courtship colors
In its breeding plumage, the male stonechat has a black head and back, with a white collar, chestnut breast, and white patches on the wings.

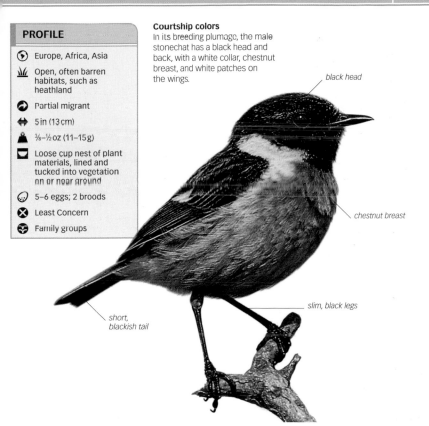

black head

chestnut breast

slim, black legs

short, blackish tail

SIMILAR SPECIES

dark cap

Whinchat Migratory, ground-nesting chat, which arrives in Europe from Africa

white underside

Pied bushchat Dark-colored chat found in Southeast Asia

Saxicola torquatus

STONECHAT

Stonechats are readily identified by their call, and by their habit of sitting bolt upright on a perch, watching for insects, spiders, and worms. At intervals, the males produce a *weet-chak-chak* call, which sounds like two small pebbles being knocked together and makes this species easy to locate.

Stonechats live in a wide variety of habitats, but grassland and heaths are among their favorites, followed by coastal scrub. Females build the nest and incubate the eggs for 14 days. However, both parents feed the nestlings. The young are fed for about 13 days, after which they begin flying and soon leave the nest.

Female stonechat
When breeding, the female is streaky brown above, and lacks the black head and white collar of the male.

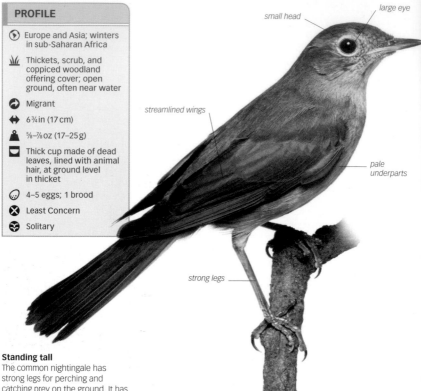

small head

large eye

streamlined wings

pale
underparts

strong legs

PROFILE

- Europe and Asia; winters in sub-Saharan Africa
- Thickets, scrub, and coppiced woodland offering cover; open ground, often near water
- Migrant
- 6¾ in (17 cm)
- ⅝–⅞ oz (17–25 g)
- Thick cup made of dead leaves, lined with animal hair, at ground level in thicket
- 4–5 eggs; 1 brood
- Least Concern
- Solitary

Standing tall
The common nightingale has strong legs for perching and catching prey on the ground. It has a brown back and a reddish tail.

SIMILAR SPECIES

Thrush nightingale
Lacks reddish tail patches

blue
bib

Bluethroat
Robinlike bird, breeding far north

Luscinia megarhynchos

COMMON NIGHTINGALE

Legendary for its melodious song, the nightingale is heard far more often than it is seen. The reason lies in its habitat: instead of living in open woodland, it breeds in low thickets and scrub, where its subdued colors make perfect camouflage. It often calls by night, but it is just as vocal by day in early spring. This bird feeds mainly on the ground, eating insects, and also fruit before its fall migration.

Nightingale nests are well hidden, and built on or near the ground. The female lays 4–5 eggs, which it incubates for about 14 days. The young leave the nest at the age of about two weeks, flying south when fully fledged.

Juvenile nightingale
Young birds have speckled upperparts and breasts, and brown tails. Unlike the adults, they do not sing.

Taking the plunge
The white-throated dipper can be seen flying over water, or bobbing up and down on waterside rocks, before plunging in and disappearing out of sight.

waterproof feathers

long legs

PROFILE

- Mainly mountainous, hilly regions of Eurasia, N.W. Africa
- Rivers and streams in or near woodland or forest, from sealevel to high mountain areas
- Partial migrant
- 7 ½–8 ½ in (19–21 cm)
- 2–2 ¼ oz (55–65 g)
- Large and spherical with side entrance, built over running water with moss, grass, and leaves
- 4–6 eggs; 2 broods
- Least Concern
- Solitary

SIMILAR SPECIES

gray plumage

American dipper Stocky, with dark gray plumage

powerful wings

Brown dipper Largest of dippers, found in rivers in Central Asia

Cinclus cinclus

WHITE-THROATED DIPPER

Many songbirds live near freshwater, but dippers are the only ones that feed while fully submerged. The white-throated dipper lives by clear, fast-flowing rivers and streams. Like its relatives, it eats insects and small fish, partly walking and partly swimming underwater, and using the current to counteract its buoyancy. Its nostrils close when it is submerged, although its eyes remain open, and it has well-oiled, water-repellant feathers that dry within minutes of returning to the surface.

The white-throated dipper nests in rocky crevices close to water. The young leave the nest when they are about three weeks old.

Juvenile dipper
The juvenile has gray upperparts, and lacks the distinct white throat seen in the adult.

Gifted singer
A melodious bird, the song thrush sings a sharp, full-throated call, which is marvelously vibrant and instantly identifiable.

pale eye-ring

pale feather tips

V-shaped, brown-black spots on underside

buff underparts, browner on flanks, white on belly

pinkish legs

PROFILE

- ⊙ Europe, N. Africa, Middle East, C. Asia; introduced in Australia, New Zealand
- 🌾 Woods, hedgerows, thickets, parks, gardens
- ◐ Partial migrant
- ↔ 8–9 ½ in (20–24 cm)
- ⚖ 2 ¼ oz (65 g)
- ▭ Cup made of plant material, lined with mud, wood pulp, or clay, in tree or bush
- ◔ 3–5 eggs; 3 broods
- ✖ Least Concern
- ❀ Family groups

SIMILAR SPECIES

distinctive pattern on wing

Mistle thrush Largest European thrush; feeds mostly on worms, insects, and berries

long, black tail

Fieldfare Common winter visitor to southern Europe, often in vocal flocks

Turdus philomelos

SONG THRUSH

Named for its celebrated song, the song thrush is a typical ground-feeding member of the thrush family, with an omnivorous appetite. In its case, the early bird does catch the worm, because earthworms are often found near the surface on damp summer mornings, making it easier for the song thrush to catch them. Although it feeds mostly on worms and snails, this bird also eats insects, and fruit in fall. Song thrushes cannot extract snails from their shells, and instead smash them open on an "anvil stone," which becomes littered with broken shells—a remarkable technique used by few other birds.

Both male and female song thrushes are similar in appearance, with mid-brown backs and spotted underparts. The female takes sole charge of making the nest. It lays a clutch of 3–5 eggs, and often produces three broods a year. Found in Europe, Africa, the Middle East, and Asia, these birds have been introduced in Australia and New Zealand.

PROFILE

- Europe, parts of N. Africa, Asia; introduced in Australia, New Zealand
- Deciduous woodland, scrub, parks, gardens
- Partial migrant
- 9½–11½in (24–29cm)
- 4oz (125g)
- Cup-shaped nest of moss and leaves, lined with grass and mud
- 3–5 eggs; 2–3 broods
- Least Concern
- Family groups

Ground feeder
The Eurasian blackbird is a medium-sized, ground-feeding thrush. It has strong legs, rounded wings, and a bright, orange-yellow bill.

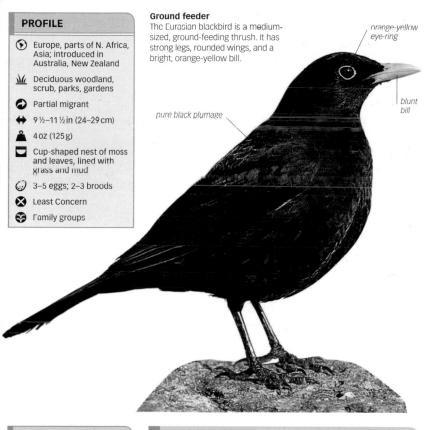

orange-yellow eye-ring

blunt bill

pure black plumage

SIMILAR SPECIES

pale black plumage

Ring ouzel Blackbirdlike thrush of European moorland, with a white chest band

Turdus merula

EURASIAN BLACKBIRD

Originally a bird of deciduous woodland, the Eurasian blackbird has been highly successful at coping with man-made changes to its habitat, and is now as common in city parks and gardens as it is in the wild. Its natural range spans much of Europe and southern Asia, but after successful introductions in the 19th century, it is also commonly seen in Australia and New Zealand, where it is prized for its musical song.

Blackbirds feed mainly on the ground, noisily throwing aside dead leaves to find earthworms and insects hidden underneath. In autumn, they feed on fallen fruit, particularly apples. The female lays eggs and the chicks leave the nest when they are about two weeks old. The young birds are speckled once they have left the nest.

Female blackbird
The female Eurasian blackbird has dark brown plumage, without the male's brightly contrasting bill.

PROFILE

- ⊙ E. North and Central America; winters as far south as Nicaragua

- 🌿 Open woodland, including orchard, plain, pasture, pine forest, and swampy ground

- ⟳ Partial migrant

- ↔ 6¾–8½ in (17–21 cm)

- ⚖ ⅞–1 ¹⁄₁₆ oz (25–30 g)

- ✉ Simple cup nest with fine lining, placed in tree-hole or nest-box

- ◔ 3–7 eggs; 2 broods

- ✖ Least Concern

- ⧟ Pairs/flocks

Return trip
The male eastern bluebird has bright blue upperparts. Eastern bluebirds are partial migrants that move northward from the southern USA each spring.

vibrant blue body

white underparts

long tail

SIMILAR SPECIES

brown patch on back

Western bluebird Partial migrant from western North America

sky-blue body

Mountain bluebird Found mainly on high ground in western North America

Sialia sialis

EASTERN BLUEBIRD

A familiar bird across much of eastern USA, this small thrush is found in farmland and open woodland, where it eats insects and fruit. Like other bluebirds, it feeds mainly from upright perches, making short sorties to the ground. Females are relatively inconspicuous, but adult males are a vibrant sky-blue, set off by pinkish red throats and breasts. Juveniles are speckled—a feature that is common in thrushes as a whole.

Eastern bluebirds are found in pairs during the breeding season. They often form flocks once the young have fledged, feeding on berries and other winter fruit. They are hole-nesters, and frequently have to compete for space with starlings and house sparrows. Eastern bluebirds were in decline, but the provision of nest boxes has helped them stage a comeback.

Female eastern bluebird
The female is grayer than the male, with pale eye-rings and less intense blue on the wings and back.

Call sign
The American robin is easily recognized by its red breast. Like many thrushes, it is a gifted singer, with a well-known, fluid song.

white ring around eye

gray-brown upperparts

red breast

long tail

PROFILE

- North America, Mexico, Guatemala
- Forest, wooded swamp, farmland, parks, urban and suburban gardens
- Partial migrant
- 10–11 in (25–28 cm)
- 2 ⅝ oz (75 g)
- Bulky nest made of twigs, grass, and mud, in a wide variety of situations at any height from ground level to treetops
- 4 eggs; 2–3 broods
- Least Concern
- Flocks

Turdus migratorius

AMERICAN ROBIN

Despite its name, the American robin is a thrush, although it shares the European robin's red breast (p.300). It has strong legs and a yellow bill, and feeds largely on the ground. It forages for earthworms among fallen leaves, and eats fruit in winter, often gathering in large roosts. Native to forests, it has adapted successfully to the growth of towns, and is now a common suburban bird.

American robins are partial migrants that spread across most of the continent as temperatures warm up each spring. They make large nests of twigs, at any height from ground level to treetops. The female incubates the eggs for about 14 days, and the young fledge in about the same length of time. American robins normally raise 2–3 broods a year.

Juvenile American robin
The young American robin has heavily speckled underparts, and scalloped coloration on its back.

black plumage

rusty brown breast

PROFILE

- ⊙ E. to S. Africa
- 〰 Savanna grassland
- ↻ Nonmigrant
- ↔ 14 in (36 cm)
- ⚖ ¹¹/₁₆ oz (20 g)
- ▭ Nest parasite, lays eggs in the nest of pytilias
- ◯ 3–4 eggs
- ✕ Least Concern
- ❂ Pairs/small flocks

Giant tail
The breeding male eastern paradise whydah has an enormously developed tail. Outside of the breeding season it loses this special plumage, and resembles the female.

long tail feathers

SIMILAR SPECIES

black breast band

Pin-tailed whydah
Bright red bill and black breast band

red bill

narrow tail feathers

Shaft-tailed whydah Golden buff breast and red legs

Vidua paradisaea

EASTERN PARADISE WHYDAH

Whydahs are remarkable songbirds that live in the savanna grasslands of Africa, forming flocks at certain times of the year. The eastern paradise whydah is one of the most widespread. The breeding male has black plumage and an enormously developed tail, almost three times the length of its body. Once the breeding season is over, the male whydah molts its special plumage, and becomes more like the female until the next breeding season begins. The sparrowlike female is about 4¾ in (12 cm) long with streaky brown plumage and a short tail.

The male whydah shows off its tail in display flights, where rival males compete for a chance to mate. Having mated, the female behaves like a cuckoo and does not make its own nest, but instead lays eggs in the nest of finches called pytilias, which raise the whydahs' young.

PROFILE

- Parts of Indonesia, most of Australia
- Open grassland, scrub near water
- Nonmigrant
- 4 in (10 cm)
- 7⁄16 oz (12 g)
- Dome of grass and twigs with side entrance, placed in tree or hollow branch
- 4–5 eggs
- Least Concern
- Large flocks

Feeding on seeds
The zebra finch has a short, conical bill for cracking open small seeds. It also feeds on insects and forages on the ground.

orange cheek patch

striped throat and breast

SIMILAR SPECIES

red face

Painted finch Prominent red face, glowing red rump

pale olive-brown wings

Star finch Pale olive-brown wings, spotted face and breast

Taeniopygia guttata

ZEBRA FINCH

With its lively behavior and colorful markings, the Australian zebra finch is popular as a caged bird, and also common in the wild. Found across most of Australia, and also in parts of Indonesia, it lives in open grassland and scrub near water, feeding on a diet of seeds, and foraging on the ground. The male zebra finch has orange cheek patches, a striped throat, and spotted flanks.

The zebra finch keeps in contact with loud, nasal calls, which sound like miniature trumpets being blown. The male uses these calls to attract a mate, with breeding taking place during most months of the year. The female lays 4–5 eggs in the breeding season. The chicks are ready to leave the nest by the time they are about four weeks old. A social bird, this species often forms large flocks.

Female zebra finch
The female is plainer than the male, with gray cheeks and flanks, and a uniformly gray throat and breast.

PROFILE

- Java, Bali; introduced in the tropics worldwide
- Lowland, grassland, and open woods; farmland
- Nonmigrant
- 6¾ in (17 cm)
- ⅞ oz (25 g)
- Bell-shaped nest made of grass; in tree tops or under eaves of buildings
- 3–4 eggs; 1 brood
- Vulnerable
- Flocks

white cheek

stout, pink bill

pinkish underparts

gray wings

Rice-eater
The Java sparrow uses its stout, pink bill to crack open the husk of rice and other grains—a habit that has led to it being persecuted as an agricultural pest.

SIMILAR SPECIES

Yellow-rumped munia
Related species with a dull crown; found in N. Australia

chestnut breast

Chestnut-breasted munia
Brown-colored species with white underparts; found in N. and E. Australia

Padda oryzivora

JAVA SPARROW

Originally from the islands of Java and Bali, this thickset and handsome finch is a popular caged bird, established in numerous regions outside its native range. The wild Java sparrow is always pearly gray and white, with a heavy, pink bill, but domestic varieties can have different hues, ranging from fawn to cream. The sexes look identical. Found in grasslands and farmlands, this bird feeds on seeds, including rice and grains. Java sparrows often feed and roost in flocks, dispersing during the breeding season as pairs prepare to raise their young.

Their bell-shaped nest is constructed in treetops. The female usually lays a clutch of 3–4 eggs, and both parents incubate them. The eggs hatch after about 18 days. The young leave the nest when they are about one month old.

Juvenile sparrows
Young Java sparrows are gray, with dull-colored bills. They mature after about six months.

red face

Rainbow colors
The male Gouldian finch has a range of facial colors but the same body markings. The female is duller, yet boldly colored when compared with many other birds.

black chin

green wings

purple and yellow underparts

PROFILE

- N. Australia
- Grassy plains with trees, savanna woodland, scrubland with spinifex grass
- Partial migrant
- 5 in (13 cm)
- ½ oz (14 g)
- Tree holes and disused termite mounds
- 4–6 eggs; 2 broods
- Endangered
- Mixed flocks

Erythrura gouldiae

GOULDIAN FINCH

Despite its small size, the increasingly rare Gouldian finch has a richness of color that few other birds can match. There are three color variants—black-headed, red-headed, and golden-headed, which is much scarcer in the wild. In all variants, the male has a sumptuous purple-and-yellow underside, while its back and wings are green. Gouldian finches feed on grass seeds, gathering at waterholes during the dry season, and nesting in tree holes and disused termite mounds.

For several decades, this species has been in a sharp decline. The reasons for this include its trapping as a caged bird, deliberate burning of its habitat, and competition from cattle, which eat the grasses on which Gouldian finches depend.

Gouldian variant
The black-headed variant makes up most of Australia's Gouldian finch population.

PROFILE

- ⊙ Originally Eurasia, N. Africa, Middle East; introduced in many other countries
- 🌾 Wide variety of habitats, tolerates extremes of climate and altitude
- ↪ Nonmigrant
- ↔ 6 in (15 cm)
- ⚖ 1 ¹⁄₁₆ oz (30 g)
- ⬒ Untidy nest of grass and leaves, often on buildings
- 🥚 3–7 eggs; 1–4 broods
- ✖ Least Concern
- ✿ Flocks

Household sparrow
One of the world's most familiar birds, the house sparrow is largely brown. The male is more colorful than the female, with a gray head and a black bib.

gray crown

brown nape

black-brown streaks on upperparts

gray underside

short tail

SIMILAR SPECIES

brown cap

Eurasian tree sparrow
Slightly smaller; males and females look alike

longer wings

Rock sparrow Found in rocky hills and mountains in Europe, northern Africa, and Asia

Passer domesticus

HOUSE SPARROW

A widespread species, the house sparrow is present on every continent except Antarctica. This extraordinary range is due to its adaptability and talent for living in cities and in towns. The house sparrow is remarkably good at life in built-up areas, finding its way into all kinds of manmade habitats, from supermarkets to coal mines. Originally a seed-eater, it can also feed on a huge range of foods, from kitchen scraps to farmland crops.

House sparrows usually nest in cavities. At just 10 days, they have one of the shortest incubation periods of any bird, and can produce up to four broods each season. With figures like these, house sparrows can quickly build up huge numbers, although they are also vulnerable to habitat change, which can trigger rapid declines.

Female house sparrow
The female's mid-brown back, wings, and lighter underparts stay the same color all year round.

PROFILE

- ⊙ Sub-Saharan Africa
- ☇ Semi-arid zones; wet and dry habitats on rare occasions
- ➍ Partial migrant
- ↔ 4¾ in (12 cm)
- ⚖ ½–1 ¹⁄₁₆ oz (15–30 g)
- ▭ Ball-shaped, woven grass nest, with entrance on upperside
- ◔ 2–4 eggs, 1 brood
- ✖ Least Concern
- ✿ Large flocks

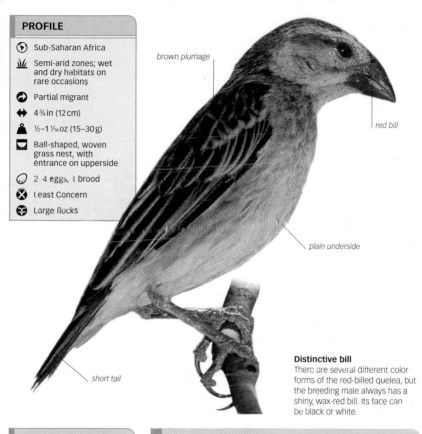

brown plumage

red bill

plain underside

short tail

Distinctive bill
There are several different color forms of the red-billed quelea, but the breeding male always has a shiny, wax-red bill. Its face can be black or white.

SIMILAR SPECIES

Red-headed quelea Found in the grasslands of East Africa

Quelea quelea

RED-BILLED QUELEA

Found in vast numbers in Africa, red-billed queleas are often seen flying in huge, synchronized flocks that can be several million strong. They roll across the ground like immense twittering clouds, settling wherever there are seeds or grain. These nomadic swarms sometimes invade farmland, where they can have disastrous effects.

Red-billed queleas belong to the weaverbird family, and like most of their relatives, they are skilled builders of woven grass nests. Males lay the foundations of the nest, while females help complete the structure. The eggs are incubated for about 12 days, and the young birds are fledged when they are just over two weeks old.

Female quelea
Unlike the male, the female is undistinguished and sparrowlike. Its bill may be yellow during breeding.

PROFILE

- Much of sub-Saharan Africa, except in desert areas
- Open woodland and forest edges; parks and gardens
- Nonmigrant
- 6¾ in (17 cm)
- 1 1/16–1 9/16 oz (30–45 g)
- Oval nest of reeds, sedges, and grasses with vertical entrance tube hanging below
- 2–5 eggs; 1 brood
- Least Concern
- Large flocks/colonies

Master builder
The village weaver tears grasses and sedges into strips, using them to weave domed nests. Its bright yellow plumage helps attract breeding females.

bright yellow plumage

compact body

streaked wings

SIMILAR SPECIES

conical bill

Cape weaver One of the southernmost weavers; builds kidney-shaped nests

black face

Southern masked weaver Wings streaked with black or green; males have black faces

Ploceus cucullatus

VILLAGE WEAVER

There are over 100 species of weaverbirds, most from the grasslands and forests of Africa, where they feed on insects and seeds. Some are restricted to small areas, but the village weaver is an abundant and widespread species. Like most other weaverbirds, the male village weaver has conspicuous breeding plumage. Females are drab, but breeding males have black faces or heads, and bright yellow bodies. Outside the breeding season, the sexes are more similar.

In the breeding season, the male village weaver builds the nest. If the female is impressed by the male's expertise, it moves in, mates, and lays the eggs. If a nest fails to attract a female, the male eventually abandons it and starts again, fluttering beneath the new nest to draw attention to its work.

Female village weaver
The female bird has a greenish yellow breast, a pale underside, and greenish gray wings.

PROFILE

- Mountainous areas of N.W. Africa, S. Europe, parts of Asia
- Mountain areas without much vegetation
- Partial migrant
- 6–6¾ in (15–17 cm)
- ⅞ oz (25 g)
- Cup nest of grass, roots, mosses, and lichens, in rock crevice
- 3–5 eggs; 2 broods
- Least Concern
- Family groups

True mountainbird
The Alpine accentor survives the harsh mountain climate by feeding and nesting on the ground, using rocks as cover from cold winds.

gray head

streaked back

red-brown streaks on flanks

dark tail

SIMILAR SPECIES

gray neck patch

Dunnock Only lowland species of accentor; also known as the hedge sparrow

Prunella collaris

ALPINE ACCENTOR

This small and unobtrusive bird is typical of the accentor family—a group of about a dozen species of small, streaky-brown birds that are easily mistaken for sparrows. Found across Europe and Asia, the Alpine accentor often lives in hills and mountains, where it finds food by hopping across the ground. This bird ranges from the Iberian peninsula in the west to Japan in the east.

The Alpine accentor is a true mountain bird, often reaching altitudes of over 8,200 ft (2,500 m). On Mt. Everest, it has even been spotted at 26,250 ft (8,000 m), which is close to a record for any songbird. Flitting among rocks and boulders, the accentor feeds mainly on small insects and spiders, although it also pecks at scraps and seeds. The Alpine accentor breeds on the ground, making cup-shaped nests in rocky crevices, using grass lined with moss and hair. The female usually lays 3–5 eggs, and often raises two broods a year. Unusual among songbirds, males have overlapping territories, and each male may have several partners in a year.

PROFILE

- Europe, Africa, Asia; some populations migrate south
- Fast-flowing upland water courses; slow and still water habitat in winter
- Partial migrant
- 6¾–8 in (17–20 cm)
- ½–¹¹⁄₁₆ oz (14–20 g)
- Cup of moss and leaves, placed in hole or ledge near running water
- 4–6 eggs; 2 broods
- Least Concern
- Family groups

Breeding colors
The gray wagtail has lemon-yellow underparts. The breeding male can be identified by its black throat—a feature that is lost in winter.

white stripe over eye

gray back

SIMILAR SPECIES

olive upperparts

Yellow wagtail Widespread migratory species of pastures, breeding mainly in Eurasia

white underparts

White wagtail Common as an urban bird; breeds across Europe and Asia

Motacilla cinerea

GRAY WAGTAIL

With its long, bobbing tail and contrasting plumage, the gray wagtail is a slim and attractive bird of riversides, lakes, and streams. It breeds in much of Europe and northern Asia, either as a year-round resident, or a summer visitor from farther south.

Instead of swimming to catch food, the wagtail flutters over rocks and boulders, deftly snapping up insects and larvae from damp ground or the water's edge. It walks or runs instead of hopping, and continuously bobs its tail, even when standing still. The wagtail makes nests in crevices, cliffs, and rocks, or sometimes under bridges. The female lays 4–6 eggs. Once the breeding season is over, migratory birds make their way to slow-flowing and still water, where they spend the winter months.

Female gray wagtail
The female has a white or speckled throat. Like the male, it has strong legs and claws.

iridescent head

tubelike downcurved bill

scarlet breast

black plumage

PROFILE

- Parts of sub-Saharan Africa
- Savanna, open land, sometimes farmland
- Nonmigrant
- 5 ½ in (14 cm)
- ⁷⁄₁₆ oz (12 g)
- Purse-shaped, hanging nest made from lichens and spiders' webs, slung from thin twig, often near wasp's nest
- 2–3 eggs
- Least Concern
- Flocks

Iridescent colors The male scarlet-chested sunbird is intensely iridescent. From some angles, its chest looks a vivid red; from others, almost black. It keeps these markings all year round.

SIMILAR SPECIES

longer bill

Malachite sunbird Metallic green, long-tailed mountain species found in Africa

Nectarinia senegalensis

SCARLET-CHESTED SUNBIRD

Small and beautifully iridescent, the scarlet-chested sunbird shares a similar way of life to hummingbirds (p.208), but comes from a very different part of the world. One of Africa's largest sunbirds, it gets its name from the male's coloration, which is almost black, apart from an intense scarlet breast and a greenish crown.

This bird feeds on insects and nectar, often gathering in small flocks on shrubs and flowering trees, making it a common sight in gardens and farms from Western Africa to Mozambique. The sunbird's nest has a porch and an entrance at one side. The nest holds 2–3 eggs that hatch after 15 days.

Female sunbird Brown overall, the female is much drabber than the male. It lacks the male's vivid scarlet chest.

PROFILE

- From Persian Gulf to India and S.E. Asia
- Dry, deciduous forest and woodland, scrub, and gardens
- Nonmigrant
- 2¾–3½in (7–9cm)
- ⁵⁄₁₆oz (9g)
- Hanging, pear-shaped nest, using spiders' webs to weave together building materials
- 2–3 eggs; 1 brood
- Least Concern
- Solitary/pairs/flocks

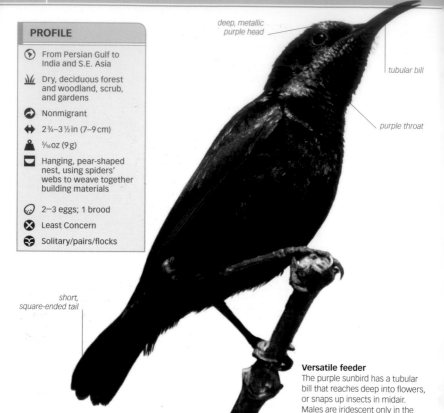

deep, metallic
purple head

tubular bill

purple throat

short,
square-ended tail

Versatile feeder
The purple sunbird has a tubular bill that reaches deep into flowers, or snaps up insects in midair. Males are iridescent only in the breeding season.

SIMILAR SPECIES

olive
upperparts

Olive-backed sunbird
Metallic blue throat and breast; yellow underparts

red upperparts

Mrs. Gould's sunbird
Colorful, long-tailed species from the forests of S.E. Asia

Cinnyris asiaticus

PURPLE SUNBIRD

This small and slender sunbird, with a range stretching from the Persian Gulf to Vietnam, is one of the most widespread species in southern Asia. Foraging alone or in pairs, the purple sunbird feeds on nectar and fruit, but it can congregate in much larger numbers to catch swarming insects such as flying ants. Extremely agile, this bird often hangs upside down as it feeds, or hovers hummingbird-style in front of open flowers.

The male purple sunbird has two types of plumage. When breeding, the male is iridescent, and its head and breast are a deep, metallic purple. Otherwise, it is largely dark. After breeding, the male molts into an "eclipse" plumage, appearing more like the female. The female lays 2–3 eggs, which hatch after about 15 days.

Female purple sunbird
The female keeps its olive-brown head, back, and wings, and creamy yellow underparts all year.

PROFILE

- S. Africa
- Fynbos shrubland, gardens, plantations
- Nonmigrant
- 11–17 in (28–43 cm)
- 1¼ oz (35 g)
- Untidy cup nest made of twigs, grass, bracken, roots, and pine needles, lined with protea down, placed in tangled or forked branches
- 2 eggs; 1 brood
- Least Concern
- Pairs/small flocks

Attractive appearance
The male Cape sugarbird becomes more eye-catching in the breeding season, when it perches on flower heads, launching display flights to attract a potential mate.

brown upperparts

white throat

buff underparts

SIMILAR SPECIES

white cheek

Gurney's sugarbird Found inland, this species lives as far north as Zimbabwe

Promerops cafer

CAPE SUGARBIRD

Sugarbirds are found only in southern Africa, where their unique shape and behavior make them hard to mistake. There are two species, both with a slim body, slender bill, bright yellow vent, and an extremely long tail in the male.

The Cape sugarbird flits busily around proteas and other plants, feeding on a mixture of sugar-rich nectar and insects, which it catches around the blooms. The main display feature of the male sugarbird is its tail, which can measure up to three times its body length, and is much longer than that of the female. The male's central feathers flick and twist during the impressive display flights. After mating, the female sugarbird nests in bushes, laying a pair of eggs and incubating them for about 17 days.

Female cape sugarbird
The female's tail is shorter than the male's, but it has a similar bright yellow vent, and head stripes.

PROFILE

- S. Canada and much of the USA; northern populations migrate south as far as N. Mexico in winter
- Woodland, farmland, gardens, and open ground with plenty of weeds
- Partial migrant
- 4¼ in (11 cm)
- ⁷⁄₁₆ oz (13 g)
- Open cup nest of bark, grass, and plant stems, placed in fork of tree
- 4–6 eggs; 1–2 broods
- Least Concern
- Small flocks

black cap

bright yellow plumage

white pattern on wings

cone-shaped bill

white rump

pinkish legs and feet

Breeding colors
In the breeding season, male American goldfinches have canary-yellow bodies and shoulders, with black caps, wings, and tails.

SIMILAR SPECIES

greenish back

Lesser goldfinch Smaller North American species; males have green or black backs

yellow wing-bars

European goldfinch
Red-faced finch; common across Europe and N. Asia

Spinus tristis

AMERICAN GOLDFINCH

This widespread seed-eater from North America is a common flock-forming bird. Frequently, if inaccurately, known as the wild canary, the American goldfinch is a partial migrant. In winter, the sexes look similar, but by spring, breeding males turn bright yellow, making them very visible as they feed. American goldfinches specialize in extracting seeds from thistles, teasels, and other late-flowering plants. To make the most of this harvest, they breed relatively late in the year.

Females build nests using spiders' silk to hold together the outer rim. Eggs hatch after about 12 days. The parents feed a milky pulp of seeds to the young that fledge when they are 17 days old.

Female goldfinch
The female has a duller, olive-green body. Unlike the male, it varies only slightly throughout the year.

PROFILE

- Europe, N. Africa, Middle East, Siberia; some populations winter in N. Africa, India
- Deciduous and coniferous woodland, farmland, parks, gardens
- Partial migrant
- 6 in (15 cm)
- ⅞ oz (25 g)
- Cup nest of moss, in fork of tree or shrub
- 4–5 eggs; 1 brood
- Least Concern
- Flocks

Familiar finch
The common chaffinch is a familiar bird in Europe and a full-time resident in many regions. Males have pale wing-bars that are conspicuous in flight.

blue-gray head

brown back

gray bill

dark tail

SIMILAR SPECIES

black back

Brambling More strongly marked migratory species

Fringilla coelebs

COMMON CHAFFINCH

One of the most common European birds, the well-known chaffinch is a frequent visitor to bird tables, feeding directly on them or on food that has fallen to the ground. Like most finches, the sexes look different, particularly during the breeding season: females are largely brownish gray, while the males have a rich color combination including a pinkish red face, throat, and breast, and pale wing-bars, which are conspicuous when they fly.

Common chaffinches eat seeds, fruit, and insects, varying their diet according to the time of year. They nest in trees or bushes, making neat, woven cups of grass, covered with lichens, and lined with feathers and hair. In most years, there is just a single brood. The young fledge in about 28 days.

Female chaffinch
The female has drabber color tones than the male. The juvenile male resembles the female until it matures.

PROFILE

- North America, Europe, Asia
- Coniferous forest
- Partial migrant
- 6¾ in (17 cm)
- 1¹⁄₁₆–1⁷⁄₁₆ oz (30–40 g)
- Small cup nest of twigs, lined with grass, placed high in tree
- 3–5 eggs; 1–2 broods
- Least Concern
- Flocks

Deep red plumage
Instantly recognizable by its cross-tipped bill, the male red crossbill is deep red during the breeding season.

dark brown wings

crossed bill tips

red rump

red plumage

SIMILAR SPECIES

pinkish red plumage

White-winged crossbill
North American crossbill with conspicuous white wing bars

large bill

Scottish crossbill Found only in the pine forests of Scotland

Loxia curvirostra

RED CROSSBILL

Crossbills get their name from their unique bills, which have crossed tips like a pair of scissors. Using this remarkable adaptation, red crossbills extract seeds from pine and spruce cones, slicing their way between the scales. While they feed, they use their feet to hold the cones in place and scoop the seeds using their tongues, before swallowing them. They also feed on insects and their larvae.

Red crossbills spend most of their lives high in trees. Portly but agile, they move easily among the branches, flying in short bursts from tree to tree. Their breeding season is linked to the ripening of cones, which can begin as early as February —a time when winter is often still underway. Females build the nest and lay a clutch of 3–5 eggs.

Female red crossbill
The female is olive-colored, with a paler rump and underside. It resembles the nonbreeding male.

Island jewel
With its brilliant scarlet plumage, and contrasting black tail and wings, the iiwi is one of the most attractive native birds found in the Hawaiian Islands.

long, curved bill

black wings

red plumage

PROFILE

📍	Hawaiian Islands
🌾	High-altitude wet forest with 'ohi'a and koa trees; also dry mamane forest
↻	Nonmigrant
↔	6 in (15 cm)
⚖	½–¹¹⁄₁₆ oz (15–20 g)
🪹	Open, loosely made cup, in tree or bush
🥚	2–3 eggs; 1 brood
✖	Vulnerable
🐦	Small flocks

Vestiaria coccinea

IIWI

A distinctive bird with bright red plumage, the iiwi is a highly specialized finch found only in the Hawaiian Islands. A nectar-feeder, it spends most of its time hidden deep among the foliage of flowering trees and shrubs. Although hard to spot, it gives a wide variety of calls and is often easier to hear. It gets its name from its creaking *ee-ee-vee* sound.

Iiwis breed when the flowering season is at its peak, making small cup-shaped nests. Females lay 2–3 eggs, which take about 14 days to hatch. When the chicks fledge, they look very different from their parents—turning bright red only once they have matured. Although still fairly common, iiwis are threatened by introduced species, including cats, rats, and mosquitoes that spread avian malaria.

Juvenile iiwi
Young birds look so different from adults that they were once thought to be a separate species.

Amazonian oropendola
The crested oropendola is a characteristic sight of the Amazon. Its crest is hard to spot and the upper part of its bill is enlarged to form a shield over the forehead.

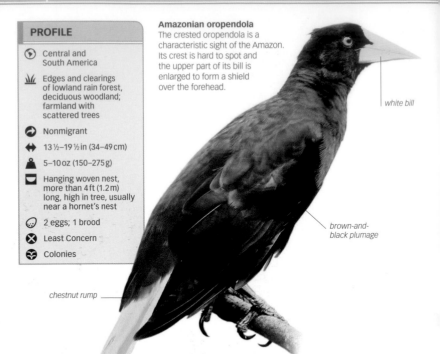

white bill

brown-and-black plumage

chestnut rump

yellow tail

Psarocolius decumanus

CRESTED OROPENDOLA

This highly gregarious bird is one of the largest icterids, or New World blackbirds—a family of songbirds that includes nearly 100 species from temperate and tropical parts of the Americas. A heavy-looking bird with a conical bill and narrow crest, it feeds in noisy groups, flying to and from the nesting tree in search of fruits, seeds, and insects.

Crested oropendolas nest in spectacular colonies in giant emergent trees. Made of plant fibers, the nests hang from the branches of the nesting trees, sometimes over 100 ft (30 m) above the forest floor. Females build the nests, laying a clutch of two eggs, which take about 18 days to hatch.

Female oropendola
The female is smaller and does not have a crest. In most colonies, females outnumber males.

PROFILE

- E. North America; winters within the southern half of its range
- Open areas, such as fields, marshes, and parks; suburban areas
- Partial migrant
- 4¾–5 in (12–13 cm)
- 3⅛–4 oz (90–125 g)
- Bulky cup nest of grass and stems, usually placed low in tree
- 4–5 eggs; 1–2 broods
- Least Concern
- Flocks

Purple haze
The male common grackle has iridescent purplish plumage on its head, neck, and breast, and sometimes across the rest of its body as well.

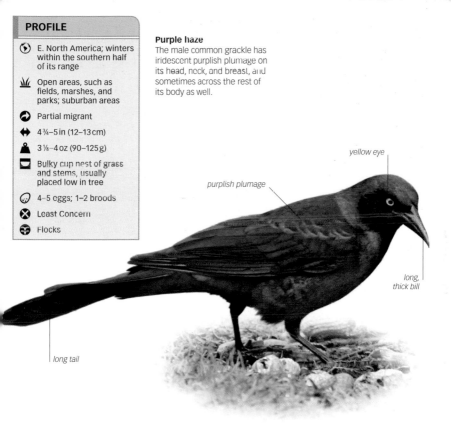

yellow eye

purplish plumage

long, thick bill

long tail

SIMILAR SPECIES

blue-black plumage

Boat-tailed grackle
Larger; from Atlantic and Gulf Coast states

longer tail

Great-tailed grackle
Larger; from southern USA to South America

Quiscalus quiscula

COMMON GRACKLE

Easy to mistake for a crow, the common grackle looks completely black from a distance. However, unlike a true crow, it has a sharp, conical bill, yellow eyes, and a long, keel-shaped tail. A highly adaptable species, it is at home in a variety of habitats. It is a noisy member of the New World blackbird family, which includes some of North America's most common flock-forming birds.

Common grackles feed and roost in large groups, and can be a problem on farms, where they eat crops and grain. They also feed on a wide range of small animals, from insects and earthworms to fish. During the breeding season, females make bulky nests, where they lay a clutch of 4–5 eggs. In northern regions, common grackles are summer visitors only, wintering in the southern half of their range.

Female common grackle
The female is slightly smaller than the male. It has duller, purplish bronze plumage and pale eyes.

- North America, Mexico, N. South America
- Native grassland, pastures, meadows, old fields
- Partial migrant
- 8½–10 in (22–25 cm)
- 2⅝–3½ oz (75–100 g)
- Domed grassy structure with entrance tunnel
- 3–8 eggs; 1 brood
- Least Concern
- Pairs/winter flocks

Two-tone plumage
The eastern meadowlark has a lemon-yellow throat, breast, and belly, and a yellow stripe above each eye. Its upperparts are camouflaged in brown with black streaks.

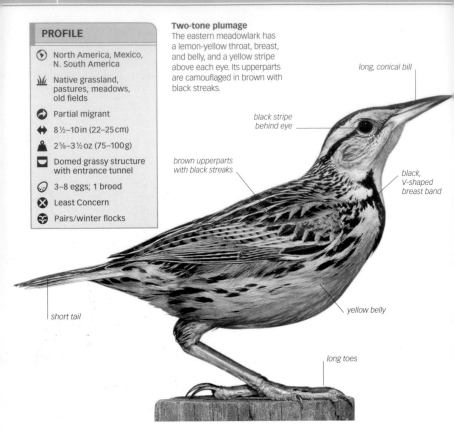

long, conical bill

black stripe behind eye

brown upperparts with black streaks

black, V-shaped breast band

short tail

yellow belly

long toes

SIMILAR SPECIES

yellow patch above eye

Western meadowlark
Almost identical species; found in western North America

Sturnella magna

EASTERN MEADOWLARK

This brightly colored bird spends most of its life on the ground. Like other American icterids (p.324), the eastern meadowlark has a sharply conical bill, which is used to collect small animals and seeds. Either a seasonal visitor or year-round resident, depending on location, the eastern meadowlark is most noticeable when it breeds because males defend territories by singing from a prominent perch or while fluttering above the ground. Their whistled song is the species' trademark, and the easiest way of distinguishing them from western meadowlarks, which otherwise look very similar.

Eastern meadowlarks nest on the ground, making domed nests with entrance tunnels, carefully hidden in dense cover. Like many farmland birds, this species benefits from the existence of open fields, but it is also harmed by mechanization, with many nests being accidentally destroyed each year.

PROFILE

- 🌐 North America to the Caribbean; winters from S.W. Canada to the Caribbean

- 〰 Breeds in dense freshwater vegetation; also occurs in fields and woodland edges

- ➤ Partial migrant

- ↔ 8–8½in (20–22cm)

- ⚖ 1⁷⁄₁₆–2¼oz (40–65g)

- ▭ Woven cup nest in reeds, grass, or bush, usually near water; built in loosely spaced colonies

- 🥚 3–4 eggs; 1–2 broods

- ✖ Least Concern

- 🔁 Flocks

Attracting attention
During the breeding season, the male red-winged blackbird sings from a prominent perch, and shows off its yellow-edged shoulder patches to attract attention from females.

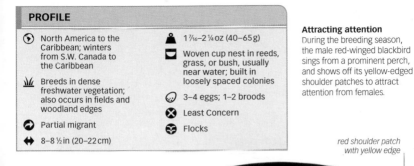

red shoulder patch with yellow edge

glossy black body

pointed bill

SIMILAR SPECIES

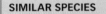

all-black body

Tricolored blackbird
Californian species with white-edged shoulder patches

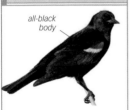

yellow head and chest

Yellow-headed blackbird
White wing patch; common in western North America

Agelaius phoeniceus

RED-WINGED BLACKBIRD

One of North America's most abundant birds, the red-winged blackbird is found in waterside habitats and open fields. Its roosting flocks can be millions strong, creating clouds of whirring wings and a deafening barrage of sound. In the north of its range, it is a seasonal migrant, while southern birds are resident all year round. It feeds on insects and seeds, traveling up to 50 miles (80km) a day to find food.

Females make nests near or over water where eggs hatch after 12 days. The young fledge within two weeks. Remarkably for land birds, the young can swim when just a few days old—an important survival aid if they accidentally fall out of the nest.

Female blackbird
Females are dark brown, with streaked undersides. Some have a faint trace of a shoulder patch.

Streak effect
The black-and-white warbler has
heavy, black streaking against a
white background. In the breeding
season, the male's throat and
cheeks become solid black.

black-and-white
stripes on upperparts

white eye-ring

slightly
downcurved
bill

black spots on
undertail feathers

white underparts
with black streaks

PROFILE

- 🌐 Central and S.E. Canada,
  and USA east of the
  Rockies; winters in
  Central and South
  America as far as Peru

- 〽️ Mature deciduous or
  mixed forest; winters
  in forest borders and
  secondary woodland

- ↻ Migrant

- ↔ 5 in (13 cm)

- ⚖️ ⅜ oz (11 g)

- ▭ Grass cup nest in hollow
  on ground, often next
  to a tree

- 😊 4–5 eggs; 1 brood

- ✖️ Least Concern

- 🔀 Migrant/winter flocks

Mniotilta varia

BLACK-AND-WHITE WARBLER

Every spring, millions of New World warblers land in
North America to breed, many after covering thousands
of miles. The black-and-white warbler is one of the most
common of these long-distance travelers. A bird of
mature broadleaved or mixed forest, the black-and-white
warbler has distinctive, easy-to-recognize, streaked
plumage. It has an unusually long hind toe and claw on
each foot, an adaptation that
lets it creep over bark in search
of insects, a way of life mirrored
by nuthatches (p.290).

Despite its arboreal lifestyle, the
black-and-white warbler makes a
small cup nest on the ground.
The eggs hatch in 10 days, and
the young fledge within 12 days,
ready to fend for themselves.

Female warbler
The female has gray cheeks
and a white throat. The
sexes look similar except
during the breeding season.

PROFILE

- Canada, USA, Central and South America; some North American populations migrate southward
- Various brushy and semi-open habitats, especially if shady and near water; mangroves
- Partial migrant

- 5 in (13 cm)
- ⅜–⁷⁄₁₆ oz (10–12 g)
- Compact cup nest in shrub, often close to water
- 4–5 eggs; 1–2 broods
- Least Concern
- Flocks

Sunlit yellow
Male yellow warblers are bright yellow overall, with olive-yellow backs and wings, and shining, black eyes.

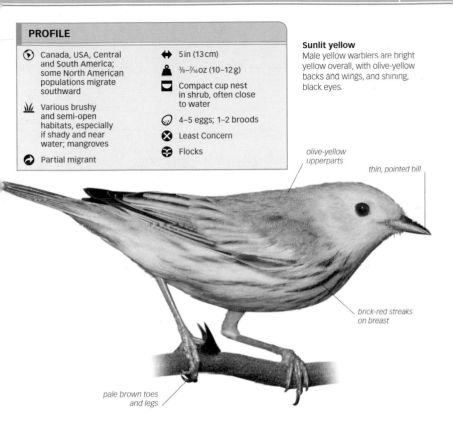

olive-yellow upperparts

thin, pointed bill

brick-red streaks on breast

pale brown toes and legs

SIMILAR SPECIES

bluish wings and tail

Prothonotary warbler
Bright yellow warbler; breeds in eastern USA

two white wing bars

Blue-winged warbler Yellow warbler with black eye-stripe, from eastern USA

Setophaga petechia

YELLOW WARBLER

This small but brightly colored bird is the most widespread North American warbler. A long-distance migrant, it arrives every spring from as far south as Brazil, ending its journey in wet and semi-open habitats, from woodlands and suburban gardens to Arctic tundra.

Once in place, male yellow warblers begin a period of intense courtship. Some have been recorded singing over 3,000 times in a single day. Like most New World warblers, this species feeds on insects, picking them off leaves and bark or snatching them up in midair. Males forage higher in trees than females— an adaptation that lets them claim a territory and find food at the same time.

Female yellow warbler
The female yellow warbler is duller than the male, and has a greenish yellow breast without streaks.

PROFILE

- North America, Caribbean Islands, Mexico, southward to Panama
- Coniferous, deciduous, and mixed hardwood forest, particularly near water, with lichens
- Migrant
- 4 ¼ in (11 cm)
- 9/32 oz (8 g)
- Hanging pouch in wooded areas, where clumps of lichen (*Usnea*) or Spanish moss (*Tillandsia*) are available
- 4–5 eggs; 1 brood
- Least Concern
- Winter flocks

Parula colors
The male northern parula has a blue-gray head and back. Each eye is surrounded by an incomplete, white ring.

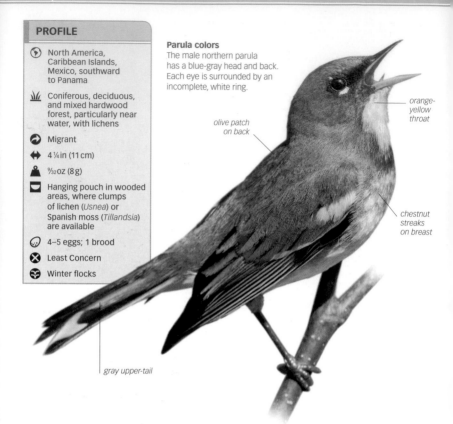

olive patch on back

orange-yellow throat

chestnut streaks on breast

gray upper-tail

SIMILAR SPECIES

darker face

Tropical parula Breeds from southern USA to South America; yellow underparts

unmarked, gray back

Yellow-throated warbler Breeds in eastern North America; feeds high up in trees

Setophaga americana

NORTHERN PARULA

This colorful bird is one of North America's smallest warblers. A summer visitor to the east of the continent, the northern parula lives in broadleaved, coniferous, or mixed woodland, particularly near water. It feeds on insects and spiders, flitting along the thinnest branches to search for food, and sometimes hanging upside down to inspect the underside of leaves.

In northern regions, the northern parula nests in beard moss or lace lichen, while farther south, this bird relies on Spanish moss, which hangs from twigs in long fronds. The female builds the pouch-shaped nest in wooded areas, lining it with feathers or hair, and often reuses it in successive years.

Female northern parula
The female is much duller than the male. An immature male resembles the female until it starts to breed.

PROFILE

- S. Canada, E. USA; winters in Central America
- Mature, deciduous, or mixed forest, with sparse shaded undergrowth
- Migrant
- 5 ½ in (14 cm)
- ¹¹⁄₁₆ oz (19 g)

- Domed structure of leaves, dry grass, and weed stems, lined with tiny rootlets, and placed on ground
- 4–5 eggs; 1–3 broods
- Least Concern
- Solitary/flocks

bold, white eye-ring

olive-brown back

black, streaked underparts

Identical sexes
Male and female ovenbirds look identical, with olive-brown backs and streaked undersides. They have rust-colored crowns, bordered by dark, parallel stripes.

SIMILAR SPECIES

white eyebrow

Louisiana waterthrush Lives in woods and swamps; breeds in eastern North America

brown back

Northern waterthrush
Ground-dwelling warbler, found foraging along northern streams

Seiurus aurocapilla

OVENBIRD

Named for its nest, which is shaped like an old-fashioned oven, this New World warbler winters in Central America, and breeds across southern Canada and the eastern USA. Instead of scaling trees, the ovenbird forages on foot, looking for insects, snails, and other small animals on the ground. Largely brown, with dark streaks on the underside, this bird can be easily overlooked due to its camouflaged plumage. However, it can be pinpointed by its song, a repeated *teacher-teacher-teacher* that steadily rises in volume.

An ovenbird's nest, constructed entirely by the female bird, is an intriguing structure, made of grass, leaves, moss, and small twigs, and built on the ground. The only entrance to it is a narrow slit, just wide enough for the ovenbird to squeeze inside. Once the nest is complete, the female lays a clutch of 4–5 eggs, rarely leaving them until the 12-day incubation period is complete. When food is abundant, ovenbirds can produce up to three broods in a single year.

PROFILE

- North America to Mexico; Central America to Nicaragua
- Widespread in open woodland, edges, grassy fields, and parkland
- Partial migrant
- 4¾–5½ in (12–14 cm)
- ⅜–½ oz (11–15 g)
- Cup nest placed well off ground in tree or shrub
- 4 eggs; 2 broods
- Least Concern
- Flocks

Breeding colors
During the breeding season, the chipping sparrow has a rusty crown and bright white "eyebrows." Once breeding is over, these markings fade away.

rusty crown

streaked upperparts

gray underparts

long tail

SIMILAR SPECIES

rusty cheek patch

Field sparrow Widespread sparrow from eastern USA

rust patch on shoulder

American tree sparrow Breeds in trees bordering the Arctic tundra

Spizella passerina

CHIPPING SPARROW

Named for its repetitive rattle—a series of *chip chip* sounds—this native species is among the most common sparrows in North America. It breeds across most of the continent, south of the Arctic timberline, and winters in the southern states and Central America. Found in many different habitats, from woodland to grassy fields, it is a frequent visitor to bird tables, particularly during the winter months, and sometimes sings at night.

Chipping sparrows feed mainly on seeds, although their diet also includes insects, especially when they are raising their young. Unlike some sparrows, chipping sparrows rarely nest on the ground. Females construct neat, cup-shaped nests in a tree or shrub, and lay a clutch of four eggs. Once the clutch is complete, they sit tight, rarely leaving the nest except to feed. The eggs hatch after about 14 days, and the young take only about 10 days to fledge. In a typical year there are two broods.

PROFILE

- N. North America, Eurasia; winters farther south
- Dry, rocky areas of the Arctic; winters in fields and on shores to the south
- Migrant
- 6–7 in (15–18 cm)
- 1¼–2 oz (35–55 g)
- Cup nest in a rock crevice
- 3–6 eggs; 1 brood
- Least Concern
- Pairs/flocks

Black-and-white breeder
Male snow buntings are black and snowy white during the breeding season to attract mates. For the rest of the year they are brownish white and black.

white head

black back

black bill

white underside

SIMILAR SPECIES

reddish nape

Lapland longspur Summer visitor to the tundra of Scandinavia and Siberia

Plectrophenax nivalis

SNOW BUNTING

The world's most northerly breeding songbird, the snow bunting nests as far north as the Arctic tip of Greenland, just a few hundred miles from the North Pole. Migrating north in the rapidly lengthening days of spring and early summer, it breeds on cliffs, among boulders, and on tundra, making a nest that is tucked away from the punishing Arctic wind. The males feed the females while the females are incubating the eggs. The young form large flocks once they have fledged and left the nest.

Snow buntings feed on seeds, insects, and spiders. They also peck up other small animals when foraging along inlets and coasts. Like many Arctic birds, they are protected by camouflage: breeding males are black and snowy white, which makes them attractive to females, but difficult to see as they forage among rocks on snow-covered ground. Females resemble males in their nonbreeding plumage, with brown heads and backs, and black-and-white wings.

PROFILE

- Europe, N. Asia
- Reeds or wet areas; also breeds among young conifers and crop
- Partial migrant
- 5 ½–6 ½ in (14–16 cm)
- ⅝–¹¹⁄₁₆ oz (17–20 g)
- Bulky nest of grass, sedge, and stems, lined with moss and hair, on or close to ground in thick cover
- 4–5 eggs; 2 broods
- Least Concern
- Small flocks

white collar

pale underparts

white outer tail feathers

Courtship colors
During the breeding season, the male reed bunting has a distinctive black head with white mustachelike stripes. Its outer tail feathers are white.

SIMILAR SPECIES

black eye-stripe

Cirl bunting
European species, with stripy-headed males

jet-black head

Black-headed bunting
Long-tailed species from Europe and the Middle East

Emberiza schoeniclus

REED BUNTING

A bird of contrasting habitats, the reed bunting lives in riversides and marshes, as well as drier places such as woodlands and fields. The boldly marked male, with a dark head and a pale white collar, is a very conspicuous reedbed bird. Reed buntings feed on small seeds and insects, collecting their food in reeds, in trees, or on the ground. Compared to some other reedbed birds, the reed bunting's song is unexceptional, but it makes up for this by flicking its tail in an eye-catching way as it calls from a perch.

The reed bunting makes a cup-shaped nest on the ground. If threatened, the parents try to distract attention from the nest by feigning injury and shuffling away. The average clutch is 4–5 eggs, and there are often two broods a year.

Female reed bunting
The female has sparrowlike markings, with a pale "mustache." It keeps these markings all year round.

bright red head and crest

white collar

gray upperparts

red breast

long legs

PROFILE

- E. Bolivia, Paraguay, Uruguay, S. Brazil, C. Argentina; introduced population in Hawaiian Islands
- Semi-open areas, with shrubbery and scattered trees, particularly near water
- Nonmigrant
- 7 ½ in (19 cm)
- 1 ⁷⁄₁₆ oz (40 g)
- Neat cup nest made of rootlets and grass, placed low in bush or a small tree
- 2–4 eggs; 2 broods
- Least Concern
- Pairs/flocks

Flame effect
The red-crested cardinal's head, throat, and breast are a brilliant scarlet, almost as if they have been dipped in colored ink. Its permanently raised red crest completes the flame effect

SIMILAR SPECIES

black upperparts

Red-capped cardinal
South American species with red head without crest

white collar

Yellow-billed cardinal South American species; yellow bill, black bib

Paroaria coronata

RED-CRESTED CARDINAL

Not to be confused with the unrelated northern cardinal of North America (p.339), this handsome bird is commonly found in the scrub and grasslands of South America, from eastern Bolivia to the pampas of central Argentina. In Hawaii, the red-crested cardinal has become one of the long list of species that has been accidentally or deliberately introduced. A gifted singer, this species was popular as a caged bird.

Often seen in pairs or small groups, red-crested cardinals form larger flocks outside the breeding season. They feed on seeds and small animals, usually in open ground. Particularly common near water, they can even walk on floating water plants, spreading their weight with their long toes. Red-crested cardinals build cup nests in trees and shrubs. Incubation takes about 14 days, and both parents feed the young once the eggs have hatched. There are two broods in a typical year.

PROFILE

- 🎯 S.E. Canada, E. USA; winters from Panama as far south as Bolivia
- 🌿 Deciduous forest; humid forest edges and secondary woodland in winter
- 🔄 Migrant
- ↔ 6¾ in (17 cm)
- ⚖ 1¹⁄₁₆ oz (30 g)
- 📭 Loose platform of twigs lined with leaves and grass
- 🥚 4 eggs; 1 brood
- ❌ Least Concern
- ✴ Mixed flocks

scarlet head and body

grayish yellow bill

black wings

black tail

Intense red
The male scarlet tanager has intense red plumage during the breeding season, with black wings and a black tail.

SIMILAR SPECIES

black back

Western tanager
Most northerly breeder of all tanagers

bright red body

Summer tanager Bright red overall; brownish legs and toes

Piranga olivacea

SCARLET TANAGER

Native to the American tropics, tanagers include some of the world's most colorful birds. There are more than 200 species, mainly full-time residents of dense forests. The scarlet tanager is different: a long-distance migrant, it winters in South America, but flies to eastern North America each spring. Here, the breeding male makes an exotic sight, with its striking red head and body. Despite this vivid plumage, its habit of perching for long periods makes it difficult to spot.

Scarlet tanagers feed on adult insects and caterpillars, often collecting their food from the underside of leaves. They build loose nests, lined with plant matter, on horizontal branches. Females incubate the eggs, which hatch after about 14 days. Both parents feed the developing young.

Female scarlet tanager
The female is olive-colored all year round. In its post-breeding molt, the male resembles the female.

PROFILE

- Cuba, Mexico to Brazil; Bolivia
- Forest edges, woodland, clearings with scattered trees, residential areas
- Nonmigrant
- 4¾ in (12 cm)
- ½ oz (14 g)
- Shallow cup nest in tree
- 2 eggs; 1 brood
- Least Concern
- Small flocks

turquoise crown

black eye-stripe

purplish blue plumage

short, black tail

Color contrast
The male red-legged honeycreeper has bright purplish blue plumage and a turquoise crown during the breeding season.

SIMILAR SPECIES

black wings

Purple honeycreeper
South American species, with yellow legs

Cyanerpes cyaneus

RED-LEGGED HONEYCREEPER

This species belongs to the tanager family, but unlike the scarlet tanager (p.336), it does not migrate. Stunningly colored, the male has vividly contrasting red legs. Unusually for a tropical bird, it molts into an "eclipse" plumage at the end of the breeding season, becoming much more like the female, until the next breeding season starts.

The red-legged honeycreeper has a thin, curved bill, which it uses to suck nectar from flowers and catch insects on twigs and leaves, or in midair. The female lays the eggs in a small, cup-shaped nest that it builds in a tree. The eggs hatch after about 14 days, and the young fledge in about the same time.

Female honeycreeper
The female is dull green, with reddish brown legs. It is similar to the male in its "eclipse" plumage.

PROFILE

- Central and N. South America
- Forest edges, woodland, scrub, gardens, and agricultural areas with scattered trees
- Nonmigrant
- 4¼ in (11 cm)
- ½ oz (15 g)
- Dome-shaped nest in sheltered nook or cranny
- 1–2 eggs; 2–3 broods
- Least Concern
- Small flocks

dark blue back and wings

yellow underparts

short tail

Fruit feeder
The thick-billed euphonia feeds entirely on fruit. It crushes its food before swallowing it—a contrast with many other fruit-eating birds.

SIMILAR SPECIES

blue hood

Elegant euphonia Colorful species from the mountain forests of Central America

yellow underparts

Violaceous euphonia Nearly identical species from South America

Euphonia laniirostris

THICK-BILLED EUPHONIA

Euphonias are some of the smallest tanagers, few measuring more than 4 in (10 cm). The thick-billed euphonia is a typical example, with a finchlike body, short tail, and a stubby bill. It feeds almost entirely on fruit, particularly of mistletoes. Unlike other fruit-eating birds, it does not down its food whole.

These birds build dome-shaped nests with an entrance on one side. Little is known about their breeding biology, although given their small size, their incubation period is likely to be short. Chicks are fed initially on insects and spiders—a high-protein diet that helps them grow—switching to fruit once they have fledged.

Female euphonia
The female euphonia is a drab olive-yellow. The young male is similar, until it develops its adult plumage.

PROFILE

- North America
- Shrubby habitat and woodland edge, often in suburban areas
- Nonmigrant
- 8 ½ in (22 cm)
- 1 ⁹⁄₁₆ oz (45 g)
- Coarse cup nest of leaves and twigs, lined with bark placed just above ground in bush
- 3–4 eggs; 1–4 broods
- Least Concern
- Solitary

pointed crest

bright red wings

black bib around bill

Scarlet splendor
The Northern cardinal is brilliant red all over, apart from a thick black patch and bib around the base of the bill.

SIMILAR SPECIES

red-tipped grey crest

Pyrrhuloxia
Gray overall; found in southwestern USA and Mexico

conical beak

Vermilion cardinal Most vibrantly red of all cardinals; found in N. South America

Cardinalis cardinalis

NORTHERN CARDINAL

One of North America's most eye-catching birds, the northern cardinal is instantly recognizable by its crest and crimson color. Its exotic appearance makes it look like a summer migrant, but it is actually a year round resident throughout most of its range. Easily spotted when feeding, it becomes even more visible in winter among snow-covered branches.

This songbird lives in woodland edges and shrubby habitats, eating insects, seeds, and fruit, often visiting suburban bird feeders when supplies of wild food run low. During breeding season, the female lays 3–4 eggs. Once they hatch, both parents take care of the young. In some years, the northern cardinal can raise 3–4 broods.

Female cardinal
Females are olive-brown, with darker wings and tails. Like males, they have conspicuous, pointed crests.

GLOSSARY

ADAPTATION
Any inherited feature of an animal's structure or behavior that helps fit it into its environment and lifestyle; also the evolutionary process giving rise to such features.

ADULT
A fully developed, mature bird that is able to breed. It is in its final plumage. See also *immature*.

ALLOPREENING
Mutual preening between two birds, the main purpose of which is to reduce the instinctive aggression when birds come in close ontact. In the breeding season, allopreening helps strengthen the pair bond between the male and female. This behavior is particularly common in parrots and estrildid finches. See also *preening*.

ARBOREAL
Living fully or mainly in trees.

AUSTRALASIA
A biogeographical region that comprises Australia, New Guinea, New Zealand, and adjacent islands in the East Indies and Polynesia.

BARRED
With marks crossing the body, wing, or tail; the opposite of streaked. See also *streaks*.

BILL
A bird's jaws. A bill is made of bone, with a hornlike outer covering of keratin.

BOND
The formation and maintenance of a strong, monogamous relationship between the male and female of a species. Also referred to as a pair bond.

BREEDING PLUMAGE
A general term for the plumage worn by adult birds when they display and form breeding pairs. It is usually, although not always, worn in the spring and summer. In most sexually dimorphic species, the male is more colorful.

BROOD
1) The young birds produced from a single clutch of eggs and brooded together. 2) To sit on nestlings to keep them warm. Brooding is usually carried out mostly or entirely by the adult female, although in some species the male takes sole responsibility for this task.

BROOD PARASITE
A bird that tricks another bird into raising its young. Some brood parasites, including the cowbirds of the New World, and many Old World cuckoos, always breed this way, laying their eggs in the nests of different species. A variety of other birds, including waterfowl, gamebirds, and songbirds, are occasional brood parasites. They usually raise their young themselves, but sometimes dump their eggs in the nest of another member of the same species instead.

CACHE
Food stored for later use.

CALL
A sound produced by the vocal apparatus of a bird to communicate a variety of messages to other birds. Calls are often highly characteristic of individual species and can help birders locate and identify birds in the field. Most bird calls are shorter and simpler than songs. See also *syrinx*.

CAMOUFLAGE
Colors or patterns that cause an animal to resemble its environment, so that it is not noticed by potential predators or prey, or both. See also *cryptic plumage*.

CANOPY
The highest layer of a forest or woodland, which is created by the overlapping branches of neighboring trees.

CASQUE
A bony extension on the head of an animal.

CLASS
A level used in classification. In a sequence of classification levels, a class forms part of the phylum, and is subdivided into one or more orders. The world's birds make up the class Aves. See also *order, family*.

CLUTCH
The group of eggs laid in a single nest, usually laid by one female and incubated together. Clutch sizes vary from a single egg in some species to as many as 28 eggs in some others.

COLOR FORM
One of two or more clearly defined plumage variations found in the same species. Also known as a color morph or phase, a color form may be restricted to a particular part of a species's range, or it may occur side by side with other color forms throughout the entire range. Adults of different color forms are able to interbreed, and these mixed pairings can produce young of either form.

CONTOUR FEATHER
A general term for any feather that covers the outer surface of a bird, including its wings and tail. Contour feathers are also known as body feathers, and help to streamline the bird.

COVERT
A small feather that covers the base of a bird's flight feathers. Coverts grow in well-defined groups on the wing and at the base of the tail.

CRÈCHE
A group of young birds of about the same age, that are produced by different parents. One or more adults guard the entire crèche. This behavior is found in penguins, flamingos, ostriches, and rheas.

CROP
A muscular pouch below the throat, forming an extension to the esophagus. Its purpose is to store undigested food, and it enables birds to feed quickly so that they can digest their meals in safer surroundings.

CROWN
The area on top of a bird's head. It is often a prominent plumage feature.

CRYPTIC PLUMAGE
Coloration and markings that make a bird difficult to see against its background.

DIMORPHISM
See *sexual dimorphism*.

DISPLAY
A form of visual communication in which a bird uses body postures, movements, and plumage to communicate, usually with another member of its species. The purpose of the display can be as part of a courtship ritual, to distract predators, or as a form of defense against a rival or a predator.

DISTRACTION DISPLAY
A distracting display in which a bird deliberately attempts to hold a predator's attention in order to lure it away from its nest and eggs. This behavior is common in ground-nesting waders, which pretend to have an injured wing to tempt a predator to follow them.

DISTRIBUTION
See *range*.

DIURNAL
Active during the day.

DOWN FEATHER
A soft, fluffy feather, lacking the system of barbs of contour or flight feathers, which provides good insulation. Young birds are covered by down feathers until they molt into their first juvenile plumage. Adult birds have a layer of down feathers under their contour feathers.

ECLIPSE PLUMAGE
An inconspicuous plumage that is worn in some birds by adult males for a short period after the breeding season is over. At this time, the males often resemble the females. The eclipse plumage helps disguise them during their molt.

ENDANGERED
A label used to describe a species that faces a very high risk of extinction in the wild in the near future. See also *IUCN*.

ENDEMIC
A species native to a particular geographic area, that is found nowhere else.

FAMILY
A level used in classification. In the sequence of classification levels, a family forms part of an order and is subdivided into one or more genera.

FERAL
An animal that comes from domesticated stock, but which has taken up life in the wild.

FLEDGLING
A young bird that is ready to leave the nest or has acquired the first set of complete flight feathers.

FLIGHT FEATHER
A collective term for a bird's wing and tail feathers, used in flight. More specifically, it also refers to the largest feathers on the outer part of the wing.

FLOCKING
Group-forming behavior in birds.

FORAGE
Activities concerned with seeking and obtaining food.

FORE WING
The front section of a bird's wing, including the primary coverts and secondary coverts. See also *hind wing*.

GALLERY FOREST
A narrow strip of forest, often along a riverbank or beside a stream, but also in savanna and other open country. Gallery forest may be an area's only forest for many miles.

GENUS
A category in classification: a group of closely related species, whose relationship is recognized by the same first name in scientific terminology.

GIZZARD
A region of the gut in which food is ground down before digestion.

GREGARIOUS
Living or congregating in large flocks or colonies.

GULAR SAC
Also known as a gular pouch, it is a large, fleshy, extendable sac just below the bill of some birds. It forms part of the throat.

HABITAT
The geographical and ecological area where a particular organism usually lives.

HIND WING
The rear section of a bird's spread wing. See also *fore wing*.

HOST
A bird, or species of bird, that is victim to a brood parasite.

IMMATURE
In birds, an individual that is not yet sexually mature or able to breed. Some birds pass through a series of immature plumages over several years before adopting their first adult plumage and sexual maturity. See also *adult, juvenile*.

INCUBATE
To sit on eggs to keep them warm, allowing the embryo inside to grow. Incubation is often carried out by the female. See also *brood*.

INTRODUCED SPECIES
A species that humans have accidentally or deliberately brought into an area where it does not normally occur.

IRIDESCENT PLUMAGE
Plumage that shows brilliant, luminous colors, which seem to sparkle and change color when seen from different angles.

IRRUPTION
A sporadic mass movement of animals outside their normal range. Irruptions are usually short-lived and occur in response to food shortage. Also called irruptive migration

IUCN
The initials used to designate the International Union for the Conservation of Nature and Natural Resources. This organization carries out conservation-related activities, including gathering and publishing information on the current status of threatened species.

JUVENILE
A term referring to the plumage worn by a young bird at the time it makes its first flight and until it begins its first molt. See also *adult, immature*.

KEEL
Enlarged "ridge" on the breastbone that anchors the muscles that are used for flight.

LEAST CONCERN
A label used to describe a species that is widespread or abundant, or which is not likely to become threatened in the near future. See also *IUCN*.

LEK
A communal display area used by male birds during courtship, where they show off their plumage, and make a variety of sounds. Females gather at the lek to watch the performance, selecting the male or males that they will mate with. Leks often remain in use over successive years.

MANDIBLE
The upper or lower part of a bird's bill, known as the upper or lower mandible respectively.

MANGROVE SWAMP
A forestlike habitat found in the tropics along muddy coasts and river mouths. It is formed by mangrove trees, which are adapted to grow with their roots immersed in saltwater. Mangrove swamps are an important habitat for nesting seabirds, herons, and egrets.

MANTLE
The loose term used to define the back of a bird, between its neck and rump.

MELANISTIC
A term describing an animal with more brown or black pigments than usual. Melanistic birds appear very dark.

MIGRANT
A species that regularly moves between geographical areas. Most migrants move on an annual basis between a breeding area and a wintering area. See also *partial migrant, sedentary*.

MIGRATION
A journey to a different region, following a well-defined route. Most birds that migrate regularly do so in step with the seasons.

MIMICRY
In birds, the act of copying the songs or calls of other species. The mimic often weaves these vocal fragments into its own usual song. Some birds, including parrots and mynas, can also copy mechanical sounds such as ringing telephones, machinery, and car alarms.

MOBBING
A type of defensive behavior in which a group of birds gang up to harass a larger predator, such as a bird of prey or an owl, swooping repeatedly to drive it away.

MONTANE
A high-altitude habitat, often forested, found in temperate and tropical parts of the world.

MOLT
The shedding of old feathers so that they can be replaced. Molting enables birds to keep their plumage in good condition, to change their level of insulation, and to change their coloration or markings so that they are ready to breed.

NEAR THREATENED
A label used to describe a species of bird that is not currently facing any serious risk of extinction in the wild, but which is considered likely to become threatened in the near future. See also *IUCN*.

NEW WORLD
The Americas, from Alaska to Cape Horn, including the Caribbean and offshore islands in the Pacific and Atlantic oceans. See also *Old World*.

NOMADIC
Being almost constantly on the move. Birds of deserts, grasslands, and coniferous forests are commonly nomadic.

OLD WORLD
Europe, Asia, Africa, and Australasia. See also *New World*.

OMNIVORE
An animal that eats both plant and animal food.

ORDER
A level used in classification. In the sequence of classification levels, an order forms part of a class and is subdivided into one or more families. The world's birds are separated into 29 orders.

ORNAMENTAL
In birds, a species that is kept for its colorful plumage.

PARTIAL MIGRANT
A species in which some populations migrate while others are sedentary. This situation is common in broadly distributed species that experience a wide range of climatic conditions. See also *migration, sedentary*.

PELAGIC
Relating to the open ocean. Pelagic birds spend most of their lives at sea and only come to land to nest.

PHASE
See *color form*.

PREENING
Routine behavior by which birds keep their feathers in good condition. A bird grasps a feather at its base and then "nibbles" upward toward the tip, and repeats the process with different feathers. This helps smooth and clean the plumage. Birds often also smear oil from their preen gland onto their feathers at the same time. See also *allopreening*.

PRIMARY FEATHER
One of the large outer wing feathers, growing from the digits of a bird's "hand." See also *secondary feather*.

RACE
See *subspecies*.

RAIN FOREST
Type of forest, usually tropical, with high rainfall, high humidity, and high temperatures year-round.

RANGE
The geographical area across which a bird species is naturally found.

RAPTOR
A predatory bird that captures prey by using its hooked claws, or talons.

RESIDENT
See *sedentary*.

RIPARIAN
On or near the banks of a river.

ROOST
A place where birds sleep, either at night or by day.

SALT MARSH
A habitat found on sheltered, flat, muddy coastlines. It consists of a wide, low-lying area colonized by salt-tolerant plants and is covered by high tides.

SAVANNA
A general term for all tropical grasslands. Most savannas have a scattering of trees or scrub.

SCRAPE
A simple nest that consists of a shallow depression in the ground, which may be unlined or lined with soft material such as feathers and grasses.

SECONDARY FEATHER
One of the row of long, stiff feathers along the rear edge of a bird's wing, between the body and the primary feathers at the wingtip. The secondary feathers are often collectively referred to as secondaries. See also *primary feather*.

SEDENTARY
Having a settled lifestyle that involves relatively little movement. Sedentary birds remain in the same area throughout their life and are also said to be resident or non-migrants. See also *partial migrant*, *migration*.

SEXUAL DIMORPHISM
The occurrence of physical differences between males and females. In birds, the most common type of sexual dimorphism is plumage variation. Other forms of sexual dimorphism include differences in bill length or body size; for example, in many birds of prey, the female is larger than the male.

SIT-AND-WAIT STRATEGY
A feeding technique in which a bird sits on a perch and waits for its prey to appear, instead of actively searching for it. Birds that use this strategy often catch their food in midair, before returning to their perches.

SOLITARY
A bird that tends not to associate with other members of its species, except to breed.

SOARING
In birds, flight without flapping of the wings. On land, birds soar using rising air currents that form over warm ground, or along cliffs and mountains. At sea, some birds are expert at dynamic soaring, repeatedly diving into the troughs between waves and then using the wind to deflect them back into the air.

SONG
A loud vocal performance by a bird, usually the adult male, to attract and impress a potential mate, advertise ownership of a territory, or drive away rival birds. Songs are often highly characteristic of individual species and can be a major aid in locating and identifying birds in the field. See also *call*.

SPECIES
A group of similar living things that are capable of interbreeding in the wild and of producing fertile offspring that resemble themselves. Species are the fundamental units used in biological classification. Some species have distinct populations that vary from each other. Where the differences are significant and the populations biologically isolated, these forms are classified as separate subspecies (or races). In situations where two individuals belonging to different subspecies meet and form a mixed pair, they are still capable of interbreeding successfully. See also *subspecies*.

SPECULUM
A colorful patch on the wing of a duck, formed by the secondary feathers. See also *secondary feather*.

STREAKS
Marks that run lengthwise on feathers; opposite of bars.

SUBSPECIES
Geographical variants of a species that are recognizably different in color, voice, or other characters. Also known as races. See also *species*.

SYRINX
A modified section of a bird's trachea (windpipe), equivalent to the voicebox in humans, that enables birds to call and sing. Membranes inside the syrinx vibrate and produce sound as air passes over them. Passerine birds have the most complex syrinx. See also *call*, *song*.

TALON
The sharp, hooked claw of a bird of prey.

TEMPERATE
The regions of the world that lie at midlatitudes, between the polar regions and the tropics and subtropics.

TERRITORY
An area that is defended by a bird, or group of birds, against other members of the same species. Territories often include useful resources, such as good breeding sites or feeding areas, which help a male attract a mate. Territories vary in size from just a few inches wide in colonial species, such as cliff-nesting seabirds, to many square miles in some large eagles.

THREAT DISPLAY
A form of defense in which a bird adopts certain postures to drive away a rival or a potential predator. These postures are often designed to make the bird appear larger than it actually is. A threat display is sometimes accompanied by loud, agitated calls.

TORPOR
A sleeplike state similar to hibernation, in which the heart rate and other body processes slow down below their normal rate. Animals usually become torpid to survive difficult conditions.

TUNDRA
A treeless habitat of low-growing, cold-tolerant plants widespread in the far northern North America and Siberia.

UNDERWING
The underside of the wing.

UPPERWING
The top side of the wing.

VAGRANT
A bird that has strayed far from its normal range. Usually, vagrants are long-distance migrants that have been blown off course by storms while on migration, have overshot their intended destination due to strong winds, or have become disoriented.

VENT
The area of feathers between the base of a bird's tail and its legs.

VULNERABLE
A label used to describe a species that faces a high risk of extinction in the wild unless prospects for its survival improve. See also *IUCN*.

WATTLE
A bare, fleshy growth that hangs loosely below the bill in some birds. It is often brightly colored, and may play a part in courtship.

INDEX

Page numbers in **bold** indicate a main profile.

ACKNOWLEDGMENTS

Dorling Kindersley would like to thank the following people at the **Smithsonian Institution** in Washington D.C:
Kealy Wilson, Product Development Coordinator
Ellen Nanney, Licensing Manager
Brigid Ferraro, Director of Licensing
Carol LeBlanc, Vice President

The **IUCN Red List of Threatened Species** is the world's most comprehensive information source on the global conservation status of plant and animal species. It is based on an objective system for assessing the risk of extinction of a species should no conservation action be taken.
IUCN 2011. IUCN Red List of Threatened Species. Version 2011.1.
http://www.iucnredlist.org.
Downloaded on 16 June 2011.

The publisher would like to thank the following people: David Burnie, the author; Jonny Burrows for design assistance and icon design; Simon Murrell for additional design help; Jamie Ambrose for proofreading; Jane Parker for the index; Lili Bryant for editorial assistance; Manisha Majithia, Jacket Editor, and Sophia Tampakopoulos, Jacket Design Development Manager.

The publisher would like to thank the following for their kind permission to reproduce their photographs:

(Key: a-above; b-below/bottom; c-center; f-far; l-left; r-right; t-top)

1 Dorling Kindersley: Frank Krahmer/Getty. **5 Alamy Images:** FLPA (bl); imagebroker (b/common quail). **Corbis:** Pam Gardner; Frank Lane Picture Agency (t/brown quail); Roger Wilmshurst; Frank Lane Picture Agency (b/female quail). **FLPA:** Malcolm Schuyl (b/asian blue quail). **12–13 Corbis:** Erich Schlegel/Dallas Morning News. **17 Jauro Torquato:** (bl). **20 Alamy Images:** Henry Westheim Photography (cl). **Getty Images:** Barcroft Media (br). **22 Corbis:** Steven Vidler/Eurasia Press (bl). **Dreamstime.com:** Awcnz62 (t). **Getty Images:** Robin Bush (br). **25 Alamy Images:** David Hosking (t); Prisma Bildagentur AG (br). **26 Dreamstime.com:** David Schliepp (br). **28 Alamy Images:** FLPA (br); Wildscotphotos (bl). **29 Alamy Images:** imagebroker (t). **Corbis:** Pam Gardner; Frank Lane Picture Agency (bl); Roger Wilmshurst; Frank Lane Picture Agency (br). **FLPA:** Malcolm Schuyl (clb). **31 Alamy Images:** Oamkumar Thottungal (cl). **Corbis:** Buddy Mays (br). **32 Alamy Images:**

David Hosking (cl). **34 Dreamstime.com:** Dohnal (br). **35 Getty Images:** Gail Shumway (cl). **36 Corbis:** Wayne Lynch/All Canada Photos. **43 Dreamstime. com:** Steve Liptrot (bl). **44 Alamy Images:** Amar and Isabelle Guillen – Guillen Photography (br). **57 Corbis:** Frans Lanting (t); Momatiuk – Eastcott (cl). **59 Corbis:** Gerald & Duff Curisl/Visuals Unlimited (br). **60 Ardea:** Alan Greensmith (bl). **61 Dorling Kindersley:** Barry Hughes (t). **62 Getty Images:** Tom Ulrich. **68 Dreamstime.com:** Dean Bertoncelj (bl). **69 Corbis:** Jason Edwards/National Geographic Society (cl). **73 Fotolia:** Stephen Crisp (cl). **75 Alamy Images:** Michael Stubblefield (br). **76 Alamy Images:** Holger Ehlers (br). **77 Dreamstime.com:** Susan Robinson (br). **78 Fotolia:** Han van Vonno (br). **80 Rhys Marsh:** (br). **86 FLPA:** Tui De Roy/Minden Pictures (br). **88 Dreamstime. com:** Chris Kruger (bl). **90 FLPA:** Pete Oxford/Minden Pictures (cl). **91 Getty Images:** James Hager (br). **98 Fotolia:** Sebastien Burel (bl); Jeffrey Ong (br). **99 Dreamstime.com:** Steve Allen (bl). **100 Getty Images:** Martin Harvey (br). **104 Alamy Images:** Bill Bachman (bl). **108 Alamy Images:** blickwinkel (bl). **109 FLPA:** Gertjan De Zoete /

Minden Pictures (bl). **110 Alamy Images:** Ann and Steve Toon (br). **111 Corbis:** Kevin Schafer (t). **Dreamstime.com:** Edwin Verin (bl). **116 Mark Tittley:** (bl). **118 Marlene Lyell:** (cl). **Patricio Fernández Mackenzie . pfmack. Patricio Fernández Mackenzie :** (bl). **122 Corbis:** Uwe Walz (br). **Dreamstime.com:** Mikhail Blajenov (bl); Loflo69 (cl). **125 Alamy Images:** A & J Visage (bl). **127 Dreamstime.com:** Veronica Wools (bl). **128 FLPA:** Colin Monteath/Minden Pictures (cl). **133 Corbis:** Theo Allofs (br). **Fotolia:** Michael Fritzen (bl). **136 Corbis:** FLPA/Neil Bowman (bl). **141 FLPA:** Gianpiero Ferrari (bl). **144 Alamy Images:** WoodyStock (cl). **Fotolia:** AustralianDream (br); Alta Oosthuizen (bl). **150 Alamy Images:** PhotoKratky - Wildlife/Nature (cl). **151 Getty Images:** Robert Harding Productions (bl). **155 Alamy Images:** Accent Alaska.com (cl). **158 Alamy Images:** Juan Manuel Menacho (br, t). **162 Patrick Ingremeau:** (br). **163 Alamy Images:** Harjono Djoyobisono (t); imagebroker (bl). **166 Fotonatur.de :** Nikolaj Ullman (cl). **167 Alamy Images:** petpics (bl). **168 Dorling Kindersley:** Alex Robinson © Rough Guides. **171 Corbis:** Ann & Steve Toon/Robert Harding World Imagery (bl). **Fotolia:** David_Steele (cl). **172 Corbis:** John Carnemolla (bl). **177 Alamy Images:** INSADCO Photography (t). **178 Alamy Images:** Juniors Bildarchiv (bl). **180 FLPA:** Pete Oxford/Minden Pictures (r). **184 Alamy Images:** Nature Picture Library (br). **185 FLPA:** Richard Brooks (br). **186 Alamy Images:** Danita Delimont (r). **188 Alamy Images:** Juniors Bildarchiv (bl). **190 Dreamstime.com:** Radu Razvan Gheorghe (bl). **Fotolia:** Petr Mašek (br). **194 FLPA:** David Hosking (bl). **197 Alamy Images:** Advance Images (br). **naturepl.com:** Murray Cooper (bl). **199 Corbis:** Eric and David Hosking (br). **200 Corbis:** Steve Parish/Steve Parish Publishing. **201 NHPA/Photoshot:** A.N.T. Photo Library (bl). **203 Corbis:** Kevin Schafer (bl). **207 Photolibrary:** BIOS/Dominique Halleux (t). **209 NHPA/Photoshot:** Bill Coster (cl). **211 Alamy Images:** Ian Butler (b). **Johann Grobbelaar:** (t). **212 FLPA:** Murray Cooper/Minden Pictures (b). **213 Corbis:** Glenn Bartley/All Canada Photos (b). **214 Alamy Images:** Rolf Nussbaumer

Photography (br). **215 Corbis:** Glenn Bartley/All Canada Photos (t). **216 FLPA:** Neil Bowman (cl). **NHPA/Photoshot:** Eladio Fernandez (t). **218 Getty Images:** Radius Images. **219 Dreamstime.com:** Neal Cooper (cl). **Getty Images:** Peter Chadwick (bl). **221 Getty Images:** Panoramic Images (br). **223 Corbis:** Pam Gardner; Frank Lane Picture Agency (cl). **226 FLPA:** Otto Plantema/Minden Pictures (cl). **228 Getty Images:** Danita Delimont (br). **229 Fotolia:** JohanSwanepoel (br). **230 Dreamstime.com:** Eric Rivera (bl). **231 FLPA:** Lesley van Loo/Minden Pictures (br). **234 Alamy Images:** Petra Wegner (b). **Corbis:** David Hosking (t). **235 Alamy Images:** Life on White (br). **238 Dreamstime.com:** Edurivero (bl). **240 Alamy Images:** Douglas Scott (bl). **242 Corbis:** Nigel J. Dennis; Gallo Images (t). **FLPA:** David Hosking (br). **245 Fotolia:** avs_lt (cl). **248 Alamy Images:** FLPA (bl). **Getty Images:** altrendo nature (t). **249 Dreamstime.com:** Nimblewit (cl). **Getty Images:** Katsumi Suzuki/A. collection (bl). **251 Alamy Images:** Krystyna Szulecka (t). **253 Alamy Images:** E.D. Torial (br). **254 Alamy Images:** Arco Images GmbH (br). **Getty Images:** Ch'ien Lee/Minden (cl). **256 Alamy Images:** blickwinkel (bl). **Dreamstime.com:** Ben Twist (br). **257 Getty Images:** Sylvain Cordier (t). **258 NHPA/Photoshot:** David Tipling (cl). **259 Alamy Images:** FLPA (bl). **261 FLPA:** Tui De Roy/Minden Pictures (b). **262 Alamy Images:** Avico Ltd (bl). **267 Dreamstime.com:** Lincurrie (cl). **268 Alamy Images:** blickwinkel (bl). **Nik Borrow:** (cl). **273 Alamy Images:** LOOK Die Bildagentur der Fotografen GmbH (cl). **NHPA/Photoshot:** Biosphoto/Alain Compost (bl, t). **275 JJ Harrison, http://creativecommons.org/licenses/by-sa/3.0/deed.en:** Grey Fantail, http://en.wikipedia.org/wiki/File:Rhipidura_fuliginosa_3.jpg (cl). **NHPA/Photoshot:** A.N.T. Photo Library (bl). **276 Alamy Images:** Juniors Bildarchiv (bl); Alistair Scott (br). **NHPA/Photoshot:** Daryl Balfour (cl). **280 Alamy Images:** Brian Elliott (cl). **281 Alamy Images:** Rick & Nora Bowers (cl). **282 Alamy Images:** Wildscotphotos (cl). **284 Ardea:** Don Hadden (bl). **287 Dreamstime.com:** Helen E Grose (t). **288 Getty Images:**

Michael Sewell (br). **291 Alamy Images:** FLPA (br). **295 Dreamstime.com:** Stubblefieldphoto (cl). **297 Dreamstime.com:** Cooper5022 (bl). **298 Corbis:** Buddy Mays (cl). **Dreamstime.com:** Picstudio (bl). **299 Corbis:** James Hager/Robert Harding World Imagery (b). **300 Fotolia:** Ornitolog82 (bl). **naturepl.com:** Aflo (cl). **301 Fotolia:** Dubults (bl). **303 Alamy Images:** Mike Lane (bl). **308 Alamy Images:** Nico Smit (bl). **309 Alamy Images:** David Hosking (cl). **Dreamstime.com:** Isselee (bl). **Fotolia:** Eric Isselée (t). **310 Alamy Images:** marek kasula (bl). **(c) Mat & Cathy Gilfedder:** (cl). **Dreamstime.com:** Lori Froeb (br). **313 Alamy Images:** FLPA (br); David Hosking (cl). **314 Alamy Images:** Arco Images GmbH (br). **Fotolia:** Linn Currie (bl); Jean-Marc Strydom (cl). **317 Fotolia:** Chris Fourie (cl). **318 Alamy Images:** Ainars Aunins (br, t); Ian Butler (cl); fotolincs (bl). **319 Alamy Images:** blickwinkel (br). **Getty Images:** Steve & Ann Toon (t). **Alan Manson:** (cl). **323 Alamy Images:** Frans Lanting Studio (br). **324 Alamy Images:** Arco Images GmbH (br). **Fotolia:** Eduardo Rivero (cl). **Dominic Sherony:** (bl). **330 Corbis:** Glenn Bartley/All Canada Photos (cl). **337 Corbis:** Kevin Schafer (cl). **Dreamstime.com:** Tzooka (br). **338 Julian Londono:** (br). **Dominic Sherony:** (cl). **339 FLPA:** Murray Cooper/Minden Pictures (bl)

Jacket images: Front: Dorling Kindersley: Brian E Small (tc), (tr/northern cardinal), Windrush Photos/David Tipling (tl); **FLPA:** S & D & K Maslowski (b); **RSPB:** Steve Round (tr); *Back:* **Dorling Kindersley:** Hanne and Jens Eriksen (tl/blue footed booby), Brian E Small (tr/California quail), Bob Steele (tl), David Tipling (tr/red-breasted goose); *Spine:* **Dorling Kindersley:** Hanne and Jens Eriksen (c), Melvin Grey (cb); **FLPA:** S & D & K Maslowski

All other images © Dorling Kindersley
For further information see:
www.dkimages.com